SENNACHERIB'S PALACE WITHOUT RIVAL AT NINEVEH

D1242466

SENNACHERIB'S PALACE WITHOUT RIVAL AT NINEVEH

JOHN MALCOLM RUSSELL

THE UNIVERSITY OF CHICAGO PRESS
Chicago and London

JOHN MALCOLM RUSSELL is assistant professor in the
department of art history and archaeology at Columbia
University in the City of New York.

The University of Chicago Press, Chicago 60637
The University of Chicago Press, Ltd., London
© 1991 by The University of Chicago
All rights reserved. Published 1991
Printed in the United States of America

00 99 98 97 96 95 94 93 92 91   5 4 3 2 1

Russell, John Malcolm.
    Sennacherib's palace without rival at Nineveh / John Mal-
colm Russell.
        p.   cm.
    Revision of author's thesis.
    Includes bibliographical references and index.
    ISBN 0–226–73175–8 (cloth)
    1. Palace of Sennacherib (Nineveh) 2. Nineveh (Ancient
City)—Buildings, structures, etc. I. Title.
DS70.5.N47R87   1991
935—dc20   90–21830
                                                         CIP

This book is printed on acid-free paper.

To Janet

CONTENTS

PREFACE

When this project was begun as a doctoral dissertation ten years ago, my intention was to study everything available on Sennacherib's palace at Nineveh. At the time, this seemed a large order, but a finite one. No new part of the palace had been investigated archaeologically since 1905, and the last substantial excavation report was Layard's *Discoveries in the Ruins of Nineveh and Babylon* in 1853. There had been no work at all on the palace site for fifteen years, and it seemed there was little chance of a resumption in the near future. Likewise, there had been no major philological studies of Sennacherib's palace building accounts since the work of Meissner and Rost in 1893, and no major new palace building account had appeared since King's publication of British Museum prism 103000 in 1909. The corpus of available material was extensive, therefore, but did not appear to be expanding significantly. Sennacherib's palace seemed to be a subject that was ready for, and would stand still for, a thorough synthesis.

Even so, I knew this could in no sense be a final synthesis. When the dissertation was written between 1982 and 1985, my research was limited by two relatively serious constraints. The first was that roughly half of the nineteenth-century drawings of Sennacherib palace reliefs are unpublished and were not available for me to study. In practical terms, this meant that in some cases I had to refer to the excavator's rather general descriptions of a room's decoration instead of to the much more specific information that might have been contained in a drawing. The other constraint was that only a selection of Sennacherib's palace texts have been published. A number of handwritten copies from the nineteenth-century excavations were still unpublished, as well as many foundation cylinders and fragments from Nineveh. Most were apparently duplicates, or near duplicates, of published texts, but a few seemed to contain new information. To edit these texts would have been a major project and largely outside the scope of the proposed study. In the dissertation, therefore, I confined myself to the published texts, but acknowledged that they might not contain the whole story.

What I failed to consider was the effect of my examination on the object of my enquiry. Under my probing and prodding, it came alive. There are now gratifying signs of life in all the areas mentioned above. In the summer of 1988 I was able to study the palace building accounts on three unpublished Sennacherib foundation prisms, as well as some fifty fragments, all in the British Museum. There were many interesting variants in these texts, but nothing that affected any of my major conclusions. The results of this research will be published in the near future. Shortly after the completion of my dissertation, the unpublished nineteenth-century drawings of Sennacherib's reliefs were made available by the British Museum for publication. I also studied these drawings in the summer of 1988 and a number of them are published here for the first time. As with the texts, they provided a wealth of new information, but did not significantly alter my original arguments.

Most exciting of all, in the spring of 1989 at the invitation of Dr. Mu'ayyad Sa'id, Director General of Antiquities in Iraq, and of David Stronach, Director of the Berkeley Expedition to Nineveh, I went to Nineveh to supervise the reexcavation of Sennacherib's so-called *bīt nakkapti*, which plays an important role in my consideration of the extent of the palace in chapter 4. The preliminary results, which are discussed here briefly and in more detail in the Nineveh excavation reports, were surprising, but further work is required to place them in context. At that time I also studied the visible remains of the palace throne-room suite, which resulted in several significant alterations to this manuscript.

Paralleling my own experience, the last ten years have witnessed a remarkable renaissance in Assyrian studies in general. We now have one complete Assyrian dictionary, von Soden's *Akkadisches Handwörterbuch*, and another, the Chicago *Assyrian Dictionary*, nearly so. Two major Assyrian text corpus projects, the Helsinki *State Archives of Assyria* and the Toronto *Royal Inscriptions of Mesopotamia*, produced auspicious debut volumes. New excavations are being conducted in Assyrian remains at Nineveh and Nimrud. The recent fabulous discoveries of gold at Nimrud are once again focusing world attention on the Assyrians to a degree unknown since the great discoveries of Layard and Smith in the mid-nineteenth century. In such a climate, the last word on Sennacherib's palace clearly has yet to be written. Still, as a synthesis of what is known and a catalyst for what will come, this book has served me well. It's time to let it go, suspecting ever more strongly that its completion marks not an end but a beginning.

ACKNOWLEDGMENTS

This study could not have been written without the assistance and encouragement of many people. Foremost among these is Irene Winter, whose creative scholarship in Assyrian art set the pattern that I have tried to emulate here. Her patience and sound judgment as supervisor of the dissertation that constituted the first version of this study are responsible for more of its strengths than I could begin to enumerate.

Pamela Gerardi and Erle Leichty assisted with Akkadian language problems on countless occasions; they also read portions of the manuscript and offered valuable suggestions and criticisms. Erika Bleibtreu and Geoffrey Turner, who are preparing the British Museum publication of the Sennacherib palace reliefs, freely shared the results of their research with me. Hermann Behrens, Robert Kraft, and Mary Griffin provided the expertise and equipment to transfer my original typescript onto computer disks, greatly facilitating the editing process. Gregory Schmitz advised and assisted me in a variety of photographic matters. Pauline Albenda, J. A. Brinkman, Richard Ellis, Mark Hall, Renata Holod, Louis Levine, Michelle Marcus, James Muhly, Nadav Na'aman, and Edith Porada also gave freely of their time and expertise.

I am indebted to others for assistance in my study of museum collections and archaeological sites: Dr. John Curtis, Mr. T. C. Mitchell, Dr. Julian Reade, and Mr. C. B. F. Walker of the British Museum; Dr. Mu'ayyad Sa'id Damerji, Dr. Behnam Abu as-Soof, Mr. Manhal Jabr, and Mr. Donny George Youkana of the Iraq State Organization for Antiquities and Heritage; Monsieur Pierre Amiet, Madame Annie Caubet, Madame Agnes Spycket, and Madame Françoise Tallon of the Louvre; Dr. Liane Jakob-Rost and Herr Wartke of the Vorderasiatisches Museum, East Berlin; Signor Walter Persegati of the Vatican Museums; Dr. Anna Mura and Signor Alessandro Fochetti of the Barracco Museum, Rome; and Dr. Prudence Harper, Dr. Joan Aruz, and Dr. Holly Pittman of the Metropolitan Museum of Art, New York.

To McGuire Gibson of the University of Chicago I owe a special debt, for it was as a member of the Oriental Institute's team at Nippur that I first visited Nineveh to study the remains of Sennacherib's palace. Likewise to David Stronach of the University of California, Berkeley, who invited me to join his new excavations at Nineveh to begin testing some of the hypotheses put forth here.

Very generous support for two research trips to Europe and one to Iraq was provided by the Samuel H. Kress Foundation. The Kress Foundation's executive secretary at the time, the late Mary Davis, was interested in Sennacherib in connection with another Kress project, the excavations at the site of ancient Lachish. Her enthusiasm and encouragement in the early stages of my research are greatly appreciated. Funding for a further trip to London was provided by the Columbia University Council for Research in the Humanities. The majority of my expenses for two additional trips to Iraq were covered by the Mesopotamian Fellowship of the American Schools of Oriental Research and grants from the Linda Noe Laine Foundation. Time for reflection and writing was provided through grants from the University of Pennsylvania, the Andrew W. Mellon Foundation, and Georgia Southern College.

Karen Wilson, Kathryn Kraynik, and Toni Ellis of the University of Chicago Press shepherded this manuscript through the press and into print. My indebtedness to them is immeasurable. I am also grateful to the College Art Association of America, Inc., for permission to reprint portions of my article "Bulls for the Palace and Order in the Empire: The Sculptural Program of Sennacherib's Court VI at Nineveh," from *Art Bulletin* 69 (1987), which appear here as parts of chapters 5, 9, and 11.

Last but certainly not least is the thanks I owe my wife Janet. Her most tangible contribution to this project was the typing of several drafts, but far more important were her patience, her encouragement, and her confidence.

1

INTRODUCTION

At the beginning of his reign, Sennacherib (704–681 B.C.) moved the capital of the Assyrian empire from the recently completed city of Dur Sharrukin to Nineveh, the ancient cult city of Ishtar. There he built a new palace that he called *ekallu ša šānina lā īšû*, the "Palace without Rival." It was built on the southwest corner of Kouyunjik, one of the two great mounds encompassed by the walls of ancient Nineveh (figs. 1, 2, plan following Index). The walls of some seventy rooms in this structure were lined with limestone slabs carved in low relief with scenes commemorating Sennacherib's royal exploits.

When Nineveh fell in 612 B.C. to a coalition of Medes and Babylonians, Sennacherib's palace was pillaged and burned; the upper story collapsed into the lower and the "Palace without Rival" lay buried and forgotten for nearly two and one-half millennia. In 1847 its remains were discovered by the British diplomat and amateur archaeologist Austin Henry Layard, who excavated the "Southwest Palace," as he called it, between 1847 and 1851. His finds there generated a wave of excitement among both scholars and the educated public seldom equaled in the annals of archaeology. The main focus of this excitement was a small inner chamber in the palace, Room XXXVI (figs. 3, 4). There Layard uncovered wall reliefs that, according to the cuneiform label, depict Sennacherib's siege of the Judean walled city of Lachish, an event also recorded in II Kings (18:13–14). Here, then, was the first archaeological confirmation of an event from the Bible. In addition to this visual account of the victory at Lachish, the palace yielded written records describing Sennacherib's siege of Jerusalem. Layard observed that the Assyrian and biblical accounts agreed not only on the unsuccessful outcome of the siege, but also even on the thirty talents of gold paid as tribute by Hezekiah of Judah to Sennacherib.[1]

1

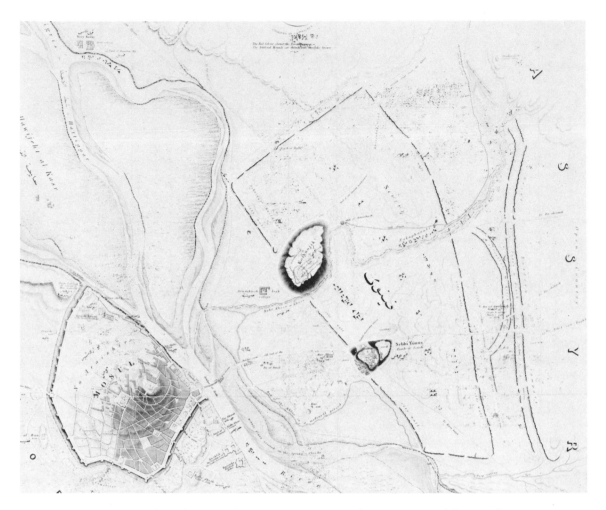

FIG. 1.   Plan of Nineveh by Felix Jones, 1852 (photo: Trustees of the British Museum).

The degree of popular interest in the palaces of Sennacherib and the other Assyrian kings can be judged, as Barnett observed, from the number and success of books on the subject that appeared within a few years of Layard's discoveries. "Thus Layard's *Nineveh and Its Remains* (1849) ran through six editions, and his *Nineveh and Babylon* (1853) had at least three popular abridgements. . . . W. S. Vaux's *Nineveh and Persepolis* (1850) had four editions and James Fergusson's *Palaces of Nineveh and Persepolis Restored* (1850) had two editions while Joseph Bonomi's *Nineveh and Its Palaces: The Discov-*

FIG. 2. Nineveh, mound of Kouyunjik, aerial view looking west, 1933 (reproduced by permission of the University of London Institute of Archaeology, University College London).

FIG. 3. Sennacherib reviewing the spoil of Lachish, detail of Slab 11, Room XXXVI, Southwest Palace, Nineveh. British Museum, WAA 124911 (photo: author).

FIG. 4. Siege of Lachish as installed in the British Museum, Room XXXVI, Southwest Palace, Nineveh (photo: author).

eries of Botta and Layard Applied to the Elucidation of Holy Writ, published in 1852, had five editions."[2]

The palaces of Nineveh were the source of a second wave of excitement some twenty years later when in 1872 George Smith, a young Assyriologist employed by the British Museum to sort and copy clay tablets, discovered that one of the museum's tablets from Nineveh contained a fragmentary account of the Deluge. Because of the uproar resulting from the announcement of this discovery, Smith was immediately dispatched to Kouyunjik to seek further portions of the account and, with incredible good luck, he succeeded in finding another fragment, largely completing the Deluge account.[3] With this event, which signaled the coming of age of Assyrian philology as well as its future potential, the primary focus of Assyriological interest shifted from palaces and their decoration to texts, a situation that still largely holds true today.

In the years since the discovery of the great Assyrian palaces, some scholars have studied the palace reliefs, concentrating primarily on their style and on their significance as illustrations of the way of life of a dead civilization. Others have studied the palace inscriptions, focusing mainly on their historical and religious content. Very few, however, have studied the images and texts *together* in their original context as integral components of the overall decorative scheme of an Assyrian palace. What is attempted in this study is an appreciation of Assyrian palace decoration as a synthesis of text and image. This, I believe, does no more than fulfill the original intention of the kings whom these images and texts jointly serve to glorify.

This work owes a great debt to a number of earlier works on a variety of subjects, and these are cited throughout in the notes. Of particular value to me were Layard's remarkably informative accounts of the excavation of the Southwest Palace (1849a, 1853a) and his publications of the palace reliefs (1849b, 1853b) and inscriptions (1851); the publication and identification of additional Sennacherib relief slabs by Gadd (1936) and Weidner and Furlani (1939); Paterson's (1915) catalog of the majority of the published Southwest Palace reliefs; Reade's (1967, 1978, 1979b) work on the location, arrangement, and subjects of the Southwest Palace reliefs; Nagel's (1967) study of stylistic development in neo-Assyrian relief from Sennacherib to Assurbanipal; Hrouda's (1965) and Madhloom's (1970) typological studies of neo-Assyrian relief; Groenewegen-Frankfort's (1951) observations on perspective in neo-Assyrian reliefs; and the programmatic studies of the reliefs of Assurbanipal's Room S[1] by Albenda (1976, 1977) and Assurnasirpal II's throne room by Winter (1981, 1983).

Since the information contained in the palace inscriptions provides the foundation for much that follows, they are treated here first. Chapter 2, "Texts and Context," considers the four most common types of texts that figure in the decorative schemes of Assyrian palaces during the period from Assurnasirpal II (883–859 B.C.) to Sennacherib: bull texts, thresholds, wall slab texts, and epigraphs.[4] This chapter has two goals. The first is to establish the architectural context of the palace inscriptions. There has been a tendency among Assyriologists to focus on the content of Assyrian royal inscriptions while largely ignoring their physical context, even though the intended location of an inscription—whether buried in a foundation, displayed on a palace bull colossus, or carved on a cliff at the frontier of the empire—largely determines its content. My other goal here is to place the palace inscriptions of Sennacherib in their developmental context in order to determine which traditional types of inscriptions Sennacherib omitted and how those types he retained were modified.

Chapters 3 to 7 bring together several kinds of evidence to reconstruct as fully as possible the appearance of Sennacherib's reliefs within their architectural context. "Excavation and Architectural Setting" gives a history of the excavation of the Southwest Palace, emphasizing particularly the aims of the excavators, and summarizes their finds there. "(Re)constructing the Palace" offers a reconstruction of the plan of the palace based on available archaeological and textual material and examines evidence for the chronology of its construction. "Quarrying and Transport" combines archaeological, pictorial, and textual evidence to determine the types of stone Sennacherib used for architectural embellishment and the manner of its procurement. "The Periods of the Southwest Palace Reliefs" assembles and evaluates the observations of several scholars who have proposed sets of criteria intended to determine which of the Southwest Palace reliefs date to the time of Sennacherib and which ones do not. "The Subjects of Sennacherib's Reliefs" considers historical, epigraphic, and pictorial evidence in an attempt to identify which campaign or campaigns were the subject of each Sennacherib relief series. Together, these five chapters give a reasonably clear overall picture of the Southwest Palace and its decoration at the time of Sennacherib.

Chapters 8 to 11 are concerned with the function of Sennacherib's palace reliefs and the associated texts. "Tradition and Innovation" seeks to clarify which conventions of Assyrian palace decoration were sufficiently established by Sennacherib's reign that they may be termed "traditional" and then examines why and how certain of these traditions were modified by him. "Space and Time" focuses on Sennacherib's innovations in the representation of spatial and temporal perspectives. "Audience" brings together various sorts of textual and pictorial evidence to determine what sorts of people would have had the opportunity to view the palace reliefs and texts. "The Message of Sennacherib's Palace" is concerned with the meaning of the reliefs and texts and their effect on the various components of their audience. Also included are two appendices, one giving transliterations and translations of the inscriptions on Sennacheribs palace reliefs, the other collecting publication references for individual reliefs on a room-by-room basis.

There is more and a greater variety of information available concerning the decoration of Sennacherib's palace than for the palace of any other neo-Assyrian king. A large part of the palace has been excavated, including nearly all of its decorated residential area. The relief decoration of many of its rooms is known from preserved reliefs, drawings, and Layard's descriptions. A good sample of the palace inscriptions has been published, including both extended texts carved on the gateway colossi and buried in the palace foundations and brief epigraphs carved on the wall reliefs. These texts provide a relatively complete picture of the events of Sennacherib's first fifteen years of rule, including very full accounts of the construction and decoration of the Southwest Palace. Thus Sennacherib's palace decoration provides an excellent opportunity to study the interconnections between text and image in a neo-Assyrian palace. What will emerge from this, I hope, is an awareness that in Sennacherib's palace neither of these decorative components is sufficient unto itself; rather, the meanings of the texts and images are inextricably entwined, in turn reinforcing and modifying one another.

2

TEXTS AND CONTEXT

A long-lived Assyrian subject granted a royal audience in the throne room of Assurnasirpal II's palace at Nimrud in 861 B.C. and granted a similar audience in 706 B.C., 155 years later, in Sargon's palace at Khorsabad, might observe that the passage of years and relocation of the capital had had little effect on the general appearance of the royal reception area. This same subject, granted another fifteen years of life and another royal audience in 691 B.C., this time in Sennacherib's palace at Nineveh, might marvel that so few years could produce such alterations—some dramatic, some subtle—to the familiar appearance of the throne room (fig. 5). These alterations are not found in

FIG. 5.   Throne room (I), Southwest Palace, Nineveh (photo: author).

7

the plan, which, insofar as it is preserved, is virtually identical to that of Sargon's palace. Rather, they are found in the decorative scheme of the throne room, particularly in the relief sculpture and inscriptions.[1] The substantial changes in the sculpture of Sennacherib's palace will be discussed later, in chapters 8 and 9. This chapter deals with the various types of inscriptional decoration traditionally found in the throne rooms of Assyrian palaces before Sennacherib and investigates Sennacherib's utilization, rejection, or transformation of these types in the decoration of his own throne room.[2]

A survey of Assyrian records, presented in chapter 10 below, suggests that the potential audience for the neo-Assyrian palace inscriptions included the king and his family, courtiers, Assyrian citizens, foreigners, future kings, and the gods. These various components of the audience will be investigated more thoroughly in that chapter. For now it is sufficient to observe that during the neo-Assyrian period, as for the ancient Near East as a whole, writing was a specialized art confined, for the most part, to the spheres of temple and palace administration. There can have been very few contemporaries who could read the messages inscribed on the walls of Assyrian palaces, and most of those who could would have been involved in state administration and thus already familiar with the messages' content. The possibility that these inscriptions were also intended to function at some nonverbal level must therefore be considered, unless they are to be dismissed as mere decoration.

As members of a society where literacy is available to everyone, it is difficult for us to view texts through the eyes of a nonliterate Assyrian. For us, the primary informational value of a text derives from its content, but this need not have been the case at all times, especially in ages when nonliteracy was the norm. Even today, texts communicate at a variety of levels, only one of which is at the overt "content" level. For example, before computers revolutionized publishing, a typeset book was valued more highly than one reproduced photomechanically from a typescript. The former, because of the greater resources required to produce it and its greater aesthetic appeal, commanded greater respect, even if the literary merit of the two books was identical. Similarly, the same text can carry different connotations if it is reproduced in gothic instead of roman type or if it is reproduced on a billboard in letters six feet high instead of on a handbill. None of these variations has anything to do with what is usually considered "content," but they affect the reader nonetheless. More important for the argument presented here, these differences are also noticeable to a perceptive nonliterate viewer and could conceivably evoke similar responses of respect or disdain.

Literacy was not a prerequisite, therefore, for satisfactory functioning of

Assyrian royal inscriptions. In addition to the overt level of "content," these inscriptions function at at least two nonverbal levels. At one level was the simple fact of the inscription's presence. In Assyria, there was generally only one person with the resources, authority, and power to order the composition of large numbers of extensive texts and have them engraved in stone. The narrative and heraldic reliefs of the palace function at this level too. One need not study the images nor read the text to appreciate that they represent enormous power, a power beyond the means of all but the king.

The other level is more difficult to define precisely. It has to do with the power inherent in the control of the craft of writing. The control of the

Fig. 6.   Inscribed cylinder ("Rassam Cylinder"), baked clay, Southwest Palace, Nineveh. British Museum, WAA 22503 (photo: Trustees of the British Museum).

scribes was itself a strong affirmation of the legitimacy of the king's rule. But beyond this is the mystical quality of writing, its ability to encode unlimited quantities of information for future use. To the nonliterate majority of courtiers and visitors, the palace inscriptions would have served as a reminder that the king controlled a vast store of information that was a symbol, as well as a source, of immense power.

Besides impressing visitors to and residents of the palace, whether literate or not, the neo-Assyrian palace inscriptions served one other important function. Many of these texts conclude with an invocation to the gods and a request that future kings preserve and restore the palace, thereby perpetuating the memory of the king who built it. These passages indicate that one of the texts' functions was to serve as a *record* of the king and his accomplishments. In Sennacherib's palace the same extended texts that were carved on the colossi at the palace doors were also inscribed on cylinders and prisms of clay that were then baked and buried in the palace foundations for future generations (fig. 6).[3] It is to these records on stone and clay that we owe most of our knowledge of the historical circumstances of Sennacherib's reign. They also provide lengthy descriptions of the construction and appearance of his palace. The palace inscriptions are therefore considered here first; the wealth of information they contain serves as a framework on which to fashion an image of Sennacherib's "Palace without Rival."

Bull Texts

The courtyard facade of the principal throne rooms of the palaces of Assurnasirpal II (Room B), Sargon II ("Court" VII), and Sennacherib (Room I) were all decorated with five pairs of bull colossi—one pair in each of the three doorways, and one antithetical pair on the face of each of the two buttresses that flanked the central door (figs. 7, 8, 9, 10). In each case, the space between the legs of the bulls carried an inscription. Since these are the first texts a visitor would have encountered when entering the throne room, they will be discussed first.

The first preserved Assyrian palace colossi are from the Northwest Palace of King Assurnasirpal II (883–859 B.C.) in the city of Kalhu, now known as Nimrud (fig. 11). The same basic text was apparently used on all of Assurnasirpal's colossi, though different amounts of the text are found on different colossi. The only preserved monument that contains the full text is the inscribed throne base from the east end of Assurnasirpal's throne room B.[4] Its beginning is identical to that of Assurnasirpal II's "Standard Inscription":

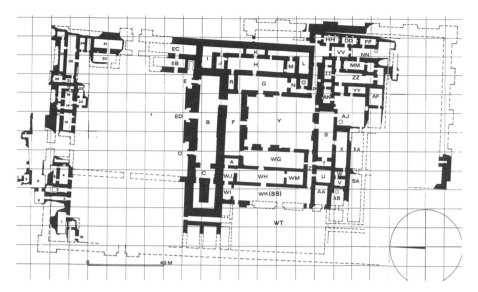

FIG. 7.   Plan of the Northwest Palace of Assurnasirpal II, Nimrud, drawn by Richard Sobolewski (from Paley and Sobolewski, *Baghdader Forschungen*, x, 1987, plan 1).

titles and epithets of the king and a geographical summary of the king's conquests. The colossus text then diverges from the "Standard Inscription," inserting more royal epithets and accounts of a campaign to the Mediterranean, the breeding and hunting of animals, and a campaign against Carchemish. Its conclusion returns to the "Standard Inscription" and recounts the building of a palace at Kalhu.

The next king for whom throne-room colossi are preserved is Sargon II (721–705 B.C.). As with the palace colossi of Assurnasirpal II, all colossi in Sargon's palace at Khorsabad (ancient Dur Sharrukin) were apparently inscribed with the same text. Unlike the Assurnasirpal II colossus inscriptions, each Sargon inscription contains the full text, distributed between the two bulls of each doorway or facade buttress (fig. 12).[5] Sargon's bull text is also somewhat different in form from Assurnasirpal II's. It commences with a brief titulary and a list of Babylonian and Assyrian cities to which Sargon granted special favors, followed by a geographical summary of Sargon's conquests arranged according to region rather than chronology. The remainder of the text is a lengthy account of the building of the new capital, Dur Sharrukin, and the conclusion is a supplication to the gods to protect the works of Sargon's hands. The proportions of this text are noteworthy: two-thirds of

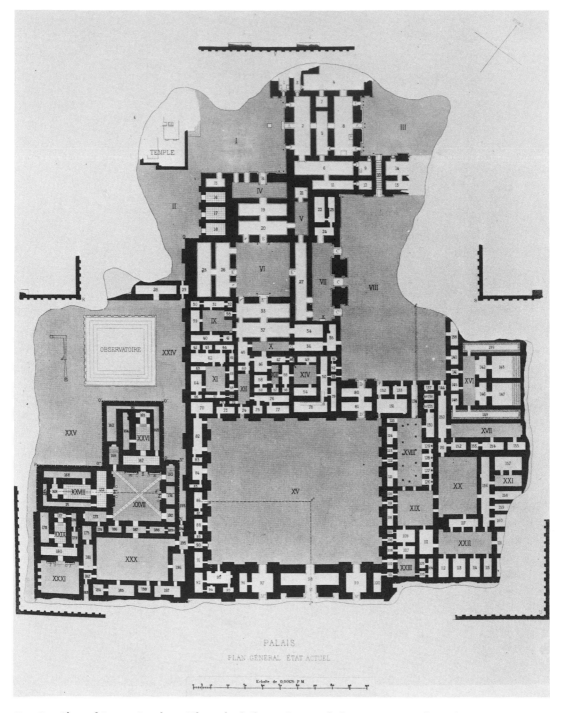

Fig. 8.   Plan of Sargon's palace, Khorsabad (from Place and Thomas 1867, vol. 3, pl. 3).

it is a building account, compared with less than one-sixth of Assurnasirpal II's colossus text. Clearly a primary function of Sargon's bull text was to commemorate the foundation of the new capital.

With Sargon's successor, Sennacherib, there was a considerable shift in the content and function of the palace bull inscriptions. Ten Sennacherib colossus inscriptions are published in whole or in part, and the majority of these

FIG. 9.   Throne-room facade, Slabs 42–57, Facade n, southwest wall of Court VIII, Sargon's palace, Khorsabad (from Botta and Flandin 1849, vol. 1, pl. 30).

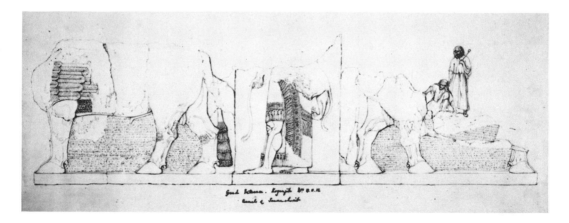

FIG. 10.   Colossi from the throne-room facade (H), Slabs 10–12, Southwest Palace, Nineveh. British Museum, WAA, Or. Dr., I, 33 (photo: Trustees of the British Museum).

FIG. 11. Bull colossus, no. 2, Door *e*, Room Y, Northwest Palace of Assurnasirpal II, Nimrud, h. 314 cm. Metropolitan Museum, 32.143.1 (photo: Metropolitan Museum of Art, Gift of John D. Rockefeller, Jr., 1932).

FIG. 12. Bull colossus, probably Gate B, inner citadel wall of Sargon's palace, Khorsabad, h. 442 cm. British Museum, WAA 118809 (photo: Trustees of the British Museum).

are from the area of the throne room (I) of the Southwest Palace. The Sennacherib colossus inscriptions have been analyzed in detail elsewhere both by Galter, Levine, and Reade (1986) and by me, so I will confine myself here to a summary account of their role in Sennacherib's palace decoration.[6] A comparison of the bull inscriptions of Sennacherib with those of his father, Sargon II, reveals considerable differences in form and content, which may in turn point to a change in intended function. The most noticeable of these differences are an increased variety of types of content and the considerably greater length of Sennacherib's bull inscriptions.

All of Sargon's palace bulls carried the same inscription. The preserved

Sennacherib bulls, by contrast, displayed a variety of texts, which conformed
to three general types. The first type—seen in Room I, Door *a*—was a detailed annalistic narrative, arranged chronologically, followed by a palace
building account (see fig. 125). Portions of this type of text may also be preserved in two unidentified casts made from Southwest Palace colossi and
published by Meissner and Rost. The second type—seen in Room I, Doors *d*
and *e*—was a brief historical summary, arranged in a mixed chronological-
geographical order, followed by a palace building account (see fig. 129).
George Smith's "Bull 3"—probably from the throne-room facade buttresses
(fig. 10)—and an inscribed fragment in Hannover were also of this type. The
third type—found in Court VI, Door *a*, and Room I, Door *c*—consisted entirely of a palace building account (see figs. 53, 126).[7]

Though the Southwest Palace bull inscriptions seem to conform to these
three general types, no two of the published texts are identical. In addition to
the orthographic variants that are the rule in Assyrian palace inscriptions,
these inscriptions also give differing versions of details, such as the dimensions of the palace; they exhibit varying degrees of abridgment; and they
seemingly intermix passages drawn from the entire corpus of palace inscriptions, both from early and later foundation texts. The inscriptions also cover
differing time periods, with some recording five and others six campaigns. In
the case of Room I, Door *d*, the historical summary covers five campaigns,
but campaigns one and four, both against Babylonia, are combined, so that
the order of presentation is one and four, followed by two, three, and five.
This is not the pattern of geographical rotation employed in Sargon's bull inscriptions, but rather a slightly modified chronological presentation. The historical summary of George Smith's "Bull 3" adds the sixth campaign, against
Babylon, but rather than combining it with campaigns one and four, it is
placed at the end. This suggests that the scribes updated the five-campaign
summary not by rewriting it, but simply by adding to it.

It appears, then, that most of Sennacherib's palace bull inscriptions were
compiled individually. We cannot know all of the considerations that applied
when each was composed, but clearly the scribes were interested in presenting information that was up-to-date, and apparently they were also aware of
the amount of space available for each inscription and tailored them accordingly.

The question of space available for inscription raises the second major difference between the bull inscriptions of Sennacherib and Sargon II, namely
their length. Unlike Sargon's bull inscriptions, which were restricted to four
rectangular panels, Sennacherib's filled the entire space under the belly and

between the legs. Furthermore, as will be seen in chapter 9, Sennacherib's elimination of the extra foreleg visible in the side view of his predecessors' colossi expanded the space available for inscription under the belly. The result of this expansion is seen not in Sennacherib's smaller bulls, where the inscriptions are only slightly longer than Sargon's, but rather in the large bulls, such as those in Door *a* of Room I, where the inscription is more than two and one-half times as long as Sargon's.

Accounting for this variety in the Sennacherib bull inscriptions, which is especially noticeable when contrasted with Sargon's use of a single text for all his colossi, regardless of size or location, remains to be done. It seems to me this variety must be viewed not simply in the context of Sargon's colossus text, but rather in the context of the entire corpus of Sargon's palace inscriptions. Sargon had different types of texts composed for different types of features of his palace decoration: bulls and the walls of Room 14 carried a historical summary, arranged geographically, plus a building account; thresholds were inscribed with a brief historical summary, or with a summary plus building account; the inscribed band between the registers of narrative relief in Rooms 2, 5, 13, and 14 carried an annalistic account of the king's reign plus a building account; the formal scenes of tributaries in Rooms 1, 4, 7, 8, and 10 were inscribed with a lengthy historical summary, arranged in roughly chronological order, plus a building account; and the narrative reliefs carried brief captions identifying the towns and peoples represented.[8]

In the palace of Sennacherib, by contrast, the only visible inscriptions were the bull inscriptions and the captions on the reliefs. Sennacherib apparently wished to retain the variety of Sargon's inscriptions, but within a more restricted range of locations. The bulls and captions, therefore, entirely usurped the functions that formerly had been apportioned to inscriptions in a variety of palace locations. Thus in Sennacherib's throne room, the bulls of Door *a* had a text similar in form to Sargon's annalistic inscriptions; in Door *d* was a summary arranged chronologically, similar to Sargon's chronological summary; and in Door *c* was a text whose principal emphasis was on the building account, similar to Sargon's bull and threshold texts. To be sure, the correspondence between Sennacherib's bull texts and the corpus of Sargon's palace texts was not complete; Sennacherib, for example, was far more interested than his father in presenting a detailed and complete account of his building activities. But it is clear that when Sennacherib sacrificed or modified a type of text, it was not because he lacked a place to carve it, but rather because he wished to express priorities different from his father's.

Thresholds

The second type of inscription a well-informed visitor to the throne room of Sennacherib's palace would have expected to find would be that on the stone threshold of the entrance. In large measure, this expectation would have been frustrated. Though inscribed thresholds were the rule in the palace decoration of all of Sennacherib's predecessors, they seem to occur infrequently in his own Southwest Palace.

Inscribed thresholds were a common feature of monumental doorways in Assurnasirpal II's Northwest Palace at Nimrud. Layard observed that "between the lions and bulls forming the entrances was generally placed one large slab, bearing an inscription." Only the threshold inscription from Door *c* of the throne room (B) has been published: it was inscribed with a portion of the annals of Assurnasirpal's fifth year.[9] Two inscribed thresholds were likewise reported from "Fort Shalmaneser," Shalmaneser III's "palace" at Nimrud.[10] Only one, from a small chamber (S4) to the west of the throne-room suite, was legible. It consisted of a brief titulary followed by an extremely condensed summary of years one to fifteen.[11]

Inscribed thresholds were also an important feature of Sargon II's palace at Khorsabad. Flandin's detailed plans show no fewer than twenty-nine inscribed thresholds, twenty-one of which are published. Each carried one of five different texts. The longest, used in monumental entrances, consists of a brief titulary and list of tax concessions, a summary of the king's military triumphs, and a detailed palace building account. The remaining four texts represent various degrees of abridgment of this long text, with occasional additions that may reflect a text's intended function.[12] The decision of which of these five texts to carve on a given threshold was influenced largely by the size of the threshold, but also probably by other factors, such as the function and decoration of the room.

It is noteworthy that while Sargon's palace thresholds are inscribed in the traditional manner, important thresholds in some neighboring buildings at Khorsabad exemplify another fashion. Three stone thresholds from Residence L carry a short inscription identifying the building's owner as Sinahu-sur, Sargon's brother and vizier, but the inscription occupies only a small part of the surface, the remainder being covered by a pattern of small rosettes enclosed in a grid. Three thresholds were also found in Residence K, and these carried no inscription at all, but rather an elaborate ornamental pattern of rosettes and alternating cone and lotus.[13]

The antecedents, if any, of these floral patterned thresholds are unknown to us. Albenda suggested that they may reflect an otherwise unknown tradition of placing floral patterned carpets in the principal doorways of important nonpalatial neo-Assyrian buildings.[14] It seems likely that these thresholds were created with the knowledge of the king, who would probably have been the only person with the resources to procure and decorate large stone slabs, but they were apparently not deemed suitable for the doorways of the royal palace itself. They are of particular interest, however, because in the palaces of Sennacherib and Assurbanipal, the floral threshold completely supplanted the traditional inscribed threshold seen in the palaces of Assurnasirpal II, Shalmaneser III, and Sargon II.

The threshold slabs in Sennacherib's Southwest Palace are fairly well known from descriptions and drawings of Layard's excavations. According to Layard, "the pavement slabs were not inscribed as at Nimroud; but those between the winged bulls at some of the entrances, were carved with an elaborate and very elegant pattern."[15] He published an engraving of only one of these thresholds, that from Room XXIV, Door *c*, whose pattern he described as "a border of alternate tulips or lotus flowers and cones, enclosing similar ornaments arranged in squares and surrounded by rosettes." In his note to this engraving, Layard stated that "many of the entrances at Kouyunjik have similar pavements" and drawings of some of these have recently been published by Albenda.[16] All of these patterns consist of various arrangements of the basic elements described by Layard for Room XXIV, Door *c*.

Concerning the thresholds of Sennacherib's throne room (Room I), Layard reported that the threshold of Door *e* (formerly *a*) was "elaborately carved with figures of flowers, resembling the lotus, and with other ornaments." Layard failed to mention that this threshold has a brief two-line inscription carved across its middle (fig. 13; see Appendix 1). This is the only inscribed threshold known from Sennacherib's palace, but there may be others. The Iraqi excavations showed that throne-room Door *a* and Room V, Door *a*, were also decorated with floral thresholds, but no inscriptions were reported.[17]

In view of the expanded format and content of Sennacherib's throne-room colossi, a similar phenomenon with respect to the threshold slabs associated with them might be expected. Such was not the case, however, as all available evidence indicates that the visible surfaces of most of Sennacherib's palace thresholds, unlike those of his predecessors, were devoid of inscriptions. The text on the only known inscribed example is very brief, stating only that Sennacherib built this palace. The implications of this modification of the tra-

FIG. 13.   Inscribed floral threshold, Door *e*, Room I, Southwest Palace, Nineveh, w. 211 cm (photo: author).

ditional role of the palace threshold will be considered in the context of Sennacherib's other palace inscriptions at the end of this chapter.

The Wall Relief Text

As with the threshold texts, our perceptive visitor to Sennacherib's palace would have noted the absence of a third type of inscription. This missing inscription was the band of text carved on the relief slabs lining the walls of the palaces of Sennacherib's predecessors. The first occurrence of this type of inscription was in the Northwest Palace of Assurnasirpal II (fig. 14). The text, known as the "Standard Inscription," is a highly condensed formulation of royal titles and epithets, a geographical summary of the extent of the empire, and a palace building account.[18] The entire text was carved across the middle

FIG. 14. Inscribed wall relief of Assurnasirpal II, Slab 30, Room I, Northwest Palace, Nimrud, w. 211 cm. Metropolitan Museum 32.143.3 (photo: Metropolitan Museum of Art, Gift of John D. Rockefeller, Jr., 1932).

FIG. 15. Relief of Tiglath-pileser III showing the booty of Aṣtartu, Central Palace, Nimrud, w. 195 cm. British Museum, WAA 118908 (photo: Trustees of the British Museum).

FIG. 16.   Siege of Pazaši, engraving of Slab 2, Room 14, Sargon's palace, Khorsabad (from Botta and Flandin 1849, vol. 2, 145).

of each of the decorated and plain wall slabs, giving the visual effect of a continuous register of inscription around the room. A similar-looking register of text was on the wall reliefs of Tiglath-pileser III's Central Palace at Nimrud (fig. 15). There are two significant differences, however, between the wall-relief texts of Assurnasirpal and Tiglath-pileser: the preserved examples of the latter are annalistic, rather than summary, in form; and this annalistic text apparently continued from slab to slab around an entire room, rather than being repeated on every slab in the room.[19]

Tiglath-pileser III's annalistic text, carved once around the walls of a room, has one disadvantage when compared to the short summary text carved on every slab of Assurnasirpal II's palace. The important passage that gave the name and titles of the king—thereby identifying the protagonist of the texts and reliefs—apparently occurred only once, at the beginning of the wall inscription, in each room of the Central Palace. If the slab bearing the royal name is overlooked or damaged, then the events described and depicted on *all* the reliefs in that room lose their particularity and risk being read as generic.[20] This continued to be a problem for Sargon II, but it was corrected by his successor, Sennacherib.

In the palace of Sargon II also, extensive inscriptions were sometimes carved on a band across the middle of reliefs in two registers or across the lower portion of formal scenes in one register (indicated by a band of parallel lines in fig. 16). These wall relief inscriptions were of two types: an annalistic account of the king's first fourteen years and a historical summary in which campaigns were arranged geographically, beginning with the east, proceeding roughly counterclockwise around the empire, and concluding with the southeast. Both of these texts conclude with an account of the building of the new palace at Dur Sharrukin.[21]

Upon arriving finally at Sennacherib's Southwest Palace, we see that, with the exception of brief epigraphs, which will be discussed below, the wall reliefs are devoid of inscriptions.[22] To be sure, Sennacherib still included annalistic and summary texts in his palace decoration, but these were now confined to the doorway bulls, which were positioned at right angles to the decorated walls of the rooms. No longer were the palace reliefs required to share space with extensive inscriptions that did little to illuminate their content. Except for the epigraphs, Sennacherib's images stood on their own, with no competition for the viewer's attention.

Epigraphs

Epigraphs are brief, purely explanatory captions applied to reliefs as labels for persons, places, and/or events depicted. They serve, in Barthes's terminology, to "anchor" an image, thereby ensuring that the literate viewer will select the correct reading from a range of conceivable alternatives. It is in the nature of images that they are *perceived* far more readily than they are *understood*. Anyone familiar with the visual code employed can read an image, but fewer will have the cultural background necessary for its correct interpretation. Viewers tend to read images in terms of their own experience, with the result that a highly specific historical image may be read at an ideal or nonhistorical level. The "anchoring" function of an epigraph ensures a specific, rather than generic, reading of the image.[23]

An epigraph can serve this function to some degree even for an illiterate, since one need not be able to read the inscription to recognize these brief, strategically placed texts as labels, and the very presence of labels connotes specificity. They serve, therefore, to arrest and focus the gaze of literate and nonliterate alike.[24] Epigraphs are particularly important to the palace decoration of Sennacherib since they constitute the only other category of text besides bull inscriptions to be used consistently. In fact, Sennacherib exploited the epigraphic label to a degree unknown in the reliefs of any of his predecessors.

Epigraphs are not found on the palace reliefs of Assurnasirpal II, though they do occur on his obelisks and bronze doors. The reason for their omission from the wall reliefs is unclear. Perhaps their designers felt that in these comparatively large-scale images, particularizing details such as costume, scenery, and architecture would have made them sufficiently specific to be readily recognizable without incorporating explanatory labels. Indeed, these reliefs probably were easily recognizable to members of and visitors to Assurnasirpal's court, viewers who either would already have a passing familiarity with the events of the day or who could readily find someone who was.

Such may well not have been the case, however, for Tiglath-pileser III and his court, who lived in Assurnasirpal's palace 150 years later. It is probable that by this time relatively few of Assurnasirpal's unlabeled images would have been recognizable because of changing artistic conventions, the changing appearance of the cities in question, and the death long ago of all those who could explain the images. For Tiglath-pileser, the "matching" of events recounted in Assurnasirpal's annalistic texts with the events depicted on the reliefs may have been nearly as uncertain a process as it is today. Tiglath-pileser III was in a position, therefore, to perceive what Assurnasirpal II could not: the difficulties of interpretation that unlabeled narrative images present for posterity.

The reliefs of Tiglath-pileser III mark the first known appearance of epigraphs on the wall decoration of an Assyrian palace. Only three of these epigraphs are known, all apparently from the same relief series.[25] Each consists only of a single city name—U-⌈pa⌉?, Gezer, and Aṣtartu (see fig. 15)—written directly above the walls of the city it labels. These brief, unobtrusive epigraphs would have ensured that Tiglath-pileser's narrative reliefs could be read at the desired level of specificity both at the time they were carved and in years to come.

A considerable number of epigraphs survive from the reliefs of the northwest wing of Sargon II's palace at Khorsabad. Most were inscribed on the reliefs of military narrative in Rooms 2, 5, 13, and 14, which were in two registers with a band of annalistic text between (see fig. 16). A few, rather longer than the rest, were found on the Room 8 reliefs, the subject of which was a single-register depiction of the punishment of captives, inscribed with a summary text. One was on a narrative relief fragment found dissociated from its original architectural context.[26] They do not occur on the procession reliefs, nor on those of which the subject is hunting. Sargon's epigraphs, then, seem to be confined to those reliefs that record his dealings with enemies of the empire.

The most obvious innovation in Sargon's epigraphs, when compared to those of his predecessor, is their greater length and detail. In Sargon's palace, the epigraphs in Rooms 2 and 5 each consist only of a single city name, as was the case with those of Tiglath-pileser III. In Rooms 13 and 14 and on the unlocated slab, however, the epigraphs instead consist of declarative sentences, two of which require two lines of text (Room 14, Slab 2; and the unlocated slab), though each still deals with only a single subject. The epigraphs of Room 8 occupy two, three, or more lines, and at least one of these (Slab 17) includes three separate subjects.

The benefit of these longer epigraphs for Sargon's campaign narratives is not clear. The only information they usually add that is not found in the shorter epigraphs is, "I besieged, I conquered." Now such information is far from inconsequential, but one would think this action is presented sufficiently by the reliefs themselves, the subject of which is unmistakably attack, surrender, and plunder. The only element that is not clear from the reliefs is the "I"—the name of the king who orchestrates the proceedings but is not always shown as an active participant in each scene of combat. The problem here is that the epigraph does not identify who this "I" is, and this information cannot be gathered easily from the central text register either, since there the name of the king is repeated only occasionally. Therefore though Sargon's longer epigraphs include somewhat more information than do his short ones, they still do not adequately identify the perpetrator of the deeds shown.

The widespread use of epigraphs continued in the narrative reliefs of the Southwest Palace and, as already seen, were one of only two traditional palace inscription types that Sennacherib continued to use extensively, the other being bull inscriptions. Unfortunately, relatively few of these epigraphs are preserved. As Layard observed, this was largely because the upper portion of most of the Southwest Palace reliefs, the location favored for epigraphs, was destroyed.[27] This loss is graphically illustrated by Slab 10 of Room XIV, where by some miracle the small portion of the top of the slab bearing the epigraph was preserved, while the remainder of the slab top was lost (fig. 17). Certainly, many similarly located epigraphs throughout the palace were less fortunate. To be sure, the tops of most of the reliefs in Sargon II's palace were also lost, but there the division of the pictorial surface into two registers increased the survival chances of the epigraphs in the lower register, and it is from the lower register, without exception, that Sargon's epigraphs derive. The elimination of register divisions in most of Sennacherib's reliefs resulted in the consignment of many epigraphs to the top, the most vulnerable portion of the slab. Nonetheless, some twenty-seven Sennacherib epigraphs are recorded from fifteen different rooms of his palace.[28]

None of Sennacherib's preserved epigraphs are of the very brief, name-only form of those of Tiglath-pileser III or Sargon II's Rooms 2 and 5. A few are of the general form of the epigraphs in Sargon's Rooms 13 and 14, such as the epigraphs stating "the city of GN, I besieged, I conquered, I carried off its spoil."[29] The majority, however, are more informative, including not only the place name and a description of the action, but also the name and titles of Sennacherib himself. In Court VI, for example, which has one of the best-preserved relief series, the royal name apparently occurred no fewer than five times between Slabs 60 and 68, while in another well-preserved series, that showing the defeat of Lachish (Room XXXVI), his name appears twice in epigraphs located near his enthroned image (see fig. 3). Despite the absence here of the central text register, there is no danger of mistaking the identity of the hero of these stories. Indeed, the epigraphs serve this important function of identification far more effectively than the text register, both because of their direct juxtaposition with the image of the king and because his name now occurs more frequently than in the annalistic or summary texts of Tiglath-pileser III and Sargon II.

Sennacherib's epigraphs, therefore, have a markedly different emphasis from those of his predecessors. While epigraphs in Tiglath-pileser III's and Sargon II's palaces were reserved solely for enemy cities and captives, Sennacherib's serve fully as much to identify the king.[30] The quarrying and transport scenes in Court VI and Hall XLIX include lengthy epigraphs describing the materials and transport procedures, as well as giving the name of the king and location of the action. The epigraphs accompanying Sennacherib's battle scenes also sometimes contain more narrative detail than those of his predecessors, such as the information that the king sat in a *nēmedu*-throne at Lachish, or that a procession represents the booty of a particular city.[31]

For Sennacherib, then, epigraphs were no longer just passive labels providing the name of the enemy, but came to serve the much more active role in the narrative of identifying the participants on both sides and giving a descriptive summary of the action depicted. To return to Barthes's terminology, Sennacherib's epigraphs not only "anchor" the image, ensuring the correct identification of the subject, they "quicken" the image as well, emphasizing for the literate viewer the most significant features of the action.[32] Because of their narrative form, Sennacherib's epigraphs are like brief excerpts from an annalistic text. They differ from the annals that accompanied the reliefs of

Tiglath-pileser and Sargon, however, in that they refer directly and solely to the action of the accompanying images. The epigraphs of Sennacherib, then, have usurped not only the identifying function, but also the narrative form of the wall relief text register of his predecessors. The narrative they contain is not the story of all the king's conquests, however, but only of the single event illustrated in the reliefs.

It is not possible to tell if every enemy city in Sennacherib's reliefs was

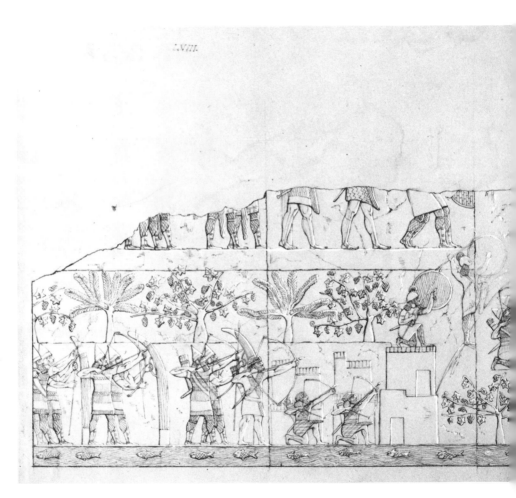

FIG. 17.   Siege of Alammu(?), drawing of Slabs 8–11, Room XIV, Southwest Palace, Nineveh. British Museum, WAA, Or. Dr., IV, 58 (photo: Trustees of the British Museum).

originally labeled with an epigraph. There are two reasons for this. First, as already mentioned, the tops of most slabs were destroyed, and thus most epigraphs located above cities are lost.[33] Second, there seems to be a tendency in Sennacherib's reliefs to shift the location of the epigraph away from the immediate vicinity of the city it labels. This can best be seen in Room XXXVI, where the city of Lachish is shown on Slabs 7 and 8, while the only preserved epigraph mentioning its name is located considerably to the right, on

Slab 12, before the image of the king. The absence of an epigraph over a city in a Sennacherib relief, therefore, doesn't necessarily mean that city was not labeled, for the label could have been elsewhere in the relief series.[34]

A comparison between those places identified by epigraphs in Sennacherib's palace reliefs and those described in the annals gives a somewhat surprising result: only three places—Balaṭai, Bīt-Kubatti, and Sahrina—are mentioned in other Sennacherib records. The remaining six—Lachish, Alammu, [Aranz]iaš, Dilbat, Kasuṣi, and Mt. Lebanon, plus one other fragmentary name—are mentioned by Sennacherib only in the epigraphs.[35] It is clear from this that the preserved editions of the annals, which were intended to be buried in the palace foundations or carved on the doorway bulls, could not also have served as the source for the campaign episodes depicted in the wall reliefs. This leaves two questions: what *was* the source for the narrative palace reliefs, and how can the differences between the events recorded in the written palace annals and those depicted by the images on the palace walls be accounted for?

The best solution to both of these problems is to postulate a lost written source from which the two differing accounts, the verbal and the visual, were derived. This source could have been in the form of detailed narratives of individual campaigns, perhaps made while the campaign was in progress, or it could have been a series of booty lists augmented by personal recollection. Either of these could later be edited into the various sorts of verbal and visual narratives and summaries with which we are familiar. Fortunately, it is possible to produce external evidence that such detailed records were made and to account for their absence from the corpus that has survived. The narrative reliefs of every Assyrian king beginning with Shalmaneser III show scribes accompanying the army on campaign, and those of Tiglath-pileser III, Sargon II, Sennacherib, and Assurbanipal show these scribes working in pairs, apparently making a record of enemy dead and captured booty (fig. 18).[36]

These images of scribes at work play an important role in the viewer's appreciation of the annalistic records that accompany the reliefs in the palace decoration. The annals include passages detailing the amount of booty taken or the number of enemy killed, and these figures sometimes seem fantastic. In the annals on his throne-room colossi, for example, Sennacherib says that Hezekiah of Judah sent him "30 talents of gold and 800 talents of silver," and that in his sixth campaign he captured "30,500 bows and 30,500 arrows." Even a credulous reader might doubt such figures, but the nearby reliefs affirm that scribes were actually there recording such things. The images of scribes counting up the booty, therefore, in effect validate the final counts

FIG. 18. Booty of Alammu(?), drawing of Slabs 13–16, Room XIV, Southwest Palace, Nineveh. British Museum, WAA, Or. Dr., I, 34 (photo: Trustees of the British Museum).

that are presented in the annals. For the literate viewer this verbal/visual parallel serves as a visual authentication of the veracity of the annals.[37]

In most of the representations of scribes, one writes on a scroll of papyrus or leather while the other writes on a hinged writing board covered with wax (figs. 19, 20).[38] Such writing boards would have had several advantages over clay tablets for a scribe accompanying the king on campaign. They could be prepared before setting out on the campaign and would then be ready for use at a moment's notice. They were lighter in weight, relative to their size, than clay tablets. Their materials were weatherproof, and since the board folded shut, the inscribed portion would have been protected from mishaps during travel. These writing boards were apparently widely used in the neo-Assyrian period, as indicated by some acquisition lists published by Parpola which suggest that roughly one-eighth of the texts originally in Assurbanipal's library were inscribed on writing boards.[39] The great disadvantage of both the scrolls and the writing boards, of course, is that in the long run they are far less durable than clay tablets and only survive in the archaeological record under unusual conditions.[40] This evidence suggests, therefore, that the original campaign records of the later Assyrian kings may have been written on perishable materials (leather or papyrus and wax on wood) and have been lost, while the epigraphs and annalistic and summary texts derived from them have been preserved on stone slabs and on prisms and cylinders of baked clay.[41]

One implication of the campaign recording procedure suggested here is that the compilation of the visual narratives with their accompanying epi-

29

graphs could have been carried out independently from that of the written narratives and summaries inscribed on the palace walls. This would seem to be the best way to account for the regular appearance in epigraphs of places not recorded in the annalistic inscriptions. Though both the visual and verbal accounts must have been derived, in part at least, from the same written sources, the visual record might have been augmented by personal recollections and/or artists' field sketches, while the verbal record too would have drawn upon additional resources, especially in the composition of the titulary and building accounts. The differing content of the visual and verbal accounts could have been governed by such factors as the date of compilation, personal choices of the compiler, and the requirements for the effective functioning of the narrative. The details of the visual account might also have been affected by the size of the room, which might have governed the number of individual events to be shown, and by the anticipated audience, which might have resulted in the graphic depiction of particular events aimed at

FIG. 19.   Scribes recording booty, detail of Slab 9, Room XXVIII, Southwest Palace, Nineveh. British Museum, WAA 124955 (photo: Trustees of the British Museum).

Fɪɢ. 20.   Hinged writing boards, ivory, Northwest Palace, Nimrud, h. 33.8 cm.
British Museum, WAA 131952 (photo: Trustees of the British Museum).

that audience—events that might have been passed over in the compilation
of the more general annalistic and summary texts. The question of audience
will be taken up again in chapter 10.

Summary and Conclusions

This chapter has been concerned with the presence or absence in Sennacherib's palace of four traditional types of inscriptions: bull inscriptions, thresholds, wall-relief inscriptions, and epigraphs. To conclude, let us return to my
hypothetical visitor to the throne rooms of the Assyrian kings. The chart on
the next page summarizes which types of texts would have been visible in
each.

In the throne room of Assurnasirpal II in the Northwest Palace at Nimrud,
our visitor would have literally been surrounded by three types of inscriptions: the summary texts on the monumental bulls of the throne-room fa-

Locations and Types of Assyrian Palace Inscriptions

Palace	Colossi	Thresholds	Wall Reliefs	Epigraphs
Assurnasirpal II	summary	annals	summary	no
Tiglath-pileser III	unknown	unknown	annals	yes
Sargon II	summary	summary	annals/summary	yes
Sennacherib	annals/summary	rare	no	yes

cade; the "Standard Inscription" on every wall relief, both outside and inside the room; and the annalistic text on the threshold. For both literate and non-literate visitors, this surfeit of inscribed surfaces makes an impressive display, connoting—as well as denoting—the vast power and authority of the king who ordered its execution.

No palace colossi or wall reliefs of Shalmaneser III are known from "Fort Shalmaneser" at Nimrud, but inscribed thresholds were found there. Tiglath-pileser III's Central Palace at Nimrud was presumably decorated with some of his relief slabs found in the area. Like Assurnasirpal's, these slabs carried a register of inscription, but Tiglath-pileser's texts were annalistic, rather than summary, in form. Tiglath-pileser's reliefs also mark the first appearance in Assyrian palace reliefs of epigraphs, consisting here of only single city names.

All four types of palace inscription were featured in the decoration of Sargon II's palace at Khorsabad. His bull colossi were inscribed with a summary text, each doorway was furnished with a stone threshold slab inscribed with one of five different summary texts, the wall reliefs in most rooms carried a single long annalistic or summary text, and epigraphs figure in virtually every relief series dealing with foreign enemies. Some of these latter are very brief, like those of Tiglath-pileser III, but others are more extended and provide basic narrative information. With respect to its inscribed decoration, then, the appearance of Sargon's palace was quite similar to that of Assurnasirpal II. Even the introduction of epigraphs into the reliefs of Sargon does not notably affect this likeness, since the epigraphs are for the most part brief and inconspicuous, blending in with the other details of the relief background.

Moving on to Sennacherib's palace, from the exterior our visitor would probably perceive few differences between its inscribed colossi and those of Sargon's palace, although the expanded text and missing fifth leg might be apparent. Proceeding through one of the throne-room doorways, however, the visitor would be struck by the almost complete absence of inscriptions inside. The threshold was now decorated with a floral pattern, occasionally framing a very brief inscription. This change is difficult to account for. Perhaps the protective or ritual role that threshold texts may originally have served was modified or eliminated, or perhaps Sennacherib decided that a royal inscription didn't really belong under the feet of his subjects and tributaries.

More noticeably, the band of text on the wall relief was missing as well. In its place was an unbroken expanse of narrative images, reaching from the floor to several feet above eye level, where the old system of composition in one or two registers had been replaced by relatively unified compositions that employ perspectival effects to utilize the entire pictorial field. This transformation in the visual imagery of Sennacherib is analyzed more fully in chapter 9. For now, it is sufficient to note that the designers of Sennacherib's reliefs evidently felt that a continuous register of text, whether carved directly on the surface of the relief or on a raised band between two pictorial registers, would have been inconsistent with the heightened illusionism that was apparently one goal of the narrative images.

The information that had formerly been provided by the annalistic and summary texts carved on the wall reliefs was now confined to the doorway bulls; extensive inscriptions were no longer permitted to compete visually with the images. The only texts that did figure in the wall reliefs were the epigraphs. Rather than distract from the image, these brief texts—by their mere presence—now served to focus attention on specific elements of the representation. In content, they now assumed the additional burdens of identifying the king, as well as his foes, and of "quickening" the narrative image through a very brief summary of the action.

The visual effect of the interior of Sennacherib's palace, then, was substantially different from that of his predecessors, and this difference is to be at least partly attributed to his elimination of a large portion of the inscriptions that before had surrounded the visitor. The texts that remained mark major doorways as entrance proclamations, on the bulls and a few thresholds, and punctuate the narrative reliefs, as epigraphs, which by their brevity and location are fully subordinated to the images on which they appear. How these texts worked with the accompanying reliefs will be one of my subjects in chapter 11, but first it is necessary to establish the architectural context of the decoration and separate the corpus of Sennacherib's reliefs from later intrusions; this will be my goal in the next five chapters.

3

EXCAVATION AND
ARCHITECTURAL SETTING

With Sennacherib's palace inscriptions at hand, let us now turn to a more thorough analysis of the palace structure. In this chapter are detailed the strategies and results of the various excavators who have worked at recovering the physical remains of Sennacherib's palace. The discoveries made by these excavators are then described and analyzed in terms of function and parallels with other excavated Assyrian palaces.

The Excavation of the Southwest Palace

The plan of Sennacherib's Southwest Palace as it is known today is the result of sporadic excavations spanning a period of 120 years, from 1847 to 1967. This section reviews the contributions of each of its excavators.

By far, the most extensive excavations in the Southwest Palace were carried out by A. H. Layard, in the course of two campaigns between the years 1845 and 1851. During his first campaign, from 8 November 1845 to 24 June 1847, Layard concentrated mainly on the ruins at Nimrud. In the early summer of 1846, however, he directed a small party of workmen in making test pits at the southern end of Kouyunjik, ancient Nineveh. This was the highest part of the mound and Layard reasoned that the best preserved remains should be found here, protected from the depredations of stonemasons and limeburners by the great accumulation of debris. His assumption was essentially correct; later work showed that this was indeed the site of Sennacherib's palace. But Layard apparently had no idea *how* deeply the remains of this edifice were buried—"20 to 35 feet below the surface"—and after a month of shallow pits and meager results, he returned to the more easily accessible rewards of Nimrud.[1]

It was not until mid-May of 1847, after closing down the dig at Nimrud, that Layard resumed work on Kouyunjik. He continued working in the same location as the previous summer, at the southern extremity of the mound. His men began digging in the deep gully that is still to be seen on the southeast edge of the mound and after several days struck a wall lined with carved alabaster slabs that led to an entrance formed by winged bulls. These were evidently Slabs 1 to 4 and Door *a* (later redesignated *e*) of Room B (later redesignated I), the throne room. In the month remaining before his departure, Layard supervised the excavation of trenches some twenty feet deep along the walls of all or part of ten rooms. Those chambers whose walls were exposed completely were Rooms I (B), III (G), IV (A), V (C), and XVII (F). Rooms only partially excavated were VI (I), XVI, XLIII (E), XLV (D), and H (fig. 21).[2]

Layard left Mosul on 24 June 1847, leaving the Kouyunjik excavations in

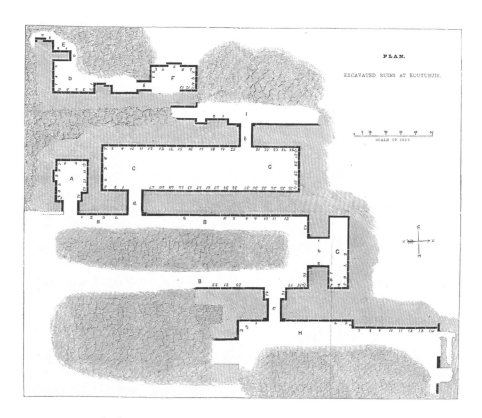

FIG. 21. Layard's first plan of the Southwest Palace, Nineveh (from Layard 1849a, vol. 2, opp. 124).

the hands of H. J. Ross. Layard's summaries of Ross's activity in the South-west Palace are complemented by Ross's letters to Layard. From these it appears that Ross was occupied in Court H, the exterior facade of the throne room, until late October 1847, but found little of interest. He then shifted his attention to the southwest side of the mound where he discovered what he believed was another palace, distinct from Layard's, but which was in reality Rooms LI(s), LII, and LIII. His career as excavator of Sennacherib's palace ended on 17 July 1848 with his departure from Mosul.[3]

During the period between Ross's departure and the return of Layard in late September 1849, work continued on a small scale on the Southwest Palace under Layard's foreman, Toma Shishman, who worked under the general control of Christian Rassam, the English vice-consul. By this time "the accumulation of earth above the ruins had become so considerable, frequently exceeding thirty feet, that the workmen, to avoid the labor of clearing it away, began to tunnel along the walls, sinking shafts at intervals to admit light and air. . . . [These dimly lit] subterraneous passages were narrow, and were propped up when necessary either by leaving columns of earth, as in mines, or by wooden beams."[4] In this manner, Toma Shishman's workers excavated all of Room XIV, and parts of Rooms XII, XIII, and Court VI.[5]

Layard returned to Mosul at the end of September 1849 and recommenced large-scale excavations on the Southwest Palace in mid-October.[6] He reported that "the accumulation of soil above the ruins was so great, that I determined to continue the tunnelling, removing only as much earth as was necessary to show the sculptured walls. But to facilitate the labor of the workmen, and to avoid the necessity of their leaving the tunnels to empty their baskets, I made a number of rude triangles and wooden pulleys, by which the excavated rubbish could be raised by ropes through the shafts, sunk at intervals for this purpose, as well as to admit light and air" (fig. 22).[7]

By the end of November, the remainder of Court VI and Room XII, and all of Room XLVIII and Hall XLIX, had been excavated, all under Layard's direct supervision.[8] In December 1849, the monumental facade of Court H was uncovered, though Layard himself spent most of that month at Nimrud. Between the beginning of January and the middle of March 1850, Layard spent much of his time at Nimrud and also visited Bavian and the neighborhood of Erbil. During this time Rooms VII, VIII, IX, X, XI, and XXII were cleared by his workmen.[9] Between 19 March and 10 May, Layard was absent on an expedition to the Khabur, having again left the Southwest Palace excavation in the charge of Toma Shishman. Layard's diary entry for 11 May indicates that during his absence Room LI(n) and parts of XIX and XLI had been excavated.

In addition to these, Rooms XXXVIII, XXXIX, XL, XLII, and part of XXIX were also excavated around this time. From mid-May to early July 1850, Layard was occupied drawing reliefs and packing them for transport, as well as continuing the Southwest Palace excavations.[10]

Photography was apparently not a practical option for Layard at the time he was excavating the Southwest Palace.[11] In any case, the dim light of the tunnels, combined with the relatively flat surface and poor preservation of the reliefs would have made effective photography very difficult. In order to record his finds, therefore, he was forced to rely on drawings made on the spot. Two artists assisted him during the excavations of Sennacherib's palace.

The first, Fredrick C. Cooper, was with him from September 1849 until July 1850, though toward the end he was too ill to work. Thomas S. Bell arrived in late February 1851 and stayed until Layard's final departure from Nineveh.[12] Layard was without an artist when he first began work on Sennacherib's palace, from May to June 1847, and again during the period between Cooper's departure and Bell's arrival. He made up for this lack by drawing many of the reliefs himself, displaying remarkable skill for an amateur (fig. 23). Since the vast majority of the reliefs were left *in situ*, these drawings are

FIG. 23. After S. C.
Malan, Layard
sketching palace reliefs
in June, 1850 (from
Layard 1853a, facing
p. 345).

Archive Chamber Kouyunjik

often our only record of their appearance. Even in the cases of slabs removed to museums, the very low relief, minute detail, and poor preservation of the surface make them very difficult to present adequately in small photographs. They too are best illustrated by drawings. Consequently, only slabs that photograph with unusual clarity or for which no drawing exists have been illustrated here by photographs instead of drawings.

On 11 July 1850, Layard left Mosul for Lake Van to escape the summer heat and did not return until 30 August. During his absence, work proceeded apace at Kouyunjik under Toma Shishman, the work force having been augmented by the addition of the laborers formerly employed at Nimrud. During this period Rooms XXIV through XXXIV, XXXVI, XXXVII, LX, LXI, and more of Court XIX were excavated. In September and the first part of October, Layard was back at Kouyunjik packing reliefs and, presumably, supervising the excavations.[13]

From 18 October 1850 until roughly 7 March 1851, while Layard was in Babylonia, work at Kouyunjik continued under Toma Shishman. Rooms uncovered from this time until Layard's final departure include XLIV, XLVI, XLVII, LXIV through LXXI, and the remainder of XLIII and XLV. With his departure from Mosul on 28 April 1851, Layard's direct involvement with the remains of Sennacherib's palace ceased. He summarized his accomplishment as follows:

> In this magnificent edifice I had opened no less than seventy-one halls, chambers, and passages, whose walls, almost without exception, had been panelled with slabs of sculptured alabaster recording the wars, the triumphs, and the great deeds of the Assyrian king. By a rough calculation, about 9,880 feet, or nearly two miles, of bas-reliefs, with twenty-seven portals, formed by colossal winged bulls and lion-sphinxes, were uncovered in that part of the building explored during my researches. The greatest length of the excavations was about 720 feet, the greatest breadth about 600 feet. (These measurements merely include that part of the palace actually excavated.) The pavement of the chambers was from 20 to 35 feet below the surface of the mound.[14]

Little new excavation was carried out on the Southwest Palace in the years immediately following Layard's departure. Control of the site reverted once again to Christian Rassam, who, under the general direction of H. C. Rawlinson in Baghdad, continued to employ a small force on the excavation, to little purpose. There were no major discoveries in Sennacherib's palace at this time, though tablets in some quantity continued to be found. Gadd noted that in the spring of 1852, Félix Thomas, the artist of the French expedition to Khorsabad, was employed in drawing the fragments being found at Kouyunjik. That summer the "outer parts" of the palace were sounded, without producing "anything that could even be drawn."[15]

With the arrival of Hormuzd Rassam (Christian's younger brother) as director of the British excavations, in mid-October 1852, work on the Southwest Palace seems largely to have ceased except for the removal and packing of sculptures already discovered, such as those depicting the siege of Lachish in Room XXXVI. Hormuzd Rassam's only significant contribution to the exploration of the Southwest Palace at this time was the discovery, in August and September 1853, of a representation of a royal procession carved on slabs that apparently originally lined one or both sides of a descending passage. They were found roughly midway between the northeast corner of the known part of Sennacherib's palace and the then unknown Ishtar Temple. Rassam concluded that "they must have been thrown down there pell-mell from different ancient buildings." The reliefs form a coherent series, however, and at least one displays Sennacherib's palace inscription, indicating that it was originally part of the palace. The find spot is consistent with an original location in the unexcavated north wall of Court H. Hormuzd Rassam left Mosul on 1 May 1854.[16] His place as principal British excavator at Kouyunjik was taken over by William Loftus, who worked on the site from June 1854 through March 1855. Loftus's main efforts were directed at Assurbanipal's North Palace, but according to his plan of Kouyunjik, he also excavated the south wall of Room LIV in the Southwest Palace.[17]

The next excavator to work in the Southwest Palace was George Smith, who led two campaigns. The first lasted from 7 May to 9 June 1873 and concentrated mainly on finding objects and tablets in rooms already partially explored by previous excavators. Though his account gives few details, Smith does record finding tablets "and numerous impressions in clay of seals, with implements of bronze, iron, and glass. There was part of a crystal throne, . . . closely resembling in shape the bronze one discovered by Mr. Layard at Nimroud."[18]

Of greater interest for the understanding of the palace as a whole is this cursory statement: "In the northern part of Sennacherib's palace I made some excavations, and discovered chambers similar to those in the south-east palace at Nimroud."[19] In the Southeast Palace at Nimrud, Smith had "opened six chambers, all of the same character; the entrances ornamented by clusters of square pilasters and recesses in the rooms in the same style. The walls were coloured in horizontal bands of red, green, and yellow on plaster; and where the lower parts of the chambers were panelled with small stone slabs, the plaster and colours were continued over these." One of these rooms had a pavement of stone slabs, in addition to a dado of the same material. Layard, who also excavated in the Southeast Palace at Nimrud, noted that the dado consisted of "plain slabs of limestone, three feet seven inches high and from two to three feet wide."[20] In the northern part of Sennacherib's palace, therefore, Smith apparently found rooms lined with a dado of plain stone slabs roughly three feet high and perhaps paved with the same material, though he gives no plan of these rooms.

Smith's second campaign at Nineveh lasted from 1 January to 12 March 1874. At this time parts of Court H and, apparently, Room I were investigated, as well as the area of the west facade, where L. W. King later found a monumental entrance. His major effort, however, was directed in the area of the "library chambers," that is, Rooms XL and XLI. Again, Smith published no plan, but he described the area of his operations as follows:

> I commenced operations by drawing an oval line about 700 feet round as the boundary of my field of operations. This line passed over the centre of the south-east court of the palace, then turning west ran along north of the long gallery where Layard found the representations of the dragging along of the winged figures and building the mounds, then turning south it went along over the chambers at the west of the palace, and turning eastward ran along to the bottom of the south-east court.[21]

This description is difficult to interpret, but clearly includes parts of Court XIX ("south-east court" and Hall XLIX ("long gallery"), and other rooms in the immediate vicinity of XL and XLI were apparently included as well. The result of this excavation was "nearly three thousand fragments of tablets" that, judging from their distribution, had apparently fallen from an upper story.[22]

Between January 1878 and July 1882, Hormuzd Rassam again directed operations in the Southwest Palace on behalf of the British Museum, though during his frequent absences work was actually supervised by his nephew, Nimroud Rassam. This activity was concerned primarily with finding tablets, considerable numbers of which apparently appeared in Rooms XXIX, LX, LXXI, and outside of Room III.[23] Of particular interest were four Sennacherib foundation cylinders excavated by Hormuzd and Nimroud during the period from December 1878 to late 1879 (see fig. 6). The documents concerning their findspots have been assembled by Reade, who concluded that one was

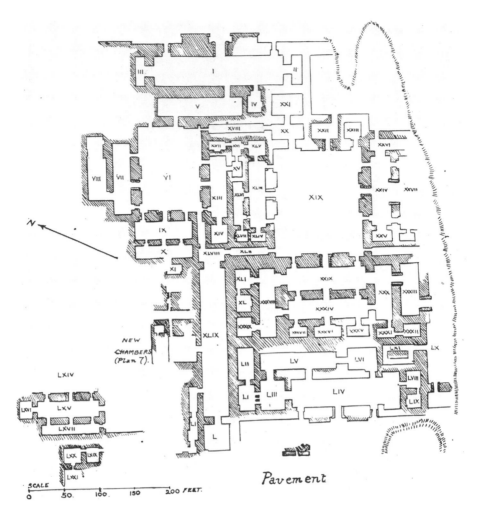

FIG. 24. Thompson's plan of the Southwest Palace, Nineveh (from Thompson and Hutchinson 1929a, plan 3).

found in the wall between Doors *g* and *h* in Room IX, one in the wall between Doors *d* and *e* of Room VII, one perhaps in the wall between Doors *c* and *d* of Room VII, and one in the wall between Rooms VII and VIII. All are dated in the eponymy of Mitunu (700 B.C.) and contain an account of the first three campaigns plus a palace building account.[24]

From January to June 1889 and from November 1890 to January 1891, E. A. W. Budge led two campaigns at Kouyunjik for the British Museum. This work consisted principally of sifting through the dumps of earlier excavators, and he was rewarded with "about 590 tablets, fragments of tablets, and other objects," more than 300 of which were from the Southwest Palace.[25]

The next excavator of Sennacherib's palace was L. W. King, who worked there between March 1903 and June 1904. His results are unpublished except for a cursory account by R. C. Thompson, though a fuller report is said to be on deposit at the British Museum. According to Thompson, King cleared parts of Rooms I, V, VI, XVI, XVII, XIX, XXIV, XXVI, XXVII, XLV, XLIX, LI, LIII, and LIV. A photograph from this time shows Room I, Slabs 14–15 and Door *d*, Bull 2 intact, but no trace of these sculptures survives today (see fig. 129). In addition, Thompson reported that King excavated a "new portion" of the western facade of the palace,

consisting of (1) an additional row of chambers beyond the wall which Layard considered to be the external wall of the palace; (2) the exterior wall of the palace on this side was sculptured with representations of his expedition to the Persian Gulf; (3) a pavement forming a terrace thirty feet broad, running along the W. front of the palace; (4), most interesting of

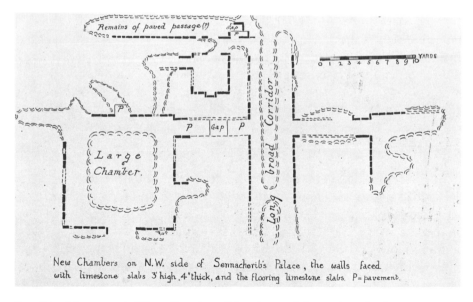

FIG. 25. Thompson's "New Chambers," Southwest Palace, Nineveh (from Thompson and Hutchinson 1929a, plan 4).

all, the main W. entrance to the palace, with two colossal bulls in place, and a colossal figure of the hero Gilgamish strangling a lion.[26]

Thompson's siting of these finds is roughly indicated in his sketch plan of the palace (fig. 24).

After King's departure, excavations were carried on until February 1905 under Thompson's direction. He discovered a series of "new chambers" on the north side of Sennacherib's palace, which he explored by the tried-and-true method of tunneling. According to his plan, the area explored measured roughly 120 by 70 feet and contained parts of some eight rooms (fig. 25). These were lined with a dado of unsculptured limestone slabs roughly three feet high and had a pavement of the same material.[27] They were apparently located north of Hall XLIX, between Rooms LI(n) at the west and XI at the east, and may be identical with the similar rooms found by Smith in the same area during his first campaign, described above.

Thompson further investigated the Southwest Palace during his 1931–32 season, sinking four test pits in the area to the north of Rooms VIII, XI, and XLIX. He found considerable evidence of walls and pavement here in the Assyrian levels, but his verbal descriptions of the finds in each pit are difficult to interpret and no plan was published.[28]

The most recent excavations in Sennacherib's palace were sponsored by the Iraqi Department of Antiquities and carried out under the direction of Tariq Madhloom. Between 1965 and 1967, Rooms I, IV, V, and perhaps III, as well as the monumental throne-room facade (Court H), were reexcavated and the fill was removed from the rooms' interiors. The surviving wall slabs were consolidated and are now displayed *in situ* under the protection of a metal roof. In 1968 the pavement of Court H was investigated.[29]

Comments on the Excavated Part of the Palace

As is clear from the preceding account, reports on the discoveries in Sennacherib's Palace are scattered in a number of places. This section gathers and summarizes the information contained in these various sources in order to present a clearer picture of its architectural features and narrative relief decoration as they are known from the excavations. Concerning the wall reliefs in each room, if drawings or photographs have been published, then only a general description is given; if not, Layard's description of the decoration is quoted in full. The material of the slabs is assumed to be "Mosul marble" unless otherwise noted. This section does not describe the apotropaic reliefs in the palace doorways, as these are treated in detail in chapter 8. A very brief summary of the doorway decoration, where known, is in Appendix 2.

Layard's two published plans of the Southwest Palace, which are cited frequently throughout this section, are reproduced here as figure 21 and on p. 344. Dimensions are given in feet, as in Layard's descriptions and plans, and in meters (rounded off to the nearest half-meter unless I took them myself). Layard did not specify the dimensions for some rooms; in such cases, the dimensions are estimated from his plans and given as approximations ("ca.").

COURT H. The west wall of this court was preserved to a length of roughly 280 feet (85 m): a monumental facade 180 feet (55 m) wide (figs. 10, 26, 93), adjoined by nearly 100 feet (30 m) of narrative relief. The north wall was excavated to a length of about 40 feet (12 m) before being abandoned as unproductive. Comparison with other Assyrian palaces shows that H was not an exterior facade, as Layard suggested, but rather the outer court of the throne-room suite, comparable to Court D-E in Assurnasirpal II's palace and Court VIII in Sargon's palace (see figs. 7, 8). The narrative reliefs, which were numbered separately from the doorway colossus slabs, showed a

FIG. 26. Throne-room facade, present state, Slabs 1–3 south, Court H, Southwest Palace, Nineveh, combined w. 12.81 m (photo: author).

FIG. 27.   Reeds and palms at bottom of defaced relief, Slab 3a north, Court H,
Southwest Palace, Nineveh (photo: author).

campaign in a district characterized by a broad river, palm trees, and reeds.
Slab 2 showed a siege and Slabs 4–7 included horsemen moving at full
speed. On Slabs 8–14 were "chariots, horsemen, archers, and warriors in
mail." Also included somewhere on this wall were processions of prisoners
and spoil, including a chained lion.[30]

The condition of these reliefs is unclear. In both descriptions of Court H,
Layard observed that the reliefs to the north of Door *c* had been deliberately
erased with a chisel, though enough traces remained to permit him to make
out the subject. The slabs to the immediate left and right of Door *c*, which are
visible today *in situ*, have the lower parts of reeds and palm trees preserved at
the bottom only, the remainder having been chiseled smooth (fig. 27). No
traces of the erased decoration are now visible on any of the exposed slabs,
but Layard's Slabs 4–7 were not reexcavated. On the basis of Layard's description and an inventory of sculptures published in *Nineveh and Its Remains*,
Reade assigned to this series several casts and fragments showing Elamite
horsemen and archers. He suggested that the erasure and recarving of these
slabs with an Elamite campaign probably dates to Assurbanipal's restoration
and repaving of Court H.[31]

In his first plan, Layard showed H as a room with one door at the west into Room I (B) and another at the south into an unexcavated area. In his second campaign he found that the "jamb" for this latter "door," Bull 12, was actually one of the pair of bulls on the outer face of the facade buttress. In his search for the east jamb of this nonexistent door, he drove a tunnel eastward nearly 100 feet across an uninterrupted pavement of square limestone slabs without encountering any walls. This pavement was reexamined by Madhloom, who reported two levels: the lower was of square baked bricks stamped with the name of Sennacherib, and the upper was of black basalt slabs, some square, some rectangular, which he assigned to Assurbanipal.[32]

In Layard's first plan, the northern part of Court H had fourteen slabs, of which numbers 8–14 were excavated by Ross. Here Ross reported finding "openings into three new chambers, one entrance having, it appears, been formed by four lion sphinxes."[33] Layard apparently had difficulty interpreting Ross's description, since no trace of these finds appears on the first plan, and in the second plan, Slabs 8–14 had been entirely deleted.

R O O M I.   (This is identified as Room "B" in *Nineveh and Its Remains;* my measurements: 51.00 × 12.25 m/167 × 40 ft.) Because of its size, plan, and location, Turner identified it as the throne room of Sennacherib's palace. Layard's plan of this room included twenty-two numbered narrative slabs, plus several slabs left unnumbered due to poor preservation. Madhloom's excavations uncovered three additional slabs to the south of Layard's Slab 22, which I have tentatively designated 23 to 25. Slabs 1–13 and 18–25 had scenes of city sieges and of skirmishes in wooded mountains (see figs. 127, 128). Slabs 14–17 showed a city on the seaside being assaulted from the right while its inhabitants escape in ships to the left (see fig. 85). Slabs 1–4, 4a, 5, 10–12, 12a, 13, and 20–25 are partially preserved and are now displayed *in situ* (see fig. 5).[34]

The plan of the preserved portion of Room I is virtually identical to that of the throne room of Sennacherib's father, Sargon II, at Khorsabad, Room VII (see fig. 8). The only significant difference is the south end of Room I, as reconstructed in Layard's second plan. This shows a shallow chamber, Room II, opening off the center of the south wall, somewhat like the alcove in the equivalent position in the throne room (M) of the North Palace of Assurbanipal, Sennacherib's grandson. But Layard's statements that the southern end of Room I "had been completely destroyed by the water-duct which had formed the ravine," and that the wall south of Doors *a* and *f* "could not be traced," coupled with his omission of any indication of architectural remains

FIG. 28.   Feet of large figure in niche, Slab 5, Room I, Southwest Palace, Nineveh, w. 251 cm (photo: author).

in this area in his first plan, make it clear that his restoration of Room II was entirely hypothetical. It was presumably based on the supposition that the south end of the room would have been symmetrical with the north, where there was such an alcove.[35] The south end of Room I, therefore, was probably similar to the southeast end of Room VII at Khorsabad, built only a few years earlier. There the southeast wall was solid and contained a shallow niche at the center, from which a rectangular throne dais of stone projected. In the case of Sennacherib's Room I, the throne dais would have disappeared with the south wall into the ravine. Another feature shared by Room VII at Khorsabad and Room I was a "tramline" of stone flags, apparently tracks for a wheeled brazier, running down the center of the room from the main entrance to the throne dais.[36]

Also in Sargon's Room VII—and in the throne rooms of Assurnasirpal II at Nimrud (Room B) and Assurbanipal at Nineveh (Room M) as well—was a shallow niche directly opposite the main entrance. At Khorsabad and Nimrud this niche was similar in form and decoration to the niche behind the throne dais, and Turner suggested that the throne might on occasion have been moved to this location to allow the king a view of the great court. Such a niche would therefore be expected opposite the central doorway in Room I. The termination of the "tramline" in this area also suggests that the king sometimes situated himself here. Though it does not appear so on Layard's plan, Slab 5, which he described as showing "the extremities of a human figure," is located directly opposite Door *a*.[37] This slab is visible today *in situ* (fig. 28). It is 48 cm thick, nearly twice as thick as the other slabs in the throne room. Its face is flush with the faces of the slabs to either side, so that its back projects well behind those of the flanking ones (fig. 29). The bottom 30 cm or so is carved with two registers of animals and other booty moving to the right. Above this, the surface is cut back a depth of 10–15 cm to form a niche somewhat above ground level. At the right side in the niche are the feet of a life-size human figure facing left. The niche occupies two slabs: the better-preserved slab on the right, just described, joined at the left to a more frag-

FIG. 29. Edge view of Slab 5, Room I, Southwest Palace, Nineveh, thickness of slab: 48 cm (photo: author).

49

FIG. 30. Tripod stand (balance?), detail of Slab 11, Room IV, Southwest Palace, Nineveh (photo: author).

mentary slab. Their combined width is 5.38 m, enough to accommodate several large figures, possibly arranged around a sacred tree as in Assurnasirpal's palace. Nothing of the other figures survives.

ROOM II.   As discussed above (Room I), there was no evidence for this room, the area of "Door *g*" more likely being solid wall.

ROOM III.   (This is identified as Room "G" in *Nineveh and Its Remains;* ca. 45 × 12 ft./13.5 × 3.5 m.) Eight slabs were preserved, all in the east half of the room (see fig. 78). The west half was "completely destroyed." The subject was the "siege and sack of a city, standing between two rivers, in the midst of groves of palm trees." The king in his chariot appeared at least twice, on Slabs 4 and 8. An epigraph on Slab 8 gave the city name of Dilbat. Room III was reexcavated by Madhloom, but it was not mentioned in his reports and none of its relief slabs are now visible.[38]

Based on a comparison of the throne-room suite of the Southwest Palace with those of Sargon's palace and Palace F at Khorsabad and Assurbanipal's North Palace at Nineveh, Turner suggested restoring a doorway opening into a stairwell at the west (destroyed) end of the north wall.[39]

ROOM IV.   (This is identified as Room "A" in *Nineveh and Its Remains;* my measurements: 5.80 × 5.80 m/19 × 19 ft.) Layard observed that Room IV contained the lower parts of fourteen slabs, on which "could be traced processions of warriors, and captives passing through a thickly wooded, mountainous country." On Slab 11, Layard reported a "eunuch," the upper body now lost, standing before what looks like a balance (fig. 30). Madhloom's excavations revealed the Room IV slabs much as Layard described them and his plan shows the shape of the room more accurately than do either of Layard's. An interesting feature, omitted from Layard's report, is that the room was paved with rectangular stone slabs. This and the presence of a drain running through a mudbrick vault behind the niche in the south wall identify this as a bathroom.[40] Just inside, to either side of the door, are un-carved areas shaped suspiciously like the profiles of the large water storage jars that might be expected in such a context (fig. 31).

Layard reported taloned bird feet on the surviving lower part of the Door *f* jambs. Madhloom's excavations showed that each jamb was actually deco-rated with *two* figures: a human-footed figure in front of a bird-footed one (personal observation). Both groups faced east, into Room I. Well-preserved examples of similar figures were found in Room XXXII (see fig. 95).[41]

ROOM V. (This is identified as Room "C" in *Nineveh and Its Remains;* my measurements: 42.25 × 7.40 m/138.5 × 24 ft.) Nearly every slab in Room

FIG. 31. Relief with uncarved area, Slab 2, Room IV, Southwest Palace, Nineveh, w. 78 cm (photo: author).

V is at least partially preserved; fifty-one whole and fragmentary slabs are on display *in situ*. The subject was a campaign along a river in a mountainous, wooded region (see fig. 80). The narrative is read from left to right and shows Assyrian soldiers capturing a city, after which the king reviews the prisoners and the army moves along to the next city. This sequence was repeated at least five, and perhaps more, times on the walls of Room V. Surviving epigraphs give the city names Kasuṣi (Slab 11) and, probably, Aranziaš (Slab 35).[42]

Room V was the "retiring room" of the throne-room suite. Based on analogy with the room in the equivalent position in Sargon's palace (Room 27) and Palace F (Room 24) at Khorsabad, we might expect a further room to open off of the north end of Room V. Neither Layard's nor Madhloom's plans show a door in this wall, but Layard could have missed a door as he reported that Slab 28 "had been entirely destroyed by a well, opened in this part of the mound, and carried through the wall." A chamber certainly existed north of Room V, as evidenced by the location of Door *b* in Court VI and this room may have been accessible from Room V as well.[43]

COURT VI. (This is identified as Room "I" in *Nineveh and Its Remains;* 124 × 90 ft./38 × 27.5 m.) The subject of Slabs 1–41, on the south and west walls, was a royal campaign in a mountainous region characterized by pines, grapevines, and dwarf oaks, and through which flowed a river (see figs. 69, 116). The Assyrian soldiers concentrated their attention not on cities, but rather pursued the enemy through the mountains. No epigraphs were preserved on these slabs. A quite different subject appeared on the north and east walls (see figs. 50, 54, 56–61): Slabs 63–68 showed bull colossi being quarried in the mountains, while Slabs 44–62 showed the transport of these colossi, first through mountains, then beside a marsh and a river. Epigraphs on Slabs 60, 66, and 68 give the setting here as Balaṭai, near Nineveh.[44]

Figure 49 is my reconstruction of Court VI. It is based on Layard's plans, descriptions, and drawings, as well as on my observations and measurements of the surviving Court VI reliefs.[45] My plan is enlarged from Layard's final plan of the palace, which is his only full plan of Court VI. It should be noted, however, that on his plan the east wall south of Door *a* is some two meters longer than Madhloom's excavations showed it to be. This suggests that Court VI was actually slightly north of where it is shown on the final plan. Also, both of Layard's plans omit the exterior buttress to the north of Door *a* (*b* in Layard's first plan), though one did exist and was reexcavated by Madhloom. Its original width is uncertain, as Madhloom's restoration did not include its north edge. Reade's restored plan of the palace includes this north buttress. Concerning the Door *a* bull colossi, Layard reported that they were poorly preserved and their heads were missing. The plan of Madhloom's excavations shows only the southern bull of Door *a* preserved, and this is the only one now visible (see fig. 53).[46]

Layard did not discuss Door *b*, but the right edge of Slab 64, now in the British Museum, shows part of a quarry scene similar to that on the face of Slab 66. Thus there was clearly some sort of opening here, apparently lined with narrative reliefs similar in subject to Slabs 66–68.

ROOM VII (100 × 24 ft./30.5 × 7.5 m). On the surviving slabs "the monarch, in his chariot, and surrounded by his bodyguards, was seen receiving the captives and the spoil in a hilly country, whilst his warriors were dragging their horses up a steep mountain near a fortified town, driving their chariots along the banks of a river, and slaying with the spear the flying enemy" (fig. 32).[47]

ROOMS VIII(E) AND VIII(W) (ca. 90 × 25 ft./27.5 × 7.5 m). Turner observed that "Room VIII" was actually *two* rooms, Layard's workmen apparently having missed a partition wall projecting between Slabs 2 and 3. These two rooms are distinguished here as VIII(w), the west end, and VIII(e), the east end. Of the fifteen numbered slabs shown in Room VIII in Layard's plan, Slabs 1, 2, and 11–15 were in Room VIII(w) (fig. 33). They showed a campaign against a maritime people. Layard remarked that their galleys and costumes were like those in Room I. Slabs 3–9 were in Room VIII(e) (fig. 34). They included a scene of a fortified camp by a stream in the mountains. There is no record of the decoration on Slab 10, which was the north jamb of the doorway connecting VIII(w) and VIII(e).[48]

Rooms VII and "VIII" conform to the most common arrangement for neo-Assyrian reception suites, Turner's "Type A," with VII the reception room, VIII(w) the retiring room, and VIII(e) the bathroom, complete with customary niche. Turner considered the function of this type of suite to have been residential.[49]

ROOM IX (82 × 26 ft./25 × 8 m). Its wall slabs were almost entirely destroyed, but surviving fragments showed a campaign in a region of wooded mountains with a broad river. "There was nothing remarkable in the dresses of the captives, or in the details, to give any clue to the conquered people."[50]

ROOM X (82 × 18 ft./25 × 5.5 m). The reliefs showed the siege and sack of a city in a mountainous region (fig. 35). The booty included camels and several statues of gods of the enemy. One slab showed an Assyrian fortified camp.[51]

FIG. 32. Sennacherib on campaign, drawing of Slabs 12–14, Room VII, Southwest Palace, Nineveh. British Museum, WAA, Or. Dr., I, 63 (photo: Trustees of the British Museum).

ROOM XI (ca. 20 × 15 ft./6 × 4.5 m). The relief subject was not recorded. Turner restored a jog at the southeast corner of this room, converting it to the standard plan for the bathroom of a residential suite. Thus Rooms IX to XI conform to the pattern of Turner's residential "Reception Suite Type A." It should be noted, however, that here the reception room and the retiring room are connected by three doors located almost directly opposite the three outer doors leading from Court VI. This arrangement, which implies greater access than in typical reception suites, is not known in other Assyrian palaces. In Sennacherib's palace, a similar pattern occurs also in Rooms LXV–LXVII, and the location of the doorways recalls that of Rooms XXIX–XXXIV and XXIV–XXVII, the function of which Turner considered to be ceremonial.[52]

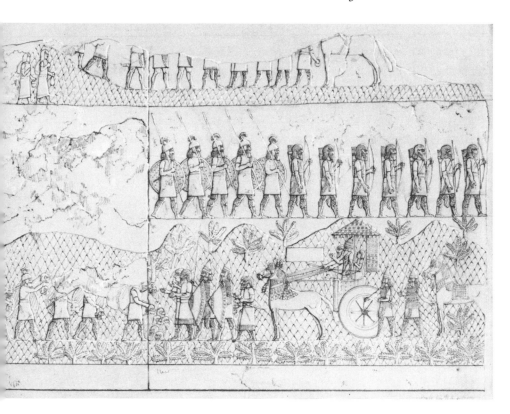

Room XII   (ca. 30 × 10 ft./9 × 3 m). This room connected the throne room precinct with Hall XLIX, the passage to the west facade of the palace. On the north wall was represented "the siege of a walled city, divided into two parts by a river" (fig. 83). Several processions of prisoners moved to the right, and the top register of Slab 15 depicted statues of gods being carried away. The south wall showed the king in his chariot surrounded by his soldiers.[53]

Room XIII   (ca. 88 × 24 ft./27 × 7.5 m) was only partially excavated and was not described by Layard.

Room XIV   (26 × 23 ft./8 × 7 m). The relief decoration of Room XIV is among the best and most completely preserved examples from the Southwest Palace. Nearly all slabs from its three principal walls were drawn and

Fig. 33.   Campaign against a maritime people, drawing of Slabs 11–13, Room VIII(w), Southwest Palace, Nineveh. British Museum, WAA, Or. Dr., IV, 68 (photo: Trustees of the British Museum).

most were transported to the British Museum where the narrative can be seen today essentially in its entirety. Its subject was the siege of a city on a mound by a river in a mountainous district (see figs. 17, 18, 121). The Assyrian army approached from the left while prisoners and soldiers carrying enemy heads marched off to the right. An epigraph on Slab 10 gave the city name of Alammu.[54]

Layard remarked that here, as in some other rooms explored, the slabs adjoining the entrance "had been purposely defaced, every vestige of sculpture having been carefully removed by a sharp instrument." It seems more likely that these slabs were never carved at all, having been obscured by some fea-

ture associated with the doorway (Room IV is another example—see above).[55]

ROOMS XV AND XVI. Room XV was wholly hypothetical. The subject of the Room XVI reliefs was not recorded. Perhaps these were among the slabs Layard reported as completely destroyed by fire. There seems to be no evidence for the wall shown separating Rooms XV and XVI, so it is possible that this was a single room of some 15 by 50 feet (4.5 × 15 m).[56]

ROOM XVII. (This was identified as Room "F" in *Nineveh and Its Remains;* ca. 27 × 14 ft./8 × 4.5 m.) The reliefs here "recorded the victories

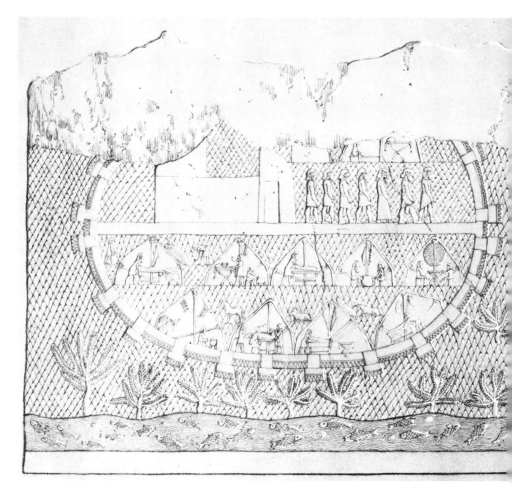

FIG. 34.   Assyrian camp in the mountains, drawing of Slabs 3–4, Room VIII(e), Southwest Palace, Nineveh. British Museum, WAA, Or. Dr., I, 38 (photo: Trustees of the British Museum).

and triumphs of the king in a mountainous country, and the siege of a city standing on the banks of a river. The king stood in his chariot, and around him were warriors leading away horses and captives, bringing heads to the scribes, and contending in battle with the enemy." The niche in the west wall of XVII suggests that it was a bathroom. If XV and XVI were a single long room, then Rooms XIII to XVII form the common pattern of Turner's "Reception Suite Type A," with XIII as the reception room, XV/XVI as the retiring

Scale Inch ½ to a foot.

room, and XVII as the bathroom. This suite was connected to a similar adjacent suite via a doorway between Rooms XVI and XLV.[57]

ROOM XVIII. (My measurement: length 22.40 m/73.5 ft., width unknown.) Layard excavated only Door *m*, the north entrance of this corridor—the remainder was hypothetical. He observed that due to the fire the walls in this part of the palace "had in many places completely disappeared." Since he discovered Room XLV by digging through the west wall of Room

FIG. 35. Deity statues and other booty, drawing of Slabs 7 and 11, Room X, Southwest Palace, Nineveh. British Museum, WAA, Or. Dr., IV, 65 (photo: Trustees of the British Museum).

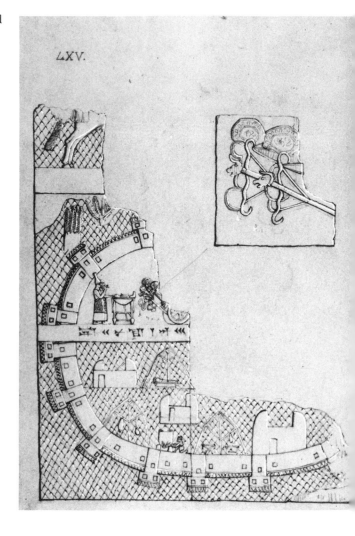

IV, he apparently dug through the south end of XVIII without noticing any trace of walls. Madhloom reexcavated the north doorway, with well-preserved reliefs on the west jamb, and the foundation of the east wall to the southeast corner (personal observation). The jamb reliefs apparently continue the campaign in the mountains shown on the south wall of Court VI. The south and west walls seem to be lost. A recarved fragment (British Museum WAA 124773) that shows an Assyrian foot soldier defeating a mounted enemy beside a reed marsh was listed by Layard as "a detached fragment

found in Chamber I" (Court VI). As there was no place for this piece in Court VI, Reade suggested that it came from a nearby room, perhaps XVIII.[58] If so, then the interior would have been decorated with a different campaign than was on the preserved door jamb.

COURT XIX (140 × 126 ft./42.5 × 38.5 m). The reliefs recorded a campaign in a region characterized by a broad river, which occupied the center one-third of the composition, and palm trees (see fig. 75). The reliefs on the west wall showed city sieges and processions of booty and prisoners, while on the preserved portion of the south wall the king and his army prepared to cross the wide central river. Layard described the decoration of Door *a* as "a pair of colossal human-headed lions, carved in coarse limestone." Elsewhere, he said all the grand entrances in this court were formed by *bull* colossi, but the former statement is more specific and therefore probably to be preferred.[59]

ROOMS XX AND XXI were wholly hypothetical.

ROOM XXII (ca. 38 × 22 ft./11.5 × 6.5 m). These reliefs recorded not military activity but rather, apparently, a peaceful procession (see fig.76). On one slab, the lower register showed a procession of spear bearers wearing feathered headdresses, while the upper had the feet of a camel preserved. The remaining slabs were devoted to a landscape in one register that included a double-walled city or camp, wide rivers, and gardens watered by what appears to be an aqueduct and canals.[60]

Layard observed that the backs of some of the slabs in Room XXII were carved with reliefs similar in style to those of the rest of the Southwest Palace. He suggested that an error had been made that was corrected by turning the slabs over and beginning the carving anew. This was not, however, the procedure followed elsewhere in Sennacherib's palace, where slabs were prepared for recarving by the simpler process of chiseling off the existing relief, as in Court H, Room XLII, and Hall XLIX. Furthermore, the obverse reliefs in Room XXII were apparently not from the time of Sennacherib and exhibited several features characteristic of the reliefs of Assurbanipal. This, together with the apparently atypical "coarse limestone" of the lion colossi in Door *a*, led Reade to suggest that Room XXII underwent architectural alterations during Assurbanipal's reign.[61]

ROOM XXIII. Except for a single doorjamb, this room was entirely hypothetical.

ROOM XXIV (98 × 27 ft./30 × 8 m). Layard reported that the "sculptured walls had been burnt to lime. On the calcined slabs, however, could still be traced Assyrian warriors mounting by ladders to the assault of besieged cities, battering-rams, long lines of archers, slingers, and spearmen, a sea with double-banked galleys similar to those frequently described, and a fortified camp, containing pavilions and tents, in which were men engaged in various domestic occupations. The king, as usual, superintended the operations from his chariot."[62]

ROOMS XXV TO XXVII. In Rooms XXV (ca. 16 ft./5 m deep) and XXVI (ca. 17 ft./5 m wide) the reliefs "had been almost entirely destroyed."

In XXVII "a few fragments, with part of a procession of captives and warriors, were alone left on the walls." Turner restored Rooms XXIV through XXVII as a "Reception Suite Type C," a suite type more fully preserved in Rooms XXIX through XLI, the function of which he felt was ceremonial.[63]

R O O M X X V I I I (70 × 12 ft./21.5 × 3.5 m). Fourteen relief slabs are preserved, of which two are devoted to a battle between Assyrians and the inhabitants of a marsh, while the remainder show processions of prisoners and booty from the battle being carried off (see fig. 77). At the bottom of the procession slabs is a small river; regularly spaced palm trees form the backdrop. The focus of at least one of these processions was the king in his chariot, on Slab 12, "which, to judge from a fragment or two found in the rubbish, must have exceeded all others in the palace, both in size and in the finish and richness of the details."[64]

R O O M S X X I X (58 × 34 ft./17.5 × 10.5 m) A N D X X X (82 × 24 ft./ 25 × 7.5 m). The walls of both rooms were "panelled with unsculptured slabs" of a "fossiliferous limestone."[65]

R O O M S X X X I (ca. 25 × 14 ft./7.5 × 4.5 m) A N D X X X I I (ca. 23 × 20 ft./7 × 6 m). The subject in XXXII was an assault on a city near a river in a wooded, mountainous district and the marching off of captives (see fig. 71). The enemy men wore a distinctive cloak of animal skin. Layard said the subject of the Room XXXI reliefs was the same as that of XXXII.[66]

R O O M X X X I I I (76 × 26 ft./23 × 8 m). As in Rooms XXIX and XXX, the wall slabs were of a limestone "full of shells and other fossils." Six slabs are preserved: the three to the west of Door *p* show the Assyrian army routing the enemy, who are driven into a river; the three to the east show a procession before the king above, and a scene of homage outside a moated city below. Epigraphs date all these reliefs to the reign of Assurbanipal: Slabs 1–3 record Assurbanipal's battle at Til Tuba in Elam, while on Slabs 4–6, the lower register is set at Madaktu in Elam and the upper register at Arbela (see fig. 65).[67]

R O O M X X X I V (58 × 29 ft./17.5 × 9 m). "Its walls had been ornamented with carved alabaster slabs, of which a few fragments remained. A fortified camp, containing the usual pavilions and tents; priests sacrificing a sheep before a fire altar; a castle on the sea shore; double-banked galleys hung round with shields; and long lines of captives (the women wearing hoods fitting close over their heads, and falling to their feet behind—the men turbans of several folds, such as are frequently represented at Khorsabad); were amongst the bas-reliefs still preserved."[68]

ROOM XXXV. Room XXXV was hypothetical. Layard reported it "had not been explored before my departure."[69]

ROOM XXXVI (38 × 18 ft./11.5 × 5.5 m). This is among the best and most completely preserved relief series from the Southwest Palace. Slabs from three walls are reassembled today in the British Museum, while the content of the fourth wall is known from Layard's description. On Slabs 1–4, now lost, were "large bodies of horsemen and charioteers." Slabs 5–13 continue the narrative, recording the siege of a city in a mountainous wooded district (see figs. 108–13).[70] The Assyrian army approaches from the left. The city, apparently double-walled, is captured by the infantry with the aid of siege ramps. Captives and booty are led off to the right before the king, who is seated on a magnificent throne. Behind him, to the far right, is the Assyrian fortified camp. An epigraph on Slab 12 identifies this representation as the fall of Lachish, in Palestine.[71]

Turner sees Room XXXVI as the focus of a "Reception Suite Type C," consisting of Rooms XXIX to XLI, the function of which he considers to have been exclusively ceremonial.[72]

ROOM XXXVII (ca. 25 × 16 ft./7.5 × 5 m). The walls of this room "had almost entirely disappeared."[73]

ROOM XXXVIII (ca. 100 × 23 ft./30.5 × 7 m). The reliefs recorded a campaign in a hilly region watered by a broad river (see figs. 72, 115). The Assyrian king and army, "the variously accoutred spearmen and the bowmen forming separate regiments or divisions," moved to the right, along what seems to be intended as the river valley, the near side of which was indicated by showing the foreground hills and trees upside down. Enemy cities were shown being captured, and the prisoners "wore a kind of turban wrapped in several folds round the head, and a short tunic confined at the waist by a broad belt." Layard also reported that "over one of the castles could be traced a few letters, giving no clue, however, to its name or site."[74] This is probably to be identified with the epigraph shown in figure 36. Though this drawing is labeled only "Old Palace, Kouyunjik," its landscape is almost certainly from Room XXXVIII.

ROOM XXXIX (ca. 28 × 21 ft./8.5 × 6.5 m). The reliefs here showed "the siege of a castle, in a country wooded with fir trees, amongst which were long lines of warriors on foot, on horseback, and in chariots. . . . [There was] no peculiarity of costume to identify the conquered people."[75]

ROOMS XL (ca. 23 × 21 ft./7 × 6.5 m) AND XLI (ca. 26 × 21 ft./8 × 6.5 m). Layard combined the descriptions of Rooms XL and XLI, without in-

FIG. 36.   Burning city, drawing of unnumbered slab, probably from Room XXXVIII, Southwest Palace, Nineveh. British Museum, Or. Dr., VI, 25b (photo: Trustees of the British Museum).

dicating whether the reliefs he described and illustrated were from XL, or XLI, or both. On the walls "could be traced a city on the shore of a sea whose waters were covered with galleys." A lithograph of one of these rooms shows, in addition to the city by the sea, men marching and leading horses through the mountains (see fig. 23). The location of the door—if it is a door—in this illustration suggests that it is a view of the northwest corner of Room XLI.[76]

Layard called Rooms XL and XLI "the chambers of records," for it was here that he found large numbers of clay tablets, piled a foot or more deep on the floors. This was a major part of the so-called "library of Assurbanipal" now housed in the British Museum. Also in this area, George Smith later found "nearly three thousand fragments of tablets." Smith believed that this vast collection of tablets was not originally stored *in* Rooms XL and XLI, but rather *above* them. He reported finding fragments from the same tablet in rooms having "no communication with each other" and concluded that the archive had been stored in an upper story that collapsed into XL and XLI when the palace was destroyed. The original use of Room XL, judging from the wall niche, was as a bathroom.[77]

ROOM XLII (72 × 11 ft./22 × 3.5 m). Layard observed that in Room XLII the "sculptured panels had been purposely destroyed." Perhaps by this he meant that the original relief decoration had been chiseled off, probably as part of the redecoration scheme that resulted in the recarving of the neighboring Court XIX and Room XXVIII slabs.[78]

ROOM XLIII. (This is identified as Room "E" in *Nineveh and Its Remains*; 96 × 23 ft./29.5 × 7 m.) In his final plan of this room, Layard used the numbers 1 to 4 twice: Slabs 1–4 in the southeast corner were found during his first campaign; Slabs 1–12 on the west, north, and east walls were found during the second. The subject was a procession of captives and booty. Some of the male captives at the west end wore a cap "not unlike the Phrygian bonnet reversed, short tunics, and a broad belt" (see fig. 91). The costume of those at the east end "bore a striking resemblance to the sculptures" of Assurbanipal from Room XXXIII (see fig. 90). These latter wore quivers topped with a circular ornament. There was no landscape background.[79]

ROOM XLIV (23 × 13 ft./7 × 4 m). "On its walls were represented a captive tribe, dressed in short tunics, a skin falling from their shoulders, boots laced up in front, and cross-bands round their legs; they had short, bushy hair and beards" (see fig. 81).[80]

ROOM XLV. (This is identified as Room "D" in *Nineveh and Its Remains*; ca. 25 × 19 ft./7.5 × 6 m.) The relief subject was the capture of a city by a river in the mountains. The army apparently approached from the right while spoil, captives, and cattle were carried off to the left, where it was received by the king in his chariot. Among the booty were fine horses and statues of deities (figs. 37, 74).[81]

ROOM XLVI (62 × 16 ft./19 × 5 m). The relief subject was said to be the same as that of Room XLIII—a procession of deportees, including some in costumes reminiscent of the Elamites in Room XXXIII, carrying round-topped quivers (see fig. 82). Though Layard also reported captives wearing the "reversed Phrygian bonnet" in this room, the published drawings show only those in Elamite costume. It may be that here, as in *Monuments of Nineveh*, Layard confused Room XLVI with XLIII, where both types of costume *were* shown and that XLVI showed only captives in Elamite costume.[82]

FIG. 37.   A captured city, drawing of Slab 5, Room XLV, Southwest Palace, Nineveh. British Museum, WAA, Or. Dr., IV, 25 (photo: Trustees of the British Museum).

ROOM XLVII   (17 ft./5 m square). "On its walls, the campaign recorded in [Room XLVI] had been continued. The bas-reliefs still preserved represented the king in his chariot receiving the captives; musicians playing on harps before him; mountains and forests, and a castle" with the presumably fragmentary epigraph "I burned with fire." The latter part of this description corresponds closely to figure 38, an unlabeled drawing of a relief from Sennacherib's palace, which I therefore attribute to this room. Rooms XLIII through XLVII show the familiar pattern of Turner's Reception Suite Type A," with XLIII as the reception room, XLVI as the retiring room, and XLVII as the bathroom. This suite communicated with a similar suite via the doorway connecting Rooms XLV and XVI.[83]

FIG. 38.   Assyrians dismantling a city, drawing of unnumbered slab, probably from Room XLVII, Southwest Palace, Nineveh. British Museum, WAA, Or. Dr., VI, 2b (photo: Trustees of the British Museum).

ROOM XLVIII (24 × 19 ft./7.5 × 6 m). Layard's plan shows sixteen slabs, numbered 1–8 and 15–22. Slabs 9–14 must have been omitted from the plan inadvertently, as at least some of them did exist (Slabs 11–13) and were drawn and described by Layard (fig. 39). The reliefs "recorded the conquest of a city standing on a broad river, in the midst of mountains and forests. The Assyrians appear to have entered the enemy's country by a valley, to have forded the stream frequently, and to have continued during their march along its banks. Warriors on foot led their horses, and dragged the chariots over precipitous rocks. On each side of the river were wooded hills, with small streams flowing amongst vineyards." The burning city was shown already in the hands of the Assyrians, who carry off furniture, some of it decorated with animal-head finials. The composition terminated with the king, enthroned in his fortified camp, receiving captives.[84]

HALL XLIX. In *Nineveh and Babylon,* Layard gave the dimensions of XLIX as 218 feet (66.5 m) long and 25 feet (7.5 m) wide. In his plan, however, its width is 35 feet (10.5 m). This discrepancy is presumably to be attributed either to a typographical error in the text or to an inaccuracy in the plan, perhaps resulting from Layard's attempts to regularize the many irregularities that characterize the mudbrick architecture of this period.[85]

At the east end of the north wall eight slabs remained in their original position. They showed the transport by sledge of an immense object with a rounded end (see fig. 86). It was drawn by means of three ropes, each pulled by a team of some sixty men, who seemed to be hauling the sledge from a body of water onto dry land. Detached fragments from XLIX showed "the king in his chariot, superintending the operations, and workmen carrying cables, or dragging carts loaded with coils of ropes, and various implements for moving the colossi." Fragmentary epigraphs mentioned the Tigris. Of the slabs still standing at the east end of the south wall, "every trace of sculpture had been carefully removed by some sharp instrument."[86]

Layard several times stated that the transport of bull colossi was shown in Hall XLIX, but all of his descriptions and drawings of bull transport scenes were from Court VI. Furthermore, the Hall XLIX epigraphs all referred to objects of wood, not stone. Perhaps this statement originated with his misidentification of the object on the sledge as "a huge block of stone . . . to be carved by the sculptor into the form of a colossal bull." As is shown on the Court VI reliefs, stone colossi were roughed out before, not after, transport.[87]

ROOM L (ca. 36 ft./11 m long). Not described by Layard.

ROOM LI(N) (96 × 13 ft./29.5 × 4 m). This was the more northern of two rooms designated "LI" by Layard. It was apparently an entrance passage that descended from XLIX to a postern gate on the west side of the mound. On its north wall was carved an ascending "procession of servants carrying fruit, flowers, game, and supplies for a banquet, preceded by mace-bearers" (see fig. 87). On the south wall, shown descending, "were fourteen horses without trappings, each horse having a simple halter twisted round its lower jaw, by which it was led by a groom." All these slabs were about six feet high, and the carved figures were 4½ feet high. These reliefs apparently recorded processions that took place in the entrance passage itself.[88]

ROOM LI(S) (ca. 38 × 24 ft./11.5 × 7.5 m). This was the more south-

FIG. 39.   Defeated city, drawing of Slabs 11–13, Room XLVIII, Southwest Palace, Nineveh. British Museum, WAA, Or. Dr., IV, 60 (photo: Trustees of the British Museum).

ern of two rooms designated "LI" by Layard. It was excavated in 1848 by Ross, who mistakenly believed it was part of a new building. Layard described it thus:

> The lower part of a long series of sculptures was still partly preserved, but the upper had been completely destroyed, the very alabaster itself having disappeared. The bas-reliefs recorded the subjection by the Assyrian king of a nation inhabiting the banks of a river [fig. 40]. The captive women are distinguished by long embroidered robes fringed with tassels, and the castles have a peculiar wedge-shaped ornament on the walls. The towns probably stood in the midst of marshes, as they appear to be surrounded

by canes or reeds, as well as by groves of palm trees. The Assyrians having captured the strong places by escalade, carried the inhabitants into captivity, and drove away cattle, camels, and carts drawn by oxen. Some of the men bear large baskets of osier work, and the women vases or cauldrons. The king, standing in his chariot, attended by his warriors, and preceded by an eunuch registering the number of prisoners and the amount of the spoil, receives the conquered chiefs.[89]

To this Ross added that "one or two castles [are] assaulted by the king in the act of drawing his bow"; that "in the army two of the circular models of towns are carried"; and that "near the castle is a field of millet in ear."[90]

71

FIG. 40.   Booty brought before the king, drawing of three unnumbered slabs, Room LI(s), Southwest Palace, Nineveh. British Museum, WAA, Or. Dr., I, 51 (photo: Trustees of the British Museum).

Ross's reference to "the king in the act of drawing his bow" is interesting, if correct, since this would then be the only instance in the known reliefs in which Sennacherib actually participated in an attack, as opposed to reviewing captives and booty afterward. The "models of towns" carried in procession were also otherwise unattested in Sennacherib's palace, though a number of examples were found in processional reliefs from Sargon's palace at Khorsabad.[91] The Khorsabad examples were never circular, however, and one wonders if Ross was here confusing the oft-recurring representations of Assyrian fortified camps with town models, though it must be admitted that his stipulation that these were "carried" poses a problem. The "millet in ear"; was almost certainly a misidentification of the canebrakes reported by Layard.

ROOM LII   (ca. 46 × 24 ft./14 × 7.5 m). Not described by Layard.

ROOM LIII   (ca. 44 × 35 ft./13.5 × 10.5 m). Its walls were panelled with unsculptured slabs of "a close-grained magnesian limestone, almost as hard as flint."[92]

ROOM LIV (ca. 120 × 40 ft./36.5 × 12 m). This was the principal room of a suite, composed of Rooms LI(s) to LIX, that opened directly off of the west, Tigris facade of the palace. As restored by Layard, this suite was completely isolated from the remainder of the palace. Though the preserved part of its plan seems to conform to his "Reception Suite Type A," Turner suggested that instead of being residential, this wing may have contained the palace shrines mentioned in Sennacherib's building accounts.[93]

ROOMS LV AND LVI (dimensions unknown) were not described by Layard. According to his plan there was no evidence for the wall shown separating them.

ROOM LVII. "LVII" is not on Layard's plan of the palace; Paterson suggested that LVII should be the alcove at the south end of Room LIV.[94]

ROOMS LVIII (ca. 25 × 20 ft./7.5 × 6 m) AND LIX (ca. 20 ft./6 m square) were not described by Layard. The niche in the north wall of LIX suggests that it was a bathroom.

ROOM LX (dimensions unknown). Layard said that the walls "had been panelled with the usual alabaster slabs, with bas-reliefs of a campaign in a country already represented in another part of the palace [Room XXXVIII], and distinguished by the same deep valley watered by a river, the vineyards and wooded mountains." One or more enemy "castles" were shown, one of which was identified as Bīt-Kubatti by an epigraph. "Whether these walls belonged to a chamber or formed part of the southern face of the palace could not now be determined, as they were on the very brink of the platform."[95] The number and location of its doors, however, are more suggestive of a room than a facade; probably it was part of the outer bank of rooms on the south side of the palace.

ROOM LXI (44 × 30 ft./13.5 × 9 m) housed an inclined passage, 9 to 10 feet wide, leading to the roof of the palace. Its walls were of sun-dried brick with three rows of regularly spaced projecting bosses, which Layard suggested were shelf supports. Here were found a large number of seal impressions, among them a single piece of clay that displayed an Assyrian stamp seal impression next to the impression of the seal of the Egyptian king Shabako (ca. 716–702 B.C.).[96]

ROOMS LXII AND LXIII (dimensions unknown) were not described by Layard. LXII may be one of Thompson's "New Chambers" (see below).

COURT LXIV (ca. 95 ft./29 m wide). Only the west wall was excavated;

FIG. 41. Assyrians attacking a city, drawing of Slabs 1–3, Room LXVII, Southwest Palace, Nineveh. British Museum, WAA, Or. Dr., IV, 38 (photo: Trustees of the British Museum).

because of their proximity to the surface, Layard judged that the sculptures of the other walls had probably not survived. The slabs to the south of Door *a* showed Assyrians in reed boats pursuing their enemy in a reed marsh (see fig. 88). Captives were marched away at right. To the north of Door *a*, by contrast, was represented "the conquest of a second nation, whose men were clothed in long garments, and whose women wore turbans, with veils falling to their feet. The Assyrians had plundered their temples, and were seen carrying away their idols" (see fig. 89).[97]

ROOM LXV (86 × 24 ft./26 × 7.5 m). Layard reported "a line of chariots in a ravine between mountains, warriors throwing logs on a great burning pile of wood, castles on the tops of hills, Assyrians carrying away spoil, amongst which was a royal umbrella, and the king on his throne receiving his army on their return from battle with the captives and booty."[98]

ROOM LXVI (26 × 19 ft./8 × 6 m). Layard says the walls "of this chamber had almost entirely disappeared. The fragments found in the rubbish showed that they also had been covered with sculpture."[99]

ROOM LXVII (82 × 16 ft./25 × 5 m). The reliefs "represented the siege of a great city, whose many-towered walls were defended by slingers, archers, and spearmen. The king himself in his chariot was present at the attack. Around him were his warriors and his led-horses" (fig. 41).[100]

ROOM LXVIII. "LXVIII" does not appear on Layard's plan, nor was it mentioned elsewhere in his published accounts. Presumably the partly excavated room to the south of Rooms LXV and LXVII was intended as LXVIII.

ROOM LXIX (23 × 19 ft./7 × 6 m). On its walls "long lines of chariots, horsemen, and warriors, divided into companies according to their arms and their costume, accompanied the king [fig. 42]. The Assyrians having taken the principal city of the invaded country, cut down the palm-trees within and without its walls. Men beat drums, such as are still seen in the same country, and women clapping their hands in cadence to their song, came out to greet the conquerors. Beneath the walls was represented a great caldron, which appears to have been supported upon metal images of oxen."[101]

ROOM LXX (24 ft./7.5 m square). The reliefs showed a battle in a reed marsh (see figs. 67, 79). Prisoners were marched off to the left into the presence of the king. "A great retinue of charioteers and horsemen appear to have followed Sennacherib to this war. Large circular shields were fixed to the sides of the chariots represented in the sculptures." An epigraph identified this as the marshes of Sahrina.[102]

ROOM LXXI (ca. 24 ft./7.5 m wide). The west end of this room was

FIG. 42. Assyrians cutting palm trees, drawing of Slabs 1–2, Room LXIX, Southwest Palace, Nineveh. British Museum, WAA, Or. Dr., IV, 56 (photo: Trustees of the British Museum).

"on the very edge of the river-face of the mound." Its walls "had been almost entirely destroyed."[103]

L. W. KING'S WEST FACADE (see description on p. 43). This was probably the same entrance partially excavated and described by Layard: "The western facade, like the eastern, was formed by five pairs of human-headed bulls, and numerous colossal figures, forming three distinct gateways."[104] Layard's plan adds the information that between these three doorways were two buttresses, each presumably decorated with two bulls and the colossal figure of a hero holding a lion, as on the throne-room (Layard's "eastern") facade. Similar facades were found elsewhere in Sennacherib's palace and in the palaces of other Assyrian kings, and in every case they were *exterior* facades. It seems unlikely that Layard's monumental west facade could have been located *inside* a room with yet another monumental facade beyond it. Furthermore, Layard carried his excavations at the west side of the palace "to the very edge of the mound," and he should have found this second major facade, had it existed. On balance, then, it seems more likely that King reexcavated the same entrance discovered by Layard, rather than that there were originally two distinct monumental west facades, one inside the other.[105]

THOMPSON'S "NEW CHAMBERS." The precise location of these rooms with respect to the rooms excavated by Layard is not certain. Thompson's own attempt to relate these new rooms to the old has his "large chamber" opening directly into Hall XLIX, while his "long broad corridor" has no opening at all in its south end (see figs. 24, 25). It appears from his plan of the "New Chambers," however, that his excavation was not carried over to the known part of the palace, and therefore the location he assigned them was hypothetical. Such a placement is consistent neither with the great thickness of the north wall of Hall XLIX, as shown in Layard's plan, nor with Layard's observation that the only opening in that wall was Door *b* into Room LI(n).[106] It seems probable, therefore, that these new rooms were located farther north than Thompson's composite plan indicates and that the only connection between the "New Chambers" and the old ones is that the easternmost of the new rooms was possibly the same as Layard's Room LXII.

Conclusion

Despite the efforts of Layard, Ross, Rassam, Loftus, Smith, Budge, King, Thompson, and Madhloom, the plan of the Southwest Palace remains incompletely known. This is largely because no excavator has set out with the primary goal of discovering the palace's limits and plan: Layard was seeking sculpture; the Iraqis were trying to halt modern development on Kouyunjik; and the others wanted tablets. Thus, 130 years later, the plan published by Layard in *Discoveries in the Ruins of Nineveh and Babylon* (1853a) still shows most of what is known of Sennacherib's palace. To improve this plan we must turn not to the archaeologist, but rather to the textual sources and to comparisons with other neo-Assyrian palaces.

4

(RE)CONSTRUCTING THE PALACE

Restoration of the Plan

To conclude his account of the excavation of the Southwest Palace, Layard wrote:

> A glance at the general plan will show that only a part of the palace has been explored, and that much still remains underground of this enormous structure. Since my return to Europe other rooms and sculptures have been discovered. Both to the north and to the east of the ruins comprised in the plan, I had found traces of chambers, and the fragments of bas-reliefs. The excavations having been carried to the very edge of the mound, to the south and the west, nothing, of course, remains to be discovered on those sides. How far any of the unexplored parts of the palace may still be preserved, it is of course impossible to conjecture.[1]

As noted in the previous chapter, knowledge of the physical extent of Sennacherib's palace based on excavations has changed little since Layard's day. There are two additional types of data, however, that permit a fuller understanding of the palace's original size and layout. These are Sennacherib's inscriptions that describe the construction and appearance of his palace; and comparisons of its excavated plan with the plans of other, more fully excavated Assyrian palaces.

Sennacherib's Building Accounts

Excavations in the Southwest Palace and its environs have yielded a series of palace building accounts—often appended to various editions of Sennacherib's annals—inscribed on dated foundation cylinders and prisms, and on the bull colossi in the palace entrances. The earliest of these texts was probably

composed in 703 or 702 B.C. and the latest in late 694 or 693.[2] Taken together they constitute a remarkable record of the development and expansion of Sennacherib's palace over the course of its construction. Of particular
interest for a restoration of the original plan of the palace are the total dimensions of the palace terrace platform as given in successive editions of the
building account, which are summarized in the following table.

Southwest Palace Terrace Dimensions in Successive Building Accounts[3]

	Date of text (B.C.)					
	703/702	702	700	697	694	694/693
Side	60 GAR	700	700	700	700	914
Front	34 GAR	—	—	—	440	440
"South" (i.e., west) Tigris front	—	386	386	386	—	—
"North" (i.e., east) front	—	162	176	176	—	—
Inner front, behind Ishtar Temple	—	217	268	268	—	—
"West" (i.e., north) inner front, behind Ishtar ziggurat	—	—	383	443	—	—
Height (layers of bricks)	170	180	180	180	190	190

Note: The cardinal points given in the texts must be shifted 90 degrees clockwise in order to
approximate more closely actual compass points. This shift has been noted in parentheses. All
dimensions are in *aslu rabītu* cubits (see below), unless noted otherwise. One GAR = 12 cubits,
but it is not possible to determine what type of cubit is intended in the 703/702 text.

The changing dimensions of the palace terrace would appear to be of significance for a study of the chronology of construction of the palace, and this
issue will be taken up again later in this chapter. For the moment, it is sufficient to note that the final total dimensions of the palace terrace platform, as
recorded on the great bulls at the entrance to the throne room, were 914
cubits on the side and 440 cubits on the front. In order to compare these dimensions with the dimensions of that part of the palace excavated by Layard,
the value of the *aslu rabītu* cubit must be determined. Fortunately, this may
be accomplished with a reasonable degree of accuracy. J. E. Reade has observed that in one of his building inscriptions, Sennacherib gives the circum-
ference of the new city wall around Nineveh as 21,815 *aslu rabītu* cubits. The
remains of this wall still survive and measure roughly 12 kilometers in cir-
cumference (see figure 1). Based on this equivalence, Reade calculated the
length of Sennacherib's cubit as approximately 55 centimeters.[4]

Using the equivalence 1 cubit equals 55 centimeters, the original extent of

Sennacherib's palace can be calculated from the figures in the latest building account as 503 meters on the side (east to west) and 242 meters on the front (north to south). These figures can be compared with Layard's final plan, where the area of excavated wall remains measured 198 meters from east to west, and 190 meters from north to south (see p. 344).[5] Thus it appears that Layard indeed excavated only a fraction of the total area of Sennacherib's palace. Though the dimensions given in the building accounts are for the palace terrace, and are therefore presumably somewhat larger than the area actually covered by the palace walls, still it appears that Layard excavated less than half of the palace's original length. To reconstruct those areas not excavated by Layard, let us turn for comparisons to the plans of the palaces of Sennacherib's predecessors.

Comparison with Other Neo-Assyrian Palace Plans

The plans of two of these palaces, the Northwest Palace of Assurnasirpal II at Nimrud and Sargon II's palace at Khorsabad, are relatively well known. Their plans are compared with that of Sennacherib's palace in figure 43, where all are shown at roughly the same scale and with their throne rooms aligned on the same axis. The most notable feature preserved in the plans of both earlier palaces that is absent from Layard's plan of Sennacherib's palace is the great outer court of the throne-room suite. This court, designated D/E in Assurnasirpal's palace and VIII in Sargon's, apparently served as an assembly area outside the throne room and was far larger than any of the interior courts in these palaces. Its equivalent in Sennacherib's palace is the partially excavated Court H. Layard excavated some 85 meters of the west wall of this court, including the throne-room facade, and dug an exploratory tunnel some 30 meters eastward into the court without encountering any further walls.[6] Sargon's Court VIII measured 112 meters wide and 61 meters deep, and its equivalent in Sennacherib's palace, Court H, should have been even larger, just as Sennacherib's throne room was larger than Sargon's. If Court H was a large rectangular court similar to Sargon's Court VIII, then this would add between 60 and 80 meters to the excavated part of the palace, bringing its estimated length up to around 260 to 280 meters. Figure 44 shows my reconstruction of Court H based on this analogy with Sargon's Court VIII. From this it appears that the relief slabs belonging to Hormuzd Rassam's "Ishtar Temple Procession" may originally have lined a passageway in the north wall of Court H.[7]

This still leaves over 200 meters of the total length of Sennacherib's palace

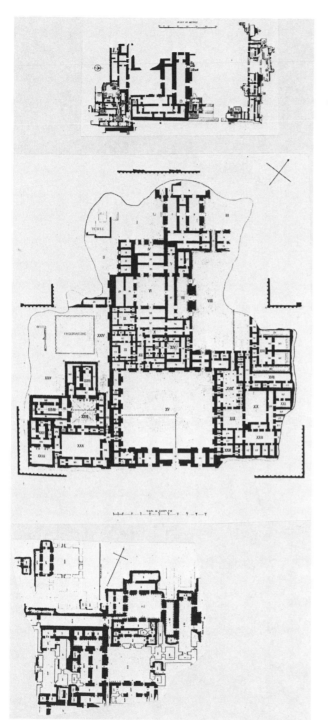

FIG. 43. Comparison of plans of palaces of Assurnasirpal II (top), Sargon II (middle), and Sennacherib (bottom), all shown to same scale (source: author).

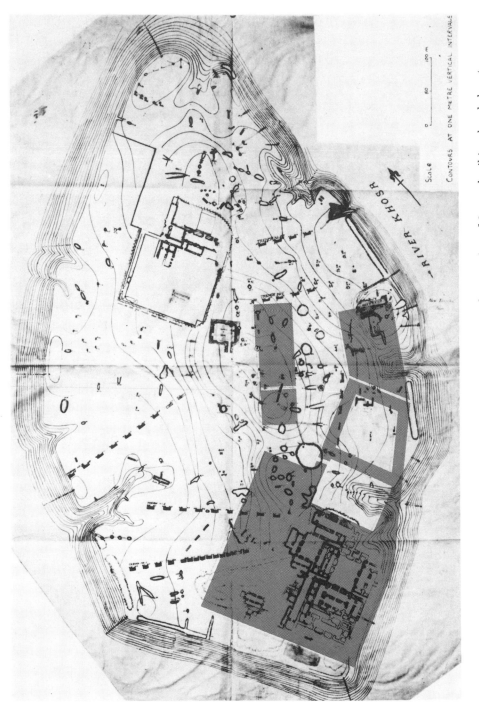

Fig. 44. Figure 45 with Ishtar Temple and Ziggurat above and my suggested restoration of Sennacherib's palace below (source: author).

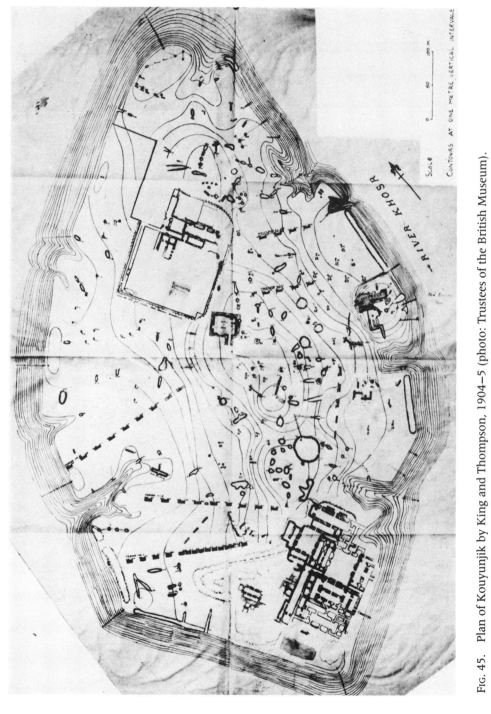

FIG. 45.   Plan of Kouyunjik by King and Thompson, 1904–5 (photo: Trustees of the British Museum).

FIG. 46. Plan of the *bīt
nakkapti*, Nineveh, 1904–5
(from Thompson and
Hutchinson 1929a, plan 7).

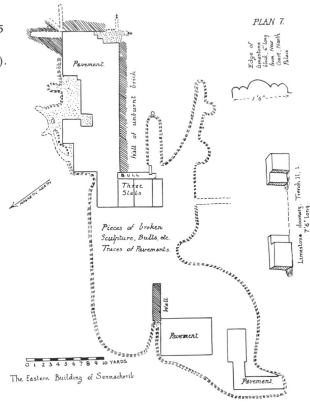

unaccounted for, assuming that the figure of 914 cubits (503 meters) in the
final building account actually represents the overall length of the palace.
Sargon's palace may also provide a key to at least a part of this difference. In
addition to the throne-room outer court (VIII), Sargon's palace had a second,
even larger, court (XV) that measured some 100 meters wide and 88 meters
long. This court, located just inside the palace's main gate and separated from
the residential areas, probably served as the administrative center for the palace services. If a similar outer court existed in Sennacherib's palace, located
to the east of Court H, then this would add another hundred or so meters,
giving a total estimated length of some 360 to 380 meters.

This hypothetical addition of two outer courts plus their subsidiary rooms
onto the excavated length of Sennacherib's palace would result in a total
length that is approximately the same as the length recorded in all but the

final building accounts, that is 700 cubits (385 meters). The latest building description, however, increased the length to 914 cubits (503 meters), and this additional 118 meters needs to be accounted for. It appears to me that this increase must represent a late addition to Sennacherib's palace built at the time the main part of the palace was near completion.

When I wrote the first version of this study, I believed this late addition to be the so-called *bīt nakkapti,* discovered in 1904 by Thompson and King at the east edge of the mound of Kouyunjik and partially reexcavated under my supervision in 1989 (figs. 45, 46, 47). This structure included a major gateway paved with three large, wheel-rutted stone threshold slabs, orthostats carved with apotropaic figures similar to examples in the Southwest Palace, and the lower part of a bull colossus, the inscription on which seems to identify the structure as a *bīt nakkapti.* The meaning of this term is uncertain. This bull text includes a description of building stones that in part repeats the list in the Southwest Palace bull inscriptions, but adds several new stones, including NA$_4$.^{d}ŠE.TIR stone from Mt. Nipur. Mt. Nipur, the modern Judi Dagh to the north of Assyria, was the location of Sennacherib's fifth campaign,

FIG. 47.   View of the *bīt nakkapti,* Nineveh, as reexcavated by the author in 1989 (photo: author).

which took place around 697 B.C., and it was probably at that time that the NA$_4$.^{d}ŠE.TIR stone was discovered. Its inclusion in the *bīt nakkapti* bull inscription suggests that this text was composed somewhat later than those on the Southwest Palace bulls. This later date for the bull text supports the suggestion that the *bīt nakkapti* was a later addition to the palace.[8]

The straight-line distance between the northeast end of the *bīt nakkapti* threshold and the east end of the north bull in throne-room Door *a* is 293.5 meters.[9] This figure, added to the length of the portion of the Southwest Palace excavated by Layard, results in a total length for Sennacherib's palace of roughly 500 meters, which is also the figure given in the building account of 694/693 B.C. Based on this coincidence of measurements, I formerly suggested that the *bīt nakkapti* should be seen not as an independent building, but rather as an extension of the royal palace, added by Sennacherib around 693 B.C.[10]

My 1989 excavations on the *bīt nakkapti* cast some doubt on this hypothesis. Based on the plans of Thompson and King, I had assumed that the *bīt nakkapti* bull colossus faced northeast and therefore formed the exterior entrance at the eastern end of Sennacherib's palace. Excavation revealed that this bull actually faced southwest, *toward* the main part of the palace, not away from it as would be expected were it an exterior entrance. If it is part of the palace, therefore, it must be an interior doorway. The alternative is that it is a doorway in a neighboring structure.

Measurements made in the course of our 1989 excavations left the matter inconclusive. On the one hand, the direct distance between the throne-room facade and the *bīt nakkapti* matches the total length given by Sennacherib for his palace. On the other hand, measurements made between the same two points, but following the curving contour of the edge of the mound, which is presumably where the outer wall of the palace would actually have been, gave a distance that exceeds Sennacherib's by some 30 meters.[11] Without knowing where the Assyrians took their measurements, the question of the relationship between the *bīt nakkapti* and Sennacherib's palace must remain open until its plan is more completely recovered.

The Siting and Plan of Sennacherib's Palace

A tentative reconstruction of the plan and siting of Sennacherib's palace, based on the textual and comparative evidence outlined above, is given here in figure 44. It can be seen there that Layard recovered most of the palace's original width—he excavated a total width of 190 meters, while the latest building descriptions give the width as 242 meters (440 cubits). The difference of fifty or so meters can easily be accounted for by completing the outer wall of Room LX and the terrace on the south and one or two ranks of rooms off of Court LXIV to the north.[12] The west side of the palace has been squared off by the addition of the paved terrace reportedly excavated by Thompson and King. The area between the throne-room facade and the *bīt nakkapti* at the east, has been reconstructed with two large courts, as suggested above.

It is clear from figure 44, and also from the building descriptions, that the plan and siting of Sennacherib's palace were influenced by several constraints. The most substantial of these was the Ishtar Temple, which occupies the center of the mound of Kouyunjik. The building description of 700 B.C., despite some difficulties of interpretation, seems to indicate that the north exterior wall of the palace was divided into two separate facades, apparently in order to accommodate the preexisting structures of the Ishtar Temple and its ziggurat. Reade has suggested that the Ishtar ziggurat was located at what is now the highest point on Kouyunjik, L. W. King's 32-meter contour, immediately southwest of the Ishtar Temple (figure 45).[13] Consequently, I have reconstructed the north wall of the palace with a jog in this vicinity.

The site of the Southwest Palace was also constrained by the southeast and west edges of the mound of Kouyunjik, bounded by the Khosr and Tigris rivers respectively. Sennacherib claims to have reclaimed land from the bed of the Khosr in order to enlarge the palace terrace along the southeast edge of the mound, but this would probably not have worked well at the west edge, where the mighty Tigris flowed in antiquity.[14]

One difficulty in reconstructing the original plan of Sennacherib's palace is posed by the most complete sets of dimensions given in the building accounts of 700 and 697 B.C. (see table on p. 79). There are essentially two problems here. First, the sum of the two northern "inner fronts" of the palace—268 and 383 cubits in the earlier version, 268 and 443 cubits in the later one— would be expected to equal its total length, 700 cubits. In fact, in the account of 700 B.C., this sum is 49 cubits (27 meters) too small, while in the 697 account it is 11 cubits (6 meters) too large.[15] Far greater is the difference between the length of 386 cubits for the west, Tigris front of the palace and 176 cubits for its east front, a difference of 210 cubits (116 meters). Even allowing for a substantial jog in the north wall of the palace in the vicinity of the Ishtar Temple, it is difficult to explain this difference fully, assuming the exterior corners of all the palace walls were square.

These discrepancies could be accounted for if some of the exterior angles of the Southwest Palace were not square and some of the exterior walls were "bent." Indeed, the orientation of the palace with respect to the contour of the southeast edge of the mound would seem to require this. Consequently, I have tentatively restored the plan of the Southwest Palace with a "bent" south exterior wall, though its original angle is uncertain. This results either in the outer court being somewhat trapezoidal in shape, or in irregularly shaped rooms on the court's south side, or both.[16]

Whether or not the various aspects of this restoration are correct can only be determined through further excavation. Such excavation is unlikely to produce substantial further discoveries of sculpture, if the palace of Sargon II is any guide. There, the great outer court (XV) and its surrounding rooms were devoid of sculptures, suggesting that their function was oriented toward palace services and administration. Excavation of the remainder of the plan of Sennacherib's palace would be highly instructive, nonetheless, for its site is fundamentally different from those of Assurnasirpal's palace at Nimrud and Sargon's palace at Khorsabad. Nimrud and Khorsabad were essentially virgin sites, and their palaces could be laid out without regard for preexisting constraints. Nineveh, on the other hand, was a city of great antiquity, and its sacred traditions had a concrete existence in the form of the Ishtar Temple. The precinct of this temple was apparently inviolable, and it would be interesting to have a clearer picture of how Sennacherib adapted the plan of this, the greatest of the Assyrian palaces, to the restrictions imposed by his chosen site.

The Sequence of Construction

There are several types of evidence for the sequence of construction of Sennacherib's palace. Foremost among these are the king's own building accounts. As can be seen in the table on p. 79, in each succeeding building account, excluding the first, the dimensions given for the palace terrace increase, suggesting that the size of the palace was increasing throughout this period. In the first building account, of 703/702 B.C., dimensions are given as 60 by 34 GAR, which converts to 720 by 408 cubits. Unfortunately, the type of cubit intended here is not specified in the text, so that these measurements cannot be compared meaningfully with the later examples.

A closer look at this earliest text indicates that it was modeled on the palace building account of Sennacherib's father, Sargon II. Indeed, the length and wording of the palace building episodes in these two accounts are in many respects identical, and phrases occur here that are dropped in Sennacherib's later accounts.[17] Of particular interest in this context is the reference in both texts to great stone slabs that were placed along the walls of the palace and upon which the king caused to be depicted "the enemy tribes whom my hands had conquered."[18] This is the only reference to the wall reliefs in Sennacherib's palace texts. One senses here that construction of the new palace has barely begun and that Sennacherib, unable yet to describe the unbuilt palace in detail, has been obliged to borrow this description from his father.

Sennacherib's next two palace building accounts, of 702 and 700 B.C., focus on the building of the palace terrace and describe the process in great detail. This account concludes, almost as an afterthought, with a phrase taken almost verbatim from Sargon's building account: "Thereon I built a palace of ivory, maple, boxwood, mulberry, cedar, cypress, and spruce, the 'Palace without a Rival,' for my royal abode."[19] The absence of any further specific information about the palace itself suggests that here, too, the construction is in its early stages. This deduction also helps to account for the varying dimensions given for the palace terrace, for at the time of these texts the terrace would have been under construction and still expanding toward its final dimensions.

Apparent confirmation that the construction of the palace was still in its early stages in 700 B.C., at the time of the third building account, was found during Hormuzd Rassam's excavations in Sennacherib's palace. As mentioned previously, Rassam found four inscribed cylinders in the walls of Rooms VII, VIII, and IX.[20] All of these cylinders bore the annals of the first three campaigns and a palace building account and were dated in the second month (equal to April–May) of 700 B.C. Evidently the walls in the Court VI area were being built at the time these cylinders were made.

Though the Rassam cylinders are apparently the only clearly provenienced examples from the Southwest Palace, there is a very considerable number of unprovenienced duplicates of these cylinders. In Borger's listing of known duplicates of the various editions of Sennacherib's texts, duplicates of the 700 B.C. cylinder far outnumber those for any other text.[21] Because the content of the building account in these cylinders deals exclusively with the palace and its surroundings, it seems probable that the origin of most or all of these duplicates was Sennacherib's palace.

Further evidence for a foundation date around 700 B.C. is in a fragmentary

eponym list, where the entry for the year 700 in part reads: "[the founda-
tions/walls(?)] of the palace in the city [of Nineveh . . .]," and then continues with a list of the same rare building materials that are described in the
later palace building accounts.[22] Consequently, it appears that the Southwest
Palace's walls were built around 700 B.C.

The next adequately published editions of Sennacherib's palace building
account, of 694 and 694/693 B.C. (see table on p. 79), contain detailed descriptions of the construction and appearance of the palace itself, from which
it may be deduced that by this time the palace was nearing completion. The
only substantial difference between these two texts is in the dimensions given
for the palace. The edition of 694 gives the same total length, 700 cubits, as
was found in the earlier editions, but this has expanded to 914 cubits in the
final version, of 694/693. As argued above, this increase probably reflects the
addition of the *bīt nakkapti*.

It was about this time that annalistic, summary, and building accounts
were inscribed on the palace's gateway colossi. The building accounts on
these colossi are chronologically suggestive since the length of the palace is
given as 700 cubits in some, while in others it is given as 914. In those cases
where an annalistic or historical summary text accompanies the building account, the five-campaign text is associated with the smaller palace length,
and the six-campaign text with the larger. This suggests that the colossi
were inscribed over a period of time that spanned the transition from the
five-campaign annalistic edition of 694 B.C. to the six-campaign edition of
694/693.[23]

Another chronological indicator is supplied by one of the special types of
stone used in the embellishment of the palace. A brief text on the back of the
colossi in Door *p* of Room XXXIII identified the stone on the walls of that
room as NA₄.ᵈŠE.TIR stone from Mt. Nipur. According to Layard, the same
stone was used to panel the walls of Rooms XXIX and XXX, where it was left
uncarved. As was noted in the discussion of the *bīt nakkapti* above,
NA₄.ᵈŠE.TIR also figured in the decoration of that structure. Though this
stone was presumably discovered around 697 B.C. during Sennacherib's fifth
campaign, to Mt. Nipur, it is not mentioned in the palace building account of
694 or in its near-duplicate of 694/693. The implication here would seem to
be that the NA₄.ᵈŠE.TIR was not installed in the palace until after the Southwest Palace building account had assumed its final form, which was probably
not long before 694.[24]

A final chronological indicator is provided by two foundation prisms—the
"Jerusalem Prism" in the Israel Museum and the "Taylor Prism" in the Brit-

ish Museum—that describe the work on Sennacherib's arsenal on the other mound in ancient Nineveh, Nebi Yunus. Both are dated in the eponymy of Bēl-īmurani, that is, from 691 to early 690 B.C. Though the month date of the Jerusalem Prism is lost, its modern editor believed it was the earlier of the two, since its building account is shorter and less elaborate than that on the Taylor Prism. It contains no mention of the Southwest Palace. By contrast, in the Taylor Prism, which was inscribed in the last month of the year (late 691 or early 690), the building account commences with the statement that after the Southwest Palace was completed, Sennacherib turned to the rebuilding of the Nebi Yunus arsenal. The omission of this claim from the Jerusalem Prism and its inclusion in the Taylor Prism suggests that during the interval between the writing of the two texts the palace was finished, though an alternative interpretation would be to see it as mere literary embellishment, without chronological significance. In any case, if the statement in the Taylor Prism is taken literally, and there is no evidence that it should be doubted, then the "Palace without Rival" was completed in, or shortly before, 691 B.C.[25]

The various types of evidence outlined above point to the following chronology for the construction of Sennacherib's palace. The earliest texts suggest that the period from 703/702 to 700 B.C. was devoted to planning the palace and preparing a suitable foundation platform, and the increasing dimensions given for the platform in successive editions of the building accounts seem to indicate that it expanded throughout this time. Inscribed cylinders dated 700 B.C. were found buried in the walls of the palace, suggesting that the construction of the superstructure began around this time. The building account appended to the annalistic edition of 694 B.C. carries the palace description essentially in its final form, which implies that work on the building was nearing completion by that time. A further increase in the length of the palace in the building account of 694/693 probably signals the addition of the *bīt nakkapti*. Finally, according to Sennacherib's arsenal text, the palace was completed by 691 B.C. It might be possible to refine this chronology through a study of the changes in the palace building account in the editions between 700 and 694 B.C., but this can only be done after the relevant texts are published.

Conclusions

To conclude, it should be noted that a primary potential source of information on the sequence of construction of Sennacherib's palace is not at present available to us and may be lost forever. This source is archaeological information on construction phases that can be derived from careful observation of such features as stratigraphy, brick size and color, and wall bonding. These details were apparently of no interest to Layard, who was tunneling his way through the Southwest Palace in search of reliefs, nor are they described in the published reports of any subsequent excavators, most of whom were in search of tablets. It is probable that some of this information is still in the ground awaiting a sympathetic interpreter, but much archaeological information must have been lost to the treasure-hunting techniques of Layard and his successors.[26]

Another potential source of information on construction sequence could be the date of the subjects shown on the wall reliefs. One could hypothesize that rooms decorated with reliefs showing the first campaign, for example, were constructed earlier than rooms showing the third campaign. This hypothesis may be correct, but it would be very difficult to prove for two reasons. First, if my reconstruction of the construction sequence based on the contemporary building accounts is correct, then Sennacherib had already completed his first three military campaigns by mid-700 B.C., the time the walls were apparently built. The annals of the first three campaigns, of 703, 702, and 701 B.C., had already been compiled and the records of all three of these campaigns would presumably have been available to Sennacherib's artists by the time the relief slabs were ready to be carved. Second, there is no necessary relationship between the placement of stone slabs along a wall and the carving of those slabs with reliefs. A room could be finished with its slabs in place months or years before the slabs were actually carved. In at least three rooms in Sennacherib's palace, XXIX, XXX, and LIII, and possibly also XXXIII, the slabs were never carved at all. It seems unlikely, therefore, that the representation of a campaign in a given room necessarily implies any temporal relationship between the date of that campaign and the date of construction of that portion of the palace.

Nevertheless, even though clear archaeological data is lacking, and even though the subjects of the wall reliefs are not reliable chronological indicators, it has still been possible—based on the known plan of the Southwest Palace, comparisons with other Assyrian palace plans, and Sennacherib's dated building accounts—to recover what appears to be a reasonably clear picture of the original plan and chronology of construction of Sennacherib's "Palace without Rival." I have attempted to demonstrate here that the dimensions of the excavated remains of the palace are consistent with the dimensions given in Sennacherib's building accounts; that the walls of the nucleus of the palace were built around 700 B.C. and that an extension, perhaps to be identified with the *bīt nakkapti,* was added to the east end of the palace around 693 B.C.; and that the total length of time required for the construction of the palace was less than twelve years, from about 703 B.C., when the palace was apparently still only a dream, until 691 B.C., when Sennacherib says it is finished. Having examined the extent and chronology of the palace walls, let us now turn to the stone slabs that covered them.

5

QUARRYING AND TRANSPORT

We have seen in chapter 2 that the great bull colossi flanking the major door-ways of Sennacherib's palace were the location of lengthy inscriptions pro-claiming the glories of Sennacherib's reign (figure 48).[1] It may well be that part of the reason the bulls continued to carry inscriptions even after texts had disappeared from other traditional locations (thresholds, wall relief text band) was because these colossi were themselves very special to Sennacherib. Sennacherib's building accounts are full of descriptions of the colossi, detailing not only their numbers and appearance, but also the types and sources of stone from which they were carved. Furthermore, these colossi were commemorated not only in the palace inscriptions, but also in an extensive series of reliefs devoted to the subject of their quarrying and transport.

This chapter is an investigation of the sources of the stone used in the Southwest Palace decoration and a description of its quarrying and transport. Surprisingly little has been written on these subjects and this aspect of neo-Assyrian architecture still awaits a comprehensive survey such as Clarke and Engelbach accomplished for Egyptian architecture and Naumann for that of Asia Minor.[2] And yet sufficient evidence exists—physical, textual, and pictorial—to reconstruct a relatively complete picture of neo-Assyrian quarrying and transport in the reign of Sennacherib.

Quarries

Sennacherib Quarries Known Archaeologically

To my knowledge, the only neo-Assyrian quarry known today is a limestone quarry near Bavian, at the head of the aqueduct completed by Sennacherib in the same year as the battle of Halule (691 B.C.). This quarry, first recorded by Wigram, was described by Bachmann as a "large U-shaped excavation in the cliff, which could be thought to be an Assyrian quarry." Jacobsen and Lloyd believed this quarry was the source of limestone for the aqueduct and suggested that during construction stone was transported along the aqueduct itself to the construction site. Unfortunately, neither Bachmann nor Jacobsen and Lloyd published adequate photos of this quarry, so it is not possible without visiting the site itself to determine what evidence for neo-Assyrian stone-working technique it contains.[3]

Layard searched for quarries in the environs of Nineveh but was unable to locate even a trace. He concluded that because stone is so abundant in the area, it could have been quarried virtually anywhere. This abundance of stone would have made deep quarries unnecessary and sites from which stone was removed would have eventually filled with soil, leaving no traces. At the time of Layard's second visit, alabaster was being quarried in the vicinity of the Sinjar Gate of Mosul, northwest of the city. Layard did report

FIG. 48. Bull colossus of Sennacherib, Nergal Gate, city wall, Nineveh, ca. 4.5 m high (photo: author).

"quarries of the kind of alabaster used in the Assyrian palaces" in the Gebel Maklub, east of Khorsabad. These quarries appeared ancient, but Layard found no Assyrian remains in them. Place described limestone quarries in this vicinity and says they contained "stones cut and made ready, but for which the Assyrian architects apparently had no need." Place found no alabaster quarries but, like Layard, observed that this stone was everywhere, literally "underfoot," and could have been quarried whenever it was convenient.[4]

Sennacherib Quarries Known from Texts

Of the neo-Assyrian kings, only Sennacherib gave detailed information on his quarries. His building accounts record five sources of stone for architectural sculpture. The quarry mentioned first in these texts is at Tastiate, "across the Tigris," which supplied *pīlu peṣû*, white limestone ("Mosul marble").[5] Sennacherib said that under his predecessors the quarry at Tastiate had supplied stone for colossi. The transport of these colossi, as related by Sennacherib, was inefficient and not without hazard. The larger figures were quite massive; Layard observed that Sennacherib's largest colossi were twenty feet square with an estimated weight of forty to fifty tons. Only at the time of the spring floods was there sufficient water in the Tigris to float these great loads safely across to Nineveh.[6]

By transporting the colossi at this time, the Assyrian engineers could have avoided the very tricky problem of safely loading such huge objects onto rafts in the river. To be sure, Layard found a solution to this problem, allowing his colossi to slide down a ramp on the riverbank onto rafts moored alongside, and it may be assumed the Assyrian engineers would have been no less ingenious. But Layard's colossi were relatively small and had been trimmed back as far as possible to reduce weight. He doubted whether this loading procedure would have worked for large colossi, as the strain on the raft from the sudden weight would have been too great. By waiting for the spring floods, he suggested, one could simply haul the stone block to the river bank, raise it enough to construct the raft under it, and wait for the flood waters to rise enough to float raft and block free. Unloading could, of course, follow the reverse procedure, grounding the rafts at Nineveh and waiting for the water to recede. Layard stated that if he had been authorized to transport the larger colossi from Nimrud, this is the procedure he would have used, and it is reasonable to suppose that this was also the Assyrian method.[7]

There would appear to have been two major problems with Tastiate as the principal source of supply of white limestone for colossi. First, the colossi could only be transported to Nineveh once a year, namely in the spring. Sennacherib required large numbers of colossi for the city gates, palace, and armory of Nineveh, and it must sometimes have been inconvenient to have to plan building projects around the annual arrival of colossi from Tastiate. Second, the flood waters of the Tigris can be treacherous, and it is likely that colossi were occasionally lost in the river, thus further delaying construction schedules.[8]

Despite Sennacherib's claims that the quarry at Tastiate was used only by his unenlightened predecessors, his remarkably detailed description of the difficulties of bringing stone from that quarry has the ring of personal experience, presumably gained as crown prince during the construction of the palace of his father, Sargon II.[9] His disenchantment with Tastiate, as buildings languished uncompleted awaiting colossi, would have made a new source of good quality white limestone on the left bank of the Tigris highly desirable. Then the only transportation requirements would be plenty of manpower—no problem for an Assyrian monarch—and dry weather, which is common enough in Assyria.

The importance to Sennacherib of a more convenient source of stone is suggested by his statement that its discovery was "by decree of the god." This new quarry was "near Nineveh, in the district of Balaṭai," and, judging from the frequency of its occurrence in the building accounts, it replaced Tastiate as Sennacherib's primary source of *pīlu peṣû* for the production of colossi. While the general area of these quarries is fairly certain, their specific location is a matter of some conjecture. Neo-Assyrian Balaṭai is generally identified with the medieval city of Balad, modern Eski Mosul, on the right bank of the Tigris some 35 kilometers upriver from Mosul.[10]

This identification may well be correct. There is evidence, however, that the quarries themselves were on the left bank. A remarkable relief series from Court VI of Sennacherib's palace shows the quarrying and transport of bull colossi for that palace (figure 49). Epigraphs on the reliefs identify the quarry as that at Balaṭai.[11] Most of the slabs from this series are preserved, either physically or in Layard's drawings, and it is possible from these to reconstruct fully its appearance. The Assyrian artist was very conscientious in recording topographic detail. The area of the quarry, at the right end of the series, has a background of wooded mountains (see figure 50). As the colossi are dragged leftwards, toward Nineveh, the background changes, first to a reed marsh, then to a tree-lined river, presumably the Tigris (see figs. 57, 58). A river-crossing scene is *not* shown, which suggests that quarrying and transport

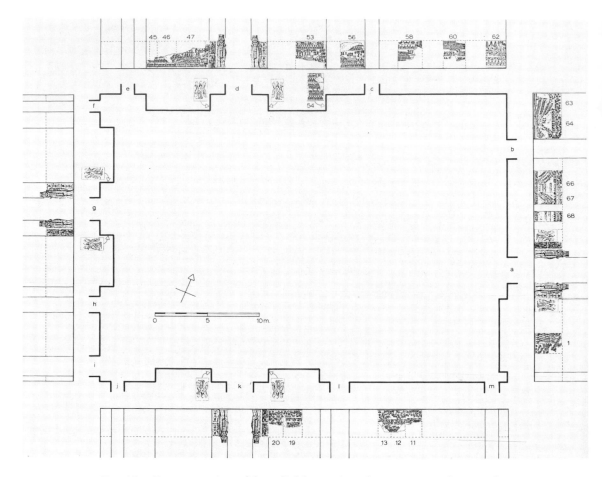

FIG. 49.   Reconstruction of the relief decoration of Court VI, Southwest Palace, Nineveh (source: author).

took place entirely on the Nineveh side of the river. Furthermore, if the images are read literally, the colossi are shown being dragged from right to left with the river above, in the background. Assuming they were being hauled south, from the vicinity of Eski Mosul, this arrangement corresponds with a quarry located on the left bank of the Tigris.

In an unpublished letter to Loftus of 4 October 1854, Rawlinson wrote, "I would particularly recommend to your examination the quarries on the river near Zigan [Jikan] (ancient Balad) from whence Sennacherib brought his hewn slabs to Nineveh."[12] Tell Jikan is on the left bank of the Tigris some fifteen kilometers north of Eski Mosul, and fifty kilometers upriver from Nineveh. While modern Eski Mosul and ancient Balaṭai may be one and the same, therefore, this identification is satisfactory only if the "district" of Balaṭai included land on both sides of the Tigris.[13]

Sennacherib brought unusual stone from three other sources, though apparently only in limited amounts. The first of these was Mt. Nipur, the Judi Dagh to the north near Cizre, Turkey. This was the location of Sennacherib's fifth campaign, which probably took place in 697 B.C. In the Judi Dagh inscriptions, Sennacherib claims to have personally led this campaign, and it may have been the king himself who noticed the fine quality NA$_4$.^{d}ŠE.TIR stone "at the foot of Mt. Nipur."[14] This stone is described as having a variegated surface that looked like grains of "mottled barley" or, in another text, cucumber seeds. Sennacherib claims that before his time NA$_4$.^{d}ŠE.TIR was prized for jewelry and so must have been considered rare. He, however, found it in sufficient quantity at Mt. Nipur to make an unspecified number of *ʃapsasāte* colossi for his palace and armory. As Reade pointed out, these figures probably *were* transported by water the considerable distance downriver to Nineveh.[15]

Reade associated the Mt. Nipur NA$_4$.^{d}ŠE.TIR stone *ʃapsasāte* with the colossi described (but not illustrated) by Layard in Door *p* of Room XXXIII of the Southwest Palace. This is almost certainly correct. Layard reported that behind these "winged lions," or "sphinxes," were inscriptions "describing the cutting of those sculptures and their transport to Nineveh," which included "the Assyrian word both for the colossi and for the stone of which they were made." The only text that fits this description was published by Rawlinson, who said it was from the "back of slabs at the entrance of Sculptured Chamber; transferred to New Gallery at the British Museum." The sphinxes at the entrance to Room XXXIII and the carved orthostats within were of the same distinctive material, a limestone "full of shells and other fossils, [having] when polished, a very pleasing appearance."[16] This accords well with Sennacherib's description of NA$_4$.^{d}ŠE.TIR. From this association, then, it is clear both that the Room XXXIII slabs in the British Museum are of NA$_4$.^{d}ŠE.TIR stone from Mt. Nipur and that the figures called *ʃapsasāte* by Sennacherib are human-headed, winged lions, presumably female, judging from the use of the feminine plural and determinative. Unsculptured slabs of this stone lined the walls of Rooms XXIX and XXX. Presumably they were left uncarved to emphasize the beauty of the stone.[17]

Another source of unusual stone was Kapridargilâ, "which is on the border of Til-Barsip," west of Assyria. From here Sennacherib says he brought great slabs of NA$_4$.DÚR.MI.NA.BÀN.DA, usually translated "breccia." Reade tentatively identified this stone with the "close-grained magnesian lime-stone, almost as hard as flint," unsculptured slabs of which lined the walls of Room LIII.[18]

Finally, Sennacherib brought *gišnugallu* stone from Mt. Ammanana, which Cogan identified with the Anti-Lebanon range west and north of Damascus. *Gišnugallu* seems to be a high-quality alabaster that Sennacherib claimed was a precious material used for inlaying weapons in the time of his forefathers. He, however, found sufficient quantities to make human-headed bull and sphinx colossi of it for his palace.[19]

Thus, of the five quarries used by Sennacherib, two were sources of *pīlu peṣû* or "Mosul marble," the material of the vast majority of the colossi and reliefs in the Southwest Palace. One of these quarries, at Tastiate, was a tra-ditional source of this stone, but transportation difficulties apparently caused Sennacherib to abandon it in favor of the newly discovered one at Balaṭai. The other three quarries, Mt. Nipur, Kapridargilâ, and Ammanana, supplied unusual stones that Sennacherib used in certain areas for special effect.

Quarrying Technique

In the reliefs of Court VI in Sennacherib's palace, we are fortunate to have a detailed representation of neo-Assyrian quarrymen at work. This illustration covers Slabs 66 to 68 of the east wall of the court (figure 50).[20] The setting is a hilly, wooded countryside. There are two representations of workmen quarrying large blocks of stone from which bull colossi are to be carved. In the better-preserved relief, on Slab 66, quarrymen are shown crouching and kneeling around three sides of the block (the fourth side is not preserved). Those below the block work singly, chipping away the rock surrounding the block. The tool of the rightmost of these figures, a relatively large pick, is fairly well preserved. The men above the block appear to be sitting on its up-per face. They work in pairs and while their tools are not clearly identifiable because of poor preservation, they are apparently not the large picks of the men below. Probably they wield smaller masons' picks with which they are roughing out the form of the bull. Two men at the left side of the block are in the same pose as the men on top, but work singly rather than in pairs— one appears to hold a small pick, very like a mason's pick.

The scene is completed by files of basketmen who carry off the rubble and dump it atop great piles of waste stone and two rows of soldiers who dis-

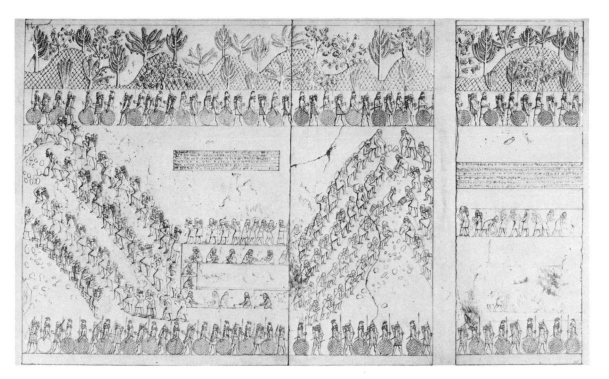

FIG. 50. The quarry at Balaṭai, drawing of Slabs 66–68, Court VI, Southwest Palace, Nineveh. British Museum, WAA, Or. Dr., I, 56 (photo: Trustees of the British Museum).

courage the workers from wandering off. Directly above the quarrymen is the caption:

> Sennacherib, king of the world, king of Assyria: At the command of the god white limestone for the construction of my palace was discovered in the district of Balaṭai. I had men from enemy towns and the inhabitants of hidden mountain regions, conquest of my hands, wield iron *qulmû* and *ak-kullu* tools (on which see below), and I had great *aladlammû* figures made for the gates of my palace.

From this it is clear that the setting is the quarry at Balaṭai and the subject is the quarrying of *aladlammû*, which the accompanying images show to be human-headed bull colossi.[21]

Comparison with actual quarries in Egypt and Anatolia aids an understanding of the procedure shown here. Based on their examination of ancient

FIG. 51. Granite quarry with unfinished obelisk, Aswan (photo: Barry Bergdoll).

quarries in Egypt, Clarke and Engelbach described the Egyptian procedure for removing limestone from surface quarries. To remove a large block from a surface quarry, trenches wide enough for a man to work in (roughly two feet wide) were cut along each of its sides. Examples of blocks abandoned after the trenches were dug were found in Anatolia at Boghazköy, site of the ancient Hittite capital, and in Egypt at Aswan (figure 51).[22] On Slab 66, the upper face of the block will become the broad side of the colossus; the desired width of the sculpture (five or six feet for a large example) determines the depth of the trench. This block, then, is seen from the side, that is, the part that will become the front of the colossus.

After all four sides are exposed, the block is detached from the stone beneath, either by driving iron wedges into slots cut at its base or by inserting wooden wedges into slots and wetting them, which caused the wedges to expand. While this step isn't shown in the preserved reliefs, a cart containing four large wedges is shown on Slab 62 approaching the quarry (see figure 56). And while sledge hammers don't figure in the quarry scene from Court VI, Layard did find several objects "resembling the heads of sledge-hammers" in Room AB of the Northwest Palace at Nimrud, and another was found at Khorsabad, indicating that this tool was used by the Assyrians.[23]

Subsequent scenes in this relief series show that the figure was roughed out, though apparently not finished, before transport. Presumably this was done both to reduce weight and to ensure that the stone was free of flaws, thereby avoiding the expense of transporting a block that may later have to be discarded. As noted above, the masons on top of the block seem to be using their small picks to rough out the form at the same time that the quarrymen below dig the separating trench with their larger picks. The caption accompanying the quarry scene specifies two types of tools, *qulmû* and *akkullu*. I would suggest that these words designate the two types of picks shown: the quarryman's pick, used to free the block from the surrounding stone, and the mason's pick, used to rough out the figure, though I cannot say which is which.[24]

Place found two types of picks in the great hoard of iron implements in Room 86 of Sargon's palace at Khorsabad. He identified the first type as a mason's pick, similar in form to the pick he observed stonemasons using in the vicinity of Khorsabad in his own day (figure 52: nos. 5–7). Some fifty or sixty picks of this type were found—Place reported that the largest examples weighed 12 kilograms, but the average seems to have been about 5 to 8 kilograms. This weight would be consistent with usage for stonecutting, where the principal effect derives from the mass of the pick rather than from the force with which it is wielded. The second type of pick was shaped like a modern mattock, with one end pointed and the other broad, and weighed 14 to 16 kilograms (figure 52: no. 4). These massive tools must have been used for quarrying or breaking stone since they are far heavier than necessary for digging earth. Perhaps these two types of picks are the *qulmû* and *akkullu* referred to in the bull quarrying caption.[25]

Also in the iron hoard were several other tools that could have been useful in the quarrying process. Place described and illustrated a sledge hammer head, which could have been used to drive wedges used to break the stone blocks free (figure 52: no. 8), and also chains and grapnels, which could have been used in moving large blocks.[26]

Other stoneworking tools are known from actual finds, descriptions, and the Court VI illustrations. Two double-handled stonecutter's saws came from Nimrud. One was found by Layard in the Northwest Palace and illustrated by him; the other was from Ft. Shalmaneser. These are probably stonecutting saws because the teeth are not set, that is, they are not alternately bent outward to prevent binding as in a wood saw. The original appearance of these saws can be seen in illustrations from Slab 53 of Court VI where two men are shown carrying similar long double-handled saws (see figure 60), though because of their context the examples in the relief may be wood saws used in preparing materials for the transport of the colossi. Stonecutter's saws would

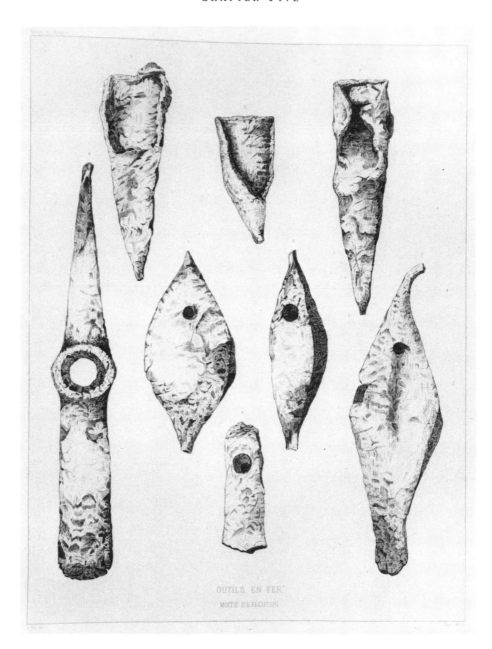

OUTILS EN FER
MOITIE D'EXECUTION

FIG. 52.   Iron picks, Room 86, Sargon's palace, Khorsabad (from Place and Thomas 1867, vol. 3, pl. 71).

have been used for cutting the stone slabs to line the walls of the Assyrian palaces.[27]

Also on Slab 53, directly in front of the man carrying three double-handled saws, are two men, each carrying a crowbar. While Layard's drawing shows these as a single long bar held by two men, it is clear from the actual relief that two shorter bars are shown. These bars could be used for raising and moving blocks in the quarry. Again, however, the context here makes it likely that these particular examples were used in the transport operation.

Transportation of Stone

To the right of the quarry scene in Court VI is a doorway containing two real colossi, a very concrete reminder of the magnitude of the project illustrated (figure 53). The reliefs continue on the east and north walls with detailed representations of the transport of stone blocks from the quarry at Balaṭai to Nineveh. The wooded, hilly background, file of soldiers, and pile of waste stone at the right in Slabs 63 and 64 suggest that the setting is still the quarry (figure 54). This scene shows the first stage of the transport of a colossus. The roughed-out bull, still on its side, has been levered onto a sledge and is being pulled up an incline out of the quarry. Four massive ropes are attached to beam ends protruding from the side of the sledge, one on each side at the front and rear. A team of men is harnessed with shoulder straps to each rope.

Fig. 53. Inscribed bull colossus, Door *a*, Court VI, Southwest Palace, Nineveh, 1. 420 cm (photo: author).

Fig. 54. Moving the bull out of the quarry, drawing of Slabs 63–64, Court VI, Southwest Palace, Nineveh. British Museum, WAA, Or. Dr., I, 57 (photo: Trustees of the British Museum).

FIG. 55.   Layard moving a colossus from Nimrud (from A. H. Layard, *A Popular Account of Discoveries at Nineveh* [London, 1851], facing p. 297).

Their efforts are coordinated by supervisors in front while overseers with whips provide encouragement from behind. The passage of the sledge is eased by wooden rollers placed under its front. Behind, a gang of men provides the initial impetus by means of a long, stout lever. Layard stated that he used "enormous levers of poplar wood" for the same purpose when moving the Nimrud colossi to the banks of the Tigris (figure 55).[28]

Atop the bull four more supervisors, two of them with megaphones or trumpets, coordinate the traction and the lever. To the right, laborers clear a path out of the quarry, carrying loose stones to the top of the waste heap. On a rise at the upper left, Sennacherib watches from his chariot. At the lower left, three men operate water sweeps, feeding a small stream that runs diagonally to the left across the contiguous Slab 62 (figure 56). This operation may or may not have anything to do with the business of transport. I will return to this question in chapter 11.[29]

Essentially the same subject is repeated three more times between Slabs 60 and 51, with alterations only in the background (figs. 57, 58, 59, 60). It is not clear whether the artist intended to show several colossi in transit or a single colossus at several stages of the journey; in either case, the repeated use of the same central motif while varying background detail admirably conveys a sense of progress along the river. The first bull in this cross-country

Fɪɢ. 56.   Workmen proceeding toward the quarry, drawing of Slab 62, Court VI, Southwest Palace, Nineveh. British Museum, WAA, Or. Dr., IV, 51 (photo: Trustees of the British Museum).

FIG. 57. Sennacherib supervising the transport of the bull colossi, drawing of Slab 60, Court VI, Southwest Palace, Nineveh. British Museum, WAA, Or. Dr., IV, 50 (photo: Trustees of the British Museum).

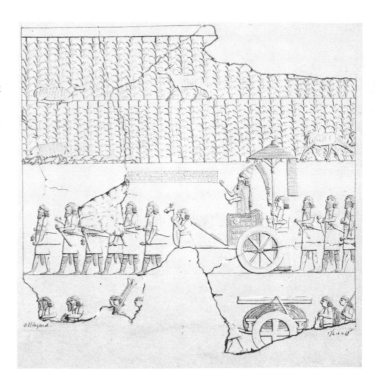

FIG. 58. (*below*) Transport of a bull colossus, Slab 58, Court VI, Southwest Palace, Nineveh, w. 224 cm. British Museum, WAA 124822 (photo: Trustees of the British Museum).

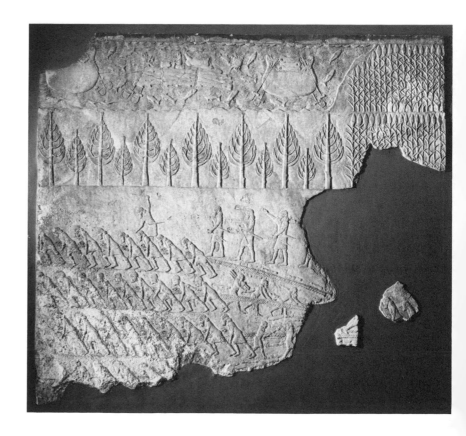

FIG. 59. Transport of a bull colossus, drawing of Slabs 54 and 56, Court VI, Southwest Palace, Nineveh. British Museum, WAA, Or. Dr., I, 55 (photo: Trustees of the British Museum).

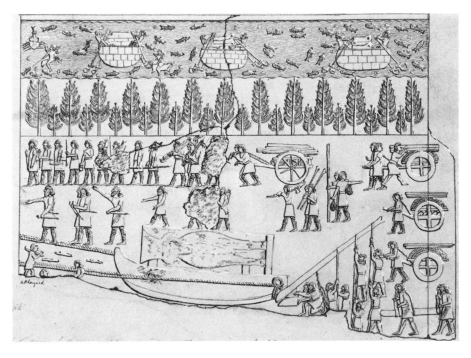

FIG. 60. Transport of a bull colossus, drawing of Slab 53, Court VI, Southwest Palace, Nineveh. British Museum, WAA, Or. Dr., IV, 49 (photo: Trustees of the British Museum).

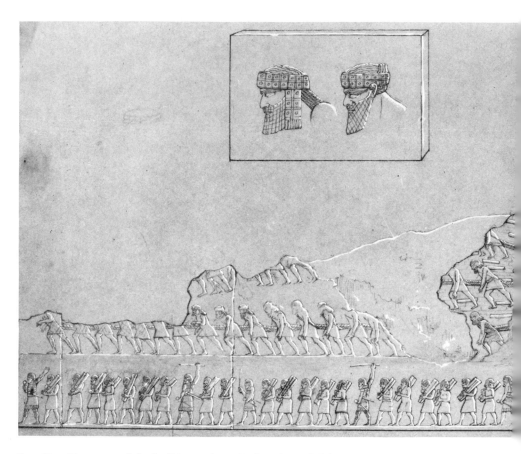

FIG. 61.   Entrance of the bull into Nineveh, drawing of Slabs 45–47, Court VI, Southwest Palace, Nineveh. British Museum, WAA, Or. Dr., IV, 48 (photo: Trustees of the British Museum).

procession, on Slab 53, is accompanied by men carrying various kinds of tools (figure 60). Since this is the front of the line, it is reasonable to assume that these men are responsible for preparing the path down which the sledge travels. Their tools seem to bear this out. Two men carry iron levers for prying out protruding stones. Two others carry saws and axes for clearing away vegetation and cutting rollers. And two carry pointed hoes and shovels for leveling the way. Also accompanying this first bull, and the others as well, are two-wheeled carts loaded with stout rope and short poles and men carrying poles with forked ends. These items seem to be shown in use at the end of the series, on Slab 47. The purpose of the short poles is not entirely clear,

however. If the images are read literally, the poles on the carts appear shorter than those used for the framework around the bull in Slab 47. Perhaps they were used instead to facilitate passage over soft ground, laid either longitudinally as tracks for the rollers, or transversely as sleepers across which the sledge could be pulled and levered without the aid of rollers.[30]

To the left of Slab 53, the series is punctuated once again by a pair of actual colossi. Then follows the final scene, on Slabs 47 to 43, apparently showing the entrance of a bull into the palace, though no background is preserved (figure 61). Still on a sledge, but now fully carved and upright, it is encased in a timber framework and steadied by men holding the aforementioned ropes and forked poles. It appears to be supported below by stacks of blocks (probably baked bricks) wedged under the body. Perhaps these were used in conjunction with levers to raise the colossus, as Loud did when moving the great Khorsabad bull, and were then left in place to provide additional support.[31]

Several features here are puzzling. First, why is this bull shown finished when the others in the series are only roughed out? Surely the best time to finish the carving would be after the figure was safely installed and was no longer subject to transportation mishaps. This could be an error by the nineteenth-century draftsman; the original drawing of Slab 56 shows that bull finished also (see figure 59), but the engraved version—presumably per Layard's instructions—instead shows it unfinished. For Slab 44, however, drawing and engraving both agree that the bull was finished. Second, why is this bull upright? One could argue that since very few of the palace doorways could admit an object 20 feet wide, a large bull could probably not pass through unless it was upright. Nonetheless, the risks of transporting such a huge and unwieldy object vertically would seem to outweigh any possible advantages. Finally, and most puzzlingly, the blocks that support this bull appear to be placed underneath its belly, overlapped by its left legs. This would not be possible with the known colossi, which have solid stone here (see figure 48). Perhaps the Assyrian or nineteenth-century artist misunderstood the function of these blocks, or perhaps this particular colossus is not stone at all, but instead is one of Sennacherib's bronze colossi.[32] This could account for all three of the relief's puzzles, since these figures were open underneath, would have appeared finished when transported from the foundry, and might best have been moved upright since the metal thickness would have been tailored for that position. This suggestion is unprovable, however, at least for the present.

These slabs show not only the transport of colossi, but also of other items apparently intended for the palace. In the river at the top of Slab 53 are three round-bottomed boats of a type still used in Iraq in Layard's day (see figure 60).[33] The one on the left carries a stack of what look like stone slabs, perhaps intended for the walls of the palace, while the other two carry oblong objects, rounded and pierced at one end—possibly door fittings. At the top of Slab 54 is a raft, buoyed by inflated animal skins, carrying what appears to be a block of stone (see figure 59). If these cargoes are stone for the decoration of the palace, then it appears that those small enough to be handled easily were transported by water; only very large stones were transported by land.

Conclusion

There is sufficient detail in the Court VI reliefs, taken together with textual and archaeological data, to permit a reconstruction of the processes of stone quarrying and transport in Sennacherib's day. Sennacherib brought sculptural quality stone from four separate quarries, but by far the greatest part probably came from the quarry at Balaṭai, which seems to have been a short distance up the river on the same side of the Tigris as Nineveh. The stone from these quarries was used to manufacture at least two types of colossal doorway figures: male human-headed bulls and female human-headed lions. The process of quarrying and transport involved a large work force of specialized and unskilled labor and utilized multiple strategies for moving the stones, with large blocks hauled overland and smaller pieces, presumably including the relief slabs, going by boat.

Sennacherib seems to have taken a lively interest in the stone used to embellish his palace. He attributed the discovery of his primary source of sculptural alabaster, the quarry at Balaṭai, to divine revelation. The other three new sources of stone—Kapridargilâ, Mt. Ammanana, and Mt. Nipur—all correspond with the locations of Sennacherib's military campaigns, the first two with the third campaign, to the west, and the last with the fifth campaign, to the north. While on campaign Sennacherib was apparently ever on the lookout for unusual stone for his palace. Evidence that the king was also interested in the actual procedures of quarrying and transport may be seen in the Court VI reliefs where, on Slab 63, Sennacherib has himself depicted in the upper left corner supervising the removal of a colossus from the quarry. Further along, on Slab 60, he is shown again, accompanying the colossi on their journey to Nineveh (see figs. 54, 57). Sennacherib's palace building accounts evidence a similar interest in the colossi, describing at length their numbers, appearance, and manufacture.[34] All of this suggests either that Sennacherib was personally very much involved in this stage of his palace construction or that he wished to convey the impression that he was thus involved.

Considering that the largest of Sennacherib's palace doorway colossi were 20 feet tall and weighed some forty to fifty tons, the king's interest in them is understandable. By virtue of their size and prominent location, the colossi would probably have been the single most impressive feature of Sennacherib's palace.[35] Even without their inscriptions, these creatures would have served as proclamations: no visitor could fail to be aware that they represent extraordinary power, and this power lies mainly not in their mythical fusion of human and beast, but rather in their great size. Their very presence marks not only a quantitative, but also a qualitative difference between Sennacherib's palace and the palaces of all foreign rivals. They serve as very concrete reminders that, like his palace, the human resources at the command of the Assyrian king are also "without rival." The different types of stone of which the colossi are fashioned likewise serve as reminders that the king's control of those resources is not only local, but extends to the very edges of the empire.

Thus the doorway colossi are a peaceful equivalent to the scenes of conquest carved on the majority of the Southwest Palace wall reliefs. Both signify the extent and magnitude of the king's authority throughout the empire. The identification of the regions and peoples depicted in those military images will be the goal of chapter 7. First, however, it is necessary to determine which of these reliefs actually date to the reign of Sennacherib, and it is to this problem that we now turn.

6

THE PERIODS OF THE SOUTHWEST
PALACE RELIEFS

Although Layard claimed to have excavated all or part of seventy-one rooms containing nearly two miles of wall reliefs, only a fraction of these are visible in any form today.[1] Not all of his seventy-one rooms contained sculptured slabs. Others may have had wall slabs, but these were not described or illustrated. Some rooms definitely had sculptured slabs, but illustrations of them have not been published, so knowledge of their subject is limited to Layard's verbal description. There are published illustrations, either in the form of drawings or photographs, of at least some of the relief slabs that decorated the walls for only thirty-three rooms. It is from these rooms that the visual corpus of Sennacherib's sculptures must be drawn. An overview of this information is presented in the table below; for room-by-room references, see chapter 3 and Appendix 2.

State of Knowledge of Relief Decoration of Southwest Palace Rooms

room not excavated	II, XV, XX, XXI, XXXV
door jambs only were excavated	XVIII, XXIII
wall slabs unsculptured	XXIX, XXX, LIII
sculptures chiseled off	XLII
no wall slabs	LXI
wall slabs destroyed	XXV, XXVI, XXXVII, LXVI, LXXI
no mention of sculptures	XIII, XVI, L, LII, LIV, LV, LVI, LVII, LVIII, LIX, LXII, LXIII
slabs shown on plan but not described	XI, LXVIII
reliefs described but not illustrated	IX, XVII, XXIV, XXVII, XXXI, XXXIV, XXXIX, LX, LXV
reliefs with illustrations	H, I, III, IV, V, VI, VII, VIII(e), VIII(w), X, XII, XIV, XIX, XXII, XXVIII, XXXII, XXXIII, XXXVI, XXXVIII, XL or XLI, XLIII, XLIV, XLV, XLVI, XLVII(?), XLVIII, XLIX, LI(n), LI(s), LXIV, LXVII, LXIX, LXX

Epigraphic evidence indicates that the reliefs of at least one of these rooms, XXXIII, are from the time of Assurbanipal. Several scholars have argued that other, uninscribed, reliefs date to his reign as well.[2] It is necessary, therefore, carefully to compare known reliefs of Sennacherib with those of Assurbanipal in order to develop criteria for determining which of the Southwest Palace reliefs date to the time of Sennacherib and which do not. To do this, two problems must be contended with: (1) classification, that is, the gathering of the reliefs into distinctive groups; and (2) periodization, that is, the association of these groups with a chronology. In suggesting a solution to these problems, I will employ two concepts that are in common use in art historical inquiry: *period* and *school.*

"Period" is the temporal and cultural context of a work or group of works. For greatest accuracy, criteria for periodization should be independent of the visual qualities of the works under consideration. Original inscriptions on the works or primary texts discussing the works are examples of useful criteria for periodization.

Once the period of a work or group of works has been established it may be possible on the basis of distinctive visual characteristics to assign other, undocumented, works to the same period. "School" is the term I propose to use as the designation for a group of works with perceived similarities. I suggest this term be used as it is used by Berenson: to designate a group of works by more than one artist that displays a cluster of similarities so pronounced that the assignment of the entire group to a single place and time seems justified.[3] Berenson's criteria were primarily aesthetic—form, tactile values, movement, and space-composition—but these could be supplemented by such nonformal criteria as subject, material, and technique. "School" used in this way is a highly subjective tool. It is unlikely that any two analysts could independently arrive at the same set of distinguishing criteria; that they would employ any given criterion in precisely the same way; that they could agree in all cases on how large a cluster of similarities is required to define a school; or that they could always agree in assigning to a school marginal works that meet some but not all of the criteria for the school.

"School" may, nonetheless, be a useful tool. It draws attention to groups of works that display such a degree of similarity that the analyst feels he or she may detect the influence of a single individual, a contemporary workshop or work group, or of a succession of pupils and masters working within a limited time at a specific place; but since distinguishing a "school" is a subjective process, the analyst must always clearly and explicitly define the criteria on which such a judgment is based.

In the study that follows, inscriptions on several reliefs will be used to distinguish two periods, the "period of Sennacherib" (705–681 B.C.) and the "period of Assurbanipal" (668–627 B.C.) On the basis of these inscribed reliefs, I will attempt to define criteria for distinguishing the reliefs of these periods from one another. Finally, these criteria will be employed to distinguish at least two schools of sculpture: one grouped around the inscribed reliefs of Assurbanipal and the other around those of Sennacherib.

Sennacherib or Assurbanipal? Criteria for Differentiation

The reliefs of Sennacherib in the Southwest Palace are the ones of principal concern for this study. As already noted, reliefs from thirty-three rooms in the Southwest Palace are preserved, but in only eight of these rooms are there inscriptions that include the name of the king. In one case, Room XXXIII, this king is Assurbanipal, and in the other seven—Rooms, I, V, VI, X, XXXVI, XLIX, and LXX—the king is Sennacherib. The sculptures from these seven rooms, then, are the basis for the study of the characteristics of the Southwest Palace reliefs during the period of Sennacherib. To elicit criteria for distinguishing reliefs of the period of Sennacherib from those of the period of Assurbanipal, the inscribed Sennacherib reliefs may be compared with examples inscribed with the name of Assurbanipal, namely those from Rooms, I, M, S[1], and V[1]/T[1] in Assurbanipal's North Palace and from Room XXXIII in the Southwest Palace.[4] It should be noted that the presence of an inscription on one relief in a room does not necessarily justify assigning all reliefs in that room to the same king. As will be seen, however, in the cases of the North and Southwest Palaces, all slabs in the rooms concerned do indeed exhibit the same characteristics that are seen on the inscribed slabs in those rooms.

The first scholar to make such comparisons for the purpose of determining the period of reliefs in different rooms in the Southwest Palace was Falkner, and further observations were contributed by Hrouda. The arguments of both writers were summarized and augmented by Nagel. Since these studies are of fundamental importance here, I will reexamine the observations and conclusions proposed in them and place them in a formal system that highlights their contributions and limitations.[5]

The criteria for distinguishing the art of Sennacherib's period from that of

119

Assurbanipal's will be divided into two general categories based on characteristics of *form* and characteristics of *fashion*. Fashion characteristics are those that vary as a result of changing fashion in the physical object represented—for example, the appearance of a chariot wheel or earring—while form characteristics vary as the result of the forms an artist chooses for representing unchanging objects and the way those forms are made to relate to each other—for example the form of a hand or the proportions of a human body.

In the analysis that follows, first characteristics of fashion and then characteristics of form that distinguish the art of Assurbanipal from that of Sennacherib are listed individually with illustrative examples from the reliefs. These characteristics are then grouped as either *diagnostic* (criteria so specific that they permit positive identification of the period of a relief) or *suggestive* (criteria not sufficiently certain to be diagnostic but that still suggest an attribution).

In some cases it is not certain whether a characteristic is related to fashion or form, that is, whether a visual difference is to be attributed to a change in the object itself or rather to a change in the way that object is depicted, and these are indicated below. Note that some criteria, particularly those of fashion, may not be derived from or applied to drawings of reliefs, since these often misrepresent the finer details of the sculptures. The notes give the rooms in both palaces where each feature was represented (SWP equals Southwest Palace, NP equals North Palace). Photographs of examples not included in the illustrations can be found by consulting Barnett's catalog of the North Palace (1976) and my Appendix 2 for the Southwest Palace (or the catalog by Bleibtreu, Barnett, and Turner [forthcoming], when it becomes available).

Fashion Criteria

Fashion criteria, if carefully chosen, might be expected to be the most sensitive for determining period, since they attempt to focus on specific objects that physically change over time, independent of individual artists or schools. Perhaps the most obvious example of this in neo-Assyrian representations is the number of spokes in the Assyrian chariot wheel: ninth-century examples have six spokes, while those of the eighth and seventh centuries have eight.[6] This change should be attributed not to the idiosyncracies of ninth-century versus eighth-century schools of sculpture, but rather to a change in the wheel of the chariot itself. As already noted, however, it is not always possible to be certain if a change in the appearance of an object is to be attributed to an actual change in fashion or rather to a change in the convention used to represent it.

ARMOR SHIRT. A distinctive difference attributable to a change in fashion is the armor shirt worn by Assyrian soldiers. In Sennacherib's period, this shirt is provided with a fringe of metal strips that extends well below the waist all around (fig. 62). In Assurbanipal's period, the shirt either ends at the waist or extends below the waist only at the back (fig. 63).[7]

HELMET. The pointed helmet worn by Assyrian soldiers changes in a way possibly attributable to fashion. Under Sennacherib, the shape of the helmet is essentially conical, the ear flaps are separate pieces attached to the helmet body with hinges, and the helmet is usually decorated with a number of horizontal incisions (fig. 62). Under Assurbanipal, the contours of the upper part of the helmet are concave, which makes the point appear more distinct and elongated. The helmet body is decorated with few or no horizontal incisions, and the ear flaps are of a piece with the body (fig. 63).[8]

STOCKING SUPPORT. Another change possibly attributable to fashion is the stocking support used by Assyrian soldiers. The stockings of Sennacherib's men are held up by a simple wide band just below the knee (fig. 62). On Assurbanipal's soldiers, the long bootlaces are carried diagonally upward to the back of the leg and are then wrapped several times around the calf just below the knee (fig. 64).[9]

BOOT. Also probably, but not certainly, attributable to a change in fashion is the cut of the soldiers' boots. Under Sennacherib, the tongue and leg of the boot are the same height and form an unbroken contour when viewed from the side (fig. 62). Under Assurbanipal, the tongue is relatively longer, resulting in a stepped appearance (fig. 64).[10] In Assurbanipal's Room XXXIII in the Southwest Palace, however, the upper contour of the boot conforms to the Sennacherib fashion (fig. 65).

ROYAL CHARIOT WHEEL. In Sennacherib's reliefs, the running surface of the wheel of the royal chariot is always smooth (fig. 66). In Assurbanipal's reliefs, it is studded with round-headed nails (fig. 64).[11]

ROYAL SUNSHADE. Under Sennacherib the rear flap of the royal sunshade is relatively long, nearly reaching the chariot box, and has a fringed lower edge (figs. 66, 67). Under Assurbanipal it is shorter and has a scalloped border on all three sides (fig. 64).[12] In Room XXXIII, Slab 6, in the Southwest Palace, the flap lacks the scalloped border, having instead a tasseled lower fringe (fig. 65).

FIG. 62.   Assyrian soldier, period of
Sennacherib, detail of Slab 13, Room
XXXVI, Southwest Palace, Nineveh.
British Museum, WAA 124913 (photo:
author).

FIG. 63.   Assyrian soldier, period of
Assurbanipal, detail of Slab 12, Room M, North
Palace, Nineveh. British Museum, WAA 124945
(photo: author).

Fɪɢ. 64.   Royal chariot of Assurbanipal, detail from drawing of Slab 13, Room M, North Palace, Nineveh. British Museum, WAA 124946 (photo: author).

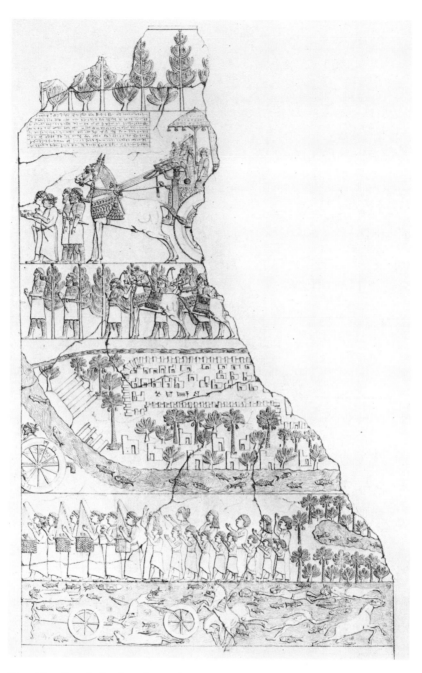

Fig. 65.   Royal chariot of Assurbanipal, detail of Slab 6, Room XXXIII,
Southwest Palace, Nineveh. British Museum, WAA, Or. Dr., II, 6 (photo:
Trustees of the British Museum).

124

F IG . 66.   Royal chariot of Sennacherib, detail of Slabs 11–12, Room XXXVI, Southwest Palace, Nineveh. British Museum, WAA 124911–12 (photo: author).

B EARDS .   The great majority of royal attendants under Sennacherib are bearded (fig. 67). Under Assurbanipal, the majority are beardless (fig. 64).[13]

R OUND - TOPPED   S HIELD .   A highly distinctive element found only in reliefs of Assurbanipal is a tall shield with a rounded top and square bottom (fig. 64). On Sennacherib's reliefs, Assyrian soldiers carry either a round shield or a very tall siege shield that stands on the ground and curves inward at the top (see figs. 50, 109).[14]

H ORSE   A RMOR .   Assyrian horses in military scenes during Assurbanipal's reign often have what looks like a large blanket, probably leather armor, on their backs (see fig. 68). This horse armor is never shown in Sennacherib's period.[15]

Form Criteria: "Form Elements or Motives"

In analyzing form criteria for determining the period of neo-Assyrian reliefs I will, following Schapiro, distinguish the categories of "form elements or mo-

Fig. 67.   Sennacherib receiving the booty of Sahrina, drawing of Slabs 3–4, Room LXX, Southwest Palace, Nineveh. British Museum, WAA, Or. Dr., I, 49 (photo: Trustees of the British Museum).

jik . No. 3.4 .

tives" and "form relationships."[16] This section is concerned with the former, the elements and motives the physical appearance of which probably doesn't change between the periods of Sennacherib and Assurbanipal, but which are represented significantly differently by these two kings' artists. "Form relationships," then, will be considered in the next section.

PALM TREE. Under Sennacherib, palm trees usually have eleven or more fronds, four clusters of fruit, and no leaves at the foot of the tree (fig. 67). Under Assurbanipal, they usually have only nine fronds and two clusters of fruit, and small leaves are often seen at the foot of the tree (fig. 64).[17]

POMEGRANATE TREE. In Sennacherib's pomegranate trees and other deciduous bushes, the branches are separated from each other by spaces and are of irregular lengths (see fig. 54). Assurbanipal's are not separated by spaces and are of roughly equal length (fig. 65).[18]

HORSE HEAD. Horses' heads in reliefs of Sennacherib have relatively heavy, rectangular muzzles, with the lower jaw nearly the same length as the upper. The brow is indicated with only a very slight projection on the forehead, and the eye exhibits relatively little foreshortening (fig. 66). In Assurbanipal's reliefs, horses have thinner muzzles and a pronounced underbite. The brow is indicated with a large bump, and the eye is noticeably foreshortened (fig. 64).[19]

KILT. Common to the periods of both Sennacherib and Assurbanipal is a type of kilt, one side of which terminates in a long fringed sash. The garment is worn so that the fringe begins at the lower hem at the back, is looped up diagonally over the belt at the right side, and the end then hangs down vertically, reaching to below the knees. From the right, one sees all of the fringe, but from the left, the diagonal loop is not visible and only the lower part of the vertical element is seen, hanging between the legs. Under Assurbanipal, this left view is always shown correctly (fig. 64). Under Sennacherib, however, the left view of the kilt often shows the diagonal loop of fringe on the left side, though the vertical portion of the fringe is still shown as if on the right side (fig. 66).[20] Since both the diagonal and vertical fringes are part of the same sash, they cannot in reality have fallen on different sides of the body. Consequently, the assumption here is that Sennacherib's artists are misrepresenting the left view of the kilt by applying the diagonal fringe as an artistic convention that has nothing to do with the kilt's actual appearance.

Form Criteria: "Form Relationships"

These criteria are the most amorphous of the categories discussed. Their definitions are relative, based on differences in degree rather than on absolute differences, and in each case one can point to exceptions to the definition. Because of this, these criteria are most useful when they can be supplemented by the less variable criteria from the categories of "fashion" and "form elements." The category of "form relationships" is nonetheless valuable, as it encourages us to look beyond the individual elements to the composition as a whole, that is, to the distinctive ways in which these elements are combined.

REGISTERS. Reliefs of Assurbanipal, with the exception of reliefs in passageways (North Palace, Rooms A, C, E, and R), are divided into two or more principal registers separated from each other by narrow uncarved stripes. These principal registers are often subdivided by means of continuous ground lines (fig. 68). Reliefs of Sennacherib often consist of a single register, especially when the background is mountains or water. Additional ground lines are used when needed, but rarely continue unbroken around a room (see fig. 54).[21]

GROUND LINES. In Sennacherib's images, people and animals are sometimes permitted to stand in a landscape without the aid of ground lines (see fig. 54). In the majority of Assurbanipal's reliefs, only trees and dead or dying people and animals "hover" above the ground lines.[22] Notable exceptions to this, however, are the hunting scene of North Palace Room S, where ground lines are dispensed with in depicting herds of gazelles and onagers, and the Ulai River battle in Room XXXIII of the Southwest Palace (Slabs 1–3).

INTERACTION OF ELEMENTS. Under Sennacherib, the organization of elements in a composition is additive, or, to use Nagel's term, paratactic. Figure types and other individual elements are used as needed, but they fail to interact with each other compositionally or psychologically. In Assurbanipal's compositions, by contrast, individual elements interact to a much greater degree. A good example is a comparison of prisoner processions. In Sennacherib's Court VI, Slabs 11 to 13, all figures but one look forward, and each prisoner or pair of prisoners is separated from those in front and behind by a discrete space, with little overlapping (fig. 69). In Assurbanipal's palace, by contrast, the prisoners from the defeated Elamite city of Din-Sharri are organized into tightly knit groups of three to five figures, interrelated by use of overlapping, turned heads, and gestures, and separated from neighboring

Fig. 68. Surrender of Din-Sharri to Assurbanipal, drawing of Slabs A–B, "Room V¹/ T¹," North Palace, Nineveh. British Museum, WAA, Or. Dr., V, 31 (photo: Trustees of the British Museum).

Fig. 69. Campaign in the mountains, drawing of Slabs 11–13, Court VI, Southwest Palace, Nineveh. British Museum, Or. Dr., I, 70 (photo: Trustees of the British Museum).

FIG. 70. Groom with two horses, detail of Slab 1, Room F, North Palace of Assurbanipal, Nineveh. British Museum, WAA 124929 (photo: author).

groups by spaces (fig. 68). The result is that Sennacherib's processions seem much more repetitive than Assurbanipal's, even though the density of figures in the latter is greater.[23]

OVERLAPPING. Another difference between the reliefs of Sennacherib and Assurbanipal, already hinted at above, is that the latter uses overlapping to a much greater degree than the former. The interest of Assurbanipal's artists in overlapping is demonstrated by two types of figure groups that first appear in the North Palace. One of these consists of a single groom leading with each hand one or a pair of horses, so that the head of one is ahead of him and the head of the other is behind (fig. 70).[24] The other type of group is a herd of cattle that uses overlapping to a degree that suggests considerable depth (fig. 68). Sennacherib, too, sometimes used overlapping in herd scenes, but never to quite this degree (fig. 69).[25] Another notable example of overlapping is in compositions showing figures marching past a row of palm trees. In Sennacherib examples, the heads of the figures rarely reach as high as the lowest fronds of the palm (fig. 67). In examples of Assurbanipal's, time, the heads of most of the figures overlap the lower fronds (fig. 64).[26]

Conclusions

It is clear, then, that the inscribed reliefs of Sennacherib and Assurbanipal exhibit a number of characteristics that are consistent within the reliefs of each king and, at the same time, clearly different from those of the other. The only case where this is not entirely so is in Assurbanipal's Room XXXIII in the Southwest Palace. These reliefs share most of the characteristics of those in the North Palace, but the boot tops of the Assyrian soldiers and the dissolution of register divisions and ground lines in Slabs 1 to 3 are characteristic of Sennacherib, while the border decoration of the flap of the royal sunshade is unique (see fig. 65). These differences between the Room XXXIII reliefs and Assurbanipal's North Palace sculptures led Nagel to assign the Room XXXIII reliefs to a period earlier in Assurbanipal's reign than that of the North Palace reliefs, a dating that, as Reade observed, seems to be confirmed by the content of one of the epigraphs.[27]

In reviewing the criteria developed above, it appears that by virtue of frequency, consistency, and ease of recognition, some will be more sensitive than others for determining the period of a given relief. Criteria so specific that the presence of even a single example permits identification of the period of the relief in question may be termed *diagnostic*. Diagnostic criteria for the art of Assurbanipal are the round-topped shield, short armor shirt, long boot tongue, studded royal chariot wheel, scalloped border on sunshade, horse armor, the groom leading horses with both hands, and the closely packed herd of cattle. Diagnostic criteria for Sennacherib are the long armor shirt, smooth royal chariot wheel, and incorrectly depicted kilt. The remaining criteria are for various reasons not diagnostic, either because they are not always readily recognizable or because there are occasional exceptions, but they may nonetheless hint strongly at an attribution, especially if several are present at once. These may be termed *suggestive*.

The Criteria Applied: The North Palace

In order to determine the period of the Southwest Palace sculptures, it is necessary to have as clear an idea as possible of the characteristics common to the art of Assurbanipal, as well as those common to the art of Sennacherib. In a foundation inscription from there, Assurbanipal says that the North Palace—which he calls the *bīt redûti*—had been built by Sennacherib and subsequently restored by himself.[28] It is entirely possible, therefore, that some of the reliefs in the North Palace are from the time of Sennacherib. The above criteria should permit a determination of whether or not this is so. Furthermore, since the body of inscribed Assurbanipal reliefs is relatively small, it will be interesting to see if other reliefs in his palace share the same characteristics, thereby validating the criteria for the art of his period. When these criteria are applied to North Palace rooms that do not contain inscriptions, the following results are obtained.

ROOM A. Boots and stocking support are Assurbanipal type. Figures

135

are more closely spaced and there is more overlapping of legs and feet than in the comparable procession of Southwest Palace Room LI(n), Slabs 1–17. Period: Assurbanipal.

ROOM B. The surviving slabs in this room are apotropaic doorway reliefs, and none of the criteria of differentiation apply. One detail, however, is worthy of note. The back half of the head of the lion-headed human figure has a border of feathers and a plain center. In this, it is similar to the same figure in North Palace Rooms K, S, and T, but different from examples in the Southwest Palace, where the back half of the head is completely covered by a feather pattern. Period: probably Assurbanipal.[29]

ROOM C. The round-topped shield, stocking support, boot contour, chariot wheel, beardless attendants, tree branches, horse heads, and groom leading horses with both hands (Slab 8) are all typical of Assurbanipal. The absence of register divisions and continuous ground lines, most notably in the scene of spectators climbing a hill (Slabs 8–9), is not typical of Assurbanipal's battle scenes, but does seem to be acceptable in hunting scenes (see Room S). Period: Assurbanipal.

ROOM E. Few of the criteria can be applied to this unusual scene. The leaves at the foot of the palm tree on what is probably Slab 13 and the manner in which heads overlap the palm branches point to Assurbanipal. A noteworthy detail is the feather headdress of the rear figure on Slab 5, which recurs on reliefs from Southwest Palace, Room XXII, and perhaps North Palace, Room I or S[1].[30] Period: probably Assurbanipal.

ROOM F. The helmet, armor shirt, stocking support, boot contour, royal chariot wheel and sunshade, beardless royal attendants, round-topped shield, horse armor, horse heads, left view of kilt, register divisions, adherence of figures to ground lines, interaction of figures in procession, and groom leading a horse in each hand all indicate the period of Assurbanipal.

ROOM G. The round-topped shield (Slab 3, lower register), short armor shirt, and pointed helmet profile point to the period of Assurbanipal.

ROOM H. The branches of the bushes, shape of horses' heads, register divisions, interaction between figures, and use of overlapping as carts and horsemen pass foot soldiers all suggest the period of Assurbanipal.

ROOM J. Virtually all of the criteria of differentiation are represented in Room J, all pointing to the period of Assurbanipal.

ROOM K. The lion-headed human of this slab, like that of Rooms B, S, and T, should probably be attributed to the period of Assurbanipal.

ROOM L. The round-topped shield, short armor shirt, helmet shape, stocking support, boot top, horse armor, shape of the palm tree, horse heads, register divisions, adherence of figures to the ground line, and heads overlapping palm branches all point to the period of Assurbanipal.

COURT O. None of the differentiating criteria are represented in the apotropaic relief from this room, so its period cannot be determined by this method.

ROOM R. The stocking support, boot tops, large number of eunuchs, shape of the horse's head, and considerable amount of overlapping point to the period of Assurbanipal.

ROOM S. The criteria here are the same as those cited for Room R, again pointing to the period of Assurbanipal. As noted for Room C above, the absence of ground lines in some parts of this composition appears to be typical of Assurbanipal's hunting scenes. The feather pattern on the heads of the lion-headed human figures from Door *d* is the same as that on examples from Rooms B, K, and T. These figures probably date to the period of Assurbanipal. Period of all Room S reliefs: Assurbanipal.

ROOM T. The head of the lion-headed human here is detailed in the same way as those from Rooms B, K, and S and therefore is probably to be attributed to the period of Assurbanipal.

ROOMS S^1 AND V^1/T^1. Nearly all of the distinguishing criteria are present in the uninscribed reliefs that had fallen into Rooms S, T, and V, and in every case they point to the period of Assurbanipal.

On the basis of the criteria for differentiating the art of Assurbanipal from that of Sennacherib outlined above, the preserved reliefs from North Palace Rooms A, C, F, G, H, J, L, R, and S, as well as those that had fallen into Rooms, S, T, and V, can be assigned to the period of Assurbanipal with a considerable degree of certainty. Only a few of the criteria apply to the Room E reliefs, but again they suggest the period of Assurbanipal. These criteria do not apply at all to the lion-headed human figures of Rooms B, K, S, and T, but the treatment of the head detail in all of these figures is identical and differs from that in examples from Sennacherib's palace. Finally, the criteria are of no help in determining the period of the Court O relief. Thus it appears that nearly all of the North Palace reliefs share the characteristics found in those reliefs known on the basis of inscriptions to date from the time of Assurbanipal. This provides an independent confirmation of the textual and archaeological evidence, which also points to Assurbanipal as builder and decorator of the North Palace.

The Criteria Applied: The Southwest Palace

When the criteria for differentiation are applied to the uninscribed Southwest Palace reliefs, the following results emerge.

COURT H. The four clusters of fruit and absence of leaves at the bottoms of the partially defaced palm trees at the bottom of the slabs to either side of Door *c* suggest that the reliefs originally in Court H date to the time of Sennacherib (see fig. 27).

ROOM III. In Layard's drawings it appears that the Assyrian soldiers have the pointed helmet, armor shirt, stocking support, and boot top typical of Sennacherib's reliefs. The royal chariot wheel and sunshade (Slab 4), palm tree, incorrect left view of kilt, and heads not overlapping palm trees are also characteristic of Sennacherib (see fig. 78).

ROOM IV. Though mostly unpublished, these reliefs are visible *in situ*. The helmet, armor shirt, stocking support, boot top, deciduous bushes, horse head, and incorrect left view of kilt are all characteristic of Sennacherib (see figs. 30, 31).

ROOM VII. The long armor shirt, smooth royal chariot wheel, fringed flap on the royal sunshade, shape of bushes, incorrect kilt (far right), and lack of overlapping in the cattle herd suggest the period of Sennacherib (see fig. 32).

ROOM VIII(e). Layard's drawing is too sketchy to trust for fine details, but it is clear that the armor shirt and deciduous bushes are typical of Sennacherib's period (see fig. 34).

ROOM VIII(w). In Layard's drawing, the armor shirt, incorrect left view of kilt, and deciduous bushes all point to the period of Sennacherib (see fig. 33).

ROOM XII. The long armor shirt, pointed helmet, stocking support, boot top, royal chariot wheel, royal sunshade, bearded attendants, horse heads, incorrect kilts (Slab 7), and lack of interaction among prisoners in procession are all typical of Sennacherib (see fig. 83). The divisions of Slabs 5–7 into continuous registers separated by raised, uncarved bands is unusual, but not sufficient in itself to alter the attribution. Period: Sennacherib.

ROOM XIV. The long armor shirt, pointed helmet, stocking support, boot top, shape of bushes, horse heads, and incorrect kilt (Slab 15) point unmistakably to the period of Sennacherib (see figs. 17, 18, 121).

ROOM XXXII. The long armor shirt, boot top, absence of horse armor, shape of bushes, absence of register divisions, and minimal interaction and overlapping in processions, are all characteristic of Sennacherib's reliefs. An interesting variation from the Sennacherib norm is the stocking support: here the boot laces pass diagonally across the calf, as in Assurbanipal's reliefs, but are tied to the wide garter normally found in Sennacherib figures (fig. 71). Another variation is in the pointed helmets, some of which have a concave profile reminiscent of Assurbanipal (Slab 8). Furthermore, the left view of the kilt is shown correctly here, as under Assurbanipal, and some of the horses' heads have the receding chin, high brow, and foreshortened eyes seen in Assurbanipal's horses. These details are not sufficient to alter the attribution of these reliefs to Sennacherib, but do recall Reade's observation that "Sennacherib's sculptors varied in standard and represented detail in a variety of ways."[31] Period: Sennacherib.

ROOM XXXVIII. The long armor shirt, pointed helmet, boot top, smooth royal chariot wheel, length of sunshade flap, shape of bushes, and absence of register divisions and ground lines, are all characteristic of Sennacherib's reliefs (fig. 72). As in Room XXXII, however, the stocking support and correct depiction of the left side of the kilt (Slab 13) are both suggestive of Assurbanipal's reliefs (fig. 73). Also on Slab 13, of the four preserved horse heads, the three to the right are characteristic of Sennacherib, while the arched brow, foreshortened eye, and receding chin of the example at left are more typical of Assurbanipal, again recalling Reade's observation quoted for Room XXXII above. Period: Sennacherib.

ROOM XL or XLI. Malan's sketch of one of these rooms is too rough to trust for information on attribution (see fig. 23).

ROOM XLIII. From Layard's drawings of these reliefs it appears that the Assyrian soldiers have the pointed helmet, stocking support, and boot top typical of Sennacherib. In addition, the absence of interaction and overlapping in the processions also points to the period of Sennacherib (see figs. 90, 91).

ROOM XLIV. In Layard's drawing, the helmet earpieces, boot top, incorrect left view of kilt, smooth royal chariot wheel, and horse heads indicate the period of Sennacherib (see fig. 81).

ROOM XLV. The long armor shirt, pointed helmet, stocking support, boot top, royal chariot wheel and sunshade, shape of bushes, form of the horse's heads, absence of register divisions and ground lines (especially in Slab 6), and minimal overlapping, are all characteristic of the period of Sennacherib (figs. 37, 74). An unusual variation is seen in the lower part of some of the armor shirts, where the fringe of metal strips is not continuous, as in other Sennacherib reliefs, but leaves the front exposed (Slabs 1–3, 5). Period: Sennacherib.

FIG. 71.   Processions of eastern prisoners, Slabs 7–8, Room XXXII, Southwest Palace, Nineveh. British Museum, WAA 124902–3 (photo: Trustees of the British Museum).

ROOM XLVI.   The observations for Room XLIII apply here also. In addition, some soldiers here wear the long armor shirt characteristic of the period of Sennacherib (see fig. 82).

ROOM XLVII(?).   The drawing lacks detail, but the armor shirt and deciduous bushes suggest the period of Sennacherib (see fig. 38).

ROOM XLVIII.   The long armor shirt, pointed helmet, form of the bushes, incorrect depiction of the kilt (Slab 11), and absence of register divi-

sions, ground lines, and overlapping are all characteristic of Sennacherib (see fig. 39).

ROOM LI(n). Few of the criteria apply here, but the squared muzzles of the horses, the absence of eunuchs (compare North Palace, Rooms A and R), and minimal overlapping and interaction among figures all suggest Sennacherib's period (see fig. 87).

ROOM LI(s). The long armor shirt, form of the pointed helmet, smooth

FIG. 72.   Counting heads before the king, drawing of Slabs 12–13, Room XXXVIII, Southwest Palace, Nineveh. British Museum, Or. Dr., I, 44 (photo: Trustees of the British Museum).

FIG. 73.   Assyrian horsemen beside a stream, fragment of Slab 13, Room XXXVIII, Southwest Palace, Nineveh. Metropolitan Museum 32.143.16 (photo: Metropolitan Museum of Art, Gift of John D. Rockefeller, Jr., 1932).

Fɪɢ. 74.   Chariot of Sennacherib, drawing of Slab 2, Room XLV,
Southwest Palace, Nineveh. British Museum, WAA, Or. Dr., IV, 23
(photo: Trustees of the British Museum).

Fig. 75. The king on campaign in Babylonia, drawing of Slabs 11–12, Court XIX, Southwest Palace, Nineveh. British Museum, WAA, Or. Dr., I, 72 (photo: Trustees of the British Museum).

Fig. 76. Riverine landscape, drawing of Slabs 2–4, Room XXII, Southwest Palace, Nineveh. British Museum, WAA, Or. Dr., IV, 77 (photo: Trustees of the British Museum).

Fɪɢ. 77. Booty from a Babylonian campaign, drawing of Slabs 7–9, Room XXVIII, Southwest Palace, Nineveh. British Museum, WAA, Or. Dr., I, 69 (photo: Trustees of the British Museum).

royal chariot wheel, bearded royal attendants, palm trees, and minimal overlapping and interaction among the figures in procession are characteristic of reliefs of Sennacherib's time (see fig. 40).

ROOM LXIV. The pointed helmet, long armor shirt, stocking support, and minimal overlapping and interaction in processions are typical of the period of Sennacherib (see figs. 88, 89).

ROOM LXVII. The pointed helmet, long armor shirt, smooth royal chariot wheel, and shape of the horse head here are characteristic of Sennacherib's reliefs (see fig. 41).

ROOM LXIX. The drawing here is sketchy, but the four clusters of dates, absence of leaves at the foot of the palm trees, and heads not overlapping palm fronds are characteristic of Sennacherib (see fig. 42).

COURT XIX (fig. 75). All of the fashion criteria: the tall half-round shield (Slabs 3, 6, 11, 15, 17, 20), short armor shirt, form of the pointed helmet, stocking support, boot tops, wheel of the royal chariot (Slabs 12, 21), royal sunshade (Slabs 12, 21), armor on horses in battle (Slabs 12, 15), and preponderance of beardless attendants (Slabs 12, 15, 21) all associate the Court XIX reliefs with those of Assurbanipal. Form criteria as well: the shape of the palm tree with leaves at its foot, the shape of the horse head (Slab 12), the correct representation of the kilt, division into continuous registers of equal width (the use of a river as the central register recalls the scene of hunting lions from a boat in North Palace, Room S, Slabs 3–5), firm adherence of figures to the ground line, lively interaction among figures in procession, and the use of overlapping, including heads overlapping palm fronds, the group of a groom with horses in both hands (Slab 23), and overlapping in herds of cattle (Slabs 1, 10) all point to Assurbanipal. An additional motif, noted by Nagel, is the group of a mother giving her child a drink (Slabs 3, 9).[32] This group is found in a similar context in the North Palace (Court J), but not in the Southwest Palace (except in Room XXVIII; see below). All of the criteria, then, indicate that the Court XIX reliefs are indistinguishable from those of Assurbanipal, but quite different from those of Sennacherib. Period: Assurbanipal.

ROOM XXII (fig. 76). Because Layard's drawings of these reliefs lack detail, few of the criteria apply here. The round-topped shield, shown in every slab, and considerable overlapping in the procession scene are both characteristic of Assurbanipal. The feathered headdresses, too, perhaps appear only in the art of Assurbanipal.[33] Period: Assurbanipal.

ROOM XXVIII (fig. 19, 77). As with Court XIX, both fashion and form criteria associate these reliefs with those of Assurbanipal. The round-topped shield (Slabs 3, 8); short armor shirt with rear flap; elongated pointed helmet with integral earflaps; stocking support; long boot tongues; palm trees with two date clusters and leaves at the base (though most have more than nine fronds); shape of the horse head (Slabs 12–14); correct rendition of the left view of the kilt; continuous register divisions and adherence to ground lines (except in the marsh scene); overlapping and interaction among figures in procession; and suggestion of depth through overlapping, notably through the devices of heads overlapping palm branches, grooms holding horses with each hand (Slab 14), and herds of cattle (Slabs 6, 7)—all of these are characteristic of the reliefs of Assurbanipal. And as in Court XIX, the group of a mother giving her child a drink appears here also (Slab 8). Layard's comment that the royal chariot on Slab 12 was the largest and most lavishly detailed in the palace becomes understandable if this is Assurbanipal's chariot, since that king's chariot representations are larger and more detailed than Sennacherib's.[34] Period: Assurbanipal.

To summarize, on the basis of both diagnostic and suggestive criteria for differentiation, the reliefs of Rooms III, IV, VII, VIII(e), VIII(w), XII, XIV, XXXII, XXXVIII, XLIV, XLV, XLVI, XLVII(?), XLVIII, LI(s), LXIV, and LXVII are all characteristic of the period of Sennacherib. Only suggestive criteria apply to Rooms H, XLIII, LI(n), and LXIX but these also point to Sennacherib. The reliefs of Court XIX, Room XXVIII, and at least some of those from Room XXII, by contrast, have the same characteristics as reliefs from Assurbanipal's North Palace.[35] None of the criteria apply to the sketch of Room XL or XLI.

Thus it seems clear that reliefs from at least two periods coexist in the palace of Sennacherib. Any attempt to evaluate Sennacherib's programmatic scheme must take care not to include unwittingly these latter intrusions. Having established a corpus of Sennacherib reliefs in the Southwest Palace, we may now proceed to consider the subjects Sennacherib caused to be depicted on them.

7

THE SUBJECTS OF
SENNACHERIB'S RELIEFS

Sennacherib's reliefs from the Southwest Palace depict incidents from at least three of the king's royal campaigns, plus scenes of procession and transportation of building materials. The reliefs showing the quarrying and transport of colossi for the construction of the palace have already been discussed in chapter 5. The focus of this chapter is the reliefs that depict Sennacherib's military campaigns at the borders of the empire and beyond. To this end, three types of evidence will be examined—annalistic, epigraphic, and visual—to determine the subject of Sennacherib's military reliefs. First, the evidence from the royal annals, which record the location and geographical extent of each campaign, is presented. Next, the city names preserved in epigraphs on the reliefs are placed into this historical framework. Finally, the corpus of reliefs from each campaign thus isolated is examined for distinctive visual features that may permit the identification of the same subjects on reliefs in rooms where no epigraphs are preserved. In the case of rooms for which no illustrations of the sculptures exist, Layard's written descriptions will be used, but it must be remembered that in such cases the sculptures might date to a later king.

This chapter has two goals. The first is to identify the subject of as many of these relief series as possible. Much of the work of identifying the specific campaigns represented in Sennacherib's reliefs has already been done by Wäfler and Reade.[1] To their observations I have added some of my own, particularly concerning the architecture and landscape characterizing images of the second and third campaigns, and the identity of one of the cities captured during the second campaign. My other goal here is to try to ascertain whether the placement of these subjects within the palace conforms to any pattern.

The First Campaign: South

Summary

Sennacherib's first campaign was to Babylonia. The primary source for this event is a foundation cylinder in the British Museum (WAA 113203). The first campaign has been dated by Brinkman as lasting from late 703 to early 702, while Levine has dated it from late 704 through all of 703. Levine divided it into three phases. In the first phase, Sennacherib's army advanced against a coalition of Chaldeans, Babylonians, Arameans, and Elamite mercenaries under the control of the Babylonian usurper Merodach Baladan and defeated them in two engagements, the first at Kutha, the second at Kish. The second phase was a sweep through Babylonia where Sennacherib reestablished his control over dozens of fortified cities. The final phase was the return northward along the Tigris, including the capture of the border city of Hirimmu.[2]

Epigraphs

The reliefs of two rooms in Sennacherib's palace bear epigraphs giving the names of cities captured during the first campaign. In Room LXX, Slab 4, the epigraph says that Sennacherib is receiving the tribute of Sahrina, which is also among the cities listed in the annalistic account of the first campaign (see fig. 67).[3] In Room III, an epigraph on Slab 8 labels the city of Dilbat (fig. 78). Dilbat is not mentioned in Sennacherib's annals, but cities in its immediate environs were captured during his first campaign, and Dilbat probably fell then too.[4]

Rooms Decorated with the First Campaign

The Babylonian landscape as represented in Sennacherib's palace reliefs is quite distinctive. In the reliefs associated with epigraphs in Rooms III and LXX, the countryside is characterized by reed marshes and rivers or canals lined with palm trees (fig. 79). The same type of landscape may be seen in preserved slabs and drawings from Rooms LI(s) (see fig. 40), the southern part of Court LXIV (see fig. 88), Room LXIX (see fig. 42), the unerased lower part of slabs in Court H (see fig. 27), on a slab that may be from Room XVIII, and it was reported as well on the unpublished West Facade. To be sure, some of these reliefs may record Sennacherib's fourth campaign, a minor raid

FIG. 78.   Sack of Dilbat, drawing of Slab 8, Room III, Southwest Palace, Nineveh. British Museum, WAA, Or. Dr., IV, 41 (photo: Trustees of the British Museum).

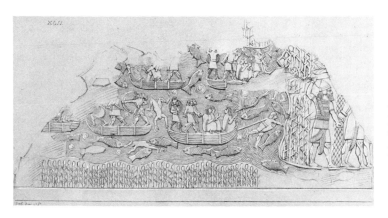

FIG. 79.   Battle in a marsh, drawing of Slab 1, Room LXX, Southwest Palace, Nineveh. British Museum, WAA, Or. Dr., IV, 42 (photo: Trustees of the British Museum).

against Bīt-Iakin also in the south, and in the absence of epigraphs no final determination is possible. It would seem, however, that the extensive and relatively successful first campaign would offer more opportunities for narrative representation than would the limited and less successful fourth campaign.[5] To summarize, Rooms H, III, LI(s), LXIV, LXIX, LXX, the West Facade, and perhaps XVIII were decorated with a Babylonian campaign, probably the first.

The Second Campaign: East

Summary

The primary source for Sennacherib's second campaign is the "Bellino Cylinder" (British Museum, WAA K1680), dated in the eponymy of Nabu-lē'i (702 B.C.).[6] This campaign, which took place in the first part of that year, opened with an assault by the Assyrian army on the lands of the Kassites and Yasubigallians in the Zagros mountains to the southeast of Assyria. The campaign continued with a march south through Ellipi and concluded with the receipt of tribute from the Medes.

Access to this area is via an important trade route, the Great Khorasan Road, which enters the Zagros by following one of the principal tributaries of the Diyala River and then proceeds toward central Iran via a series of mountain passes and river valleys. Sennacherib seems basically to have followed this road as far as Ellipi, capturing cities that resisted and turning them into fortified Assyrian outposts. This campaign seems to have accomplished two things: it established Assyrian control over this essential trade route, and it brought Ellipi into the Assyrian sphere as a buffer area between the Assyrian province of Harhar—established during the reign of Sargon II—and the powerful independent kingdom of Elam.[7]

Levine has argued that the second campaign was a continuation of the first. In support of this he observes that geographically the location of the initial engagement of the second campaign is very close to that of the final engagement of the first and that, temporally, the apparent dates of the first and second campaigns would have allowed very little time for the army to make the round trip to Assyria and back. Apparently contradicting this argument, however, is the cylinder that records just the first campaign, which concludes with the statement, "I returned to Assyria."[8] One must also try to explain why an account of the "first campaign" should have been composed at all if the king and army had not yet returned from the field.

On balance, it would seem that after the Babylonian campaign, much of the army may have remained in the south and wintered in the vicinity of Hirimmu, and consequently were already in position at the start of the second campaign. The king himself, however, apparently returned to the capital, perhaps to check on the progress of his new palace, and he doubtless had other business to attend to as well. The cylinder that records the first campaign concludes with the earliest account of Sennacherib's palace, thereby suggesting that this cylinder was intended for its foundations. The commencement of work on the "Palace without Rival" may, therefore, have been the direct stimulus for the composition of this earliest edition of the annals.

To summarize, the division of Sennacherib's annalistic account of the expedition to the southeast into two discrete campaigns may have been primarily the result of an immediate need for a palace foundation text, regardless of whether the army had yet returned from the field. Since these texts were composed for specific construction-related functions, the timing of the need for one may not always have corresponded well with that of the historical events it records. Any synthetic study of the various editions of the annals must therefore consider not only the content of each edition, but also the circumstances of its composition.

Epigraphs

The sculptures of three rooms in Sennacherib's palace display epigraphs that seem to label cities defeated during the second campaign. The most complete example, in Room LX, labels the city of Bīt-Kubatti. According to Sennacherib's annals, this city was captured during the first part of the second campaign.[9] A damaged epigraph from Room XIV records the siege of a city

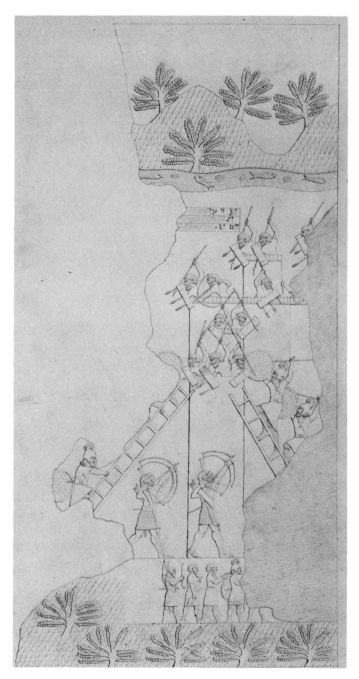

FIG. 80. Assault on [Aranz]iaš, drawing of Slab 35, Room V, Southwest Palace, Nineveh. British Museum, WAA, Or. Dr., IV, 19 (photo: Trustees of the British Museum).

whose name is almost certainly to be read as Alammu (see fig. 17). This would seem to be identical with the city Alamu, otherwise unattested, mentioned as the hiding place of Urzana of Muṣaṣir in a letter to Sargon II dealing with eastern affairs.[10] A badly damaged epigraph from Room V gives a city name ending in [. . . z]i-a-šu (fig. 80). This ought to be Aranziaš/Erinziaš, which in the annals of Sargon II is mentioned in connection with Harhar and Ellipi. This city is not included in Sennacherib's annals, but its location suggests that it was captured toward the end of the second campaign.[11] Also from Room V was an epigraph labeling a city the name of which is possibly to be read Kasuṣi, which is otherwise unattested. Since it is in a room decorated with the second campaign, it must be an eastern city.[12]

Rooms Decorated with the Second Campaign

Of the rooms containing epigraphs, no slabs have been published from Room LX, so their subject is known only from Layard's written description of the setting as a river valley surrounded by mountains covered with trees and grapevines.[13] For Rooms V and XIV, we are more fortunate. In both, a good selection of slabs is preserved and the reliefs share a number of characteristics. In both, the setting is a river valley between wooded mountains. The walls and towers of the cities under siege are pierced only by doorways; there are no windows of any sort. Some of the male captives from the reliefs in

FIG. 81. Assyrians receiving eastern prisoners, drawing of Slabs 1–2, Room XLIV, Southwest Palace, Nineveh. British Museum, WAA, Or. Dr., I, 66a (photo: Trustees of the British Museum).

FIG. 82.   Deportation of easterners, drawing of Slabs 6–7, Room XLVI, Southwest Palace, Nineveh. British Museum, WAA, Or. Dr., I, 67 (photo: Trustees of the British Museum).

each room are shown wearing a distinctive cloak of animal skin, tied at the neck and hanging loosely down the back (see fig. 18). Even though there may be some uncertainty about the restoration of the city names on the epigraphs, the skin cloaks are clear proof that these captives are easterners, for Sargon II used the same convention to distinguish easterners on his Khorsabad reliefs (see fig. 123).[14]

The same conventions of river valley, windowless architecture, and skin cloaks all occur in the reliefs from Rooms XXXII and XLV, and these rooms therefore must also record the second campaign (see figs. 37, 71). Captives in skin cloaks also figured in the decoration of Room XLIV (fig. 81). The second campaign should also be the subject of the unpublished reliefs from Room XXXI, which Layard said showed the same campaign as Room XXXII.[15]

A distinctive feature of enemy archers in several of the rooms is their rounded quiver cover. These archers are shown in action against the Assyrians on the reliefs from the south and west walls of Court VI (see fig. 69). Two factors argue in favor of identifying these reliefs as well with the second campaign. First, the landscape, a wooded river valley, is consistent with the second campaign.[16] Second, archers with round-topped quivers appear in the

Room XXXVI reliefs of the siege of Lachish, but there they are shown fighting *in* the Assyrian army (see fig. 109). Since these foreign archers must have been impressed into the Assyrian army before the third campaign, and since the Court VI reliefs show them to be mountain dwellers, their capture can only have occurred in the second campaign.[17] Similar archers also figure in the booty processions from Room XLVI and the east end of Room XLIII, so these reliefs also presumably record the second campaign (figs. 82, 90). Layard reported that the subject of Room XLVII was the same as XLVI, and a drawing attributed to this room shows windowless architecture, while a probable fragment includes a river (see fig. 38). This room too probably showed the second campaign.[18]

Several other rooms—VII, VIII(e), IX and XVII—showed a campaign in a wooded river valley in the mountains (see figs. 32, 34). These may be representations of the second campaign, but the landscape would also be appropriate for portions of the third campaign and in the absence of more detailed information their subject must remain uncertain.

To summarize, then, the following rooms seem to have been decorated with representations of the second campaign: V, VI, XIV, XXXI, XXXII, the east end of XLIII, XLIV, XLV, XLVI, XLVII, and LX.

The Third Campaign: West

Summary

The primary source for Sennacherib's third campaign is the "Rassam Cylinder" (British Museum, WAA 80–7–19, 1), dated in the eponymy of Mitunu (700 B.C.), and its numerous duplicates (see fig. 6). As summarized by Na'aman, the third campaign, of 701 B.C., fell into three phases. First, Sennacherib's army marched down the Phoenician coast, collecting tribute along the way. Next came the recapture of Philistia, in the course of which Sennacherib defeated an Egyptian army at Eltekeh. The final phase was an apparent attempt to subjugate Judah, where Sennacherib's offensive succeeded in capturing a number of Judean fortified cities, but failed to conquer the capital city Jerusalem.[19]

Epigraphs

Only one set of reliefs bears an epigraph identifying a city captured in the third campaign. These are in Room XXXVI, and according to the caption they show the Judean city of Lachish (see fig. 3). Lachish is not mentioned by name in Sennacherib's annalistic account of the third campaign, but that it fell in the course of that campaign is confirmed by the biblical account of the same event. Evidently Lachish was among "46 of Hezekiah's strong, walled cities" that Sennacherib claims to have captured during the third campaign.[20]

Two fragmentary epigraphs from Room I (the throne room) apparently originally contained the names of cities captured during the third campaign, but these names are now too badly damaged for restoration. Also in this room the Iraqi excavators reported finding a representation of the "Jewish city of Lagash" [Lachish?], but the preliminary report did not mention the basis for this identification and no epigraph labeling Lachish is visible on these reliefs as now displayed.[21]

Rooms Decorated with the Third Campaign

Several features of the Room XXXVI Lachish reliefs are of use in identifying uninscribed representations of the third campaign in other rooms. The landscape is mountainous, without rivers, and dotted with shrubs and vines (see fig. 113). The walls of the city are characterized by numerous windows and by rows of round shields placed defensively on the ramparts. Small balconies project to either side at the tops of the towers (see fig. 110). Virtually identical architecture is shown on buildings from Rooms I and XII, and the reliefs from XLVIII show a similar, though more elaborately fenestrated, building type (see figs. 39, 83, 85). The architecture in Room LXVII is also similar, but lacks the shields and balconies, and no landscape information was included in Layard's drawing or description (see fig. 41).

The male captives from the Room XXXVI Lachish reliefs wear a short tunic bound by a broad belt and a turban with earflaps (Fig. 84). The same costume is worn by some of the captives in Room XLIII and by the enemy in the reliefs from Room XXXVIII, where the mountainous landscape includes a broad river (see figs. 91, 115). Male prisoners in Room XXXIV wore what Layard described as "turbans of several folds, such as are frequently represented at Khorsabad."[22] Female captives from Lachish wear a long dress and a hood that covers the head and hangs down the back almost to ankle level (fig. 84). This costume is also worn by women in Rooms X, XXXIV, and LXIV (see figs. 35, 89).

The Room I reliefs, which are clearly associated with the third campaign on the basis of landscape and architecture, introduce additional features characteristic of the third campaign. These include a scene of a city beside a

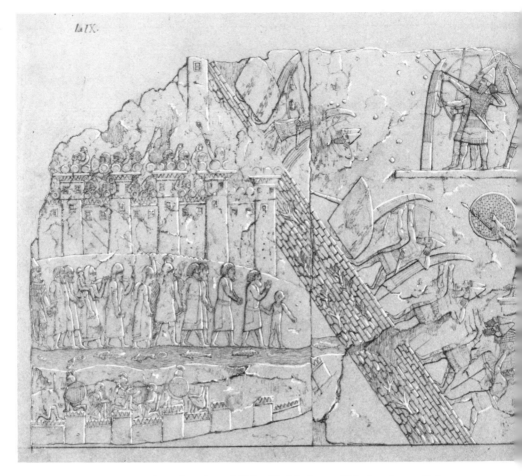

FIG. 83. Western campaign, drawing of Slabs 12–15, Room XII, Southwest Palace, Nineveh. British Museum, WAA, Or. Dr., IV, 59 (photo: Trustees of the British Museum).

sea filled with galleys, a setting that is clearly Phoenician (fig. 85). Similar examples were recorded in Rooms VIII(w) (see fig. 33), XXIV, XXXIV, and XLI. Some of the women in the Phoenician scene in Room I wear a tall cylindrical headdress with a veil falling down the back. Similar examples also occurred on women in Rooms VIII(w) and XII (fig. 83). Elsewhere in Room I is a captive shown wearing a soft cap with a pointed top that flops backward, a type that Layard said looked "not unlike the Phrygian bonnet reversed."

This same cap was also found on some of the prisoners from Room XLIII, where it appeared together with turbans having earflaps.[23]

The preserved Room IV slabs show no river, nor was one reported in the mountainous landscapes in Rooms XXXIX and LXV, which suggests that the third campaign was shown in these rooms also, but the evidence is negative and may be defective.

To summarize, it seems reasonably certain that all of the reliefs in Rooms

I, VIII(w), X, XII, XXIV, XXXIV, XXXVI, XXXVIII, XLI, XLVIII, and LXVII, and some of the reliefs from Rooms XLIII and LXIV, were devoted to Sennacherib's third campaign, to the west.

Later Campaigns

All of the known military narrative reliefs in Sennacherib's palace can be identified with one of the first three campaigns. Still, it is possible that later campaigns were represented as well. The texts on the palace gateway bulls record either five or six campaigns, indicating that the earliest examples were inscribed after the fifth campaign (about 697 B.C.), and the latest immediately after the sixth (694 B.C.).[24] Consequently, representations of the fourth campaign, to Babylonia (700 B.C.), and the fifth campaign, to the mountainous Judi Dagh in the north, might be expected to be included in the palace decoration. Indeed, the fourth campaign, despite its small scale and relative lack of success, may be the subject of some of the Babylonian scenes in the palace; in the absence of epigraphs it cannot be certain that such a scene represents the first rather than the fourth campaign.

The fifth campaign, however, which militarily was also relatively insignificant, may because of its late date be completely absent from the reliefs. This is because of the lag between the carving of the sculptures, which seem to

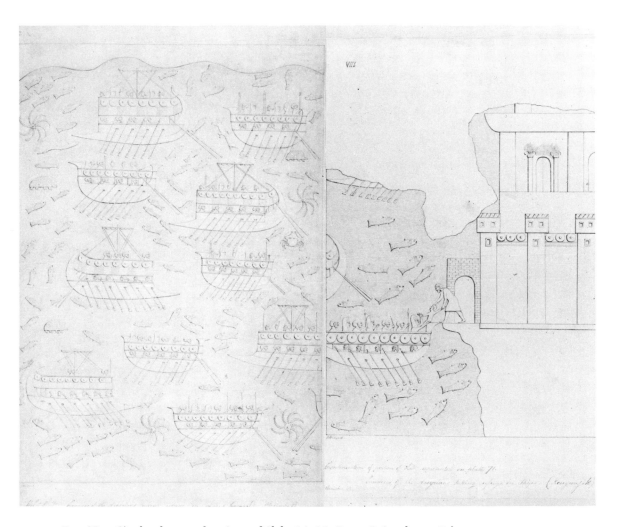

FIG. 85.   City by the sea, drawings of Slabs 14–15, Room I, Southwest Palace, Nineveh. British Museum, WAA, Or. Dr., IV, 7–8 (photo: Trustees of the British Museum)

165

have been completely finished before being inscribed, and the carving of the text, which was already well underway shortly after the end of the fifth campaign. This latter seems usually to have been the final step in the building of a palace, thereby insuring that the enduring record of the palace inscriptions was as up-to-date as possible.[25] In any event, all particularizing details of architecture and costume in those Sennacherib reliefs showing mountainous settings can be comfortably associated with either the second or third campaigns, and it therefore seems reasonably certain that the fifth campaign was not included in the sculptural program. As seen in chapter 4, however, the fifth campaign is represented after a fashion by uncarved slabs of decorative $NA_4.^dŠE.TIR$ stone—discovered during that campaign—which lined the walls of Rooms XXIX, XXX, and XXXIII.

Other Subjects

Construction

Two areas in Sennacherib's palace were decorated at least in part with scenes related to palace construction. The best preserved series is from the north and

east walls of Court VI, fully discussed in chapter 5, which shows the quarrying and transportation of bull colossi for the palace doors. Captions give the location of the quarry as Balaṭai, which was probably a short distance north of Nineveh on the east bank of the Tigris, and the destination of the colossi as Sennacherib's palace at Nineveh.[26] Manpower for the quarrying and transport operations is supplied by captive foreign labor. While the garb of many of these laborers is nondescript, some wear headgear that identifies them as captives of the third campaign, to the west. All of the quarrymen are shown wearing the floppy-topped "reversed Phrygian bonnet" seen also in a few of the third campaign reliefs, and some of the men who haul the colossi wear the turban with earflaps seen also in the Room XXXVI Lachish series and elsewhere.[27]

The other construction-related scene is from the north wall of Hall XLIX (fig. 86). There captives are shown hauling a large unidentified object on a sledge. Once again, some of the laborers wear the western turban with earflaps.[28] These images, therefore, clearly affirm that prisoners from the third campaign were used in the construction of the palace.

Fig. 87.   Procession of food bearers, drawing of Slabs 13–17, Room LI(n), Southwest Palace, Nineveh. British Museum, WAA, Or. Dr., IV, 70 (photo: Trustees of the British Museum).

Processions

The relief decoration of two passageways in the Southwest Palace was devoted to royal processions that apparently took place in or about the palace. In Room LI(n), a descending passage leading to the edge of the mound, one wall was decorated with a procession of horses being led out by grooms, while the opposite wall showed servants entering the palace with provisions for a feast (fig. 87). The other procession lined a corridor that may have connected Court H of the palace with the Ishtar Temple. The subject here is the

168

king with his attendants and bodyguard. As R. D. Barnett pointed out, the turban with earflaps worn by the defenders of Lachish is also worn by some members of the royal bodyguard here.[29] Whether this is sufficient evidence to identify these guards as Lachishites is debatable, however, since it would seem they could as easily be from any of the other forty-five Judean cities Sennacherib claimed to have captured during the third campaign.

Rooms with Multiple Subjects

The preserved evidence, combined with Layard's observations, suggests that the reliefs in the vast majority of Sennacherib's rooms showed only a single subject.[30] There are only three known exceptions to this. Two of these are courtyards: Court VI, which contained scenes of the eastern campaign on one side and palace construction on the other; and Court LXIV, which showed a Babylonian campaign on the south side and the western campaign on the north side. In the case of Court VI this juxtaposition of subjects may be seen as a summary of Sennacherib's accomplishments in the military and civic spheres, and I will return to this theme in chapter 11. In the case of Court LXIV, the reliefs seem to express the geographical extent of the empire

Fɪɢ. 88.   Campaign in marshes, drawing of Slabs 5 and 7, Room LXIV, Southwest Palace, Nineveh. British Museum, WAA, Or. Dr., IV, 33 (photo: Trustees of the British Museum).

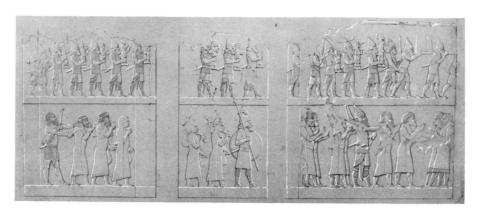

FIG. 89.   Western prisoners and gods, drawing of Slabs 1–3, Room LXIV, Southwest Palace, Nineveh. British Museum, WAA, Or. Dr., IV, 32 (photo: Trustees of the British Museum).

FIG. 90.   Eastern deportees, drawing of Slabs 1–2 east, Room XLIII, Southwest Palace, Nineveh. British Museum, WAA, Or. Dr., IV, 28 (photo: Trustees of the British Museum).

FIG. 91.   Western prisoners, drawing of Slab 2 west, Room XLIII, Southwest Palace, Nineveh. British Museum, WAA, Or. Dr., I, 66b (photo: Trustees of the British Museum).

170

(figs. 88, 89). The opposition of western and southern campaigns would then be the visual equivalent of the familiar formula inscribed on Sennacherib's palace gateway bulls, "From the upper sea of the setting sun (Mediterranean) to the lower sea of the rising sun (Persian Gulf), (Aššur) made all the rulers in the world bow down at my feet."[31] Evidently the great size and conspicuous central location of the courtyards made them a suitable location for these ideologically motivated visual juxtapositions of subjects.

The third room that appears to contain more than one subject is Room XLIII, a large reception room opening off of the north side of Court XIX. Here Layard recorded processions of figures wearing eastern garb on reliefs from the eastern end of the room and western garb at the western end, and it might be deduced from this that both of these campaigns were included in this room (figs. 90, 91). Reade observed, however, that the preserved slabs show neither fighting nor landscape background and suggested that the subject of Room XLIII was deportation of prisoners. This room apparently showed no particular campaign, then, but rather processions of captives from several parts of the empire in a nonhistorical setting.[32] This atypical subject in such a conspicuous location raises the question of the function of Room XLIII. It is tempting to speculate that the king reviewed foreign prisoners and booty in this very room, but supporting evidence is completely lacking.

Conclusions

The rooms in Sennacherib's palace for which the subject of the relief decoration is known with reasonable certainty are shown in figure 92. Though little or nothing is known about the decoration of a number of rooms, enough *are* known to permit several general observations regarding the organization of the subject matter in Sennacherib's palace.

One puzzling feature noted by Reade is the relative paucity of rooms decorated with Babylonian campaigns. The importance of the south is clearly indicated by its choice as the subject of the two surviving exterior facades of the palace, and yet it seems to appear infrequently elsewhere in the palace. The evidence here may be defective, however. The very poorly known suite of rooms at the western side of the palace (Rooms LIs to LIX) definitely contained at least one room decorated with a southern campaign (Room LIs), and it is possible that other rooms here originally contained the same subject. Also, Reade has suggested that Court XIX and the corridors leading into it, later recarved by Assurbanipal, may originally have been decorated with Sennacherib's Babylonian campaigns. Possible support for this suggestion is

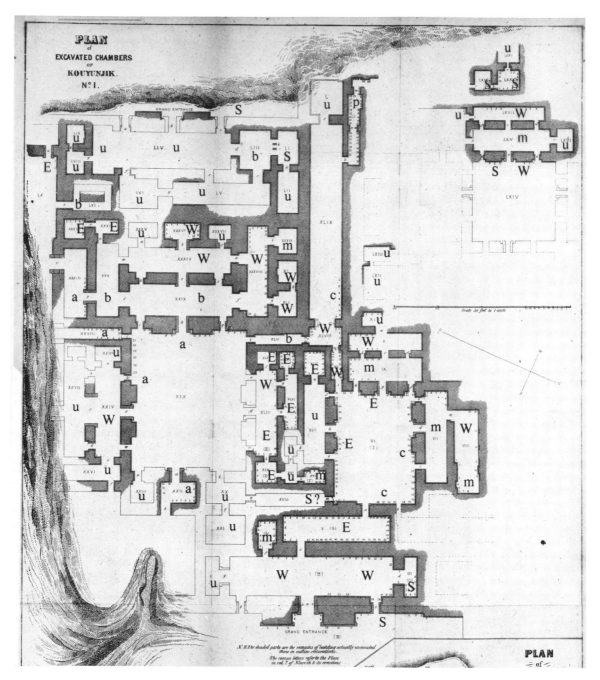

FIG. 92. Distribution of subjects in the Southwest Palace, Nineveh; S: south,
E: east, W: west, m: mountainous, c: construction, p: procession, b: blank,
a: Assurbanipal, u: unknown (source: author).

172

a recarved slab attributed by Reade to one of these corridors, XVIII, which originally showed a Babylonian campaign, probably Sennacherib's.[33]

It can be seen in figure 92 that the throne-room suite (Court H and Rooms I–VI) enjoyed great variety in its subject matter. Proceeding inward from the outer court we encounter first Babylonians (Court H), then westerners (Throne Room I), then easterners (Room V and Court VI), then construction (Court VI). The mixture of such a variety of subjects within a single suite seems not to occur elsewhere in the palace and attests to the all-encompassing function of the throne-room suite as a whole.

The pattern in the other suites that lead off of Inner Court VI is not as clear. In the north suite—composed of Rooms VII, VIII(e), and VIII(w)—the subject of only Room VIII (w), the western campaign, is known for certain. In Room VII, the presence of a river and general similarities to the campaign reliefs in Court VI suggest, but cannot confirm, an eastern campaign. The subject of Room VIII(e) is a campaign in the mountains and could be either east or west. The case of the west suite, formed by Rooms IX to XI, is similar. Once again, the presence of a river suggests that the subject of Room IX may be eastern, while that of Room X is definitely western, and that of Room XI is unknown. If the subject of Rooms VII and IX is eastern, and this is uncertain, then these two suites would show a mixture of eastern and western campaigns similar to that in the neighboring throne-room suite.

A different pattern seems to prevail in at least two of the suites opening off of Court XIX. Though the original decoration, if any, of Court XIX itself is unknown because of later recarving around the time of Assurbanipal, the suites to the north and west of the court still contained fairly well-preserved reliefs of Sennacherib. With the exception of the western half of Room XLIII, every recorded room in the northern suite (Rooms XII–XVII, XLIII–XLVII) was decorated with reliefs showing the second campaign, to the east. In addition, Layard's mention of a river in the reliefs of Room XVII suggests, though doesn't prove, that this room also showed the east.

The suite to the west of Court XIX (Rooms XXIX–XLI), by contrast, seems to have been decorated almost exclusively with scenes from the third campaign, to the west. This is especially true if Room XXXIX, the decoration of which apparently did not include a river, and Room XL, the decoration of which Layard lumped together with that of XLI, both also showed the western campaign. The only exceptions to this rule in this suite would then be Rooms XXXI and XXXII, which showed the east.

In each of the preserved suites opening off of Court XIX, then, the decoration seems to have been dominated by a single campaign, in contrast to the mixture of campaigns observed in the throne-room suite and perhaps also in the northern and western suites opening onto Court VI. The explanation for these apparent patterns of distribution is far from clear. The value of showing a mixture of campaigns in the throne-room suite, the hub of the empire, is obvious; this principle was applied previously on the throne base of Sargon II and possibly in the decoration of the throne room of Assurnasirpal II.[34] The reason for the almost exclusive representation of a single campaign throughout an extensive suite of rooms, as in the case of the Court XIX suites, is less clear. Three very tentative hypotheses suggest themselves.

First, the subject chosen for the decoration of a suite might have been determined on the basis of the chronology of the construction of the palace itself. In this case, a suite whose subject is the second campaign might have been decorated prior to the conclusion of the third campaign, and the subject chosen would therefore have been the most recently completed campaign. The apparent occurrence of captives from the third campaign in Room XLIII, in a suite otherwise decorated exclusively with the second campaign, argues against this view, but they could have been added later.

A second possible hypothesis is that the decoration selected for a suite of rooms might somehow reflect its function. Thus, a suite decorated with the second campaign, to the east, might have functioned primarily as the administrative center for the eastern portion of the empire, or alternatively, it might have served as the primary reception suite for eastern visitors.

A third hypothesis might be that the decoration of an entire suite with a single campaign serves an extended narrative function. Only the largest rooms in Sennacherib's palace could accommodate the number and variety of distinct episodes necessary to convey the full story of a campaign. It may be that, in decorating an entire suite with a single campaign, Sennacherib's artists were using the extensive amount of wall space available to present a much more detailed picture of a single campaign than could have been achieved in a single room and thereby composed an expansive visual counterpart to the detailed verbal campaign narratives presented on the bulls.

Since most of the walls of the palace were apparently constructed after the third campaign, as discussed in chapter 4, the first alternative seems unlikely. The choice of one or both of the other alternatives, or of entirely different ones, may not be made until the quality of the evidence is enhanced by the full publication of the nineteenth-century drawings of the sculptures and perhaps also by renewed excavations in the sculptured portions of the palace itself. It is only in this way that questions of subject matter can be answered with a greater degree of certainty.

8

TRADITION AND INNOVATION

If we as modern viewers wish to attempt to experience something of the effect of Sennacherib's palace reliefs on their original viewers nearly 2,700 years ago, then we must first establish what that audience, or rather what different components of that audience, had been conditioned to expect in the way of palace decoration and how Sennacherib's reliefs diverged from those expectations.[1] That is to say, we must determine how Sennacherib's palace decoration is similar to that of earlier Assyrian palaces and how it is different. In the discussion that follows, I will consider these similarities and differences in terms of "tradition" and "innovation," concepts that will be developed more fully below. This chapter, then, does for images what chapter 2 did for texts by highlighting the ways in which Sennacherib's palace decoration conforms to and diverges from previous Assyrian practice.

Tradition

A number of features that first appear in the palace decoration of Assurnasirpal II recur in the palaces of his successors, Shalmaneser III, Tiglath-pileser III, and Sargon II.[2] These recurrent features fall into three general categories: architectural form, layout of decoration, and subject matter.

"Architectural form" refers to the plan of the palace. The most striking feature here is the plan of the suite of rooms that included the throne room, known in the palaces of Assurnasirpal II (Room B), Shalmaneser III (Room T1), and Sargon II ("Court" VII; see fig. 43).[3] This most important of reception areas was a long, relatively wide room—the largest roofed space in the palace. Its principal access was on its long northeast wall via three doors, a monumental portal flanked by two subsidiary ones, opening off the palace's large outer court. The throne was located at the short southeast end of the room, while the opposite (northwest) short wall opened into a small cham-

175

ber that gave access to a stairway. The throne room's long southwest wall, opposite the principal entrances, contained a door leading to a smaller room that in turn opened onto the palace's inner courtyard, or, in the case of Fort Shalmaneser, onto a terrace. In Sargon's palace, the southwest wall of the throne room also contained a second entrance that led into a bathroom. In each of these palaces, then, the general layout and orientation of the throne-room suite were very similar.

"Layout of decoration" refers to the distribution of various forms of decoration throughout the palace. Here again, there are marked similarities in the decorative schemes of Assurnasirpal II's and Sargon II's palaces.[4] In both cases, the lower eight to ten feet of the walls of the courtyards and principal rooms of the palace were covered with stone orthostats carved in low relief, and in both cases major doorways were decorated with pairs of stone colossi, the largest of which were nearly twenty feet high. Once again the throne room displays the clearest example of similarities. In Assurnasirpal's palace, the throne-room facade was apparently originally decorated with one pair of colossi in each of the three exterior doors and one pair on the face of each of the two great buttresses that flank the central doorway for a total of five pairs of colossi, though some are now lost. The walls flanking the two side doorways were covered with orthostats carved with procession scenes.[5] This arrangement of colossi and orthostats is precisely the same on Sargon II's throne-room facade as well (see fig. 9).

The palaces of Assurnasirpal II, Tiglath-pileser III, and Sargon II also display similarities in the ordering of the narrative and nonnarrative compositions on the wall slabs. In nearly every case, slabs carved with nonnarrative subjects—which include apotropaic, ceremonial, and processional scenes—are composed in a single register, with larger than life-sized figures depicted (see fig. 122).[6] Slabs carved with narratives, however, are nearly always composed in two registers separated by a band of text, with figures shown well under life-size (see fig. 16).[7]

Another similarity in the decorative layout of Assurnasirpal II's and Sargon II's palaces, analyzed already in chapter 2, was in the location of inscriptions. In both palaces, three locations were reserved for long texts: door thresholds, the spaces between the legs of the doorway colossi, and the horizontal band separating registers of relief on the wall slabs.

"Subject matter" refers to specific subjects and motifs introduced in the palace reliefs of Assurnasirpal II that recur regularly in the reliefs of his successors, Tiglath-pileser III and Sargon II. The primarily nonnarrative subjects in the palaces of all these kings were apotropaic, ceremonial, and processional scenes, while the primary narrative subject was royal military exploits, shown with particular attention to details of costume and landscape. These narratives are often organized according to a compositional principle that equates progression through space with temporal sequence.[8] Narratives of the royal hunt also occur in both Assurnasirpal's and Sargon's palaces, though the quarries are different: lions and bulls for Assurnasirpal; small game for Sargon.[9] Specific motifs that figured prominently in the decorative schemes of Assurnasirpal II, Sargon II, and apparently also Tiglath-pileser III were the winged human-headed genie with bucket and cone, the winged eagle-headed genie, the so-called "sacred tree," and the winged human-headed bull gateway colossus.[10]

It is tempting to ascribe the consistency in these aspects of the reliefs to a tradition of neo-Assyrian palace decoration, but the actual explanation would seem to be more complex. Implicit in "tradition" is the idea of sequence: to qualify as traditional, a custom or usage is usually thought of as having been handed down by one generation to another generation or by one's predecessors.[11] No such sequence is to be observed among the earlier neo-Assyrian palaces. Fort Shalmaneser, which Shalmaneser III refers to as his "palace," included neither wall reliefs nor gateway colossi.[12] There is no evidence of further palace building activity in the capital until the reign of Tiglath-pileser III, seven kings and nearly 150 years after the date that Assurnasirpal II's palace was begun. Its relief decoration seems to have duplicated many of the forms established by Assurnasirpal's palace, but the amount of time elapsed between the building of these two structures and the lack of intervening examples make one hesitate to attribute these similarities to a tradition of palace building. Instead, Assurnasirpal's palace, occupied in turn by each ruler from Shalmaneser III to Tiglath-pileser III, *becomes* the "traditional" Assyrian palace and consequently was the natural model for the decoration of Tiglath-pileser's new palace.[13]

Sargon II (721–705 B.C.) restored and lived in Assurnasirpal's palace and seems to have been copying it in his own new palace at Khorsabad, thereby perpetuating certain features that, by virtue of this repetition, become "traditional." In the case of Sargon II, however, this copying may have gone beyond simple imitation of established forms to a conscious emulation of Assurnasirpal's deeds. Assurnasirpal's records indicate that he founded a new capital, Kalhu (Nimrud), around his fifth year. This remained the Assyrian capital until Sargon II duplicated this achievement by founding a new capital called Dur Sharrukin (Khorsabad), also in his fifth year. Sargon could well have been consciously patterning this major event in his reign on the similar event from the reign of Assurnasirpal II. If so, he seems to have even emulated Assurnasirpal's timing.[14]

By the time of the construction of Sennacherib's palace, it probably *is* appropriate to speak of a tradition of palace decoration, since two of his immediate predecessors, Tiglath-pileser III and Sargon II, had also erected similarly decorated palaces. This would seem to fulfill the requirement of sequence necessary for "tradition." Sennacherib's palace presents a number of features that by now appear to be traditional. Its architectural form is similar to that of the palaces of his predecessors, with ranks of rooms grouped around central courts of various sizes. The similarity is most pronounced in the plan of Sennacherib's throne-room suite, the preserved part of which is virtually identical to that of Sargon II, though somewhat larger.

The layout of the decoration of Sennacherib's palace is also in most respects similar to that of Sargon's palace. Sennacherib too used carved stone orthostats to cover the lower part of the walls of his principal rooms and courts, as well as stone bull colossi in important doorways. His throne-room facade, with its human-headed bull colossi, colossal figures of lion-clutching heroes, and carved orthostats, is very similar in appearance to the throne-room facade of Sargon's palace (see fig. 10). As seen in chapter 2, Sennacherib also continued Sargon's use of the spaces between the legs of the doorway colossi as the location for lengthy texts.

The subject matter of Sennacherib's palace decoration is also in many ways similar to that of Sargon. Sennacherib's palace reliefs included royal processions and apotropaic figures, as did Sargon's palace reliefs, and Sennacherib's artists continued the tradition of representing these subjects in a single register. Some of the apotropaic figures in Sennacherib's reliefs are also traditional types, notably the winged human-headed bull colossus and the winged human-headed and, perhaps, eagle-headed genies. Finally, the vast majority of wall reliefs in Sennacherib's palace depict royal military campaigns, which is also the most popular narrative subject in the reliefs of his predecessors, and like those of his predecessors, many of these images are organized according to the traditional principle that equates spatial progression with temporal sequence. Sennacherib's artists, however, exploited this principle to an unprecedented degree, a point that will be taken up again below. The format of Sennacherib's narrative reliefs is also considerably changed from that of earlier examples. This and other innovations are the subject of the remainder of this chapter, but it is important to remember that these innovations only stand out because they are silhouetted against the backdrop of tradition.

Innovation

Despite its maintenance of a number of now traditional features, one of the most remarkable aspects of Sennacherib's palace decoration is his transformation of a number of the standard elements in the palaces of his predecessors. This transformation may be termed *innovation*, "the alteration of what is established by the introduction of new elements or forms."[15] Innovation is generally understood as a conscious process that is to be distinguished from the unconscious process of mutation. The innovations in Sennacherib's reliefs, when compared to Sargon's reliefs, fall into two general categories: subject matter and composition. The first of these is dealt with here, while the second is the subject of the next chapter.

In Sennacherib's reliefs, there are innovations in both the apotropaic and narrative subjects.[16] Two of the most common apotropaic figures in the reliefs of Assurnasirpal II and Sargon II, the winged human-headed genie with the cone and bucket and the winged human-headed bull gateway colossus, also figure prominently in Sennacherib's portal decorations (figs. 48, 93). Other apotropaic figure types that occur in one or more ninth- and eighth-century Assyrian palaces, and recur in Sennacherib's palace, are the genie with a fish-skin cloak, the figure of a hero strangling a lion, and probably the eagle-headed winged genie (see figs. 10, 22).[17]

FIG. 93.
Winged figure, drawing of Slab 4 south, Court H, Southwest Palace, Nineveh. British Museum, WAA, Or. Dr., IV, 1 (photo: Trustees of the British Museum).

To these traditional types, however, Sennacherib added several that had apparently not occurred in the reliefs of earlier palaces. One of these is a man with six large curls at the back of his head who wears a kilt and holds vertically a standard shaped like a spear (fig. 94). A second new type is an empty-handed man with a horned crown and a long tress of hair bound at the back of the neck, which sometimes appears with another new type, a lion-headed,

FIG. 94. Doorway guardian figure (*lahmu* or *apkallu*), lower part of Slab 21, Court VI, Southwest Palace, Nineveh. British Museum, WAA 124792 (photo: Trustees of the British Museum).

FIG. 95. Door way guardian figures (*ugallu* and *Lulal?*), west jamb, Door *o*, Room XXXI, Southwest Palace, Nineveh. British Museum, WAA 118932 (photo: Trustees of the British Museum).

eagle-footed man holding a mace and upraised dagger (fig. 95). Yet another new figure has a "human head and the feet of a lion" (fig. 96; for a better-preserved Assurbanipal example, see fig. 97).[18] The "sacred tree," however, which figured prominently in the relief decoration of Assurnasirpal II and continued to be used occasionally in the corners and doorways of rooms decorated with nonnarrative scenes in Sargon's palace, was completely absent from Sennacherib's palace reliefs.[19]

Finally, Layard reported a number of gateway colossi that had human heads and winged-lion bodies. He usually called these figures "human-headed" or "winged" lions, but once referred to some examples excavated by Ross as "sphinxes" and apparently used the terms "winged sphinxes" and "winged lions" interchangeably when describing the gateway colossi from Room XXXIII. Sennacherib's inscription on the back of this latter pair of colossi identified them as *ªapsasāte,* a term that occurred in neo-Assyrian building accounts only during the reigns of Sennacherib and Esarhaddon.[20] Though no illustration of the Room XXXIII colossi has been published, the feminine plural and determinative used in the writing of their name suggests that these winged lions (or sphinxes) were female. Concerning their posture,

FIG. 96. Doorway guardian figures (*uridimmu* and *apkallu?*), drawing of slabs attributed to Door *a*, Room XIV, Southwest Palace, Nineveh. British Museum, WAA, Or. Dr., II, 43 (photo: Trustees of the British Museum).

it seems that those examples that served as doorjambs were standing, while those functioning as column bases were recumbent, though in the absence of illustrations of any examples from Sennacherib's palace, it is not certain that this was true in all cases. It is clear in Sennacherib's texts that *ʃapsasāte* could serve either as door jambs or as column bases—the term apparently refers only to the type of figure and not to its posture or location.[21] Standing or crouching, these female lion sphinxes apparently have no precedent either in Sargon's palace, where no human-headed lions were reported, or in Assur-nasirpal's palace, where the only lion colossi were male-headed.

It remains to attempt to account for the introduction of these new figure types in the palace decoration of Sennacherib. Reade and Winter have suggested that the female sphinx may derive from examples in North Syrian palaces, such as the double-sphinx column bases from Sakçegözü and Zinçirli.[22] That the later neo-Assyrian kings were interested in North Syrian architec-

ture is demonstrated by their borrowing of the North Syrian *bīt-hilāni* structure for use in their own palaces, beginning with Tiglath-pileser III and described also in the palace building accounts of Sargon II, Sennacherib, and
Assurbanipal.[23] Perhaps the female sphinx is another example of direct borrowing at this time.

Sources for the remaining new figures may be found closer to home. In
fact, all of these "new" figures are existing Assyrian apotropaic types that,
before the time of Sennacherib, functioned not as subjects for stone relief
sculpture, but rather as clay figurines buried at strategic points under the

FIG. 97. Doorway
guardian figure
(*uridimmu*), Slab 1,
Door *a*, Room I, North
Palace of Assurbanipal,
Nineveh. British
Museum, WAA, Or. Dr.,
VII, 10 (photo: Trustees
of the British Museum).

pavement of a room to ward off evil forces. Assyrian caches of these protective figurines predating Sennacherib's palace have been found in Shalmaneser III's (858–824 B.C.) "Southeast Palace" at Nimrud; in phases E and F—dating respectively to the reigns of Adad-nirari III (810–783 B.C.) and Sargon II (721–705 B.C.)—of the Burnt Palace at Nimrud; and in Sargon II's palace at Khorsabad.[24] There are also lengthy texts from Assur and Nineveh recording rituals for the protection of houses and the healing of the sick, and these describe the manufacture, appearance, and placement of such figurines. Two of these texts are dated: one was written during the reign of Shalmaneser III and recopied for Assurbanipal, and the other dates to 750 B.C.[25]

Botta's plans of Sargon's palace show the location of a considerable number of figurine caches, which are usually buried under the pavement directly in front of each door jamb.[26] At least two, and perhaps three, of the "new" Sennacherib figures occurred in Sargon's deposits. One of these is the kilted, six-curled genie holding a spear-shaped standard. On the basis of inscriptions on similar figurines from Assur, this type can be securely identified with a figurine described in the apotropaic ritual texts whose name has been read either *apkallu* ("sage") or *lahmu* (possibly "hairy one"; fig. 98).[27] The type itself is ancient, occurring already on Akkadian cylinder seals, where it often holds a gatepost. The triangular top of the object held by the Assyrian figures is not unlike the top of the doorposts shown in the Akkadian seals. One of the figurine texts describes this figure's attribute, but the sign is damaged—the preserved traces have been restored as GIŠ.⌈MAR⌉ (*marru*: "spade"). Wiggerman observed that if this is a spade, then it might serve to place the house under the protection of Marduk, whose symbol is the spade.[28]

Another Sennacherib apotropaic figure type that appeared in the foundation deposits of Sargon is the lion-headed, eagle-footed human (fig. 99). Woolley suggested that this was the *ugallu* ("great lion" or "great storm-demon") of the Assur figurine texts, and Green was able to confirm this identification on the basis of two inscribed clay figurines of this type from Fort Shalmaneser at Nimrud. In the Assur texts the *ugallu* is described as carrying a dagger in its right hand and a weapon in the left. Certainly these attributes correspond well with those held by this figure in Sennacherib's reliefs.[29]

It is not clear whether the empty-handed genie with the horned cap and bound hair is represented among the surviving foundation figurines. A figure with a horned crown and similar pose was found in the Khorsabad deposits, but its hairstyle, though poorly preserved, appears different (fig. 100). Indeed, none of the published surviving figurines with horned crowns seem to have this distinctive hairstyle, though the hairstyle itself is worn by certain

FIG. 98. (*left*) Protective figurine (*lahmu* or *apkallu*), unfired clay, Sargon's palace, Khorsabad, h. 23.4 cm. Louvre, N 8283 (photo: Musée du Louvre/AO).

FIG. 99. (*right*) Protective figurine (*ugallu*), unfired clay, Sargon's palace, Khorsabad, h. of figure: 21.5 cm (from Botta and Flandin 1849, vol. 2, 152).

deities on much earlier cylinder seals. Perhaps the hairstyle is not an essential attribute of this figure, which Wiggerman identified with the god Lulal in the figurine texts.[30]

Sennacherib's fourth "new" apotropaic type, the human genie with the legs and feet of a dog or lion, was not reported among the surviving figurines from Khorsabad, but does occur at Nimrud and Ur (fig. 101). Wiggerman suggested this figure is the *uridimmu* ("mad dog/lion") of the Assur figurine texts. This too, therefore, is an extant Assyrian apotropaic figurine type appropriated by Sennacherib as a doorway relief subject.[31]

FIG. 100. (*left*)
Protective figurine
(*Lulal?*), unfired clay,
Sargon's palace,
Khorsabad, h. 22 cm.
Louvre, N 3152 (photo:
Musée du Louvre/AO).

FIG. 101. (*right*)
Protective figurine
(*uridimmu*), unfired clay,
Burnt Palace, Nimrud,
excavation no. ND 4112,
h. 14 cm. (information
courtesy British School of
Archaeology in Iraq,
excavation archives).

Clearly, the apotropaic figures on Sennacherib's palace reliefs were not new types at all, but rather existing types newly applied in a new context. Their already well-established protective roles were now employed on a different scale and in a different medium. Though the evidence from both palaces may be defective, it is at least suggestive that three of the four clay figurine types from Sargon's palace later turn up on the doorway reliefs of Sennacherib's palace.[32] One wonders whether the absence of any reported figurine deposits in Sennacherib's palace might be because nearly all of the traditional figurine types were instead prominently displayed on the reliefs of various doorways. Whether or not this is the case, it appears that in decorating his doorways, Sennacherib made visible that which had previously been invisible—that is, he displayed on the door jambs powerful apotropaic figures that had formerly been buried under the pavement.[33] This innovation may or may not have been more efficacious where incorporeal visitors were concerned, but it certainly would have provided an impressive effect for corporeal ones.

The absence of the "sacred tree" from the corner slabs of the rooms of Sennacherib's palace may be attributed to Sennacherib's exclusive use of continuous military narrative, which allows no place for such a nonnarrative motif (Sargon II didn't combine the "sacred tree" with military narrative either). Its absence from doorways, however, which in Sennacherib's palace are usually decorated with apotropaic figures, suggests that the "sacred tree" had been entirely replaced by other types of figures, at least in large-scale wall reliefs.[34]

Sennacherib's innovations in subject matter were not confined only to the protective figures in the doorways, but extended to the narrative subjects that decorated the room walls as well. He apparently completely omitted three subjects that had had important roles in the palaces of Sargon II and Assurnasirpal II. One of these was processions of tribute from various parts of the empire. Such processions had flanked the two side entrances in the facade of Assurnasirpal's Northwest Palace throne room and had lined several courts and rooms in Sargon's palace at Khorsabad (see figs. 122, 123).[35]

Another "traditional" subject omitted in Sennacherib's palace decoration is hunting scenes. Lion and bull hunts held a place of honor next to the enthroned king himself in the throne room of Assurnasirpal II and were found in the ruined "west wing" as well. In Sargon II's palace, Room 7, which was apparently a bathroom in the private rear wing of the palace, was decorated with scenes of a small game hunt set in a forest of conifers. Lion hunts were also prominent in the passageways and private rooms of the later palace of Assurbanipal at Nineveh. No hunting scenes of any sort, however, were reported in Sennacherib's palace, though the rooms that by analogy should have contained them were excavated by Layard.[36]

The third subject omitted by Sennacherib is scenes of royal banqueting. This may have been shown in the large-scale reliefs in Assurnasirpal's Room G, and was definitely the subject of the smaller-scale reliefs in Sargon's Rooms 2 and 7; it reappears in Assurbanipal's palace among the reliefs that had fallen into Room S. Once again, no banquet scenes were reported by Layard, though Room LI(n) does show a large-scale procession of servants bringing foodstuffs into the palace.[37]

There is one subject that Sennacherib emphasized far more than did his predecessors: the transport of building materials for the construction of the palace. The cutting of timber, possibly for palace construction, is shown in a single relief of Assurnasirpal II, which is probably from the west wing of the Northwest Palace.[38] The transport of roofing timbers is the subject of a more extensive relief series from the northwest wall of Court VIII in Sargon's palace at Khorsabad (see fig. 107). The context of this series, however, which was accompanied elsewhere in the court by processions of tributaries, makes it unclear whether it was intended primarily as a scene of procurement of building materials or rather as one of tribute from a timber-rich part of the empire.

No such uncertainty holds for Sennacherib's construction procurement scenes, however, which covered two walls of Court VI, the inner court of the throne-room suite, and part or all of the walls of Hall XLIX, the great hallway connecting the central areas of the palace with the southwest terrace. These showed the quarrying and transport of stone gateway colossi and the transport by water of a large but unidentifiable piece of wood or stone. Not only were the reliefs in both of these rooms labeled with epigraphs stating that the materials shown were intended for the construction of Sennacherib's palace, but in Court VI the identification between the objects in the reliefs and their intended function was made visually explicit by juxtaposing them with the actual colossi themselves, which stood in the doorways of the same court and at one point actually interrupted the narrative series (see fig. 49).

As with the new doorway figures, one must try to account for Sennacherib's choice of narrative subjects. Why did his palace relief decoration omit several traditional subjects (tribute, hunting, banquet), while considerably expanding the use of another subject that previously had been used sparingly (procurement of building materials)? It seems that no single explanation is adequate to account for all of this. Reade suggested that some traditional subjects were dropped because they were relatively unsuited to the "elaborate and detailed compositions" that emphasize the king's "visible achievements" favored by Sennacherib's artists.[39] This could at least partially account for the omission of tribute processions and banquets, which offer little potential for narrative action, perspective space, and topographic detail, and could also account for the expansion of the construction procurement sequences, which provide ample scope for all of these.

Reade's suggestion does not explain the absence of hunting scenes, which are ideal narrative subjects, and it is here, I think, that the question of the personality of Sennacherib himself must be introduced. It is not known whether Sennacherib enjoyed hunting or considered himself an accomplished hunter, but if he did his surviving texts do not mention it. This is in marked contrast to the texts of Assurnasirpal II and Assurbanipal, both of whom detail their hunting exploits in images *and* texts.[40] It appears that whether or not Sennacherib actually hunted, he did not consider the hunt an important part of his royal image. This is a reminder that while there are certain constants in the Assyrian ideal of kingship, most notably service to the gods and the maintenance of the realm, the holder of the office is an individual who will, to some degree at least, interpret this ideal to suit his personal interests and goals.

This may help explain Sennacherib's emphasis on construction in his palace reliefs. His building texts are longer and more involved than those of any of his predecessors. More important, on several occasions they explicitly describe the king's involvement with various aspects of the construction.[41] It appears that Sennacherib was personally interested in the building process, and as I shall show in chapter 11, he seems to have viewed royal construction as a more significant component of his imperial policy than did his predecessors.

Summary

Sennacherib's palace represents a complex fusion of tradition and innovation. The plan of his throne room (I) is virtually identical to that of his father, Sargon II. Sennacherib retained his predecessor's monumental throne-room facade with its five pairs of colossi, but the flanking orthostats were carved with a royal campaign, rather than with processions. Similarly, a large number of Sennacherib's rooms were decorated with wall reliefs, but the division of the narrative reliefs into two registers had been abandoned, as had the central band of text. The colossi were still carved with long texts, but the texts on the thresholds had been largely replaced with floral patterns. Sennacherib continued the tradition of carving protective figures on doorways and employed such traditional types as the winged human-headed bull colossus and the winged human-headed and eagle-headed genies, but the "sacred tree" is gone, and a number of new protective types, apparently derived from foundation figurines, appear instead. Sennacherib's reliefs show such traditional subjects as military narratives and royal processions, but the hunt is missing, and a new narrative subject, procurement of palace building materials, assumes a prominent role.

In conclusion, it should be stressed that the king of Assyria was a man as well as an office and that royal pronouncements—verbal or visual—should be expected to bear the stamp of the king's individual personality, as well as that of royal "tradition." The decoration of the Assyrian palaces shows ample examples of variation, both in content and composition; since each palace is the work of an individual king, built primarily as his personal residence, it is here, rather than in a truly traditional structure such as a temple, that we would expect to find the clearest expression of the king's personality. Thus, if certain subjects fail to appear in a given palace, this may not be because they haven't been excavated yet, but rather because they were never there at all, having played no part in the image the king wished to express. These same observations may also help explain innovations in relief composition, and it is to these that I now turn.

9

SPACE AND TIME

Compositional innovations in Sennacherib's palace may be divided into two general categories: representation of space and representation of time. I will show that, while neither of these types of representation were invented by Sennacherib's artists, they did take a distinctive form in the decoration of his palace.

Space

One of the most remarkable features of the narrative reliefs in Sennacherib's palace is their perspective. While not rigorously coherent or "scientific," like Renaissance linear perspective, it often provides an effective suggestion of depth.[1] In considering perspective, two points must be kept in mind. First, though some perspective systems provide a more convincing illusion than others, no such system is inherently "correct." This is because in perceiving spatial relationships, we rely not only on spatial indicators such as recession, overlapping, and diminution, which can be approximated in a planar representation, but also on bifocal vision, head movement, and shifting viewpoint, none of which have planar equivalents.[2] The best that a perspective image can hope to achieve is an *approximation* of nature that may function illusionistically under certain predetermined conditions.

The other point is that the Renaissance tradition of painting, reinforced now by the omnipresence of the photographic image, has conditioned modern viewers to accept the "correctness" of one-point perspective construction. This tends to prevent us from being convinced by the illusion presented by other perspective systems, but this would not have been the case for pre-quattrocento viewers who would have brought different expectations to their viewing of a perspectival representation. We need only recall Boccaccio's praise of Giotto, who, he says, "painted anything in Nature, . . . and painted them so like that they seemed not so much likenesses as the things themselves; whereby it often happened that men's visual sense was deceived, and they thought that to be real which was only painted."[3] Few modern observers would apply this particular praise to Giotto who, as one eighteenth-century critic observed, "would today hardly be considered fit to paint a signboard."[4] Though this criticism was evidently intended to be derogatory, it also was—and still is—a simple statement of fact, emphasizing the differing background and expectations of the pre-quattrocento versus the post-quattrocento observer.

It would seem, then, that in order to appreciate ancient perspective, Renaissance-conditioned perception must be put aside and a more flexible set of perceptual criteria substituted. The essential test of any perspective system, ancient or modern, I would suggest, should be: how easy is it for the viewer intuitively to construct a coherent space consistent with the perspectival cues presented in the image? Or to put it differently, how closely does the visual information conform to an intuitively possible view of the world? The emphasis here on the perception, as opposed to the construction, of a perspective image permits one to judge the success of the image not according to how well it fits a preexisting system or set of requirements (such as one-point construction), but rather on how well it functions visually, independent of other criteria.

Thus prepared, let us turn now to the neo-Assyrian palace reliefs. The narrative reliefs of Assurnasirpal II, Tiglath-pileser III, and Sargon II all follow essentially the same compositional system. The spatial inconsistencies in the wall reliefs of all three kings result, in particular, from two aspects of the conceptual approach of their designers. First, with a single exception, the narrative reliefs of Sennacherib's predecessors are all divided horizontally into two registers by a raised band of inscription, resulting in a register that is only tall enough to accommodate comfortably the height of a standing figure.[5] The artist sees this register not as a window through which to view an approximation of three-dimensional space, but rather as a field to be filled. With this approach, the lower and upper borders of the register function as compositional boundaries, with the lower serving as the ground line and the upper as the axis of isocephaly. For example, in a common type of scene, an Assyrian siege of a city, the lower border of the register serves as ground line for the Assyrian infantry, siege machines, and bottom of the city wall, while the upper border determines the level of the heads of the same infantrymen, siege machine operators, and defenders of the wall, though the figures themselves are shown at quite different scales (see fig. 16). The problem with these images is that they are spatially incoherent, that is, it is quite impossible to visualize a space in which figures as tall as the full height of the register can cross swords with figures represented as one-third their size. This is not to say that the action itself is unclear, but some viewers may nonetheless have found the giant-versus-midget aspect of these conflicts to be a distraction from the intended message.[6]

The other preconception carried by the Assyrian artist into the design of the wall reliefs is that one of the best ways to insure that the king dominates the composition is to make his figure among the largest. Likewise, lower-ranking Assyrians are often smaller than high-ranking ones, while enemy peoples are smaller than Assyrians. This tendency is most pronounced in the reliefs of Assurnasirpal II, but may be observed to some degree in those of Tiglath-pileser III and Sargon II as well (see fig. 118).[7]

Despite these limitations, the artists of Assurnasirpal II, Tiglath-pileser III, and Sargon II constructed several images that are spatially remarkably coherent and which foreshadow the compositions of Sennacherib. To indicate spatial relationships in the long, relatively narrow field of the register, the Assyrian artist employed one of two conventions. The first was by far the most frequently used before Sennacherib. Here, virtually all figures are located on a single ground line—usually the lower border of the register—and depth is indicated by having closer figures overlap more distant ones. With the second convention, which was favored by Sennacherib, depth is indicated by placing distant figures higher than closer ones. Figures may be located anywhere in the register; often they are anchored to and organized by an overall background pattern, such as mountains or waves. With the first convention, the principle of spatial organization is horizontal overlapping; with the second, it is vertical stacking. Either can produce an effect of spatial recession, that is, the illusion of the third dimension on the flat picture surface.

Conceptually, the primary difference between these two spatial conventions is the implied viewpoint, that is, the viewpoint that would have to be assumed to experience a similar spatial effect when viewing nature. In compositions where all figures are placed on a single ground line, the implied viewpoint is very low. It is only with one's eye at ground level that the receding ground plane does not appear to rise, and all objects, both near and far, appear to be located on a single ground line. This low viewpoint has been termed "worm's-eye" perspective.[8] In compositions where the ground plane rises sharply, by contrast, and figures appear to be stacked vertically on the picture surface, the implied viewpoint is high. We seem to look down on the scene from above, from a "cavalier" or "bird's-eye" viewpoint.[9]

FIG. 102.   Battle, Slab 4a, Room B, Northwest Palace of Assurnasirpal II, Nimrud,
w. 215 cm. British Museum, WAA 124553 (photo: Trustees of the British Museum).

In a chariot pursuit scene from Assurnasirpal's Northwest Palace, overlapping of the three teams of horses and diminution—the horses further away are slightly smaller than the closer ones—are combined to achieve an effect of recession (fig. 102). The effectiveness of the illusion is lessened, however, by decapitated enemy bodies of various sizes that "hover" in the space above the chariots. While these figures could conceivably be read as existing in the deep background, there is a spatial conflict between the horizontal recession of the ground line, which supports the three overlapping chariots, and the ground plane, which should rise from lower foreground to upper background in order to support the decapitated bodies.[10]

This conflict is perspectivally irreconcilable and highlights the primary shortcoming of adhering a composition to the ground line, as in most of the narrative reliefs of Assurnasirpal II, Tiglath-pileser III, and Sargon II: placing too many figures on the ground line sets up the expectation of recession on a horizontal plane perpendicular to the picture surface at the level of the ground line. That is to say, if *some* figures overlap and recede at the level of the ground line, then *all* figures in the composition, both foreground and background, must adhere to the ground line if the representation is to have spatial coherence. Since the ground line will accommodate relatively few figures and permits only a certain degree of overlapping before the composition becomes saturated, this virtually eliminates the possibility of representing anything but a shallow space. This type of representation is ideal for shallow subjects, such as tribute and prisoner processions, but is inadequate for showing scenes characterized by complex landscapes and large numbers of figures, such as battles.[11]

Assurnasirpal's artists overcame the tyranny of the ground line only twice, and in both cases the setting is a body of water. One of these scenes shows three enemy men swimming a river or moat while Assyrian archers fire at them from the banks (fig. 103); the other shows the Assyrian army crossing a river.[12] In both cases the overall water pattern serves as background for figures distributed freely across the field, and in both cases it is relatively easy to imagine a deep space that fits the visual information. Neither of these images, however, is a thoroughly convincing spatial representation, mainly because the scale of the figures is not consistent.

The compositions of Tiglath-pileser III are also generally organized on the ground line, but there are several notable exceptions. In one of these, the artist again takes advantage of a maritime setting to present a remarkably convincing bird's-eye view (fig. 104). This relief is too poorly preserved to determine whether it originally bore an overall wave pattern as background for the other compositional units, but in other reliefs of this king, a bird's-eye view is achieved without the aid of a unifying background pattern. The subject of these reliefs is usually booty processions, and the best examples achieve, through a combination of vertical stacking and diminution, a remarkably illusionistic representation of deep space. In one of these reliefs, as Groenewegen-Frankfort has observed, background animals recede along a

FIG. 103. Enemy fleeing to an island city, Slab 17a, Room B, Northwest Palace of Assurnasirpal II, Nimrud, w. 224 cm. British Museum, WAA 124538 (photo: Trustees of the British Museum).

FIG. 104. Island city, engraving of a relief from the Central Palace of Tiglath-pileser III, Nimrud (from Layard 1849a, vol. 2, 395).

FIG. 105. Sheep and goats taken as booty, Central Palace of Tiglath-pileser III, Nimrud, w. 160 cm. British Museum, WAA 118881 (photo: Trustees of the British Museum).

Fig. 106.   Carrion bird following a battle, Central Palace of Tiglath-pileser III, Nimrud, w. 183 cm. British Museum, WAA 118907 (photo: Trustees of the British Museum).

gradual diagonal; in another, sheep and goats are arranged in an approximation of perspectival diminution to give a composition that is virtually seamless (fig. 105).[13]

The spatial coherence of these images is achieved primarily through two means. First, the size of all the figures relative to the height of the register is reduced. This prevents the foreground figures from dominating the composition and also allows for sufficient "stacking" of figures vertically to create a clear sense of middle ground and background. Second, the artist minimizes overlapping of figures on the lower ground line, thereby minimizing the effect of recession at the level of the ground line. Indeed, it appears as if the artists of these reliefs were aware of the incompatibility of worm's-eye and bird's-eye views, since compositions that employ vertical stacking use a minimum of overlapping, while compositions that for various reasons are tied to the ground line also employ a much greater degree of overlap while avoiding the use of "hovering" figures (except flying birds, which emphasize that the upper space is *intended* as air and not solid ground; fig. 106).[14]

The perspective of Tiglath-pileser's reliefs still isn't completely convincing. The city siege scenes in particular still suffer from pronounced inconsistencies in the scale of the figures and shift between bird's-eye and worm's eye viewpoint from slab to slab.[15] But, in general, it is easier to comprehend the space represented in Tiglath-pileser's reliefs than in Assurnasirpal II's.

With one notable exception, the palace reliefs of Sargon II, like those of Assurnasirpal but unlike Tiglath-pileser's, adopt a ground-level viewpoint. The majority of figures shown elevated above the ground line are those standing on some sort of eminence—such as a hill or city wall—and those that fall from the walls of besieged cities. On a few occasions, however, Assyrian soldiers and siege machines climb the face of a city mound, and one pursuit sequence shows hovering dead enemies (see figs. 16, 120).[16] This predominant use of the low viewpoint gives Sargon's reliefs a consistency that was lacking in the reliefs of his predecessors, but it also emphasizes the two principal drawbacks of this low viewpoint. First, the pictorial space looks extremely shallow, with all compositional elements sticking to the picture plane. Second, the discontinuity in scale between figures in a single composition is now worse than ever. This is because Sargon's artists show enemy cities at a scale even smaller than did their predecessors, apparently in order to maximize the amount of particularizing details, such as high mounds and multiple walls. At the same time, attacking Assyrians are still shown standing the full height of the register; it is hard to see how they could do otherwise, assuming the artist wished to retain the low viewpoint, since reducing the attackers to the scale of the defenders would have left large amounts of empty surface at the tops of the slabs, to say nothing of making the Assyrians look insignificant.

The result of Sargon's combination of a low, worm's-eye view and inconsistent figure scale is that many of these reliefs are spatially completely incoherent. While straightforward compositions such as processions are clear enough, the space represented in more complex examples, such as battle scenes, is impossible to interpret on purely perceptual grounds. That is to say, no amount of study will enable the viewer to visualize a coherent space that will account for the optical data. Indeed, though the consistency of viewpoint in Sargon's reliefs may be seen as an advance over Tiglath-pileser's, the latter's reliefs are generally easier to read. The disturbing effects of the incongruities of scale in Sargon's reliefs may have played a role in Sennacherib's abandonment of this perspective in favor of a different one.

In terms of representing space, one of the major problems with the narrative reliefs of Assurnasirpal, Tiglath-pileser, and Sargon is the relief format itself. The two narrow registers that remained after the slab was divided by the text band were simply not tall enough to permit the representation of deep space while maintaining a reasonably monumental figure scale. One relief series in Sargon's palace confronted this problem in a new way. At the east end of the north wall of the outer court (VIII) of Sargon's throne room was carved a narrative series showing the sea transport of roofing timber (fig. 107).[17] The most novel feature of this series is that the slabs are not divided horizontally by a band of inscription; rather, a single composition covers the

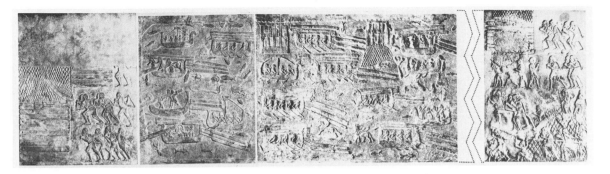

FIG. 107. Transport of timber as reassembled by Albenda, Slabs 0–4, Facade n, northwest wall of Court VIII, Sargon's palace, Khorsabad. Louvre AO 19888–91 (from Albenda 1983, pl. 8–9, courtesy of Pauline Albenda; photos from Musée du Louvre/AO).

entire three-meter height of the slab. Here, Sargon's artist adopted a high viewpoint that allowed him to depict a very deep space through the use of vertical stacking of compositional elements. The central slabs of the series show boats in an island-studded sea or river. The entire height of these slabs is covered with a wave pattern, reminiscent of that in Assurnasirpal's river-crossing scene. Boats, logs, marine life, and island cities are arrayed freely across the central slabs in a much-expanded version of Tiglath-pileser's maritime scene. To either side is a single slab, one showing the embarkation, the other the debarkation, of timber. The perspective of these end slabs is consistent with that of the central ones—a bird's-eye view of workmen moving logs. Some of these workmen stand against a scale pattern representing mountains, while others are placed against a neutral background.

This relief series is innovative for several reasons. First, by omitting the text band, the entire height of the slab is made available for the construction of a deep space. Second, it adopts a high viewpoint, which is used consistently throughout the series. Finally, there is very little disproportion in the scale of the figures. Though the figures on land are shown slightly larger than those on the water, the difference is not sufficiently dramatic to disrupt the spatial integrity of the composition. Though the artist makes no effort to indicate perspectival diminution—the foreground figures are the same size as those in the background—this scarcely affects the spatial illusion. The reason for this would seem to be that the combination of high viewpoint and small figure scale have the effect of distancing the viewer from the scene; diminution is not so apparent when a subject is viewed from a distance.[18] Furthermore, though this is not apparent from a small-scale reproduction, the con-

199

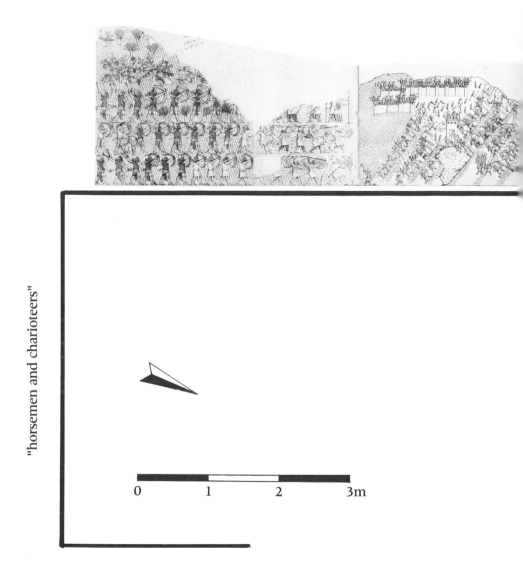

"horsemen and charioteers"

0   1   2   3m

FIG. 108. The siege of Lachish as reassembled by the author, Room XXXVI, Southwest Palace, Nineveh.

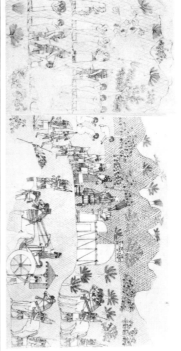

siderable height of the slabs, three meters, would result in some degree of natural diminution, at least from close up, since the top of the slab will be farthest from the viewer's eye.

This was the most consistent and most convincing representation of deep space yet to appear in an Assyrian palace, and in view of the conservative perspective of the remainder of the narrative reliefs in Sargon's palace, its appearance is cause for some surprise. It is possible to account for the absence of the text register here by observing that none of Sargon's courtyard reliefs bore inscriptions. This does not help explain why such a narrative scene should have been chosen for this location in the first place, since all of Sargon's other courtyard reliefs depicted single-register tribute processions. It is tempting to see the hand of the crown prince, Sennacherib, here. Indeed, it is known that he was involved in the construction of his father's palace, but what role, if any, he played in the design of the reliefs is unknown.[19] What does seem clear is that Sargon's timber transport relief series influenced the composition of the reliefs of the next Assyrian palace, that of Sennacherib at Nineveh.

Sennacherib's spatial innovations have less to do with the "invention" of a deep perspectival space, which was used to some degree by all of his predecessors, than with the consistent and widespread application of this type of perspective. By virtually eliminating the traditional subjects of tribute processions, banquets, punishment of captives, and worship, Sennacherib was also eliminating the very subjects that benefit from a shallow, low-viewpoint perspective. The subjects that remain—battle and building—are those that because of their spatial complexity had proven least satisfactory in the low-viewpoint, narrow-register format. Sennacherib, or his artists, must have considered this problem, for the central text register has been eliminated from all of his wall reliefs. To this expanded surface his artists applied a perspective very similar to that of Sargon's timber transport reliefs, combining a high viewpoint, relatively small-scale figures, and minimal overlapping.

The best-preserved relief series from Sennacherib's palace, the Room XXXVI reliefs showing the siege of Lachish, serves as an excellent illustration of Sennacherib's perspective construction (figs. 108, 109, 110, 111, 112, 113). Room XXXVI was a relatively small room and the Lachish episode occupied all four walls. The setting is a wooded mountainous landscape, indicated by the traditional scale pattern covering nearly the entire height of the slabs. This scale pattern is bounded at the top of the slabs by an undulating line that defines the contours of the mountains in the background. This upper contour, which functions as a horizon, is something new in Assyrian re-

F<small>IG</small>. 109.   The siege of Lachish, drawing of Slabs 5–6, Room XXXVI, Southwest Palace, Nineveh. British Museum, WAA, Or. Dr., I, 58 (photo: Trustees of the British Museum).

liefs. In "correctly" constructed perspectives, the horizon defines the level of the viewer's eye, and here too the high horizon serves the viewer as a confirmation of the high viewpoint implied by the sharply rising ground plane below it.

The majority of figures here are arranged on a series of ground lines, which serve to organize the spatial recession vertically. Unlike the inflexible register divisions in the reliefs of his predecessors, however, Sennacherib's ground lines are never allowed to assume an identity independent of the figures, and they may slant, shift, or terminate to suit the requirements of the figural arrangement. The figures themselves are relatively small, their height rarely exceeding one-fifth of the height of the slab. Most figures are roughly the same size. The soldiers who man the siege ramps and the defenders of the city are somewhat smaller than the figures on neighboring slabs, but the visually disruptive effect of the scale pattern that separates the larger and smaller figures makes the discrepancy less noticeable than it might be otherwise.

The composition is read from left to right. The preserved portion com-

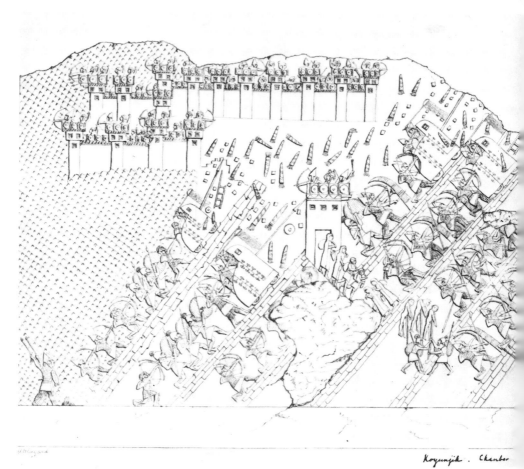

FIG. 110.   The siege of Lachish, drawing of Slabs 7–8, Room XXXVI, Southwest Palace, Nineveh. British Museum, WAA, Or. Dr., I, 59 (photo: Trustees of the British Museum).

mences with three files of Assyrian attackers, each occupying a ground line. This pattern of horizontals is then interrupted by the dramatic diagonals of the siege ramps, followed by two files of defeated Lachishites moving right. These files slant gradually upward and eventually converge on a hillock represented by a single ground line located midway up the slab. Atop this is the king, further elevated above his surroundings by the high throne on which he sits. Also setting the figure of the king apart from the rest is a pair of epigraphs that horizontally bracket his head and signify to literate and nonliter-

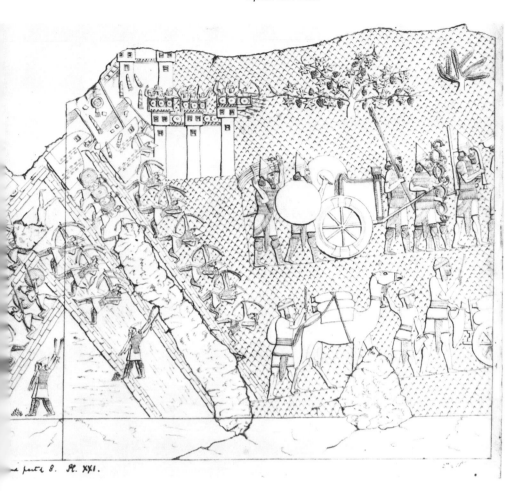

ate alike that *this* figure is someone special (see fig. 3). The king emerges as the single most prominent figure in the composition, not by being shown physically larger than his fellows, but rather because he occupies a visually privileged space.

Ussishkin's recent excavations at Tell ed-Duweir, ancient Lachish, have provided convincing evidence that Sennacherib was concerned with spatial verisimilitude not for its own sake, but rather as a means of constructing the image of a very particular place. Those excavations showed that in the Assyr-

FIG. 111. The siege of Lachish, drawing of Slabs 9–10, Room XXXVI, Southwest Palace, Nineveh. British Museum, WAA, Or. Dr., I, 60 (photo: Trustees of the British Museum).

FIG. 112. The siege of Lachish, drawing of Slabs 11–12, Room XXXVI, Southwest Palace, Nineveh. British Museum, WAA, Or. Dr., I, 61 (photo: Trustees of the British Museum).

ian period, Lachish was a double-walled city high atop a mound. Its only approach was via a ramp that ran diagonally up the side of the mound to a towered gate in the outer wall. The Assyrians breached the inner wall by building against it a massive siege ramp, portions of which still survive, at the southwest corner of the mound (fig. 114).[20]

The double walls and the locations of the approach ramp, towered gate, and siege ramp all correspond closely to Sennacherib's picture of the event in Room XXXVI. Ussishkin suggested that the Assyrian relief artists attained this degree of accuracy by working from drawings made on the spot during the campaign, but I am not sure this hypothesis is defensible. The only evi-

FIG. 113.   The siege of Lachish, drawing of Slab 13, Room XXXVI, Southwest Palace, Nineveh. British Museum, WAA, Or. Dr., I, 62 (photo: Trustees of the British Museum).

FIG. 114. Lachish, modern aerial view of mound (reproduced courtesy of David Ussishkin).

dence for such drawings is the apparent accuracy of the finished reliefs in details such as costume, topographical details, and architecture. In the Lachish reliefs, however, there is a significant difference between the excavated outer city wall, which appeared to be little but a low, unfortified retaining wall, and the outer wall as represented in the reliefs, shown fortified with regularly spaced towers full of defending Lachishites.[21] This, it seems to me, is the sort of discrepancy one would hardly expect to find in a drawing made on the spot, but which might occur in a written description of the city translated into visual terms. In this latter scenario, it is easy to imagine "wall" in a written description being translated into its most familiar visual form, that is, a towered fortification, even if this convention does not in fact correspond to the appearance of the original.

The details that do exist in the reliefs could, I believe, have been drawn wholly from written campaign accounts and interviews with participants from both sides. In this context two things should be remembered. First, many inhabitants of captured cities were deported to Assyria, so it should not have been difficult to locate Lachishites to interview; Barnett observed that men wearing the costume of the Lachishites were shown among the laborers in the bull-hauling scenes of Court VI and in the royal bodyguard in the Ishtar Temple procession. Second, Sennacherib's palace was being built and decorated at the same time the first few campaigns were being conducted; the relief designers could draw on recent memories, unclouded by time, to insure the accuracy of their images. Thus we might expect to find greater accuracy in the early campaign reliefs of Sennacherib than in those of Assyrian kings whose palaces date to the later part of their reign.[22]

Whatever the explanation for this accuracy, it is clear that the Lachish shown in the relief is intended to be recognizable. Indeed, its combination of topography, costume, and architectural features is so specific that it seems probable that anyone who had seen the city itself would recognize its image in the reliefs, whether or not he or she could read the captions. This degree of visual specificity was without precedent in Assyrian reliefs and was only made possible by the expanded pictorial field available to Sennacherib's artists.[23]

The spatial organization of most of Sennacherib's narrative reliefs is essentially comparable to that of the Lachish series, with most variations attributable to attempts to show different types of topography. In the throne room (I), for example, which also depicted the campaign to the west, most slabs are covered with the same scale pattern found in the Lachish room. Two slabs (numbers 14 and 15) in this series, however, which apparently show the city of Tyre, are decorated with a maritime scene very similar in composition and detail to Sargon's timber-transport scene (see fig. 85). Nowhere else was Sennacherib's debt to the palace relief of his predecessor expressed more clearly than here.

An unusual variation of the western landscape was found in Room XXXVIII. Here Sennacherib's army is shown marching through a river valley in mountainous countryside (fig. 115). The nature of this landscape, which rises sharply to either side of the wide river that meanders in the center, is expressed above with the usual mountainous contour defining a horizon near the top of the slab and below by a similar contour representing mountains that point *downward* from the river and likewise define a horizon. That is, the composition shows essentially symmetrical trees and mountains, those above pointing up and those below, down, with the central river serving as the axis of symmetry. From the vantage point of the viewer, standing outside looking in, this is not a very convincing perspective, but it is a remarkably accurate approximation of the view experienced by the figure of the king in the composition, who is marching down in the valley by the river. In other words, the perspective presented here is subject-centered, instead of being viewer-centered, the subject here being the king, and the view is the one experienced by the principal figure within the composition itself.[24]

The mountainous countryside of Sennacherib's second campaign, to the

209

FIG. 115. Assyrian army marching along a river, drawing of Slabs 14–15, Room XXXVIII, Southwest Palace, Nineveh. British Museum, WAA, Or. Dr., I, 45 (photo: Trustees of the British Museum).

east, is presented using essentially the same conventions as were used for the west, except that all of the representations of the eastern campaign include a small river the course of which the Assyrians seem to follow. This feature is not unexpected since, as was seen in chapter 7, access to this portion of the Zagros is via the Diyala River and its tributaries.[25] In one room showing the eastern campaign, Room LX, the artist may have resorted to the inverted foreground mountains of Room XXXVIII to represent this river valley. In the rooms for which eastern campaign slabs or drawings are preserved, however, the mountains are all shown upright, while the river may flow across the foreground, middle ground, or background of the slab, or even, in the course of a complete relief series (Room V), may meander from foreground to background.[26]

The most remarkable such series, though only partially published, is that from the south and west walls of Court VI. The first scene, on Slab 1, estab-

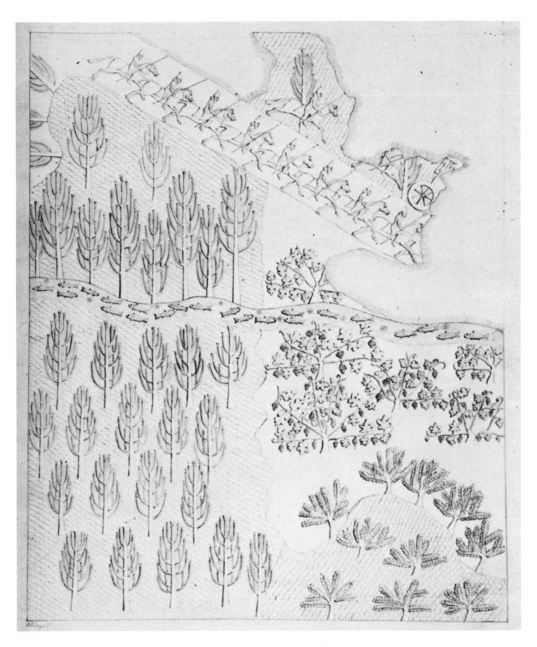

F<small>IG</small>. 116.   Assyrian army in the mountains, drawing of Slab 1, Court VI, Southwest Palace, Nineveh. British Museum, WAA, Or. Dr., IV, 43 (photo: Trustees of the British Museum).

lishes the setting (fig. 116). Nearly the entire height of the left half of this slab is covered with conifer-studded mountains, represented by the scale pattern traditional in Assyrian art, in the midst of which flows a small river. The right half of the slab opens out into a river valley filled with grapevines and bounded by low hills in the foreground.

Into this broad valley ride the minute figures of the Assyrian king and army, entering the composition from the upper left corner and galloping diagonally down across the mountains. Never before in Assyrian art had the image of the king been so thoroughly dominated by his surroundings. And yet, visually, the accomplishment of the king has not diminished with his apparent stature, for the point of this image is one that often recurs in the Assyrian annals—that the king with his army mastered the mountains themselves, on the way to further triumphs over the peoples beyond them. Visitors unfamiliar with Assyrian spatial conventions might see little glory in crossing mountains that appear to rise no more than knee-high, which is the effect of

FIG. 117. Sargon II in the mountains, engraving of Slab 7, Room 13, Sargon's palace, Khorsabad (from Botta and Flandin 1849, vol. 2, 143).

the mountain-crossing scenes of Sennacherib's predecessor (fig. 117). It is only through the use of this deep perspective that Sennacherib's artist is able to present to all viewers a visual approximation of the verbal boast inscribed on the colossi at the main entrance to the throne room: "In the mountains, I rode on horseback over difficult terrain; in extremely rough areas, I charged through on foot like a wild bull."[27]

The immediate continuation of this slab is, unfortunately, lost, but further along in the series is the same landscape of low hills in the foreground with open river valley above (see fig. 69). Distributed across this space are Assyrian soldiers and their enemies, fighting in the hills and along the river or forming processions of booty and prisoners. The figures are all roughly the same scale, and once again the consistent use of a high viewpoint, with figures stacked above one another in the composition, results in a visually intelligible representation of deep space.

The landscape of the third area in which Sennacherib campaigned, Babylonia, required somewhat different representational conventions. The flat terrain of this region, the principal natural feature of which is the date palm, did not lend itself to the sort of overall background pattern employed in mountain or maritime scenes. To be sure, a background pattern of water and reeds could be employed in representations of marsh battles, as in Rooms LXIV and LXX, but such scenes seem to have occupied, at most, only two or three slabs in any given series (see fig. 88). The remainder of the Babylonian slabs show city sieges and booty processions against a background of palm trees, and these seem usually to be organized into registers. Reade has suggested that in Room III, a natural feature—a small river—replaces the inscribed text band of Sennacherib's predecessors as a means of dividing the composition into two independent registers (see fig. 78).[28] This may be correct, but it is also possible that here Sennacherib's artist is using these strips of water as a means of organizing what is intended as a single coherent space, rather than two unrelated registers. The problem in understanding the spatial organization of the Babylonian scenes results in part from too few of these slabs being published. It is not yet possible to reconstruct any of these series sufficiently to determine whether a consistent perspective was used, or intended, throughout.

One of Sennacherib's most remarkable perspective representations was that of the colossus quarrying and transport scenes, already discussed in chapter 5, on the north and east walls of Court VI. In these scenes, Sennacherib's artists present views of various landscapes from the vicinity of Nineveh itself. The beginning of the series shows the mountainous landscape around the Balaṭai quarries, and as the viewer moves leftward through the transport series, the landscape shifts first to a reed marsh and then to a conifer forest with a large river, probably the Tigris, in the background (see figs. 50, 57, 58). All of these landscapes are viewed from a consistently high angle, with figures more or less freely disposed in space. In one scene, as Groenewegen-Frankfort has observed, files of figures are arranged in diagonals without the benefit either of ground lines or of an overall background pattern (see fig. 54). Here the artist demonstrates that figures alone, without other conventions, may *define* pictorial space, rather than simply exist in it.[29] The result is a space that is remarkably coherent, even by post-Renaissance standards.

I can suggest two nonexclusive explanations for Sennacherib's frequent use of this new type of spatial representation. First, the king seems to have been interested in projecting an image of himself as an innovator. In his palace building accounts, Sennacherib boasts that he discovered new quarries, developed a new method of casting bronze, and designed a new type of well structure, and he also claims other innovations in materials or methods.[30] This emphasis on the king's innovative contributions to the building process is itself an innovation and contrasts with the building texts of earlier kings, which are little more than straightforward descriptions of the structure with no reference to the king's role in its construction. Sennacherib's introduction of new spatial effects is consistent with this pattern; for viewers accustomed to traditional Assyrian spatial conventions, this would have been a clearly visible innovation.

A second explanation could be that Sennacherib felt that reliefs organized on the new spatial principles would function better than the previous ones. This proposal is difficult to investigate, since the intended function of these reliefs is unknown. Narrative reliefs are only specifically mentioned twice in Assyrian texts: once in Sargon II's palace building account and again in a Sennacherib foundation text that was modeled on the Sargon account.[31] In both cases the reliefs are only briefly described, with no reference to their purpose.

In order to determine if Sennacherib's reliefs might function more successfully than those of his predecessors, it is necessary to know who their audience was, and that is the subject of the next chapter. For the moment, it is sufficient to mention two points. First, to our eyes, Sennacherib's perspective seems to be a step toward greater naturalism, toward presenting the world as it actually looks, or might look, to an observer. This more "natural" perspective appears concurrently with another remarkable feature in Sennacherib's sculptures that suggests an interest in greater naturalism. The human-headed bull and lion colossi of Sennacherib's predecessors were furnished with five legs, apparently in order to insure that both the front and side views would be complete (see figs. 11, 12). Though this may be a logical solution to the requirement of two ideal views, from non-ideal vantages the viewer is confronted with the anomaly of a five-legged bull. Sennacherib deleted the fifth leg, creating a bull that is less perfect conceptually (the side view shows only three legs), but far more convincing perceptually (see fig. 48). One might argue, then, that Sennacherib's new perspective was similarly conceived as an effort toward greater naturalism.

The second point is that what we may see as "greater naturalism" is not necessarily synonymous with "greater legibility," at least not for all audiences. A member of the Assyrian court at the beginning of Sennacherib's reign would have been familiar only with the narrow registers, low viewing angle, and overlapping figures of the narrative reliefs of Assurnasirpal II, Tiglath-pileser III, and Sargon II. To a viewer accustomed to these conventions, the considerably wider register of Sennacherib's reliefs, with figures scattered helter-skelter across its surface, might initially have made very little sense. To communicate his exploits visually to this audience, Sennacherib might have been better off retaining the familiar conventions of spatial representation of his predecessors. Audiences unfamiliar with the earlier Assyrian spatial conventions, by contrast, approaching Sennacherib's narrative reliefs with fewer preconceptions, might well have found them as legible as the earlier reliefs, but we cannot know this for certain since we cannot judge the degree of visual literacy of such audiences.[32]

Evidence that Sennacherib's perspective may have been considered successful is to be found in Room XXXIII of the Southwest Palace. There his grandson, Assurbanipal, carved a representation of the Ulai River battle, which also employs Sennacherib's spatial conventions. Assurbanipal's later North Palace reliefs, however, return to the format of two or three discrete registers, and overlapping once again becomes the preferred means of indicating depth. This abandonment of Sennacherib's more dramatic innovations suggests that for some viewers Sennacherib's reliefs may have been insufficiently intelligible.[33]

Time

In a number of Sennacherib's reliefs, space is used as an analogue of time, that is, the progression of figures through the continuous space represented in the reliefs is used to express temporal sequence. This in itself was not Sen-

215

FIG. 118.   Assurnasirpal II on campaign, Slabs 3b–7b, Room B, Northwest Palace, Nimrud, total w. 10.64 m. British Museum, WAA 124549, 124552, 124554, 124556, and Or. Dr., III, NW 10 (photos: Trustees of the British Museum).

FIG. 119.   Shalmaneser III on campaign, Band II, bronze gates, Balawat, w. of flat (left) part: 145 cm (photo: Trustees of the British Museum).

nacherib's invention—the same usage occurred in the reliefs of his predecessors. Sennacherib, however, applied the idea on such a grand scale and with such consistency as to make most earlier efforts appear somewhat tentative by comparison. The general development of the representation of sequence in Assyrian art has been studied by Reade, so I will only discuss here those aspects that are of particular importance for an appreciation of Sennacherib's art.[34]

Sennacherib's artists use two different techniques for representing temporal succession through spatial progression. One of these is to show several consecutive narrative episodes within a single unvarying landscape setting, while the other is to repeat the same subject several times while varying the background detail. The earliest clear occurrence of the first technique in an Assyrian palace is on the lower register of Slabs 3 to 7 of Assurnasirpal II's Northwest Palace throne room (fig. 118).[35] This series, which is read from

right to left, commences with an Assyrian attack on an enemy city and concludes with a procession of prisoners marched into the presence of the king.
The visual indicators that this represents two episodes of the same event are,
first, the continuity of direction, with most figures proceeding from right to
left, and second, continuity of space, that is, the space of the second episode
continues that of the first without visual disruption.

The same sequence recurs, in expanded form, on several of the bronze
bands of the gates of Shalmaneser III from Balawat. The most complete representation of a single event, in terms of sequence, is from the lower register
of Band II (fig. 119).[36] The action here proceeds from left to right and shows
the approach of the Assyrian chariotry, cavalry, and infantry, the attack on an
enemy city, and the marching off of prisoners and booty after the battle. The
elements of this sequence, as will be seen, are virtually identical with those
of Sennacherib's Lachish series (Room XXXVI).

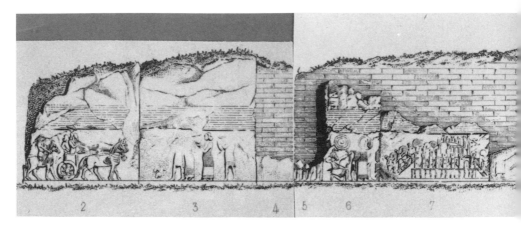

FIG. 120. Sargon II on campaign, Slabs 2–12, Room 2, Sargon's palace, Khorsabad (from Botta and Flandin 1849, vol. 1, 52).

This sort of temporal sequence also occurs in the palace reliefs of Tiglath-pileser III, though the evidence is fragmentary. In one example, the effectiveness of the Assyrian attack is emphasized by showing the image of the enemy city twice, instead of only once as in the examples of Assurnasirpal II and Shalmaneser III already discussed. Here the preserved part of the sequence begins with the traditional Assyrian siege of a city vigorously defended by its inhabitants, then follows a second image of the same city, but this time defeated and deserted, and only then comes the usual procession of prisoners and booty before the king.[37]

In the palace reliefs of Sargon, the most extended preserved temporal sequence dealing with a single event is in the lower register of Slabs 2 to 12 of Room 2, which shows the siege of Harhar (fig. 120). This series, which occupies a long stretch of wall between two doorways, is read from right to left. It shows the king in his chariot in the field running down eastern foes who retreat toward the city of Harhar, followed by the siege of the city itself, and concludes with booty and prisoners being marched before the king, who thus appears twice in the series. Similar battle sequences also occur elsewhere in Sargon's palace. A variation of this type of temporal sequence is in Sargon's Room 7. The entire lower register of this small room's reliefs was devoted to the relatively peaceful pastime of a royal hunting expedition. The landscape background throughout this series is a conifer forest, presumably not far from Khorsabad. Reade has observed that three successive stages of the

hunt—the approach, the hunt itself, and a procession to a pavilion—are shown progressing from left to right against this constant background.[38]

The relatively small size of Room 7 facilitates the concise development of this narrative without the danger of overextending the length of any of its component episodes. That is to say, the long narrow format of Sargon's wall reliefs somewhat limits the length of these temporal narratives, since to devote too much wall space to any single episode, as would be necessary in a large room, might result in the viewer losing the narrative thread. This may be one reason why in larger rooms, such as in Rooms 2 and 5, the artist does not show a single temporal sequence, but rather combines several of these sequences into a series depicting passage through both time *and* space. These will be discussed later.

The best-preserved example of a temporal sequence dealing with a single event in Sennacherib's palace is the Lachish series in Room XXXVI (see fig. 108). As with Sargon's Room 7, all the Room XXXVI reliefs are devoted to this single narrative, presenting the event in the now standard sequence of approach, attack, and aftermath. There are two features, however, that distinguish Sennacherib's presentation of this sequence from that of his predecessors. First, in Sennacherib's reliefs the vertical expansion of the picture field permits the artist to include greater narrative detail without extending the horizontal length of each segment to the point where the coherence of the narrative is in danger. Second, the more expansive landscape patterns of

FIG. 121. Assyrian army approaching city of Alammu, drawing of Slabs 4–6, Room XIV, Southwest Palace, Nineveh. British Museum, WAA, Or. Dr., IV, 57 (photo: Trustees of the British Museum).

Sennacherib's reliefs provide a strong visual link between segments, emphasizing the continuity of location from one segment to the next and thereby strengthening the unity of the narrative.

This sort of temporal record of the capture of a single enemy city seems to have been the subject of choice for most of the smaller rooms in Sennacherib's palace. An example from Room XIV, showing the siege of Alammu, is largely preserved (see figs. 17, 18, 121). Structurally, its layout is very similar to the siege of Lachish and is of interest because it includes more of the episode showing the approach of the Assyrian army than is preserved in the Lachish series. Several other similar examples are known as well, either from Layard's drawings or from written descriptions.[39]

The second type of temporal narrative repeats essentially the same subject several times while varying background detail. This is the sort of narrative usually chosen for rooms whose walls are too long to sustain the sort of simple sequence just discussed. The most extensive pre-Sennacherib examples were in Rooms 2 and 5 of Sargon's palace (see fig. 120).[40] In the reliefs of both of these rooms, the spatial and temporal progress of the Assyrian king and army on campaign is indicated by showing the king and army repeatedly, always proceeding in the same direction, against a background that changes to show the various cities that are captured in the course of the campaign. The emphasis in these sequences is primarily spatial, that is, the changing background documents the progress of the Assyrians from point to point through space. The repetition of individual elements such as the figure of the king, however, serves as a cue that these sequences also have a temporal component, since no figure can exist simultaneously in two places. In these reliefs, then, progress through time is the inevitable corollary of progress through space and is in contrast with the type of sequence first discussed, where space is a metaphor for time.

Sennacherib's artists employed this same sort of sequence in the relief decoration of the larger rooms of the Southwest Palace.[41] In Room V, where reliefs from all four walls were drawn or described by Layard, the Assyrian army is shown moving rightward through mountainous countryside capturing the enemy cities in its path. The figure of Sennacherib occurred at least five times and, with each occurrence, serves as a visual milestone along the temporal path of the army, just as the succession of defeated cities serves to punctuate the army's progress through space.[42]

An interesting variation of this more extended sort of spatial/temporal sequence occurs in the colossus transport series of the north and east walls of Sennacherib's Court VI. In this peaceful scene, the spatial progress of the colossi is indicated not by a succession of different cities against a constant landscape background, but rather by varying the landscape itself. As already noted in the discussion of the perspective of this series, the action commences in mountainous countryside and progresses first past a reed marsh and then through a forest by a river.[43]

These dramatic shifts in landscape, each of which might ordinarily characterize an entire region, may seem surprising in view of Sennacherib's statement that the Balaṭai quarries were "near Nineveh."[44] In fact, however, Sennacherib's artists are here depicting a very particular landscape—one presumably familiar to anyone who had traveled in the immediate northern environs of Nineveh. This familiarity on the part of both artist and a large part of the audience encouraged a particularity of detail that would have been neither practical nor desirable in the representations of distant landscapes, where a more generic approach would be more likely to insure at least general recognition of the subject region among audiences who may never have been there. That is to say, in depicting very familiar landscapes the artist may emphasize particularizing features, such as an abrupt shift from mountain to marsh, and this would only serve to aid the viewer's own identification of the setting, but in the case of representations of distant landscapes traversed by the king on campaign, the same sort of shift, even if it reflects the actual terrain, would probably be interpreted by the unsuspecting viewer as a spatial leap from one corner of the empire to another.

In addition to showing spatial progress in an unusual way, the colossus transport series also places much more emphasis on temporal sequence than do other examples of this sort of extended narrative. This is accomplished not by repeating the same central, but unchanged, figures periodically throughout the series, as was done with the king and army in Room V, but rather by varying the appearance of the central figure, here the bull colossus, to reflect different stages of completion. Thus, at the beginning of the series the bull is but a block in the quarry, for transport its form is roughed out, and it takes on its final appearance only in the final scene as it is dragged into the palace (see figs. 50, 60, 61). The subject of this series, then, itself exhibits a process of temporal evolution that is the by-product of its spatial progress through the narrative. In short, this series represents not only the passage of a subject through time, but the effect of time on that subject as well. In this respect it foreshadows narrative sequences of Assurbanipal, notably the Ulai River battle and lion hunts, where a single subject, such as a lion or enemy king, is represented several times, successively transformed by the temporal progress of the narrative.[45]

Summary

Sennacherib's artists, taking advantage of the greatly expanded pictorial field made available by the deletion of the text band, refined their predecessors' experiments in the representation of space and time and presented narrative sequences that in their overall spatial and temporal coherence were unprecedented. Sennacherib's palace reliefs are the first in Assyrian art to employ consistently a high viewpoint and surface patterning in order to represent a visually satisfactory perspective. They are also the first (as in the colossus transport series) to depict a temporal narrative sequence in which both the background and the subject are transformed as the sequence progresses.

In order to appreciate the purpose and effect of Sennacherib's innovations, however, it is necessary not only to be able to define these innovations, but also to know something of the goals of the king responsible for them and to know something of the audience to which they were addressed. These are the subjects of the next two chapters.

10

AUDIENCE

It is characteristic of a message delivered via any medium of communication that we cannot begin fully to understand its intended meaning or meanings unless we can also determine to whom that message is addressed. This is because the basic elements of the medium—be they groups of words or arrangements of forms—that are combined to express the message are liable to carry different connotations for different receivers. This is particularly true for visual media, where the image itself is universally accessible, though its intended meaning may not be. Thus, to take a hypothetical example, an Assyrian relief that shows the king defeating inhabitants of the Zagros would mean quite different things to different viewers. For a tributary from the Zagros visiting the capital, such an image would serve as a warning to keep up payments and not interfere in the affairs of Assyria. For an Assyrian official from the provincial capital of Arrapha, at the foot of the Zagros, the message would be one of reassurance that foreign neighbors are under control and that the borders are secure. And for a functionary stationed at the royal court in Nineveh itself, the image would serve as an affirmation of the magnitude and extent of the power of Assyria and particularly of its head, the king.

The precise function of every decorated room in each Assyrian palace may never be known, and therefore it may not always be possible to determine who would have been permitted to see a given relief series. Nevertheless, there are numerous references in both texts and images to classes of people who either visited or lived in the palaces and who consequently would have been exposed to at least some of the reliefs in the more public areas. These people would constitute the *actual* audience for these reliefs, though that doesn't necessarily mean that the reliefs were *intended* for each and every one of these groups. That is to say that though a list of people who could have been impressed by the reliefs can be assembled fairly readily, it is more difficult to determine who the reliefs were actually meant to impress. The former, those who might have seen the reliefs, is the subject of this chapter, while the latter, those who were supposed to see the reliefs, will be considered in the next.[1]

The Neo-Assyrian Sources

Information concerning visitors to and inhabitants of the royal palace in the Assyrian capital can be gleaned from a variety of original sources. These sources are first treated individually below, and the information on audience thus gathered is then synthesized and summarized at the end of the chapter.

The "Banquet Stele"

The text on this slab, which was found in the outer court of Assurnasirpal II's Northwest Palace at Nimrud (ancient Kalhu), describes the building of Kalhu and the consecration of the new palace therein.[2] The portion dealing with the consecration of the palace is particularly interesting in the present context since it gives a fairly detailed list of the numbers and types of people who were invited to that celebration. These consisted of "47,074 men and women from all districts of my land; 5,000 foreign dignitaries, envoys of the people of the lands Suhu, Hindanu, Patina, Hatti, Tyre, Sidon, Gurgum, Malatya, Hubushkia, Gilzanu, Kummuh, and Muṣaṣir; 16,000 people of the city Kalhu; and 1,500 functionaries from all my palaces." In all, the text reports, 69,574 people from Kalhu and "all lands" were hosted for ten days, after which Assurnasirpal sent "them back to their lands in peace and joy."[3]

Though the dedication of a new royal palace was not an event that recurred regularly in the reign of an individual king, it is nonetheless of great importance for an investigation of the audience for neo-Assyrian reliefs, for it was probably the single largest gathering of guests that a palace was likely to experience.[4] To be sure, the text does not specifically state that all of these people actually toured the palace. In view of the nature of the celebration, however, which would appear to have been to show off the new building, it seems reasonable to suppose that many, if not all, of the guests saw at least the most public areas, namely the outer court (D/E) and the throne room (B; see fig. 7). These, as it happens, are the very areas decorated with those subjects (namely, tribute processions and campaign narratives) that would be expected most successfully to impress a wide range of viewers. The potential impact of this single event is emphasized, moreover, by the statement that all of these visitors returned to their own lands and were thus allowed to spread the word of the magnificence of the king's new palace.

There is one other passage in the "Banquet Stele" that is of interest in an investigation of audience. The text states that at the time the new palace was consecrated, Assurnasirpal "invited inside Ashur, the great lord, and the gods of the entire land."[5] While it is difficult to determine to what degree the reliefs were "intended" for the gods of Assyria, it is clear from this text, as well as from others to be discussed below, that the gods were considered to be residents of, or at least occasional visitors to, the palace, and therefore they too were a potential audience for the reliefs.

The Royal Annals

Assurnasirpal II

The "Nimrud Monolith," erected by Assurnasirpal II at the entrance to the Ninurta Temple in Nimrud, concludes its account of the building of the Northwest Palace with a lengthy passage beginning, "May a later prince restore its weakened (portions and) restore my inscribed name to its place."[6] The passage then continues with a description of how this "later prince" should restore the palace in order to earn Assurnasirpal's blessing and also what he must not do to avoid Assurnasirpal's curse. This message, addressed to future users of the palace, indicates that for Assurnasirpal posterity played an important role in the preservation of his palace, and therefore future kings would likewise have formed one component of the audience for the reliefs.

The role of future kings as audience for the reliefs is made even more explicit in another text that contains a very brief account of the building of the Northwest Palace: "I built that palace for the gaze(?) of rulers and princes forever (and) decorated it in a splendid fashion."[7]

Sargon II

The next king whose annals provide information on audience is Sargon II. Since all of this king's Khorsabad texts are closely related, they will be dealt with as a group here. In Sargon's palace, the annalistic text band of Rooms 2, 5, 13, and 14, as well as the summary text from Room 14, concludes with the request that a "future prince among the kings, my sons, restore the ruins of that palace."[8] All of the wall text bands, as well as the gateway bull text and two of the threshold texts, report that upon the completion of the palace the gods were invited inside. The most specific account, the summary text of Room 14, states, "I invited Assur, father of the gods, the great lord, and Ishtar, who dwell in Assyria, into its midst."[9] Both future kings and the gods, therefore, were still parts of the audience for Sargon's reliefs, just as they had been for those of Assurnasirpal.

Also like Assurnasirpal, Sargon reports a great festival at the dedication of his palace. To this, according to the annals and summary text, were invited "kings from (foreign) lands; the governors of my land; the overseers, commanders, nobles, high officials, and elders of Assyria."[10] One of the threshold texts furnishes further information about these foreign kings, stating that they were "princes of the four quarters (of the world), who had submitted to the yoke of my rule, whose lives I had spared."[11] As with Assurnasirpal, then, the dedication of the new palace provided an opportunity to gather together people from all parts of the empire and beyond.

An indication of another possible audience for Sargon's palace reliefs is given at the beginning of the palace building inscription in many of Sargon's Khorsabad texts: "with the (labor) of the enemy peoples my hands had captured, I built a city . . . and called its name Dur-Sharrukin."[12] Some part of this labor force would presumably still have been working on the palace during and after the time the reliefs were carved. Though it seems doubtful that these captive workers were part of the intended audience for the reliefs, they would nonetheless have been an interested audience, for the foreign cities carved on the reliefs would have been their own home towns, and the events depicted would have included their own capture at the hands of the Assyrian king. If any of these foreigners stayed on in the palace after its completion, say as craftsmen or servants, they would have been particularly able interpreters of the reliefs for visitors unfamiliar with their content.[13]

Sennacherib

The palace building accounts appended to Sennacherib's annals provide much the same information concerning audience as do those of Assurnasirpal II and Sargon II. Like his predecessors, Sennacherib invited the gods into his palace upon its completion, and he includes a message addressed to future kings concerning the restoration of the palace. He also records a celebration at the dedication of the palace to which were invited "the people of my land."[14]

Sennacherib, too, states that his palace was built with the help of foreign labor, and his account is of interest in that it gives the nationality of these foreigners. In his earliest palace building account, composed soon after the first campaign, Sennacherib says, "The people of Chaldea, the Aramaeans, the Manneans, (the people of) Que and Hilakku, who had not submitted to my yoke, I removed them hither, and made them carry the basket and mold bricks."[15] Where did Sennacherib find these workers? His first and only campaign at this point had been directed against the south. There he encountered Chaldeans and Arameans and he says that he took large numbers of them prisoner. He does not, however, mention Manneans or Cilicians among the enemy in that campaign. Indeed, he did not campaign against Hilakku and Que (Cilicia) until 696 B.C., after his fifth royal campaign, and even then he did not personally accompany his army. Furthermore, he apparently never campaigned in Mannea at all.[16] Since this earliest building account was probably composed around 703 or 702 B.C., and in any event could not have been composed as late as 696, the best way to account for the captives from Mannea, Que, and Hilakku this early in Sennacherib's reign is to assume that they were left over from the reign of Sargon II, who did campaign in these areas.[17]

One wonders if these captives possessed some special building skills that would account for their presence in the king's work force. Sennacherib specifies the task only of the Chaldeans—to transport reeds from the marshes in the south for the construction of the palace.[18] If the captives from Mannea, Que, and Hilakku date to Sargon's reign, then they may well have had considerable experience with Assyrian palace construction. Sargon's principal campaigns in these areas were in his sixth through ninth years, while the foundation of Dur Sharrukin (Khorsabad) dates to his fifth year. Captives from these campaigns, therefore, would have been among the most likely candidates for deportation and resettlement in Dur Sharrukin and probably constituted the main work force for the building of the new capital. This force may well have continued to work at Dur Sharrukin—perhaps under the supervision of the crown prince Sennacherib—until its dedication in Sargon's sixteenth year (706 B.C.). Two years later, when Sennacherib began the construction of his own new capital, Sargon's seasoned work force could have been transferred to Nineveh for that project.[19]

Later annals indicate that captives from at least one of Sennacherib's subsequent campaigns augmented this work force. In the palace building account appended to the annals composed in 700 B.C., soon after the third campaign to the Levant, the peoples of Philistia and Tyre are added to the above list.[20] These are certainly captives from the third campaign and their inclusion here apparently reflects Sennacherib's interest in keeping his building accounts up-to-date and accurate. The later building account on the bull colossi, written around 693 B.C., states simply that "the enemy population which my hand had conquered" were forced to work on the palace.[21] I am not certain whether the more general character of this statement is to be attributed to the difficulty of listing all the captives accumulated after eight campaigns (including the two led by Sennacherib's generals), or rather to the condensed nature of the bull text, as discussed by Levine, though I suspect the latter.[22]

Two new types of statements of use for an investigation of audience appear in the annals of Sennacherib. The first of these occurs in Sennacherib's earliest account of the building of the Southwest Palace, appended to the annals of the first campaign. Here Sennacherib says that his predecessors "yearly without interruption, had received (at Nineveh) an unceasing income, the tribute of the princes of the four quarters (of the world)."[23] To be sure, the text does not specify that this yearly tribute was delivered to the palace, but as will be seen while considering the royal letters and procession reliefs below, the palace was its probable destination, and consequently the foreign bearers of this tribute may well have been exposed yearly to at least some of the palace reliefs.

The other new type of statement occurs in the account of Sennacherib's encounter with Hezekiah of Judah. Sennacherib admits that his siege of Jerusalem was unsuccessful, but he claims that after the Assyrian withdrawal, Hezekiah sent messengers with rich tribute to Sennacherib at Nineveh.[24] This seems to be the first occurrence in the Assyrian annals of the claim that the king of an autonomous foreign region voluntarily sent tribute all the way to the Assyrian capital. Formerly, nonsubject kings are said to have waited until the Assyrian king and army approached their neighborhood before dispatching tribute in an effort of appeasement.[25] In the annals of Sennacherib's successors, such accounts of voluntary tribute sent to the capital become more frequent and serve as additional evidence for the presence of nonsubject foreign visitors at the royal palace.

Esarhaddon

The annals and building accounts of Esarhaddon provide little new evidence for the audience for the neo-Assyrian palace reliefs, but rather follow the pattern established by his predecessors. His building accounts contain a message for future kings and record that at the dedication of the Nineveh arsenal the gods were invited inside and a great festival was held. To this festival were invited "all of the magnates and people of my land."[26] Except for the omission of foreign dignitaries, these would seem to encompass all of the types of people invited to the palace dedications of Assurnasirpal II and Sargon II.

Esarhaddon also states that he used captive labor for the restoration of the Nineveh arsenal, and some of these foreigners would have been exposed to his reliefs there. He further notes, in his "Letter to Assur," that some of the captives from his campaign against Šupria were apportioned "to my palaces," evidence that at least some of the palace servants were foreigners.[27]

Esarhaddon mentions tribute brought to Nineveh from specific areas several times. Of Na'id-Marduk of the Sealand, he reports, "Yearly, without fail, he came to Nineveh with his rich gifts and kissed my feet." Two foreign kings, Hazael of Arabia, and Laialê of the city Iadi', came to Nineveh to reclaim the gods of their land, which had been carried off by Sennacherib and Esarhaddon. In each case, Esarhaddon restored the gods, after adding his own inscription to them, and imposed a tribute upon that king. To prevent Esarhaddon from invading their lands, the Elamite and Guti princes "sent their messengers to me in Nineveh to establish friendly relations and peace, and took an oath (to that effect) by the great gods." Finally, several Median kings brought gifts to Nineveh hoping to enlist Esarhaddon's aid against their neighbors. Esarhaddon sent some provincial forces to help them, and adds, "My royal tribute and tax I imposed upon them, yearly."[28] The most probable location at Nineveh for these meetings between foreign princes and the Assyrian king would seem to be either the royal palace or the arsenal, both of which were decorated with reliefs.

Assurbanipal

Assurbanipal's annalistic and palace building accounts provide no new evidence for audience. In his account of the building of the *bīt redûti*, Assurbanipal stated that he too used captive foreign labor, mentioning specifically captured Arabian kings who were made to help with the building. He also included a message to future kings, asking them to restore his work.[29]

Like Sennacherib and Esarhaddon, Assurbanipal records voluntary tribute and oaths of loyalty from the kings of both subject and autonomous foreign lands. These include Egypt, Arvad, Tabalu, Hilakku, Mannea, Babylonia, Nabatea, and Lydia.[30] In all these cases either the foreign king himself or his envoys traveled to Nineveh for a personal audience with the Assyrian king, and in three cases (Arvad, Tabalu, and Nabatea), Assurbanipal then imposed a yearly tribute on that foreign land. On this evidence, then, foreigners bringing tribute or swearing fealty would have constituted a significant component of the audience for the palace reliefs of this period.

Palace Administrative Texts

In *The Nimrud Wine Lists* (1972) and *The Tablets from Fort Shalmaneser* (1984), Kinnier Wilson, Dalley, and Postgate published a series of wine ration lists discovered during Mallowan's excavations of Shalmaneser III's "palace," later called the *ekal mašarti* ("arsenal") at Nimrud.[31] The majority of these texts seem to fall into two general groups, the earlier dating to the end of the reign of Adad-nirari III (810–783 B.C.) and the beginning of the reign of Shalmaneser IV (782–773 B.C.), and the later to the second half of the reign of Tiglath-pileser III (744–727) and the first half of the reign of Sargon II (721–705).[32] Though there is much in these texts that is still obscure, when taken together with a few others that present similar sorts of information, they provide a more detailed look at several of the groups mentioned in the palace inscriptions.

There is, however, a difficulty with using the wine lists as evidence for the audience for palace reliefs: since they were found in the arsenal, they may give rations only for the arsenal staff. Nevertheless, many of the people and professions recorded in them appear to have had duties that would have been required in any court setting. Furthermore, we cannot be certain that the wine list rations were intended exclusively for the arsenal staff. Two of the lists explicitly state that a certain ration was for recipients "on the citadel."[33] It is not clear whether this was an exception to the usual practice, or whether other rations were understood to be for the palace as well. The discussion that follows focuses mainly on those members of the royal household that on the basis of their titles or professions would seem to have been associated with the palace. It must be emphasized, though, that the precise duties that many of these titles entailed are still uncertain and, consequently, so too is the degree to which their bearers might have been exposed to the palace reliefs.

The first group discussed by Kinnier Wilson that can be associated with the palace is the king and his senior officers, ministers, and advisors—that is, the "magnates" (literally "the great ones"). The king himself does not figure in the wine lists, but the magnates do. Particularly informative in this respect are two other texts that deal with the magnates. The first text, K8669 from Nineveh, describes the protocol for a great royal feast held in the winter month of Tebet. The name of the king and year are not specified, or at least not preserved, nor is the location of the meal. According to the text, furniture was brought into the room by servants. The king was the first to enter and take his place. Next his high officials (magnates) entered, one at a time, and then the crown prince followed by the rest of the king's sons. The middle portion of the text gives instructions for the servants who tended the incense burners, heating brazier, handwashing water, torches, and fans. After the feast, the diners dispersed and the furniture was removed from the room.[34]

Though this text may refer to a particular feast, there is no reason to suppose that this type of feast did not occur regularly. Kinnier Wilson has suggested that it was an annual occasion to mark the end of the campaigning season.[35] This text may, on the other hand, have been intended as general instructions for any gathering of the king and his ministers, such as the royal banquet illustrated in the upper relief register of Room 2 in Sargon's palace at Khorsabad.[36] In any case, the only reasonable location for such an event would have been in the throne room or one of the other large reception rooms in the royal palaces, and in the residential palaces these were invariably lined with reliefs. Indeed, the relief decoration of two reception rooms has led Reade to suggest that they were the location of such banquets: Room G in Assurnasirpal II's Northwest Palace, which is decorated with formal reliefs that include the king holding a bowl, and Room 2 in Sargon's palace, just mentioned.[37]

The number and identity of the magnates seem to be provided by the second text, K1359 from Nineveh, edited by Kinnier Wilson. It gives the names and titles of over 150 officials of the king, and many of these seem to be magnates. Kinnier Wilson suggested that this may have been a sort of guest list for a great royal feast. It is unlikely that all of these officials would have congregated in the palace very often, but the wine lists assign a small daily ration to unnamed magnates, and others were apparently included by name separately on the lists.[38] It is clear, therefore, that the high officials of the king were legion and constituted a significant and very powerful component of the audience for the reliefs.

Another group occupying the palace would have been the remainder of the royal family. The wine lists provided rations for the queen and her entourage and also for the harem of the palace. It seems unlikely that reliefs in this area would have been visible to any but a very select company.[39]

The royal attendants assigned to the palace would have formed another component of the audience for the reliefs. This group would have included the attendants of the *bītānu*, the private apartments around the inner court of the palace. In the early tablets they are listed under the "overseer of the *bītānu*."[40] To the outer areas of the palace Kinnier Wilson assigned the *ša rēšī*, usually, but perhaps not always correctly, translated as "eunuch," under the supervision of the "chief of the eunuchs." Some or all of the eunuchs shown in attendance on the king in the procession reliefs of Sargon II must belong to this group. Also among the royal attendants would have been the *ša šēpē* and *qurbūtu*, members of the king's personal bodyguard, who would presumably have been stationed in the palace when the king was in residence.[41]

The royal scribes would have been another group situated in the palace. In the earlier lists, the palace scribes seem to have been grouped together under the "chief scribe." The later wine lists do not mention the "chief scribe," but designate scribes according to their language. Aramean scribes are included in a number of wine lists of this group, though none are mentioned in the lists of the earlier group. One of the latest lists (732 B.C.) records not only Aramean, but also Egyptian and Assyrian scribes.[42] Finds at Assurnasirpal II's Northwest Palace at Nimrud suggest that scribes were situated on the north side of the outer court of the palace, near the main gate in the area centered on rooms ZT 4 and 5 (see fig. 7).[43] Anyone stationed in this area of the palace would have been exposed daily to at least some of the palace reliefs, especially those located on the throne-room facade directly across from them in the outer court.

Another group presumably stationed in the palace was the household staff, including food preparers, housekeepers, and servants. In one of the earlier wine lists are foreign "palace servants," subdivided into Arameans, Kassites, and men of Madira. Also in the earlier group is a profession usually translated as "bread bakers," comprising Assyrians, Arameans, and men from Suhu. One lists a "cook" and "bread baker," both Chaldean.[44] Some of these servants may have been exposed to some portion of the reliefs in the course of their daily duties, though many may have had only "below stairs" status.

The wine lists include a considerable number of other foreigners at court, and in some cases their professions are also given. Diviners appear in both groups of lists. In the earlier group, and possibly in the later, Kassite diviners were listed separately from other diviners. Also in an early list were bird augurs from Kummuh.[45] Another group composed largely of foreigners was the royal singers. In the earlier lists the singers, who all seem to be male, are subdivided into Assyrians, Kassites, Syrians (Hatti), Chaldeans, and men from

Tabalu and Kummuh. In the later lists are male Assyrian, Aramean, Kassite, Syrian (Hatti), and possibly Malatyan singers. Female singers, probably from Arpad and Hatti, appear in the later lists.[46]

In addition to all these professions, and a number of others that have not been included here since their connection with the palace was not clear, in both the early and late lists there was a substantial daily ration allotted to the "wine steward." In the later lists he has a "deputy," who received a similar ration.[47] Presumably these rations were distributed directly by these officials to meet unexpected demand, such as might be occasioned by the arrival of guests.

There is one other class of foreigners included in the wine lists, usually located near the end. They are listed only by their place of origin and not by profession as is done elsewhere in the lists. The preserved names are summarized in the chart on the following page.

Most of these foreigners are listed only by place name, without any indication of their function. Two of the recently published lists, however, seem to resolve this question. One tablet in the early group gives the information that the foreigner is the "ambassador of Elam," while one in the late group identifies others as the "envoy of Moab" and the "sheiks of Itu'a."[49] Presumably all or most of the other such entries likewise designate diplomatic missions. It would appear, therefore, that visiting foreigners must always have constituted an important part of the audience for the royal palace reliefs.

The final palace profession discussed by Kinnier Wilson is the "interpreter." In view of the large number of foreigners apparently in the palace, whether employed as scribes or musicians or just passing through as visiting envoys, the presence of official interpreters is not surprising. They are of more than incidental interest for a study of audience since it seems natural that at least part of their function would have been to serve as tour guides for visiting foreigners, and this could have included interpreting the reliefs for foreigners unable to read the Akkadian captions.[50]

Royal Letters

A number of letters that deal with the delivery of *madattu* ("tribute") and *nāmurtu* ("gifts") to the Assyrian king in the capital have been assembled by J. N. Postgate in *Taxation and Conscription in the Assyrian Empire* (1974). His primary interest was in the process of the payment and this is also of importance for a survey of audience for Assyrian palace reliefs. The term *madattu* refers to compulsory payments made by foreign territories that were subject

Origin of Foreigners Receiving Wine at Nimrud (arranged chronologically according to the scheme of Parpola; date included when known)[48]

#	Names occurring in one list only	Names occurring in two or more lists									
		Elam	Guti	Samaria	Dan	Carchemish	Šupria	Sam'al	Malatya	Mannea	Tabalu
					Early Group						
#124:	Manisa(?), Suhu										
#145 (784):	Elam										
#119:	Harhar, Zurzukaza(?), a-MAŠ-qa-a-a(?), sa-qa-a-a(?)										
#144:	Hubuškia		Guti								
#120:				Samaria							
#1:	Andia				Dan						
#18:	Arpad, Madira		Guti,		Dan,						
#4:	Hazazu, Muşaşir			Samaria,			Šupria(?)				
#23:	Babylon, Borsippa						Šupria,		Malatya(?),	Mannea,	Tabalu
#5 (779):	Urartu										
#6:									Malatya,	Mannea	
#11:											Tabalu
					Late Group						
#21:		Elam									
#8 (735):		Elam,		Samaria,		Carchemish,		Sam'al,		Mannea	
#142:	Bunisa	Elam,		Samaria(?)		Carchemish(?),		Sam'al,		Mannea(?),	
#13:	Media, Sangibutu										
#122:	Elam ša kiki	Elam									
#9 (732):	Kush										
#136:	Andia										
#135:	Ashdod, Edom, Gaza, Judah, Ulimaya(?), Ekron(?)										
#143:	Itu'a, Moab, Nuqudina(?)										

to the Assyrian king but which had not been absorbed into the administrative structure of Assyria itself. The term often appears in the royal annals in the context of a description of the amount and type of tribute imposed by the Assyrian king on captive cities and countries.[51]

Postgate observed that while bulky or less valuable items may have been delivered to the nearest provincial capital, the more valuable items were delivered to the king in person. The annals indicate that this delivery was an annual event (examples cited above in "The Royal Annals"), and several letters suggest that it was timed to coincide with the New Year festival, which began on the first of Nisan (March/April).[52] Thus in a letter to Sargon we read, "On the 23rd of Addaru (12th month) the Šuprian emissaries arrived in Šabirēšu," that is, they entered Assyrian territory and seem to have been bearing gifts or tribute.[53] In another letter, the writer refers to "the message the king my lord sent (saying): 'Come into Calah on the first of Nisan.'"[54] In two letters to Sargon II, Aššur-bēl-uṣur—apparently an eastern tributary—claims that the tribute for the previous year had been delivered in Nisan and that the current shipment is bogged down in the mountain snow, which also points to a delivery in early spring.[55] It appears, then, that the arrival of at least a portion of the tribute was timed to coincide with the festivities of the New Year.

The people who delivered the tribute are usually called *ṣīrāni*, and seem to have been foreign envoys of high rank.[56] We have already encountered the *ṣīrāni* at the dedication festival of Assurnasirpal II's palace. In the late Assyrian letters dealing with the delivery of tribute, Postgate noted *ṣīrāni* from eighteen different locales, all of them states on the borders of Assyria.[57] Not surprisingly, many of these place names also occur on the Nimrud wine lists as designations of visiting foreigners. When the *ṣīrāni* arrived in the capital with their tribute they seem to have had an audience with the king, referred to in the letters as going into the palace or before the king *ana šulmi* ("to ask his health"). According to some of these letters, royal audiences were held in the palace, presumably in the throne room, and would have served as important opportunities for the wall reliefs to be viewed by high-ranking foreigners.[58]

The congregation of so many foreign dignitaries in the capital at one time must have been quite a spectacle. This event seems to be reflected in a letter from an official to the crown prince, Assurbanipal: "Just as today the ambassadors (*ṣīrāni*) of all the lands passed (in procession) before your father, so may they pass before the king's son for one thousand years."[59] It is this congregation of foreign tributaries that seems to be illustrated in the courtyard reliefs of Sargon II's palace at Khorsabad, to be discussed next.

Tribute Procession Reliefs

There is one other source for the audience of neo-Assyrian palace reliefs. These are some of the reliefs themselves, located on the walls of the palace courts, which show processions of foreign tributaries bearing gifts as they approach the entrances of the throne rooms. The earliest examples of these processions are in the outer court (D/E) of the throne room (B) of Assurnasirpal II's Northwest Palace at Nimrud (figs. 7, 122). They are located on slabs flanking the throne room's two subsidiary entrances, *c* and *d*. The reliefs at the west entrance (*d*) show a procession of turbaned foreigners bearing apes and jewelry approaching from the right. From their costume, they should be westerners. At the head of the procession are four Assyrian officials, divided by the doorway into two groups of two, who present the tributaries to the king, facing left, on a slab that is now lost.

By contrast, the reliefs at the east entrance (*c*) show two processions of foreigners, one approaching from the left, the other from the right, converging on the doorway.[60] They are similar in appearance to the tributaries at Door *d*, but they wear headbands instead of turbans. Unlike Door *d*, how-

FIG. 122. Western tributaries, Slab 7, Court D, Northwest Palace of Assurnasirpal II, Nimrud, w. 214 cm. British Museum, WAA 124562 (photo: Trustees of the British Museum).

FIG. 123.   Western (top) and eastern tributaries, engravings of Slabs 6–7, Room 10, Sargon's palace, Khorsabad (from Botta and Flandin 1849, vol. 2, 128–29).

ever, the figure of the king is not included in the procession of Door *c*. This difference in the decoration of Doors *c* and *d* is striking; it would seem that the reason the image of the king is absent from the Door *c* decoration is because the *person* of the king, whose throne was located just inside this doorway, is the focus of the procession here. This association of procession reliefs with the facade of the throne room can hardly be accidental. They seem, rather, to be evidence that one of the functions of the throne room was as a reception room for foreign tributaries.

The same sort of reliefs decorated part of the throne-room outer court in Sargon II's palace at Khorsabad (figs. 8, 123). Here the tribute scenes were not on the facade of the throne room itself, but rather on the adjacent northwest wall of the court. The left half of this wall showed a procession of western tributaries with horses, bowls, and city models, facing right, being presented to the image of the king, facing left. The right half of the wall showed the timber transport discussed in the previous chapter, proceeding left. Separating these two relief series is a doorway opening into Corridor 10, a hallway that connects the throne-room court with an inner court and secondary throne room (8). Both walls of Corridor 10 are decorated with tribute processions in two registers, with the processions shown as filing inward toward the secondary throne room. On both walls, the upper register shows western tributaries, recognizable by their turbans, while the lower register shows easterners wearing skin cloaks.[61]

Postgate suggested that these procession reliefs illustrate an actual event that took place in the palace, namely the annual tribute delivery at the time of the New Year's festival referred to in the annals and letters.[62] If so, then these reliefs would have served a dual purpose. First, they served as a year-round affirmation of the power at the center of the realm, which extends so effectively to the eastern and western extremities of the realm. Second, they functioned for visiting foreigners as a reminder of the obligations of tributary states. Thus, at the time of the annual tribute delivery, visiting foreign dignitaries would have served simultaneously as subject of and audience for these highly visible reliefs.[63]

Summary

In reviewing the evidence presented here, it appears that the actual audience for the neo-Assyrian palace reliefs falls into twelve groups. The majority of these groups lived or worked in the palace and would have been exposed to at least some of the reliefs in the course of their daily activities. The remainder entered the palace as visitors. These twelve groups are listed individually below, with a brief summary of the evidence for each as part of the audience for the palace reliefs.

1. KING. The highest ranking component of the reliefs' audience would have been the king himself, who built and lived in the palace.

2. CROWN PRINCE/ROYAL FAMILY. The queen and harem figure prominently in the Nimrud wine lists. The crown prince and brothers and sons of the king, while they do not figure in any of the evidence outlined above, must have been at least occasional visitors to the palace. As was proven by the circumstances surrounding Sennacherib's demise, the importance of this group's support for the king cannot be overemphasized.

3. COURTIERS. Assyrian high officials and palace functionaries were among the guests at the dedications of Assurnasirpal's and Esarhaddon's royal palaces. Fairly extensive lists of these officials are given in Sargon's palace dedication account and in the Nimrud wine lists.

4. SERVANTS. Several groups of palace servants and attendants are included in the Nimrud wine lists.

5. FOREIGN EMPLOYEES. The Nimrud wine lists indicate that many of the scribes, musicians, and diviners employed at court were foreigners.

6. FOREIGN PRISONERS. The annals of Sargon II, Sennacherib, Esarhaddon, and Assurbanipal all state that captive foreign labor was used in the construction of the royal palaces. Esarhaddon also states that captives from one of his campaigns were apportioned to his palaces, presumably as servants or laborers.

7. FUTURE KINGS. Nearly all of the building accounts contain a message directed specifically at the king's posterity, requesting that the palace be restored to its original condition.

8. GODS. The building accounts of Assurnasirpal II, Sargon II, Sennacherib, and Esarhaddon specify that when the palace was finished, the gods of Assyria were invited inside. It is uncertain what this means in practical terms. Perhaps it indicates that statues of gods were moved into the palace shrines, such as those found inside or adjacent to the palaces of Assurnasirpal, Sargon, and Sennacherib.[64]

9. ASSYRIANS. The palace dedication accounts of Assurnasirpal II, Sargon II, Sennacherib, and Esarhaddon state that the people of Assyria were invited to the festivities. The Nimrud wine lists twice give rations for people—presumably visitors—from the Assyrian city of Arrapha.[65]

10. PROVINCIALS. Since the provinces were considered to be part of Assyria itself, the "Assyrians" in the preceding section undoubtedly included former foreigners. The palace dedication account of Sargon II specifically mentions the provincial governors.

11. SUBJECT FOREIGNERS. Subject foreigners visiting the palace as envoys or to deliver tribute are prominent in the annals of all of the Assyrian kings. A number of these foreigners are listed individually in Assurnasirpal II's "Banquet Stele," and other examples occur in royal letters concerning tribute, on procession reliefs from the palaces of Assurnasirpal II and Sargon II, and apparently also in the Nimrud wine lists.

12. INDEPENDENT FOREIGNERS. Envoys from countries not subject to Assyria's direct political control are mentioned in the annals of Sennacherib, Esarhaddon, and Assurbanipal, and also in Assurnasirpal II's "Banquet Stele" and in the Nimrud wine lists.

These, then, are the people who according to the preserved records would probably have been exposed at some point to some or all of the palace wall reliefs. To conclude this survey, it might be useful to speculate which of these groups would be expected to enjoy a sufficient degree of literacy in Akkadian to be able to read the texts that accompany the reliefs.[66] For these purposes, there are essentially two kinds of text. The first are the long annalistic and summary texts that are placed next to the reliefs, but are largely independent

239

in content from them. These include the bull and threshold inscriptions and the text band running across the center of the relief slabs. Only a highly literate viewer would be able to read these texts with any facility, and this would appear to exclude just about everyone except the scribes.

The other type of text associated with the reliefs are epigraphs—brief captions inscribed directly on the reliefs. Because of their relatively simple vocabulary and emphasis on place names, the epigraphs might be more readily accessible to marginally literate viewers than the longer texts would be. More important, because the epigraphs are brief and essentially identical in content with the accompanying images, they would readily lend themselves to memorization by members of the palace staff who worked in these rooms. These functionaries could then recite the epigraphs, or at least explain their content, for the benefit of interested visitors. Thus in the case of very short texts, at least, illiteracy would be no barrier to understanding, as long as there was someone handy who could explain them.[67]

These various groups of people that compose the actual audience for the reliefs would have possessed varying degrees of visual, as well as verbal, literacy. As I suggested in chapter 9, it is possible that the groups with the greatest verbal literacy, namely scribes and residents of the palace with access to scribes, might have had some difficulty "reading" Sennacherib's highly innovative visual language, which was very unlike the images they were accustomed to. At the same time, the groups with the lowest verbal literacy, namely those outside the palace circle, might have found the images relatively easy to read, since these groups' perceptions were less likely to have been conditioned by previous Assyrian representational conventions.

In closing, it must be reemphasized that this chapter has been concerned with determining the categories of people who would have had occasion to see at least some of the neo-Assyrian palace reliefs, that is, their *actual* audience. The determination of which groups were supposed to see the reliefs, their *intended* audience, is a much more difficult problem. The texts are of assistance for only one of the twelve groups outlined here. As seen above, many of the texts displayed with the reliefs in the Assyrian palaces conclude with a passage addressed specifically to future kings. Clearly then, future kings were an essential part of the intended audience for these texts, and it seems reasonable to infer that the accompanying reliefs were addressed in part to them as well. The problem of which of the other eleven groups constituted the intended audience for the reliefs is not so easily solved; I will return to this question in the next chapter.

11

THE MESSAGE OF
SENNACHERIB'S PALACE

"Sennacherib, King of the World, King of Assyria":
Imperial Priorities and Goals

Thus far in this study I have concentrated on reconstructing the physical presence of Sennacherib's palace, its decoration in the form of reliefs and inscribed texts, and its potential audience. It remains now to attempt to determine the intended effect of this ensemble, that is, what was its purpose and what was its message? While not much is known about Sennacherib the man, his public image is documented in a relatively large corpus of royal inscriptions. The majority of these were buried in, or inscribed on, the palaces, walls, roads, and canals of his capital city, Nineveh. The Nineveh texts record the events of Sennacherib's reign from its beginning in 705 B.C. until about 690 B.C. and therefore cover the full period during which the Southwest Palace was being built. In this chapter, I will first examine the image Sennacherib presented through his official titles and then compare that with the apparent content of the palace reliefs. My goal is to determine how the sculptural program participated in the expression of the king's public image—an image that, as I hope to demonstrate, differs markedly from that of his predecessors.[1]

Sennacherib's Titles

The portion of Sennacherib's texts that is most useful in reconstructing his public self-image is the titulary. This section at the beginning of each text was the king's official introduction and took the form of an abstract, formulaic summary of Sennacherib's status and accomplishments. Because of its conventional character, it is tempting to view the titulary as little more than a formality, devoid of any real meaning. This would be a mistake, however, for

241

FIG. 124. Base of sawn-off colossus in main entrance of throne room, north jamb, Bull 7, Door *a*, Court H, Southwest Palace, Nineveh, 1. 602 cm (photo: author).

Sennacherib evidently took his titulary seriously and chose each of its component titles and epithets with care.

In an exemplary study of Sennacherib's titles, Liverani has demonstrated that changes in the titulary, far from being arbitrary, often accompanied major accomplishments of Sennacherib's reign. He notes, for example, that in the earliest texts, written after the first and second campaigns, Sennacherib referred to himself simply as "unrivaled king." In texts written after the third campaign, after the force of his arms had been widely felt, he added the title "king of the world." In texts written after the fifth campaign, "unrivaled king" was replaced by "king of the four quarters (of the earth)." This last was a popular royal title and had in fact been used by Sennacherib's father, Sargon II, but Sennacherib added it to his titulary only in 697 B.C., after he had led campaigns to the south, east, west, and north.[2] Similarly, the title that boasted of the submission of princes "from the upper sea of the setting sun, to the lower sea of the rising sun" did not appear until 694 B.C., after Sennacherib had carried his conquests to both the Mediterranean Sea and the Persian Gulf.[3]

Liverani points out a second shift in the titulary as well: from *"pious* shepherd, *fearful* of the great gods" in the earlier editions, to *"expert* shepherd, *favorite* of the great gods" (my emphasis) in editions after 697 B.C.[4] As with "king of the four quarters," the title "favorite of the great gods" was also used by Sargon II, and again Liverani argues that the reason Sennacherib did not employ it from the beginning was because its use was not yet justified. Only after several years of successful rule did Sennacherib replace the earlier, more subservient titles with the similar, yet far more confident formulation.

Liverani's observations are of value in that they establish the credibility of the titulary as a personal statement that may be taken seriously in an evaluation of Sennacherib's royal self-image. On the basis of this evidence, it is fruitful to examine the highly visible titularies inscribed on the human-headed bull colossi of two adjacent exterior portals—designated "*a*" and "*c*" by Layard—of the Southwest Palace throne room (Room I; figs. 124, 125, 126). The inscription on the Door *a* colossi records six military campaigns and the building of the palace; the one on the Door *c* colossi is a palace building account only. The proximity of these texts to one another, in neighboring doors, and the use of the same set of palace dimensions in the building accounts of both inscriptions indicate that they were probably inscribed at about the same time.[5] The inclusion of the sixth campaign in the Door *a* inscription suggests a date of 693 B.C. or slightly later, around the time the palace was being completed.[6] Taken together, these two titularies should constitute a fair expression of Sennacherib's public self-image in the late 690s B.C.

The titularies of both the Door *a* and Door *c* inscriptions start with the phrase "Palace of Sennacherib," thereby identifying these texts as intended for display in the palace.[7] In nearly every other Assyrian royal titulary, the name of the king is followed by a brief genealogy of the form "son of PN$_1$, who was son of PN$_2$," stressing the legitimacy of the king. As Tadmor has observed, such a statement never appears in the titulary of Sennacherib. This omission is surprising since Sennacherib was unquestionably the legitimate heir of Sargon II. Tadmor suggests that Sennacherib omitted his father's name either because of disapproval of Sargon's policies or because of the shameful manner of Sargon's death (after his defeat and death on the battlefield, his body was abandoned by the retreating Assyrian army).[8]

This may be, but it is important to note that Sargon also omitted the genealogy from his own titulary, presumably because, contrary to his name (Sargon is the biblical form of *Šarru-kēn*: "the king is legitimate"), he was evidently not truly the legitimate ruler. Perhaps Sennacherib wished to avoid drawing attention to a flawed genealogy. The only way Sennacherib could credibly have used the standard genealogical formulation would have been with a statement such as "Sennacherib, son of Sargon, who was *not* the son of Shalmaneser," or "who was son of a nobody," and this is clearly worse than nothing at all.[9] Thus, Sennacherib's refusal to mention the name of his father may be the result of a desire to make his dynasty appear legitimate by passing silently over its weak link. Whatever the reason for Sennacherib's avoidance of Sargon's name, the fact that he did so is of interest since it may

FIG. 125.   Text panels sawed from colossus in main entrance of throne room, south jamb, Bull 6, Door *a*, Court H, Southwest Palace, Nineveh. British Museum, WAA 118815a+b (left, w. 290 cm), and 118821 (right, w. 170 cm) (photo: author).

be connected to his removal of the capital from Dur Sharrukin, founded by Sargon and charged with his memory, to Nineveh, where there is little evidence of Sargon's activities.

Both texts continue: "great king, mighty king, king of the world, king of Assyria, king of the four quarters (of the earth), favorite of the great gods."[10] These are standard titles that we might take for granted had we not already seen that half of them did not appear in Sennacherib's early texts, indicating that they were *earned* by the king, not automatically bestowed by the gods. As it stands, this final formulation combines titles that are status-oriented (great, mighty, favorite) and territorial (world, Assyria, four quarters). Liverani observes that this aggregate of territorial titles is in no way redundant, nor is their order without significance, for they progress from an unstructured, abstract totality (world), to an organizing center (Assyria), to a concrete totality, dependent upon, and structured with reference to, the center (four quarters).[11]

At this point the titularies of the two texts diverge dramatically. The tone
of the inscription carved on the colossi of Door *a* is militaristic:

> Sennacherib, . . . wise, expert, heroic warrior, foremost among all rulers,
> the bridle that curbs the disobedient, the one who strikes the enemy with
> lightning. Assur, the great god, gave me a kingship without rival; against
> all those who sit on daises he made my weapons strong; from the upper
> sea of the setting sun to the lower sea of the rising sun, he made all rulers
> in the world bow down at my feet.

Liverani describes this type of phraseology as "competitive-submissive."[12]
The emphasis here is on how Sennacherib, with the support of the god Assur,
subdues all foreign rivals. Sennacherib is presented not as the sole king, but
as one king among many, providing in effect a quantitative basis for the assertion that he, by virtue of military control, is the greatest of them.

245

FIG. 126.   Colossus from subsidiary entrance of throne room, north jamb, Door *c*, Court H, Southwest Palace, Nineveh, 1. 345 cm (photo: author).

The titulary of the inscription on the colossi of the adjacent Door *c* continues in quite a different vein:

> Sennacherib, . . . wise stag, prudent ruler, shepherd of mankind, leader of widespread peoples, am I. Bēlet-ilī, lady of living creatures, duly looked upon me in the womb of the mother who bore me and created my features. Ea gave me wide knowledge, equal to that of the sage Adapa, and granted me broad understanding. Assur, father of the gods, made all of mankind bow down at my feet; he elevated me to be shepherd over the land and people. He gave me a just scepter that enlarges the land, and put into my hands an unsparing sword for the overthrow of the enemy.

Liverani terms this a "phraseology of stable and peaceful control."[13] It consists of two distinct components. One of these is the claim of divine election, that is, the gods chose Sennacherib as ruler even before his birth. This passage seems to be a substitute for the traditional genealogy used in the titulary of other kings, replacing the human (dynastic) formula of legitimacy with a divine one.[14]

The other component is the claim of Sennacherib's universal rule, made possible by the support of the gods who affirm his authority. The competitive ("foremost among all rulers") and punitive ("who strikes the enemy with lightning") epithets of Door *a* are replaced by the universal ("leader of wide-spread peoples") and protective ("shepherd of mankind"). References to other kings are absent from this portion of the Door *c* titulary, in contrast to the equivalent passage in Door *a*, and the prosperity and stability that come from Sennacherib's peaceful rule over united mankind are emphasized instead. The only reference to destabilizing forces is abstract ("enemy") rather than specific ("rulers"). In the Door *c* titulary, then, Sennacherib's rule is presented as universal and unchallenged; its purpose is not, as in the Door *a* titulary, to subdue foreign rulers, but rather to govern all peoples.

One may well wonder why the titularies on the colossi of Doors *a* and *c* are so different from each other. It would seem that the explanation is to be found in the content of the succeeding narrative texts. The text of the Door *c* colossus inscription deals solely with public works: the palace, gardens, and irrigation system of Nineveh. Public works are one of the specific benefits of peaceful government, and therefore the Door *c* titulary is appropriate for the accompanying text. The text on the colossi of Door *a*, by contrast, is an annalistic account of Sennacherib's first six royal campaigns, and only at the end is a palace building account included. Here, too, the militaristic tone of the titulary with its emphasis on the domination of enemy rulers is appropriate for the text, which confirms with specific examples the general claims in the titulary.

Further evidence that the titulary was tailored to the narrative content of the rest of the text may be seen in an inscription carved on another of Sennacherib's throne-room colossi, this one from Door *d*. As with Door *a*, its somewhat abridged titulary emphasizes dominance over kings rather than peaceful government: "Assur, father of the gods, among all rulers he duly looked upon me; against all those who sit on daises he made my weapons strong."[15] Again, this is appropriate to the text that follows, which consists of a summary of the first five military campaigns. There seems to be a definite correlation, therefore, between the royal titles selected for a given text and the narrative substance that follows.

Features from two additional Sennacherib titularies deserve consideration, since they serve to highlight certain aspects of his reliefs. The first of these is a colorful passage found in the standard titulary that accompanied the text of Ninevite foundation cylinders inscribed in 697 B.C. and later. The passage, which is of the "competitive" type, describes the reaction of foreign rulers to Sennacherib's approach: "Strong princes feared my battle, deserted their

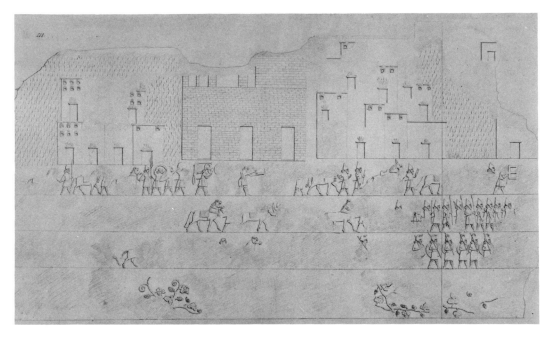

FIG. 127.   Defeated city, drawing of Slabs 1–2, Room I, Southwest Palace, Nineveh.
British Museum, WAA, Or. Dr., IV, 3 (photo: Trustees of the British Museum).

dwellings and, like bats, alone they fled to an inaccessible place."[16] Liverani
observed that this pattern of behavior of the enemy king, first stated in the
titulary in general terms, is then restated in the form of specific examples in
the account of every one of Sennacherib's royal campaigns. It would seem
that for Sennacherib this was perhaps the ultimate tribute to his military
prowess, for to defeat an enemy in battle is a great thing, but to defeat him
with the mere threat of your battle is surely greater still. This theme of fearful
enemy kings running away is developed also in the reliefs, two examples of
which are preserved among the surviving reliefs from Room I, the throne
room: On Slab 1 an epigraph reports that the king abandoned his city and
people and fled to the mountains, which are depicted on Slab 3 as crawling
with pursuing Assyrian soldiers (figs. 127, 128). On Slabs 14–15, the inhabitants of a Phoenician city abandon it and take to their ships. Though no epigraph is preserved, Barnett plausibly suggested that this represents the flight
of King Luli of Sidon (figs. 85, 129).[17]

The other titulary of interest in this context is from Assur, cult city of the
state god, on a stela commemorating the restoration of the *bīt akīti*, the

248

Fig. 128.   Rounding up enemy soldiers in the mountains, drawing of Slab 3, Room I, Southwest Palace, Nineveh. British Museum, WAA, Or. Dr., IV, 4 (photo: Trustees of the British Museum).

"Temple of the New Year's Festival." Except for the first six titles, which by now are standard ("great king, mighty king," etc.), this is completely different from the Ninevite titularies. Of particular interest is a passage that lists public works:

> Sennacherib, . . . who builds Assyria, who completes its cult cities; . . . who digs canals, opens irrigated fields, and makes irrigation ditches murmur (with water); who established prosperity and abundance in the wide croplands of Assyria; who put irrigation water in the fields of Assyria where, from days of old, no one had seen, no one had known, those who preceded me had not made, canals and irrigation in Assyria; the one who builds masonry structures, from works for the living to tombs befitting the dead, out of limestone, which none of the kings who preceded me had done in Assyria.[18]

Three features are of note here. First, this titulary accompanies a building account, so it contains little of the militaristic phraseology that is familiar from annalistic texts and concentrates instead on praising Sennacherib's pub-

FIG. 129.   L. W. King photograph of throne-room colossus, 1903–5, east jamb, Bull 2, Door *d*, Room I, Southwest Palace, Nineveh (photo: Trustees of the British Museum).

lic works. Second, the emphasis is on two specific types of public works: building of structures and cities, and irrigation.[19] Both of these types of construction facilitate, and are symptomatic of, internal prosperity; that is, they indicate a type of expansion that results from good government of the people. It is this type of expansion that is the theme of the *bīt akīti* titulary, as opposed to the other type, territorial expansion achieved through force of arms, which is the main theme of the more militaristic titulary of Sennacherib's father, Sargon II.[20] Building and, as will be seen, irrigation are also the subject of half of the reliefs from Court VI in the Southwest Palace. The third feature of interest in the *bīt akīti* titulary is the repeated assertion that Sennacherib has outdone his royal predecessors. This motif, which Liverani terms "heroic priority," also recurs throughout Sennacherib's annalistic and

250

building accounts and is even implicit in the name of his palace, "Palace without Rival."[21]

To summarize briefly, then, the titularies of Sennacherib's royal inscriptions present two different aspects of the king's rule. On the one hand, titularies that accompany annalistic accounts emphasize Sennacherib's control over the empire, especially its extremities ("the four quarters"), through military prowess. Titularies that accompany building accounts, on the other hand, emphasize the king's good government, which benefits all mankind. I shall return to this dualism later, as it is also one of the primary messages of the palace reliefs.[22]

The Message of the Southwest Palace Reliefs

Preliminary Considerations

Any attempt to define the principles of organization and articulate the message of Sennacherib's palace reliefs must first acknowledge two serious difficulties. The first is the fragmentary nature of the evidence. It is rarely possible to reconstruct the sculptural decoration of even an entire room, let alone a suite of rooms, and consequently the principles of organization that may originally have dictated the subject for a given room or suite are in most cases very difficult to recover. The second difficulty is that while it is possible to reconstruct the actual audience for the palace reliefs, that is, those people who *could* have seen the reliefs, it is much more difficult to determine the intended audience, that is, the people who were *supposed* to see them.

The only way at present to deal with the first difficulty is to focus on rooms and suites the decoration of which is well known. In practice, this means that I will be considering Room XXXVI, showing the siege of Lachish, and the throne-room suite, including its inner court (VI).

The second difficulty is less easily skirted. The only portion of the palace that may reasonably be termed "public" is the outer throne-room court (H), but the relief decoration there is poorly known. The throne room (I) as the site of royal audiences would presumably have been accessible to a select but still wide-ranging group of people, including courtiers, provincial officials, and foreign diplomats. Access to the inner portions of the palace beyond the throne room must have been very restricted, and we may wonder who, if anyone, outside the court circle would have seen the reliefs there. The safest assumption, then, would seem to be that the primary audience for the majority of the preserved reliefs would have been the king and his court and, at a more abstract level, future kings and perhaps the gods.

251

In practice though, a combination of royal vanity and hospitality probably insured that favored visitors to the palace did not leave without being shown at least a sampling of its inner splendors. In this context, it is useful to recall that when Hezekiah, king of Judah during Sennacherib's reign, received envoys from Babylon, he "showed them all his treasury, silver and gold, spices and fragrant oil, his armory and everything to be found among his treasures; there was nothing in his house and in all his realm that Hezekiah did not show them."[23] Sennacherib on occasion must also have been subject to the urge to show off his palace and treasures. He himself says that after his palace was finished, he "filled it with splendor for the astonishment of all people."[24] This "astonishment" could only occur if the palace and its contents were somehow displayed to at least some of Sennacherib's subjects. Indeed it is only through such displays that allies, as well as potential troublemakers, could be made fully aware of the wealth and power of the Assyrian king. Thus it seems a reasonable hypothesis that while the reliefs of the inner part of the palace were probably intended primarily for the eyes of the king and court, their potential effect on visitors, both Assyrian and foreign, must have been considered as well.

Room XXXVI

The relief decoration of Room XXXVI was given an unusual prominence by its architectural setting. The room occupied the third, inner, rank of rooms in the suite west of Court XIX. Access to Room XXXVI from Court XIX was gained by passing through a series of three monumental portals, designated *h*, *e*, and *b*. Each of these doors was decorated with a pair of human-headed bull colossi, which decreased in size from 18 feet high in Door *h*, to 12 feet high in Door *b*. Since these doorways were all located on a single axis, the visual effect when standing in Court XIX and looking in toward Room XXXVI was an accelerated perspective, a sense of dramatic convergence toward the scene depicted on the rear wall of Room XXXVI, namely the image of the besieged city of Lachish (fig. 130). Nowhere else in the preserved portion of the palace were colossi used to highlight a room in this way.[25]

As was seen in chapter 7, Room XXXVI was located in a suite of rooms that was decorated almost exclusively with scenes of Sennacherib's third campaign, to the west. Since its combination of central location and perspective effects makes Room XXXVI the focal point of this entire suite, a visitor might justifiably conclude that the surrender of Lachish was the high point of the western campaign. What a surprise, then, to turn to the annalistic ac-

FIG. 130.   Battle for Lachish, detail of Slab 7, Room XXXVI, Southwest Palace,
Nineveh. British Museum, WAA 124906 (photo: author).

count of that same campaign—inscribed on the bulls at the throne-room entrance—and discover that Lachish is not mentioned at all!

It appears that Sennacherib has here taken advantage of the strengths of two greatly different narrative media, image and text, to tell what is essentially the same story in two very different ways. An extended verbal narrative requires a "story line," that is, a series of links that relates each episode to the one that follows, and a coherent overall sequence, that is, an intelligible temporal relationship between episodes. In these terms, the campaign against Judah, which included the capture of Lachish, does not make a very inspiring story since its apparent objective, the capture of the capital city Jerusalem, was not attained.[26] A reasonably full written account of this phase of the third campaign would have to describe the capture of Lachish, and perhaps other important cities as well, and then culminate with the account of the unsuccessful siege of Jerusalem. This climax would be anticlimactic at best and risks making the considerable effort that went before appear wasted. Sennacherib chose instead to make the written narrative of this portion of the third campaign very brief, mentioning only that a number of cities—which are not named—were captured and that Jerusalem was not captured but paid tribute anyway. The importance of this part of the campaign is minimized, both by treating it in vague terms and by permitting it to occupy only a minimal amount of space in the overall narrative.

In this context, it is necessary to consider the audience for these written narratives. It must be remembered that at this time literacy was confined almost exclusively to the scribes. Sennacherib's colossus texts are so lengthy and specialized that they probably could be read with facility only by the Assyrian court scribes who composed them. Any outside visitor would face at least five substantial difficulties in interpreting them. First, most outsiders would not be literate. Second, if they could find someone to read the text, most foreigners—and even many Assyrian visitors—could probably not understand Akkadian, which was gradually being supplanted by Aramaic as the primary spoken language of the empire. Third, even Assyrian visitors who understood Akkadian might have difficulty understanding the palace inscriptions, which were almost always written in the Babylonian dialect rather than in the Assyrian. Fourth, few visitors, even if they passed the first three obstacles, would have the time required to read these texts, which are very long and involved. Finally, very few people outside the court would have the cultural background necessary to comprehend fully even the titulary, which presupposes a high-level familiarity with Assyrian imperial ideology. The annalistic portions of the texts might be somewhat easier for the unindoctrinated to understand, but the technical language of the building accounts would probably also be incomprehensible to those unfamiliar with Assyrian palaces.[27]

Consequently, it is unlikely that a visitor to the palace, even a literate one, could have the time or expertise to wade through the tremendous number of Assyrian victories recorded in these texts in order to discover that the Judean campaign was less than successful. The verbal narrative of the Judean campaign, therefore, must have been intended mainly for the Assyrian administrative elite, a group that was already thoroughly familiar with the story. For this audience, the seemingly unbiased written account of this campaign establishes the credibility of the text and, by extension, of the king who ordered its composition and display.

The potential impact of the palace inscriptions and reliefs on Sennacherib's courtiers, who might be exposed to them continually, should not be overlooked. Reade was correct when he observed that in the case of courtiers the reliefs were "preaching to the converted," rather than serving as propaganda, but one must keep in mind the importance of *maintaining* the fidelity of this powerful component of the audience.[28] For in this period the greatest threat to the safety of the king of Assyria was not foreigners on the fringe of the empire, notwithstanding the death on the battlefield of Sennacherib's father, Sargon II. Rather, as Garelli observed, the real threat to the king was at home in his own palace, in the form of jealous courtiers and ambitious kin. There is no better example of this than the fate of Sennacherib himself, who stabilized the borders of the empire only to be assassinated in Nineveh by a disaffected son.[29]

The visual narratives in Sennacherib's palace, by contrast, lend themselves much more readily to an episodic treatment. While an extended visual narrative consisting of a number of consecutive linked episodes is possible in the larger rooms of Sennacherib's palace, the smaller rooms often have space for only a single episode. Now, while it was apparently desirable for visual narratives within a single room to display some degree of continuity, there is no necessity, nor even any logic, in requiring this sort of continuity to extend between rooms. This is because, unlike texts, where the writing system dictates the order in which the narrative will be read, there is no way to insure that a narrative spread over the walls of a suite of rooms will be read in the correct sequence. Without some sort of guidance, a visitor to the suite cannot know which rooms to visit and in what order. There are universally acknowledged rules for reading a text, but none for walking through a building.[30]

Faced with these considerations, Sennacherib's artists seem to have adopted overall subjects for certain suites of rooms—in this case the western campaign—but not to have attempted a complete sequential narrative. Instead, their treatment of the decoration was episodic, a display of "highlights" from the campaign. The capture of Lachish probably was in fact one of the highlights of the third campaign and must have been *the* highlight of its final phase against Judah. It is of interest here that in the biblical account of this campaign, only Jerusalem, Lachish, and Libnah were considered worth mentioning.[31] Recent excavations at Lachish, concentrating on the city walls and the remains of the Assyrian siege ramp, taken together with the picture of the siege in Room XXXVI, show that Sennacherib concentrated immense resources and expended tremendous energy in its capture.[32]

Furthermore, as discussed in chapter 4, the dates of Rassam's foundation cylinders and the eponym chronicle indicate that the walls of the palace were being built in 700 B.C., the year after the western campaign. Assuming that the relief carving was carried out shortly thereafter, the victory at Lachish may well have been the last great triumph in Sennacherib's most recently completed campaign and might thereby have gained the place of honor in this suite. While in a written narrative the glory of the capture of Lachish might have been overshadowed by the disappointment of the failure at Jerusalem, in Room XXXVI the visual account of this single episode is unencumbered by concerns for the sequel, and the success at Lachish is permitted to shine forth untarnished.

The visual record of this success was presented in a way that would insure maximum recognizability, through highly specific costumes and scenery, and verisimilitude, through exploitation of perspective effects in a unified field. This narrative would have been intelligible to a much broader audience than would the verbal one, including not only literate courtiers, but also nonliterate foreign visitors, some of whom may have recognized their own people and land in this highly specific image. There is no hint of failure here—the Assyrian victory is conclusive and unalloyed. The image of the fall of Lachish confirms for foreign visitors and subject peoples what they already know—or at least what the Assyrian king wants them to believe—namely that Assyrian might is invincible and that the price of resistance is inevitably defeat. For courtiers, by contrast, these images would have been a pleasing reminiscence of an Assyrian victory, as well as a cautionary reminder of the forces at the king's command.

Thus the campaign against Judah was commemorated quite differently in the verbal and visual accounts. This difference is not—to cite Barth's formulation of the elements of narrative—in the "tale" (Judah campaign), nor in the "teller" (Sennacherib), but rather in the "told," that is, the way of telling.[33] In addition to considerations of audience, another probable reason for this difference is the differing amount of space required by the verbal and visual modes. This is a matter of both spatial scale (the reliefs are large-scale; the inscriptions, small-scale) and relative economy. No image can hope to match the narrative economy of an annalistic statement of the form "the cities of W, X, Y, and Z, I besieged, I conquered, I carried off their spoil." Such a statement carries both a description of each episode (the capture of each city) and an implied sequence (the order in which the cities are listed). A visual image, to convey the same amount of information, would require four separate episodes, which in the wall-relief format would fill a large room. The primary emphasis in the verbal narratives, therefore, is on the broad sweep of an entire campaign, while that in the visual ones is on the detail of individual, and presumably select, episodes.

The Throne-Room Suite

Because it is the most important section of the palace, it might be expected that the decoration of the throne-room suite would have been planned with particular care. A look at its subjects and the principles upon which they are organized would seem to bear this out (see fig. 92). The suite consists of four rooms—I (the throne room), III, IV, and V—and two courts—an outer court (H) and an inner court (VI). The wall reliefs in this suite include examples of each of the visual narrative subjects found in the palace: a Babylonian campaign in Court H and Room III, the western campaign in the throne room, the eastern campaign in Room V and on the south and west walls of Court VI, and palace construction and irrigation on the north and east walls of Court VI.

There are interesting parallels between the decoration of the throne-room suite, taken as a unit, and the main points of the titularies carved on the bulls at its entrances. In approaching and passing through this suite, one encounters a sequence of three campaigns, beginning with Babylonia (Court H— first campaign), then the Levant (throne room—third campaign), and finally the Zagros (Room V—second campaign). I have suggested that these first three were the only campaigns surely represented in the Southwest Palace decoration, and it was only after the third that Sennacherib began to call himself "king of the world."[34] Since the planning of the palace decoration apparently occurred at about the same time that Sennacherib adopted the new title, this selection of images of Sennacherib dominating the edges of the empire may be seen as the visual equivalent of the verbal concept "king of the world."

The campaign to Mt. Nipur in the north is not depicted in the throne-room suite, nor for that matter in any of the surviving palace reliefs, but it is represented after a fashion by the plain slabs of NA$_4$. ^{d}ŠE.TIR stone, which a caption identified as originating at Mt. Nipur, on the walls of Rooms XXIX, XXX, and XXXIII. It is not clear why these slabs were never carved; perhaps the polished fossiliferous stone slabs were deemed sufficiently attractive without further embellishment, or perhaps they were installed in the palace only at a late stage in its construction and there wasn't the time, or inclination, to design and carve relief subjects on them. In either event, the incorporation of these slabs from the north into the decoration of the palace sometime after the fifth campaign effectively expanded the range covered by the palace wall slabs to include the northern campaign as well, thereby providing a visual counterpart for another new title, this one added after the fifth campaign, "king of the four quarters of the earth."

The militaristic tone of the titulary and annalistic text in throne-room Door a finds parallels in the scenes of military conquest that fill the walls of the throne-room suite and most of the rest of the palace. Reade has observed that the reliefs of Sennacherib, a king whose reign was relatively peaceful by Assyrian standards, seem "paradoxically full of scenes of military narrative."[35] The paradox is only apparent, however, for an ever-popular method of maintaining peace is through the threat of war, and this would be the effect of these scenes of conquest, at least for that component of the audience composed of potentially disruptive foreigners.

For members of the court, these images would serve as a gratifying record of Assyrian triumphs and simultaneously as a reminder that the king controls the army, the bulwark of power in Assyria. As already noted, the extensive texts inscribed on the doorway bulls must have been intended primarily for this audience as well. As both authors of and audience for these texts they would already have been thoroughly familiar with the ideology governing their content. Liverani refers to this reinforcing relationship as "self-indoctrination by the ruling class," the purpose of which is to keep reminding the elite of what they already "know," namely that the Assyrian cause is just and that their own status, security, and wealth derive wholly from the king.[36]

The peaceful phraseology of the titulary and building account in throne-room Door c finds its parallel on the north and east walls of Court VI. Here

FIG. 131.   Water sweeps, detail of Slab 63, Court VI, Southwest Palace, Nineveh. British Museum, WAA 124820 (photo: author).

was a series of scenes of which the primary subject is the quarrying and transport of colossi for the building of Sennacherib's new palace at Nineveh. A subsidiary subject in the same series is irrigation works, shown by a group of water sweeps raising water into a canal that eventually runs into a swamp populated by deer and a wild pig with her young (figs. 54, 56, 57, 131). Jacobsen was apparently the first to suggest that this is the artificial swamp created by Sennacherib as an outlet for the overflow from his Kisiri canal irrigation system. The building account for the Door *c* colossus states:

> To calm the rush of the waters for the orchards, I created a swamp and planted a canebrake in it. Herons, wild pigs, and deer I turned loose therein. . . . The canebrakes flourished luxuriantly, the high-flying heron built his nest there, and the wild pigs and deer multiplied abundantly.[37]

The primary purpose of the Kisiri canal was not to water the swamp, however, but to water the fields and orchards of Nineveh. This project apparently benefited all the residents of the city. In an early building account, Sennacherib says, "For the planting of orchards, I subdivided land from the plain above the city into plots of 2 PI each for the citizens of Nineveh and handed

259

(them) over to them." And in another text describing the swamp, Sennacherib writes that, thanks to the Kisiri canal, "In the summer I watered all of the orchards; in the winter, a thousand fields in the plain above and below the city I watered, yearly."[38] It is difficult to imagine a clearer or more concrete statement of the value of benevolent and stable government, a government that serves not just the king and court, but *all* of the governed. The images of building and irrigation in the Court VI reliefs, then, are the visual equivalent of the ideals of good government in the Door *c* bull titulary and are closer still to the specific examples of good government—building and irrigation—enumerated in the somewhat later titulary from the *bīt akīti* in Assur.

One other aspect of the construction scenes from Court VI is worthy of note. By means of costume and captions, Sennacherib identifies the laborers in the quarry and the men hauling the bull colossi as "inhabitants of hidden mountain regions, conquest of my hands."[39] Other reliefs in the same court show battle and deportation of captives in the mountainous country at the eastern border of the empire (see fig. 69). The implication of this opposition is clear: the enemies who once threatened Assyria from the periphery now build the capital at its center.[40]

Conclusions

In the Court VI reliefs Sennacherib's two major goals, the stabilizing of the borders and the creation of a center, are explicitly linked. The motivating force behind these two processes is revealed in the flow of the two narrative sequences in that court: both originate at the monumental doorway in the east wall of Court VI and proceed outward in opposite directions around the walls (see fig. 49).[41] This doorway is the entrance that connects Court VI with the throne-room suite whose occupant, Sennacherib, is thus designated as the single source of these two contrasting policies: conquest at the periphery, construction at the center.

The imperial priorities exemplified by the Court VI reliefs therefore harmonize with the priorities expressed in the titularies of the texts on the throne-room colossi, some of which emphasize dominance over foreign rulers while others stress good government; they likewise harmonize with the narrative portion of these same colossus texts, some of which chronicle conquests while others describe the building of the "Palace without Rival" and other public works in Nineveh. In all of these cases there is a balance between military conquest and domestic construction. This bilateral image of kingship was not idle rhetoric; from the beginning of his reign, Sennacherib divided his attentions between military campaigns directed at pacifying the borders of the empire and building campaigns aimed at the creation of an unrivaled capital.

The significance of this new capital was not merely symbolic; like the military campaigns, it also played an active role in Sennacherib's imperial scheme. The creation of a new capital is of little help in the process of expanding an empire and indeed might place an unwanted drain on resources needed for the support of the army. A magnificent capital closely identified with the ruling monarch can, however, be a very useful tool for *maintaining* an empire. Subject peoples visiting the capital would have been greatly awed by the power implied by the sheer bulk and splendor of the monuments of Nineveh, thus reinforcing their inclination to submit rather than to rebel.

The construction of the new capital, then, was not a simple matter of royal vanity, but was instead an integral part of Sennacherib's imperial policy. In the course of his reign, Sennacherib made Nineveh the center of the world, and what is more, he made it a fitting center, the greatest city the world had ever seen. It was not by accident that Nineveh was chosen as the target of Jonah's prophecy in the Old Testament; it could hardly have been otherwise.

The reliefs in Sennacherib's palace likewise actively participated in the maintenance of the realm. In comparing the pictorial decoration of Sennacherib's palace with that of his father, it appears that there has been a fundamental shift in the function of palace decoration. Sargon II's palace reliefs balance narratives of conquest with images of tribute processions in an expression of an Assyrian ideal order based on the expansion of the empire and the voluntary delivery of tribute. Sargon's reliefs present this ideal as a universally acknowledged fact, though the historical record shows that not all of his expansionist campaigns were successful, nor was all tribute surrendered voluntarily. Thus in Sargon's palace reliefs a statement of the way things *ought* to be was presented as though it was a statement of the way things *are*, regardless of whether this assertion was fully supported by the facts.

By comparison with this expression of a desired ideal, which characterized not only Sargon II's palace reliefs but also those of the throne room area of the palace of Assurnasirpal II, the reliefs in Sennacherib's palace appear more pragmatic.[42] Gone are the images of lengthy tribute processions in the outer, more public areas of Sargon's palace—winding around the courts, through the corridors, and into the throne room. They are replaced in Sennacherib's palace by expansive narratives of military conquest.

The key to understanding these images would seem to be not in their subject matter, but rather in their audience and function. The reliefs in the more public areas of Sennacherib's palace, such as the outer court and throne room, seem to be directed more to outsiders than insiders, and their predominant message is one of warning rather than affirmation. One of their principal functions is apparently to insure the stability of the borders of the empire through the threat of violence expressed in graphic and easily perceptible terms. The ideal of maintaining the flow of tribute from the edges of the empire to its center has not changed, but the reliefs now take a more active part in this process. Rather than presenting visitors to the more public spaces with passive images showing universal submission as a *fait accompli*, Sennacherib's reliefs sharply confront them with the consequences of rebellion.

In the more private inner parts of the palace, by contrast, Sennacherib's reliefs balance these images of conquest at the periphery with images of construction in the center, emphasizing for insiders not only the risks involved in rebellion but the benefits of good government as well. Thus, for audiences both outside and inside the palace circle Sennacherib transformed the role of palace reliefs from affirmations of universal rule into tools to help maintain that rule.

12

PALACE WITHOUT RIVAL

In the introduction to this study I set forth the (apparently) modest goal of achieving "an appreciation of Assyrian palace decoration as a synthesis of text and image." I chose to try to make this case with Sennacherib's palace at Nineveh for the stated reason that its decoration is relatively fully documented, but I hope it has become clear that another reason for my choice is because the palace and the king who built it are so remarkable.

My investigation commences with Sennacherib's palace inscriptions, which serve as a primary source of information for much that follows. In order to understand the potential impact of these texts, it is first necessary to see them in their temporal and physical contexts. In neo-Assyrian palaces before Sennacherib, historical texts were consistently inscribed in three locations: on doorway colossi, on thresholds, and on a text band running across the center of the wall relief slabs. Different kings, however, placed different forms of texts in these standard locations. In Assurnasirpal II's palace, the colossus and wall slab inscriptions were general summary texts and the threshold texts were annalistic in form, while in Sargon II's palace the wall slabs carried an annalistic text and the colossi and thresholds displayed summary texts. Virtually all of these texts include, in addition to their historical component, an account of the building of the royal palace that they adorn. In the palaces of Tiglath-pileser III and Sargon II, a fourth type of inscription appeared: epigraphs, that is, brief explanatory captions carved on the background of the relief images.

In Sennacherib's palace long texts were confined to the colossi, the other two traditional text locations having been replaced by floral patterns on the thresholds and expanded narrative imagery on the wall slabs. To compensate for this restriction in the number of inscribed spaces, Sennacherib's colossi did not display the standardized summary text of Assurnasirpal or Sargon, but rather a variety of texts, ranging from long annalistic texts, to shorter summary texts, to pure building accounts with no military component. These texts, too, all contained an account of the building of the palace. Sennacherib also continued the use of epigraphs, but in his palace these captions were transformed from his predecessor's one-line identification of an enemy city or a friendly camp into sometimes lengthy descriptions of the individuals and actions depicted in the accompanying images.

Thus, in the arrangement of texts and images in his palace, Sennacherib and his advisers accomplished two things: they divorced specific visual images from unrelated general texts, placing each in its own clearly defined space; and they expanded those short texts that directly enhance the flow of the visual narratives of the reliefs. This separation benefited primarily the reliefs, which no longer had to compete with unrelated texts for the viewer's attention, and which were now no longer constrained by the cramped two-register format imposed by the central text band. All of this suggests that Sennacherib felt that easily readable images were more likely to convey his message than were texts.

I then turn from Sennacherib's texts to his palace reliefs and their architectural context. The strategies and goals of various excavators of Sennacherib's palace are outlined and their results are summarized. We see from this that the excavation techniques employed were generally primitive and that no excavator had the principal goal of recovering the palace plan, which explains why our knowledge of the architecture of the excavated part of the palace is still so sketchy.

The inadequacies of the excavation record are compensated for to some degree by extensive textual evidence that can be used to reconstruct the extent of Sennacherib's palace and the chronology of its construction. On the basis of measurements contained in Sennacherib's building accounts, it is clear that the portion of the palace excavated by Layard represents only a fraction of its original extent and that a structure excavated to the northeast of the palace, the so-called *bīt nakkapti*, may originally have been part of the palace. Concerning the chronology of the palace's construction, a fragmentary eponym canon and dated foundation cylinders excavated in the palace indicate that the foundations of the palace were laid around 700 B.C. Palace dimensions given in the throne-room bull texts suggest that the eastern extension must have been added after 694. A foundation prism dated 691 indicates that the palace was complete by the end of that year.

The quarrying and transport of the stone colossi for the palace doors are investigated using as primary evidence a relief series in Sennacherib's palace that depicts this process, supplemented by texts that record at least four, and perhaps five, distinct sources of stone for his palace decoration. Sculptural alabaster, the most common stone for wall slabs and colossi, was found near to hand, divinely revealed in the area of the city of Balaṭai, which appears to have been on the east bank of the Tigris across from modern Eski Mosul. By contrast, sources of three unusual types of stone were located at the fringes of the empire, evidently discovered in the course of the royal campaigns to the west and north.

To appreciate Sennacherib's palace reliefs, they must first be distinguished from later reliefs in the same palace. To this end, the observations of several scholars who have dealt with this problem are examined. I concur with their conclusions that while the reliefs in the majority of the rooms in the South-west Palace date to the time of Sennacherib, the reliefs in four rooms, XIX, XXII, XXVIII, and XXXIII, do not. Only one of these, Room XXXIII, is securely dated to the time of Assurbanipal on the basis of epigraphs. The reliefs in the other three rooms, though very similar to securely dated reliefs in Assurbanipal's North Palace, are uninscribed. Their ascription to Assurbanipal must therefore remain tentative, but in any case they were certainly created after Sennacherib's reign.

A corpus of Sennacherib reliefs having been defined, we are then able to consider their subjects and their distribution throughout his palace. On the basis of historical, epigraphic, and pictorial evidence, it appears that only Sennacherib's first three, or perhaps four, campaigns were represented in the reliefs. In addition to these scenes of military narrative, which comprise the vast majority of the Southwest Palace reliefs, there are also two examples each of royal processions and palace construction scenes.

Concerning the distribution of the relief subjects the evidence is far from complete, but it appears that in two cases large suites of rooms were decorated with a single campaign, while in a third case, the throne-room suite, a different campaign was shown in each room, and this mixture of subjects was further diversified by showing palace construction scenes in the inner court (VI) of this suite. Most rooms in Sennacherib's palace apparently displayed only a single subject; there are only three known exceptions. One of these was a reception room that showed processions of eastern and western captives. The other two were courtyards where the juxtaposition of two narrative subjects in a single space serves to express imperial ideology: the excellence of the king as military leader and civil administrator in the case of Court VI and the all-encompassing extent of the empire in the case of Court LXIV.

Finally, I consider the principles of organization—the program—of the

Southwest Palace reliefs and texts and their intended meaning. I begin by distinguishing those features in Sennacherib's palace decoration that were taken over from the palaces of his predecessors from those features that were new. By thus highlighting both traditional and innovative forms, the character of Sennacherib's decoration as uniquely expressive of his goals and ideals as Assyrian king begins to come into focus. Sennacherib, it appears, retained the general forms of his predecessors, for example in the layout and facade decoration of this throne room and in the use of carved wall slabs, while altering their content, as in the introduction of new protective figures and palace building scenes, and their structure, through the use of a consistent perspective and coherent temporal sequences.

To this point, I have considered Sennacherib's palace decoration pretty much in isolation, but there can be no expression without an audience. This raises the question of the people in the palace. A survey of neo-Assyrian texts and images reveals what types of people would have had access to at least some portion of the palace reliefs—their actual audience. The principal components of this audience were the king, the royal family, courtiers, servants (both Assyrian and foreign), future kings, gods, Assyrians, provincials, subject foreigners, and independent foreigners. It is less certain which of these groups the reliefs were created for—their intended audience. Sennacherib's boast that he furnished his palace to the astonishment of all people suggests that at least part of the purpose of the reliefs was that they be shown off. Thus it is probably justifiable to suppose that these images were directed at a broad audience, for whom the denoted meaning would remain constant, though the connoted meanings would of course vary for different segments of that audience.

The threads thus far spun are finally drawn together in order to articulate the meaning of Sennacherib's palace decoration. Sennacherib's public image as it emerges from his words and pictures is that of a ruler who strove for peace but did not hesitate to fight, a stabilizer of the borders whose principal interest lay in the creation of a capital. For the majority of the Assyrian empire, Sennacherib's reign was a period of unprecedented peace, and the new capital city of Nineveh was the focus of a series of building projects that were likewise unprecedented in ancient Mesopotamia and which transformed the ancient cult city of Ishtar into the greatest city in the world. These same bilateral concerns are expressed in the palace inscriptions, where the titularies and the accompanying texts exemplify this equilibrium between military and civic affairs, and in the palace's relief decoration, which balances scenes of conquest at the borders with scenes of construction in the capital.

The contrast in Sennacherib's reliefs between battle and building, juxta-posing the risks of insurrection with the benefits of good government, would only have been seen by viewers with access to the more private areas of the palace interior, chiefly those inside the palace circle. In the more public outer areas, Sennacherib replaced the tribute processions that were in the equiva-lent locations in Sargon II's palace with military narratives, which served as explicit reminders to visitors of the consequences of rebellion or nonpayment of tribute. In Sennacherib's palace, then, the reliefs were called upon to play an active role in the keeping of the peace, serving outsiders as a deterrent to thoughts of revolt and insiders as a reminder that the prosperity of Assyria is dependent on its king.

The decoration of Sennacherib's "Palace without Rival" was thus a re-sponse to and an expression of a series of linked oppositions. Its audience consisted of insiders and outsiders: Assyrians and foreigners, residents of and visitors to the palace. The media are text and image, each exploited with a clear awareness of its strengths and limitations, each displaying marked in-novations when compared with examples by Sennacherib's predecessors. The subjects are Sennacherib's military and civic accomplishments, con-trasted and balanced in both the texts and images. And the message—ex-pressed in the reliefs and in the texts displayed on the bull colossi—was that Sennacherib's aims were twofold: the maintenance of the boundaries of em-pire and the creation of a center. In the decorative program of Sennacherib's palace, these dual aims were inextricably entwined, as nonsubmissive peoples from the periphery of the empire served as labor for the construction of the palace at its center, while the palace in its awesome magnificence in turn served to reduce potential troublemakers to submission.

APPENDIX 1

Epigraphs on Sennacherib's Palace Reliefs

The following is a listing of all known Sennacherib epigraphs from the Southwest Palace, as well as the inscriptions on the backs of the sculptures. The inscriptions on the colossi are too lengthy to include here; references for them are given in chapter 2, notes 7 and 8.

COURT H

Slab 2 north: Fragmentary epigraph from "bas-relief representing Siege" (Layard 1851, 75:C):

(1) [. . .]MAN ŠÚ MAN ⟨KUR⟩ *aš+šur* URU.MEŠ
(2) [. . .]-*ti a-na ka-šá-di il-la*[*k*]
(1) [Sennacherib], king of the world, king of Assyria, the cities of
(2) [PN or GN] he goes to conquer.

ROOM I (B)

Door *e*, threshold: Brief inscription in the center of the floral threshold (see figure 13). It is a rough duplicate of Sennacherib's palace brick inscription (Layard 1851, 82:B; Luckenbill 1924, 126, "Ill"). This transliteration was made from the original.

(1) ᵐᵈ30-PAP.MEŠ-SU MAN ŠÚ MAN KUR *aš+šur*
É.GAL ZAG.DI.NU.TUK.A
(2) *a-na mu-šab* ⌜*be*⌝-⌜*lu*⌝-*ti*-⌜*šú*⌝ *qé-reb* NINA.KI *eš-šiš ú-še-peš*
(1) Sennacherib, king of the world, king of Assyria: a palace without rival
(2) for ⌜his lordly⌝ dwelling inside Nineveh he caused to be built anew.

Door *e*, reverse: "behind the bulls, was a short inscription, containing the name and titles of the king" (Layard 1849a, vol. 2, 126; Layard 1851, 75:D). The same text was on the backs of the wall relief slabs (figure 132):

269

Fɪɢ. 132. Inscription on back of wall slab, detail of Slab 4, Room I, Southwest Palace, Nineveh (photo: author).

Fɪɢ. 133. Fragmentary epigraph, detail of Slab 1, Room I, Southwest Palace, Nineveh (photo: author).

Fɪɢ. 134. Fragmentary epigraph, detail of Slab 4a, Room I, Southwest Palace, Nineveh (photo: author).

(1) É.GAL ^{md}30-PAP.MEŠ-SU   Palace of Sennacherib,
(2) MAN GAL MAN *kiš-šá-ti*   great king, king of the world,
(3) MAN KUR *aš+šur dan-dan-nu*   king of Assyria, the almighty one,
(4) *e-til kal mal-ki*   the lord of all kings.

Slab 1: Epigraph, "almost illegible," still visible *in situ* at the upper right above the city (figure 133; Layard 1849a, vol. 2, 125f.). The preservation is very poor. A bad copy is published in Layard (1851, 85:b). This provisional transliteration and translation were made from the original with the assistance of Pamela Gerardi and John MacGinnis. Signs marked with an asterisk (*) were restored from Layard (1851, 85:b):

(1) [^{md}30-PAP.MEŠ-SU] ⌈MAN⌉ ŠÚ MAN KUR *aš*+[*šur* ^mx-x-(x)]-*e*
(2) [LUGAL URU x-x]-⌈KI *ti-ib*⌉ *ta-ha-*[*zi-ia e-dúr*]-*ma*
(3) [*gi-mir*] ⌈*el-la*⌉-*te-šú e-*⌈*zib*⌉-[*ma* x-x-(x)]-⌈*te*⌉-*te*
(4) ⌈*ú*⌉-[*ša*]-⌈*aṣ*⌉-*bit ba-hu-la-*[*te-šú* x-(x)]-⌈*ta*⌉-*šú*
(5) *a-na zuq-ti* KUR-*i* [x-x-x]-SAG
(6) *ip-par-*⌈*šid*⌉ *ar-ki-šú* [*ar*]-⌈*di**⌉-*ma*
(7) *i-na zuq-ti* KUR-*i* [*áš*]-⌈*ta**⌉-*kan*
(8) ⌈*tah*⌉-*ta-šú-un* URU ⌈*il*⌉-[x]-⌈KI⌉
(9) ⌈URU⌉ LUGAL-*ti-šú i-na* ^dGIŠ.BAR [*aq-mu*]
(1) [Sennacherib], king of the world, king of Assyria: [PN],
(2) [king of GN], the onslaught of [my] ⌈battle⌉ [he feared] and
(3) [all of] his ⌈troops⌉ he ⌈deserted⌉. [. . .]
(4) ⌈I caused to be seized⌉. [His] soldiers [. . .]
(5) To the summit of the mountains [. . .]
(6) he fled. After him [I followed];
(7) at the top of the mountains [I] ⌈brought about⌉
(8) their defeat. The city [GN],
(9) his royal city, with fire [I burned].

Slab 4a: Fragmentary epigraph still preserved on the first slab to the north of Door *e*, apparently not recorded by Layard (figure 134). This transliteration was made from the original, which is very badly worn:

(1) URU *a-ta?-un?*-[. . .]   The city of [GN]
(2) *al-me* KUR-[*ud*]   I besieged, I conquered.

Slab 9: Epigraph over the head of the king enthroned in his fortified camp (Layard 1849b, 77): *uš-man-nu šá* ^{md}30-PAP.MEŠ-SU MAN KUR *aš+šur* (Camp of Sennacherib, king of Assyria).

FIG. 135. Fragmentary epigraph, detail of Slab 24, Room I, Southwest Palace, Nineveh (photo: author).

Slab 24: Epigraph on very badly damaged slab, subject uncertain, previously unpublished (figure 135). This rough transliteration was made from the original. Because of its fragmentary condition, I am unable to offer a restoration or translation.

(1) *me-re-*⌈x⌉-[. . .]
(2) *ma-ra-*[. . .]-⌈x-x-x⌉
(3) *un-*⌈x⌉-[. . .]-⌈x⌉-*un*
(4) *ana* ᵐ⌈*ni*⌉-[. . .]-*ir*

ROOM III (G)
Slab 8: Epigraph (see figure 78; Layard 1851, 82:A):

(1) *dil-bat*-KI *al-me* KUR-*ud*   Dilbat I besieged, I conquered,
(2) *áš-lu-la šal-la-su*   I carried off its spoil.

ROOM V (C)
Slab 11: Epigraph "over the king in a chariot" (figure 136; Layard 1851, 75:E, where it is mislabeled as Room III, Slab 2—see chap. 7, note 12). This transliteration was made from the original, except for the PAP.MEŠ in line 1, which is now missing from the original but is preserved in Layard's copy (1851, 75:E:1):

(1) ᵐᵈ30-PAP.MEŠ-SU MAN [ŠÚ]   Sennacherib, king of [the world]
(2) MAN KUR *aš*+*šur*-KI ⌈*šal-la-at*⌉   king of Assyria, ⌈the booty⌉
(3) URU *ka-su-*⌈*și*⌉   of Kasuși (?)
(4) *ma-har-šu* ⌈*e*⌉-[*ti*]-⌈*iq*⌉   ⌈passed in review⌉ before him.

272

Slab 30: Above the king was an epigraph that Layard said "had been entirely defaced," previously unpublished (figure 137; Layard 1849a, vol. 2, 133). This transliteration was made from the original:

(1) [ᵐ]ᵈ[30-PAP].⌈MEŠ⌉-[SU MAN ŠÚ]
(2) MAN KUR [aš + šur-KI šal]-⌈la⌉-[at]
(3) ⌈URU⌉ [x-x-x-(x)]-⌈bu-x⌉
(4) [ma-har-šu e]-ti-iq
(1) S[ennacherib, king of the world]
(2) king of [Assyria, the boo]ty
(3) of [GN]
(4) passed in rev[iew before him].

Slab 35: Fragmentary epigraph, still visible on slab *in situ* (see figure 80; Layard 1851, 81:B):

(1) [URU a-ra-an-z]i-a-šu   [The city of Aranz]iaš
(2) [al-me KUR]-ud   [I besieged, I conqu]ered,
(3) [aš-lu-la šal]-la-su   [I carried off its sp]oil.

Note: The first sign is *nam* or *zi*, followed by *-a-šu*. The only city name known to end this way is Aranziaš/Erinziaš. Elenzaš is also possible, but is not attested with these signs (Parpola 1970, 23, 123, 126).

Slab backs: Madhloom (1969, 48) reported inscriptions on the backs of the Room V slabs. Presumably this duplicates the text of Room I, Door *e*.

FIG. 136.   Epigraph giving city name Kasuṣi, detail of Slab 11, Room V, Southwest Palace, Nineveh (photo: author).

FIG. 137. Fragmentary epigraph, detail of Slab 30, Room V, Southwest Palace, Nineveh (photo: author).

COURT VI (I)

Slab 60: Epigraph (G. Smith 1878, 160–61; copy in Meissner and Rost 1893, 43, pl. 10:1; original visible in Paterson 1915, pl. 29).

(1) ᵐᵈ30-PAP.MEŠ-SU MAN ŠÚ MAN KUR *aš* + *šur* ᵈALÀD.ᵈLAMMA.MEŠ

(2) GAL.MEŠ *ša i-na er-ṣe-et URU ba-la-ṭa-a-a*

(3) *ib-ba-nu-ú a-na* É.GAL *be-lu-ti-šú*

(4) *ša qé-reb* NINA.KI *ha-di-iš ú-šal-da-da*

(1) Sennacherib, king of the world, king of Assyria: great bull colossi,

(2) which were made in the district of Balaṭai,

(3) to his lordly palace,

(4) which is in Nineveh, joyfully he had them dragged.

Slab 62: Two four-line epigraphs, illegible in the drawing, perhaps duplicates of the epigraph on Slab 60 (see figure 30; Layard 1853b, 17).

Slab 66: Epigraph (Meissner and Rost 1893, 43, pl. 10:2):

(1) ^{md}30-PAP.MEŠ-SU MAN ŠÚ MAN KUR *aš* + *šur* NA$_4$ *pi-i-lu pe-ṣu-ú*

(2) *ša ki-i ṭè-im* DINGIR-*ma a-na šip-ri* É.GAL-*ia ina er-ṣe-*[*et*]

(3) URU *ba-la-ṭa-a-a in-nam-ru* UN.MEŠ *da-ád-me*

(4) *na-ki-ri ù* ERÍN.MEŠ *hur-šá-a-ni pa-az-ru-ti* KUR-*ti* ŠU^{II}-*ia* [*ina*]

(5) *qul-me-e ù ak-kul-la-ti* AN.BAR *ú-šá-áš-*[*šu-nu-ti*]

(6) ^{d}ALÀD.^{d}LAMMA.MEŠ GAL.MEŠ *a-na* KÁ.MEŠ É.GAL-*ia ú-še-e-*[*piš*]

(1) Sennacherib, king of the world, king of Assyria: white limestone

(2) which, at the command of the god, for the construction of my palace had been discovered

(3) in the district of Balaṭai; I had men from enemy towns

(4) and the inhabitants of hidden mountain regions, conquest of my hand,

(5) wield iron picks and mason's-picks(?),

(6) and I had great bull colossi made for the gates of my palace.

Slab 68: Six-line epigraph (visible in Paterson 1915, pl. 36; transliterated in V. Scheil, *Recueil de travaux*, XV, 1893, 149); duplicate of Slab 66, with the following variants:

line 3: *ba-hu-la-ti* (soldiers), instead of UN.MEŠ (men)

line 4: *la kan-šu-ti* (rebellious), instead of *pa-az-ru-ti* (hidden)

line 6: *ib-tu-*[*qu*] (they carved), instead of *ú-še-e-*[*piš*] (I had made)

ROOM VII
Slab 14: Illegible unpublished epigraph in front of the king in his chariot (see figure 32; Layard 1853b, 29).

ROOM X
Slab 7: Fragmentary epigraph (see figure 35; Layard 1853b, 50): *uš-man-nu ša* ^{md}30-[. . .]   Camp of Senn[acherib . . .]

ROOM XIV
Slab 10: Epigraph (see figure 17; S. Smith 1938, pl. 63):

(1) [URU] *al-am-mu al-me* [KUR-*ud*]

(2) [*aš*]-*lu-la šal-l*[*a-su*]

(1) [The city of] Alammu I besieged, [I conquered,]

(2) [I] carried off ⌜its spoil⌝.

ROOM XXXIII

Slab backs: "On the back of each slab were inscribed [Sennacherib's] name and usual titles" (Layard 1853a, 459), evidently the same text as in Room I, Door *e*.

Door *p*: Inscription "behind the winged lions at the entrance" (Layard 1853a, 459; Rawlinson 1861, vol. 1, 7:E):

(1) É.GAL ᵐᵈ30-PAP.MEŠ-SU MAN GAL

(2) MAN *dan-nu* MAN ŠÚ MAN KUR *aš+šur* NA₄.ᵈŠE.TIR

(3) *šá* (v. *ša*) GIN₇ *še-im ṣa-ah-ha-ri ši-kin-šú* (v. GAR-*šú*)

(4) *nu-us-su-qu ša ina* (v. *i-na*) *tar-ṣi* LUGAL.MEŠ

(5) AD.MEŠ-*ia ma-la* NA₄ GÚ *šu-qu-ru* (v. *aq-ru*)

(6) *i-na* GÌRᴵᴵ KUR *ni-pur* KUR-*i* (v. *šad-di-e*) *ra-ma-nu-uš*

(7) *ud-dan-ni a-na* ꜟÁB.ZA.ZA-*a-ti*

(8) *ú-še-piš-ma ú-šal-di-da* (v. -*id*)

(9) *qé-reb* URU *ni-na-a*

(1) Palace of Sennacherib, great king,

(2) powerful king, king of the world, king of Assyria: NA₄.ᵈŠE.TIR stone,

(3) whose appearance is like that of mottled barley(?),

(4) which in the time of the kings,

(5) my fathers, was valued only as a necklace stone,

(6) revealed itself to me at the foot of Mt. Nipur.

(7) I had female sphinxes

(8) made of it and had them dragged

(9) into Nineveh.

Slabs 1–6: Eight epigraphs, all dating to the reign of Assurbanipal (Gerardi 1988). These postdate Sennacherib and therefore are not included here.

ROOM XXXVI

Slab 12: Epigraph in front of enthroned king (see figures 3, 112):

(1) ᵐᵈ30-PAP.MEŠ-SU MAN ŠÚ MAN KUR *aš+šur*

(2) *ina* GIŠ.GU.ZA *né-me-di ú-šib-ma*

(3) *šal-la-at* URU *la-ki-su*

(4) *ma-ha-ar-šu e-ti-iq*

(1) Sennacherib, king of the world, king of Assyria,

(2) sat in a *nēmedu*-throne and

(3) the booty of Lachish

(4) passed in review before him.

Epigraph over the tent (see figures 3, 112):

(1) *za-ra-tum*   Tent
(2) *šá* md30-PAP.MEŠ-SU   of Sennacherib
(3)LUGAL KUR *aš+šur*   king of Assyria.

ROOM XXXVIII

"Over one of the castles could be traced a few letters, giving no clue, however, to its name or site" (Layard 1853a, 342). This is probably to be identified with the epigraph shown in figure 36:

(1) URU [. . .]   The city [. . .]
(2) [. . .]   [. . .]

ROOM XLV

Mostly defaced epigraph shown in slab drawing (see figure 74):

(1) [. . .]   [. . .]
(2) [. . .]   [. . .]
(3) *šal-la-*[*at* . . .]   the booty [of GN]
(4) *ma-ha-⌈ar⌉-*[*šu e-ti-iq*]   [passed in review] before [him].

ROOM XLVII

Near the "castle" was a (presumably) fragmentary epigraph (Layard 1853a, 584): *ina* ᵈGIŠ.⌈BAR⌉ ⌈*aq*⌉*-mu* (I burned with fire). This is probably to be identified with the epigraph shown in figure 38, the provenience of which is given only as "Old Palace—Kouyunjik":

(1') [*aš-lu*]*-⌈la šal-la⌉-*[*su*] ⌈*ap-pul*⌉
(2') ⌈*aq*!⌉*-qur ina* ᵈGIŠ.⌈BAR⌉ [*aq*]*-⌈mu*⌉
(1') ⌈I carried off its spoil, I tore (it) down,⌉
(2') ⌈I⌉ demolished (it), with fire ⌈I burned (it)⌉.

HALL XLIX

Layard published only Hincks's translations of three detached fragmentary epigraphs (all from Layard 1853a, 118):

(1) "Sennacherib, king of Assyria . . . (some object, the nature not ascertained) of wood, which from the Tigris I caused to be brought up (*through?*) the Kharri, or Khasri, on sledges (or boats), I caused to be carried (or to mount)."
Note: After consulting Hincks's syllabary (*Transactions of the Royal Irish*

Academy, vol. 22, 1855, 349), Paterson (1915, 11) concluded that the uncertain river name was probably *harru* ("canal") and not "Khosr," which is written ÍD *hu-su-ur* (Luckenbill 1924, 124:43).

(2) "Some objects also of wood 'brought from Mount Lebanon, and taken up (to the top of the mound) from the Tigris.'"

(3) "Similar objects are described as coming from or up the same Kharri or Khasri."

ROOM LI (n)

Paterson (1915, 4) reported a plaster cast of an inscription from the back of Slab 28 (formerly Kouyunjik Gallery 39) in the British Museum. The text was said to be the same as the one behind the bulls of Room I, Door *e*.

ROOM LX

Slab 2: Epigraph "over one of the castles captured and destroyed by the Assyrians" (Layard 1853a, 460; G. Smith 1878, 52; location given in Layard's ms. copy—British Museum, WAA, Ms. A, 57 verso):

(1) URU É-ᵐ*ku-bat-ti al-me* KUR-*ud*
(2) *áš-lu-la šal-la-su ina* ᵈGIŠ.BAR *aq-mu*
(1) Bīt-Kubatti I besieged, I conquered,
(2) I carried off its spoil, with fire I burned.

ROOM LXX

Slab 4: Epigraph in front of Sennacherib in his chariot (see figure 67):

(1) ᵐᵈ30-PAP.MEŠ-SU MAN ŠÚ MAN KUR *aš + šur*
(2) *šal-la-at* ÍD *a-gam-me*
(3) *ša* URU *sa-ah-ri-na*
(4) *ma-ha-ar-šu e-ti-iq*
(1) Sennacherib, king of the world, king of Assyria:
(2) the booty of the marshes
(3) of Sahrina
(4) passed in review before him.

"ISHTAR TEMPLE PROCESSION"

At least one slab was reported to carry "Sennacherib's palace inscription" (Gadd 1936, 94; see Room I, Door *e*).

APPENDIX 2

Publication References for Southwest Palace Sculpture,
Including a Concordance of Rooms and Figures in This Book

Assembled here are references for all published sculptures for which the original location is known. For doorways, brief descriptions of their decoration are also given. Fragments of uncertain provenience are not included. When the same reproduction of a sculpture has been published several times, only the best or most accessible version is cited. When a sculpture has been reproduced in several forms—e.g., drawing, engraving, and/or photograph—all are cited. All room and door designations are those used in Layard's final plan (following Index); if he used a different designation in his first plan (see figure 21), this is shown in parentheses.

COURT H

Door *a:* Door jambs: two bull colossi, two winged figures with cone and bucket, two pairs of six-curled figures (Layard 1853a, 135f.; Layard 1853b, 6b; fragments with inscription: Brit. Mus., WAA 118815 a & b, 118817, 118819, 118821)

> **Slab 4:** my figure 93
> **Bull 6:** my figure 125
> **Bull 7:** my figure 124
> **Slab 9:** Gadd 1938, pl. XVIII

Buttresses: pair of antithetical bull colossi, between which was a colossal hero grasping a lion (Layard 1853a, 136)

> **Slabs 1–3:** my figure 26
> **Slabs 10–12:** my figure 10; Gadd 1938, pl. XVIII; Layard 1853a, 135, 137

Door *c:* Two bull colossi (my figure 126; Layard 1849a, vol. 2, 129f.; el-Wailly 1965, Arabic section, figure 2 following p. 9)

Door ?: "four lion sphinxes"—not on Layard's plans (Layard 1849a, vol. 2, 137)

279

Slabs 1–3 north: Recently reexcavated; oblique views in Madhloom 1972, pl. 22, right; and el-Wailly 1965, Arabic section, figure 2 after p. 9

Slab 3a north: my figure 27 (first slab north of Door *a*)

ROOM I (B)

Door *d* (*b*): two bull colossi (my figure 129; Layard 1849a, vol. 2, 128)

Door *e* (*a*): two bull colossi (Layard 1849a, vol. 2, 126; el-Wailly 1966, Arabic section, figure 5 before p. 1)

Door *f*: each jamb had a human-footed figure in front of a bird-footed one (Layard 1849a, vol. 2, 124; personal observation)

Slabs 1–2: my figures 127, 133; Layard 1849b, 74

Slab 3: my figure 128; ibid., 69

Slab 4: my figure 132; el-Wailly 1966, Arabic section, figure 5 before p. 1

Slab 4a: (first slab north of Door *e*): my figure 134; see Door *e* above

Slab 5: my figures 28, 29

Slab 9: Layard 1849b, 77

Slab 13: ibid., 70; el-Wailly 1965, Arabic section, figure 4, following p. 9

Slab 14: my figures 85, 129; Layard 1849b, 71; Barnett 1969, pl. I.2

Slab 15: my figures 85, 129; Barnett 1969, pl. I.2

Slab 21?: el-Wailly 1965, Arabic section, figure 3 following p. 9

Slab 24?: my figure 135

Slab 25?: Madhloom 1967, pl. X

ROOM III (G)

Slab 4: Layard 1849b, 72

Slab 8: my figure 46; ibid., 73; Reade 1980a, pl. 7

ROOM IV (A)

Slab 2: my figure 31

Slab 10: A distant view is in the right foreground of Madhloom 1972, pl. 28:left (printed backwards)

Slab 11: detail: my figure 30

ROOM V (C)

Slab 1: detail: Madhloom 1967, pl. VIII:A (verified on site)

Slab 5: Layard 1849b, 79

Slab 6: ibid., 78; Reade 1980a, pl. 2

Slab 7: detail: Layard 1849a, vol. 2, 184 (verified on site)

Slab 11: detail: my figure 136

Slab 30: Layard 1849b, 80; detail: my figure 137

Slab 35: my figure 80

Slab 36: ibid., 68; Madhloom 1972, pl. 27

Slab 37: Madhloom 1967, pl. XI (verified on site)

Slab 41: Layard 1849a, vol. 2, 469 (verified on site)

COURT VI (I)

Doors *a* (*b*), *d*, *g*, *k*: two human-headed bull colossi, to each side one colossal winged figure carrying a cone and bucket and one pair of six-curled figures (figures 49, 53, 94; Layard 1853a, 71, 102, 229; Gadd 1936, 167f.)

Door *b*: The right edge of Slab 64, which should be in the north jamb of this door, shows part of a quarry scene similar to Slab 66

Doors *c*, *e*: "Colossal winged figures" (Layard 1853a, 229)

Door *i*: "Six colossal figures, three on each side. The upper part of all of them had been destroyed. They appear to have been eagle-headed and lion-headed monsters" (ibid., 73)

Door *j*: "A small doorway" (ibid., 72)

Door *m*: The west jamb shows Assyrian soldiers on a campaign in wooded mountains (personal observation).

Slab 1: my figure 116; Layard 1849b, 81

Slabs 11–13: my figure 69; Layard 1853b, 37

Slabs 19–20: ibid., 38

Slabs 45–47: my figure 61; Layard 1853b, 16

Slab 53: my figure 60; Hall 1928; pl. 31; Layard 1853b, 12:b (Brit. Mus., WAA 124823)

Slabs 54, 56: my figure 59; Layard 1853b, 13

Slab 58: my figure 58 (Brit. Mus., WAA 124822)

Slab 60: my figure 57; Paterson 1915, pl. 29; Layard 1853b, 12:a (Brit. Mus., WAA 124824)

Slab 62: my figure 56; Layard 1853b, 17

Slabs 63–64: my figures 54, 131; Layard 1853b, 15 (Brit. Mus., WAA 124820)

Slabs 66–67: my figure 50; Layard 1853b, 14 (Brit. Mus., WAA 124821)

Slab 68: my figure 50; Paterson 1915, pl. 36; Layard 1853b, 14 (Istanbul, Museum of Ancient East, 2)

ROOM VII

Slabs 12–14: my figure 32; Layard 1853b, 29 (identified by E. Bleibtreu, personal communication, letter of 22 January 1987)

ROOM VIII (w)

Slabs 11–13: my figure 33; fragment of 11: S. Smith 1938, pl. 40 (Brit. Mus., WAA 124772)

ROOM VIII (e)

Slabs 3–4: my figure 34

ROOM X

Slabs 7 and 11: my figure 35; Layard 1853b, 50

ROOM XII

Slabs 5, 6: Gadd 1936, pl. 15; fragment: S. Smith 1938, pl. 44 (Brit. Mus., WAA 124783)

Slab 7: Gadd 1936, pl. 15; fragments: S. Smith 1938, pls. 45, 46 (Brit. Mus., WAA 124779, 124780)

Slabs 12–15: my figure 83; Layard 1853b, 18

ROOM XIV

Door *a*: On each jamb "two colossal figures, whose lower extremities alone remained, the upper part of the slabs having been destroyed: one appeared to have been eagle-headed, with the body of a man, and the other a monster, with human head and the feet of a lion" (Layard 1853a, 72); this is probably my figure 96

Slabs 4–6: my figure 121; S. Smith 1938, pl. 56 (Brit. Mus., WAA 124784)

Slabs 8–11: my figure 17; Layard 1853b, 39; S. Smith 1938, pl. 60 (Brit. Mus., WAA 124785)

Slabs 13–16: my figure 18; 13–14 only: S. Smith 1938, pl. 42 (Brit. Mus., WAA 124786); 15 only: S. Smith 1938, pl. 43 (Brit. Mus., WAA 124787)

COURT XIX

Door *a*: "A pair of colossal human-headed lions, carved in coarse limestone" (Layard 1853a, 230)

Doors *g, i, k, m*: "Formed by gigantic figures" (ibid., 442, 445)

Door *h:* Two bull colossi of "fossiliferous limestone" (ibid., 445), each flanked by a winged figure with cone and bucket (Gadd 1936, 166; Gadd 1938, pl. 17)

Door *j:* "Formed by colossal figures" (Layard 1853a, 442)

Door *l:* "A center portal flanked by winged bulls" (ibid., 442)

Slabs 1–8: W. S. Smith 1960, figure 4; fragment of 3: ibid., figure 1 (Boston, Museum of Fine Arts 60.133); fragment of 8: *Illustrated London News,* 7 November 1959, 601, lower right (Brit. Mus., WAA 132814)

Slab 9: Gadd 1936, pl. 14; fragment: *Archaeology* 8 (1955): 80 (Royal Ontario Museum, no. 950.86)

Slab 10: Gadd 1936, pl. 14; Paterson 1915, pl. 43; mislabeled "13" (Brit. Mus., WAA 124825)

Slabs 11–12: my figure 75; Layard 1853b, 42; Paterson 1915, pls. 40–41 (Brit. Mus., WAA 124825)

Slab 14: Gadd 1938, pl. 17

Slabs 15–16: Layard 1853b, 43

Slabs 17–19: S. Smith 1938, pls. 48–47 (Brit. Mus., WAA 124782)

Slabs 20–21: Layard 1853b, 41

Slab 22(?): fragment: E. Terrace, *Bulletin of the Museum of Fine Arts* 58 (1960): 36, figure 5 (Boston, Museum of Fine Arts 33.684). **Note:** Gadd (1936, 166) said this was from Slab 22; W. S. Smith (1960, 51) and Reade (1979b, 88) said Slab 24.

Slab 23: Layard 1853b, 41

ROOM XXII

Slabs 2–4: my figure 76; Layard 1853a, 232
Slab 8: Layard 1853a, 231
Slab 10: Layard 1853b, 44

ROOM XXIV

Doors *a, e:* "Guarded by colossal figures" (Layard 1853a, 442).

Door *c:* "Pair of human-headed lions" (ibid., 442; Layard 1853b, 56)

Door *d:* "colossal figures, amongst which was the fish-god" (Layard 1853a, 442)

ROOM XXVIII

Slabs 2–6: S. Smith 1938, pls. 49–55; Layard 1853b, 25, 26 (Brit. Mus., WAA 124774)

Slabs 7–10: my figures 19, 77 (7–9 only); Paterson 1915, pls. 53–56; La-yard 1853b, 35, 36a (Brit. Mus., WAA 124953–124956)

Slabs 11–14: Paterson 1915, pls. 56–58 (Brit. Mus., WAA 124957–124960)

ROOM XXXI

Door *n:* Similar to Door *o* (Layard 1853a, 462)

Door *o:* my figure 95 (Brit. Mus., WAA 118932); Layard 1853a, 462

ROOM XXXII

Slabs 1–3: Layard 1853b, 31; fragment of 2: Porada 1945, 158 (New York, Met. Mus. 32.143.15)

Slabs 7–8: my figure 71; Layard 1853b, 19 (Brit. Mus., WAA 124902, 124903)

ROOM XXXIII

Door *c:* "On each side, a block of plain limestone," perhaps a statue base (Layard 1853a, 460)

Door *p:* Formed by "sphinxes" or "winged lions" of "a limestone abound-ing in fossils" (ibid., 446, 459)

Slabs 1–3: Layard 1853b, 45, 46; Paterson 1915, pls. 62–64 (Brit. Mus., WAA 124801)

Slabs 4–6: Layard 1853b, 47–49; Paterson 1915, pls. 65, 66 (Brit. Mus., WAA 124802); 6 only: my figure 65

ROOM XXXIV

Door *b:* Two bull colossi, each about 12 feet high (Layard 1853a, 445)

Doors *c, e, k:* Decorated with "gigantic figures" (ibid.)

Door *l:* Two bull colossi, each about 15 feet high (ibid.; Paterson 1915, 9)

ROOM XXXVI

Slabs 5–6: my figure 109; Layard 1853b, 20; Paterson 1915, pls. 68–69

Slabs 7–8: my figure 110; Layard 1853b, 21; Paterson 1915, pls, 69–71; detail of 7: my figure 130

Slabs 9–10: my figure 111; Layard 1853b, 22; Paterson 1915, pls. 71–72; detail: my figure 84

Slabs 11–12: my figure 112; Layard 1853b, 23; Paterson 1915, pls. 73–75; details: my figures 3, 66

Slab 13: my figure 113; Layard 1853b, 24; Paterson 1915, pls. 75–76
Note: These slabs are Brit. Mus., WAA 124904 through 124915. New drawings and photographs of the series are in Ussishkin (1982, 77–93).

ROOM XXXVIII

Doors *g, i:* "Each entrance was formed by two colossal bas-reliefs of Dagon, or the fish-god" (Layard 1853a, 343; my figure 22)
Slabs 3–5: Gadd 1936, pl. 18; fragment of 4: ibid., pl. 18 (Brit. Mus., WAA 123339)
Slabs 8–9: my figure 59; Reade 1980a, pl. 1:b; Layard 1853a, 341
Slabs 12–13: my figure 72; fragment of 13: my figure 73 (New York, Met. Mus. 32.143.16); joins fragment published by D. Opitz, *Archiv für Orientforschung* 6 (1930–31): 299
Slabs 14–15: my figure 115
Slab ?: my figure 36

ROOM XL OR XLI

See my figure 23

ROOM XLIII (E)

Slabs 1–3 east: my figure 90 (1–2 only); Layard 1849b, 82c, 83
Slabs 2, 4 west: my figure 91 (2 only); Layard 1853b, 33:c and b

ROOM XLIV

Slabs 1–2: my figure 81

ROOM XLV (D)

Slab 2: my figure 74
Slab 5: my figure 37; Layard 1849b, 75
Slab 6: ibid., 76
Slab 7: ibid., 67:2
Slab ?: S. Smith 1938, pl. 39 (Brit. Mus., WAA 124777, 124778; identified in Gadd 1936, 165; 124778 is now in Edinburgh—Barnett, *British Museum Quarterly* 26 [1962–63]:93)
Slab ?: S. Smith 1938, pl. 41 (Brit. Mus., WAA 124789; identified by Erika Bleibtreu from an unpublished L. W. King photograph shown to the Columbia University Seminar on the Archaeology of the Eastern Mediterranean, Eastern Europe and the Near East, New York, 7 April 1988)

ROOM XLVI

Slabs 1–2: Layard 1853b, 34a

Slabs 4–7: my figure 82 (6–7 only); ibid., 34b

Slabs 9–11: ibid., 33a

Slabs 13–14: ibid., 33d; fragment of Slab 13: J. B. Stearns, *Reliefs from the Palace of Ashurnasirpal II,* Graz, 1961, pl. 93 (Hartford, Wadsworth Atheneum)

ROOM XLVII

Two probable slabs, both unnumbered: my figure 38, and Gadd 1936, pl. 20 (Brit. Mus., WAA 124947)

ROOM XLVIII

Slabs 11–13: my figure 39; Layard 1853b, 40; fragment of 12: Weidner and Furlani 1939, fig. 16 (Vatican 14983)

Slab 20: Layard 1853b, 36 (identified Gadd 1936, 227)

HALL XLIX

Door ?: In this unlabeled doorway connecting XLVIII and XLIX, "stood two plain spherical stones about three feet high, having the appearance of the bases of columns" (Layard 1853a, 103)

Door ??: lion-headed man, original location uncertain: ibid., 104, opp. 104; S. Smith 1938, pl. 36 (Brit. Mus., WAA 124826)

Slabs 1–8: my figure 86 (2–4 only); Layard 1853b, 10–11; fragments: Weidner and Furlani 1939, figures 22, 23, 24, 25 (Vatican 15000, 15004, 15005, 15003); ibid., figure 55 (Como); A. Pohl, *Archiv Orientalni* 17, no. 2 (1949): opp. 294 (Florence)

Slab ?: Weidner and Furlani 1939, fig. 74; Reade 1972, 109, pl. 34:b; Porada, *Anatolian Studies* 33 (1983): pl. III:a

ROOM LI(N)

Slabs 1, 2, 4–9: Layard 1853b, 8

Slabs 10–11: ibid., 8; S. Smith 1938, pl. 68 (Brit. Mus., WAA 124799)

Slabs 12–17: my figure 87; Layard 1853b, 9; Slab 13: S. Smith 1938, pl. 69 (Brit. Mus., WAA 124798)

Slabs 26–27(?): S. Smith 1938, pl. 65 (Brit. Mus., WAA 124795)

Slabs 28–29: S. Smith 1938, pl. 67 (Brit. Mus., WAA 124797); Layard 1853a, opp. 340, left (identified in Gadd 1936, 168)

Slabs 30–32: Layard 1853b, 7; S. Smith 1938, pl. 66 (Brit. Mus., WAA 124796)

Slabs 33–36: Layard 1853b, 7

ROOM LI(S)

Door *b:* "Formed by plain, upright slabs of a close-grained magnesian limestone, almost as hard as flint; between them were two small, crouching lions, in the usual alabaster" (Layard 1853a, 68f.)

Slabs ?–??: my figure 40; *Illustrated London News,* 7 November 1959, 601, top left (Ashmolean 1979.994) evidently fits in the gap between the left and center slabs in figure 40

ROOM LIV

Doors *a, b, c:* "five pairs of human-headed bulls, and numerous colossal figures," as on the throne-room facade (Layard 1853a, 645)

ROOM LX

Door *a:* "A pair of winged bulls" (Layard 1853a, 460)

Door *b:* Four figures on each jamb, including fish-man and lion-headed bird-footed man (ibid., 460)

COURT LXIV

Door *a:* "Formed by winged lions" (Layard 1853a, 584)

Doors *b, h:* Decorated with "fish gods" (ibid., 584).

Slabs 1–3: my figure 89; Layard 1853b, 30; fragments of 2: Weidner and Furlani 1939, figure 104 (Newbury 2); Falkner 1952–53a, figure 2 (Venice, Correr 47)

Slabs 5, 7: my figure 88; Layard 1853b, 27

ROOM LXVII

Slabs 1–3: my figure 41; fragment of 3: Weidner and Furlani 1939, figure 43 (Rome, Barracco 58)

ROOM LXIX

Slabs 1–2: my figure 42; Layard 1853a, 588

ROOM LXX

Door *a*: "Formed by colossal winged figures" (Layard 1853a, 586)

Door *b*: "Guarded by colossal eagle-footed figures" (ibid., 588)

Slab 1: my figure 79; Layard 1853b, 28

Slab 2(?): *Illustrated London News,* 7 November 1959, 601, center left (Royal Ontario Museum, no. 932.6; W. S. Smith 1960, 57, n. 15)

Slabs 3, 4: my figure 67; fragment of 3: Weidner and Furlani 1939, figure 72 (Ashmolean 1933.1575)

Slab 11(?): Layard 1853a, 587 (identified in Reade 1979b, 90)

Slab 12: fragment: Reade 1972, pl. 36:a (Boston, Museum of Fine Arts 33.683)

"ISHTAR TEMPLE PROCESSION"

Original arrangement: Gadd 1936, 172f., 176f., 215–17; Reade 1967, 45–48

British Museum

WAA 124900: Gadd 1936, pl. 21

WAA 124901: *Reallexikon der Vorgeschichte,* VII, Berlin, 1926, pl. 158b (also Paterson 1915, pl. 99)

WAA 124948: Hall 1928, pl. 38:2; Gadd 1936, pl. 22 (drawing of whole)

WAA 124951: Hall 1928, pl. 38:1

WAA 135200: Weidner and Furlani 1939, fig. 70 (formerly Royal Geographical Society 8)

Berlin

VA 953: three slabs: F. Wetzel, *Assur und Babylon,* Berlin, 1949, pl. 21 (partial view)

VA 955: Gadd 1936, 216f., pl. 23 (drawing); G. R. Meyer, *Altorientalische Denkmäler im Vorderasiatischen Museum zu Berlin,* 1965, pl. 150 (photo)

VA 957: *Reallexikon der Vorgeschichte,* VII, Berlin, 1926, pl. 158a

VA 958: W. Andrae, *Das wiedererstandene Assur,* Leipzig, 1938, pl. IIa

NOTES

Chapter 1

1. Layard 1853a, 144f.; II Kings 18:14; Luckenbill (1924), 70:31–32.
2. Barnett 1976, 21.
3. Ibid., 21f.
4. The designation of "types" here refers solely to the original location of a text, not to its form or content.

Chapter 2

1. Other types of decoration, such as wall painting and textiles, doubtless contributed significantly to one's general impression of the throne room (Reade 1979a, 18f.; 1980b, 81). Unfortunately, these types of decoration rarely survived the destruction of the palace, and when they have, they have usually been too fragmentary to permit a reconstruction.

2. This chapter is based on a larger study, tentatively titled "Neo-Assyrian Palace Inscriptions: Their Content and Architectural Context" (hereafter "Russell, forthcoming"), to be published separately.

3. Throughout this section, a "text" is a verbal composition, composed to suit a specific or general need, while an "inscription" is the physical result of duplicating all or part of such a text in some durable medium.

4. According to Layard, the same text appeared "on Bulls and Lions at Entrances a, c and d, Chamber B, Entrances b, c and f, Chamber Y, and Entrance a, Chamber BB" (1851, pl. 45). It was also found on the colossi of Door *e*, Room Y (Gadd 1936, 127; King 1902, 189, n. 1: "No. 76"). The throne-base text was published, without translation, by J. N. Postgate as *The Governor's Palace Archive* (Hertford, 1973, no. 267). It is translated as text CI:2 in Grayson (1976, §§ 594–602, 650–53).

5. Text (eleven exemplars): Botta and Flandin 1849, vol. 3, pls. 22–62; transliteration and translation: Lyon 1883, xii, 40–47; English translation: Luckenbill 1927, §§ 92–94. The typical text distribution may be seen in Botta and Flandin, vol. 1, pl. 30;

the only published exception is Door *M,* where each colossus is carved with the entire inscription (Botta and Flandin, vol. 3, pls. 24–27).

6. Russell 1985, 19–47, 499–513. At least three further Sennacherib colossus texts copied by Layard—from Room I, Door *e;* Room LX, Door *a;* and Court LXIV, Door *a*— are still unpublished, except for an excerpt from the latter in Galter, Levine, and Reade (1986, 32, Appendix). These are discussed more fully in Russell, forthcoming.

7. **Room I, Door** *a:* Rawlinson 1870, 12–13; Luckenbill 1924, "F1," 21, 66–76, 117–25 (as variants).

Meissner and Rost 1893, 6–7, 8; Russell 1985, 505–12, "Appendices 2–3."

Room I, Door *d:* Layard 1851, 59–62; Russell 1985, 499–504, "Appendix 1."

Bull 3: G. Smith 1878, 3, 30–31, 51–52, 67–68, 86, 88–89; Luckenbill 1924, "F2," 76–78.

Hannover: E. Unger, "Keilschrift," *Reallexikon der Vorgeschichte,* edited by M. Ebert, vol. VI, 1926, pl. 61b; Russell 1985, 513, "Appendix 4."

Room I, Door *c,* **and Court VI, Door** *a:* Layard 1851, 38–42; Luckenbill 1924, "I1", 21, 117–25.

For all these inscriptions, see also Galter, Levine, and Reade 1986; and Russell, forthcoming.

8. Bulls: see note 5. Thresholds: see note 12. Annals and summary texts: see note 21.

9. Layard 1849a, II, 261; Door *c:* Layard 1851, pls. 48–49, 84 bottom. Translation: Grayson 1976, §§ 567–70, 572–73, 612–13.

10. Shalmaneser referred to this structure only as an *ekallu* (É.GAL = "palace"; Laessøe 1959, 38:1; Hulin 1963, 52:1). Adad-nirari III restored parts of it (Mallowan 1966, vol. 2, 384); a wine list from his reign (dated 784 B.C.) found in Fort Shalmaneser calls it an *ekal mašarti* ("arsenal, inventory palace"; Kinnier Wilson 1972, 130:no. 3:i 11), as did Esarhaddon, who also restored it (Mallowan 1966, vol. 2, 376). Its distinctive plan, with three great courts and few residential suites, and its location off the citadel suggest that it may never have been a residential palace (Mallowan 1966, vol. 3, plan VIII; reproduced in Pritchard 1969, 368f.). It seems probable, therefore, that it served as an *ekal mašarti* for Shalmaneser III also, but since this cannot be proven, I will refer to it here as a "palace" in quotes.

11. Mallowan 1966, vol. 2, 393, fig. 319. Laessøe 1959, 38–40. See also Schramm 1973, 86, no. 5a. The titulary was incorrectly restored by Laessøe (38:1); the correct form is found in Shalmaneser's throne base (Hulin 1963, 52:1).

12. Botta and Flandin 1849, vols. 1 and 2. Summary of locations in Winckler 1889, vol. 1, x. Winckler omits mentioning the inscriptions from Doors *d* and *p,* both of which are variants of his "Pp 3," and gives an incorrect publication reference for Door *G* (should read "5," not "15"). Texts and transliterations in Winckler 1889, vol. 1, 136–62; vol. 2, pls. 37–40; English translations in Luckenbill 1927, §§ 96–102.

13. Residence L: Loud and Altman 1938, pls. 36, 66; Albenda 1978, 12f. Residence K: Loud and Altman 1938, pl. 30; Albenda 1978, 12f.

14. Albenda 1978, 1–3. Indeed, Richard Ellis observed that the inscribed palace thresholds could also have been covered and protected by rugs (private communication, letter of 6 October 1988).

15. Layard 1853a, 652.

16. Layard 1853a, 442; 1853b, 7, pl. 56. Albenda 1978, 14–16, pls. 8–15.

17. Layard 1849a, vol. 2, 126; el-Wailly 1965, 6; Albenda 1978, 14, pl. 8. There are undecorated thresholds in Doors *c* and *f* (el-Wailly 1965, Arabic section, fig. 2 following p. 9; Madhloom 1967, pl. IX).

18. Grayson 1976, §§ 650–53; Paley 1976; de Filippi 1977.

19. The text edition by Rost (1893—transliteration: vol. 1, 2–40; text: vol. 2, pls. I–XXIVB) is unreliable and outdated, as is Luckenbill's English translation (1926, §§ 762–79), which is based on Rost. A new edition is being prepared by H. Tadmor (see his "Introductory Remarks to a New Edition of the Annals of Tiglath-pileser III," *Proceedings of the Israel Academy of Sciences and Humanities*, vol. 2, no. 9, 1969, 10–19).

20. R. Barthes, "Rhetoric of the Image," in *Image, Music, Text* (New York, 1977), 38–40 (originally published as "Rhétorique de l'image," *Communications*, vol. 4, 1964).

21. **Annals, Rooms 2, 5, 13, 14:** text: Winckler 1889, vol. 2, nos. 1–54; transliteration and translation: ibid., vol. 1, 2–79; Lie 1929, 2–83; Luckenbill 1927, §§ 4–51.

Summary, Rooms 1, 4, 7, 8, 10: text and transliteration: Winckler 1889, vol. 1, 96–135, and vol. 2, nos. 63–78; translation: Luckenbill 1927, §§ 53–75.

Summary, Room 14: text: Botta and Flandin 1849, vol. 3, pl. 67–68, and vol. 4, pl. 159b–161; transliteration: Weissbach 1918, 176–85; translation: Luckenbill 1927, §§ 77–90.

22. Layard's (1849a, vol. 2, 139) report of a band of inscription in Room LI(s), excavated in his absence by H. J. Ross, was based on a misunderstanding of Ross's letter describing the room. Ross actually reported slabs that "consist of a double series of tablets, . . . and across the tablets are the remains of inscriptions," that is, a composition in two registers with epigraphs (Ross 1902, 149). When Layard later examined this room himself, "not a vestige of inscription" remained, the upper register and epigraphs having by then disappeared (Layard 1853a, 67f.).

23. Barthes (as cited in note **20**), 38–40; first cited in this context by Winter (1981, 25). I am also indebted here to conversations with Renata Holod, who helped me articulate this function of epigraphs.

24. The power of epigraphs to arrest and focus is discussed by Gerardi (1988).

25. Tadmor's "Series A" (see note **19** above). Photos of the epigraphs are in Barnett and Falkner (1962, xix, 41, pls. XXXVIII, LXIX, LXII).

26. The original publication of the text of Sargon II's epigraphs is in Botta and Flandin (1849, vols. 1, 2, and 4, *passim*). The epigraphs were edited and studied by M. el-Amin, in "Die Reliefs mit Beischriften von Sargon II. in Dur-Sharrukin," *Sumer* 9 (1953): 35–59, 214–28, and *Sumer* 10 (1954): 23–42. Amin's conclusions are summarized and augmented by Reade (1976), who also identified the epigraph on the loose fragment.

27. Layard 1853a, 148.

28. Sennacherib epigraphs are assembled in Appendix 1.

29. Rooms I:4a, III:8, V:35, XIV:10.

30. Epigraphs that label the king are in Rooms I:9, V:11, V:30, VI:60, VII:14, XXXVI: 12, and LXX:4.

31. Lachish: Room XXXVI:12. Booty: Rooms V:11, XXXVI:12, LXX:4.

32. R. Barthes, "The Photographic Message,' in *Image, Music, Text* (New York, 1977), 25 (originally published as "Le message photographique," *Communications*, vol. 1, 1961); first cited in this context by Winter (1981, 25).

33. Epigraphs known to have been located above the city image are those of Rooms I:1, III:8, V:35, XXXVIII, and LX.

34. Other displaced epigraphs containing city names are those of Rooms V:11 and LXX:4, and probably also V:30 and VII:14.

35. Balaṭai: 108:62, 121:50, 129:63, 132:74; Bīt-Kubatti: 26:73, 27:5, 58:25, 67:10; Sahrina: 52:38 (all from Luckenbill 1924). Alammu is mentioned in a Sargon II letter (Waterman 1930, vol. 2, no. 891:5). Dilbat is mentioned by Tiglath-pileser III, Sargon II, Esarhaddon, and Assurbanipal (Parpola 1970, 103); Mt. Lebanon by Assurnasirpal II, Shalmaneser III, Tiglath-pileser III, Esarhaddon, and Assurbanipal (ibid., 221f.); and Aranziaš by Shalmaneser III, Tiglath-pileser III, Sargon II, and Assurbanipal (ibid., 23, 126). Kasuṣi and Lachish occur in no other neo-Assyrian sources. The city of *A-ta?-un?-*[. . .] also apparently does not occur elsewhere. For room numbers, see Appendix 1.

36. Shalmaneser III: Pritchard 1969, fig. 364. Tiglath-pileser III: ibid., fig. 367. Sargon II: ibid., fig. 370; Botta and Flandin 1849, vol. 2, pl. 146. Sennacherib: Layard 1849a, vol. 2, 184; Layard 1853b, pls. 19, 29, 50. Assurbanipal: Layard 1853b, pl. 49; Barnett 1976, pls. XVII, LXVII. Possibly Assurbanipal: Layard 1853b, pls. 26, 35, 42. The Shalmaneser III relief cited above shows artists, as well as scribes, accompanying the king on campaign, and Madhloom (1970, 121f.) has argued that the man with the scroll in the reliefs of Tiglath-pileser III through Assurbanipal is actually an artist making field sketches. Apart from the general, and at present unanswered, question of whether field sketches were ever made or used in the designing of the palace reliefs (for which, see below, chapter 9, note 21), it should be noted that the man with the scroll is shown exclusively in booty recording scenes. Thus the only "field sketches" he could be making are of enemy heads, prisoners, cattle, and other booty. Since most of these items are hardly distinctive, and since many of them would have been brought back to Assyria as spoil anyway, it is difficult to demonstrate convincingly the need for an artist here. The identification of this figure as an Aramaic scribe composing a booty list, as does his Akkadian comrade, seems preferable.

37. Luckenbill 1924, 70:31, 76:103. This is not to say that these figures necessarily *are* accurate, only that the reliefs make it appear as though they *ought* to be.

38. D. J. Wiseman, "Assyrian Writing Boards," *Iraq* 17 (1955): 3–13, esp. 12. The

detail of a Southwest Palace relief, probably of Assurbanipal (Room XXVIII:8), reproduced by Wiseman as plate III:2, shows the hinged board with great clarity.

39. S. Parpola, "Assyrian Library Records," *Journal of Near Eastern Studies* 42
(1983):1–29, esp. 8.

40. The only surviving examples known to me are from the well in Room AB of the
Northwest Palace at Nimrud, dating to the reign of Sargon II (Wiseman, as in note **38**,
3f.), and from the fourteenth-century B.C. shipwreck at Ulu Burun (G. Bass, "Oldest
Known Shipwreck," *National Geographic* 172 [1987]: 730–31).

41. I am indebted to Pamela Gerardi for the suggestion that one common source for
the epigraphs and palace texts could have been writing boards.

Chapter 3

1. Nimrud: Layard 1849a, vol. 1, 21; vol. 2, 147. Nineveh: ibid., vol. 1, 123, 131f.;
Layard 1853a, 589.

2. Layard 1849a, vol. 2, 117, 120–37. In his first report on the Southwest Palace,
Nineveh and Its Remains (1849a), Layard used letters to designate individual rooms, as
he also did for Assurnasirpal II's Northwest Palace at Nimrud. In his final publication,
Discoveries in the Ruins of Nineveh and Babylon (1853a), he instead used Roman numer-
als, redesignating all the earlier rooms except Court H accordingly.

3. Layard 1849a, vol. 2, 137–40, 147. Layard 1853a, 67–69. Ross 1902, 52, 56–
60, 144–52, 154.

4. Layard 1853a, 69.

5. Ibid., 67, 69–74.

6. Ibid., 37, 96f.

7. Ibid., 75.

8. Ibid., 74, 101–3.

9. Ibid., 135–38, 168, 228–30.

10. Ibid., 236, 335–47, 364f.; Barnett 1976, 6, n. 3.

11. The first excavator to use archaeological photography in Iraq was Victor Place,
who photographed the monumental portals of Sargon II's palace at Khorsabad in
1852–53 (reproduced in M. Pillet, *Une Pionnier de l'Assyriologie: Victor Place* [Paris,
1962]). William Boutcher attempted to photograph a few of the wall reliefs from Assurbanipal's palace at Nineveh in 1854, but the results were unsatisfactory and the
sculptures still had to be drawn (Barnett 1976, xi, pls. XX, XXXVI).

12. Layard 1853a, 2, 214, 365, 411, 582. Bell drowned in the Gomel river three
months later. The original drawings ("Or. Dr.") by Layard and other nineteenth-
century artists who worked in Assyria are preserved in seven folio volumes in the
Department of Western Asiatic Antiquities of the British Museum. They are discussed
by E. Bleibtreu, in "Layard's Drawings of Assyrian Palace Reliefs," in *Austen Henry*

Layard: Tra l'Oriente a Venezia ([papers of an international symposium held in Venice, 26–28 October 1983], edited by F. M. Fales and B. J. Hickey [Rome, 1987], 195–201).

13. Layard 1853a, 365, 436–63.

14. Ibid., 465, 576–88, 664; quote from p. 589.

15. Gadd 1936, 72, 78, 80, 83–85.

16. Rassam 1897, 3f., 7f., 39; Gadd 1936, 88, 94f., 174, 215. The find spot was the large circular pit, roughly 70 m northeast of the palace, shown in my figure 45. This locus has been incorporated into my reconstruction of Court H (fig. 44). See also Appendix 2, "Ishtar Temple Procession."

17. Barnett 1976, 11, 16, 21, text-plate 9.

18. G. Smith 1875, 94, 96, 98, 103. Cf. Layard 1853a, 198f.

19. G. Smith 1875, 102.

20. Ibid., 77–79; Layard 1849a, vol. 2, 37–40. For this lesser-known "palace," see also D. Oates, "The Assyrian Building South of the Nabu Temple," *Iraq* 20 (1958): 109–13; J. N. Postgate and J. E. Reade, "Kalhu," *Reallexikon der Assyriologie*, vol. 5 (Berlin, 1977), 304–6, 316.

21. G. Smith 1875, 134, 143f., 148, 150. Quote: ibid., 145.

22. Ibid., 144.

23. Rassam 1897, 199f., 306, 365, 393, 422; Barnett 1976, 23f.

24. Three of the cylinders are British Museum WAA 22501, 22503, and 22504. The fourth is in Istanbul. J. Reade, "Foundation Records from the South-West Palace, Nineveh," *Annual Review of the Royal Inscriptions of Mesopotamia Project* 6 (1986): 33f.; Rassam, 1897, 222, 365; Luckenbill 1924, 60f., 102; Borger 1979, vol. 1, 68–77, 87.

25. E. A. W. Budge, *By Nile and Tigris*, vol. 2 (London, 1920), 22, 67f., 83.

26. Thompson and Hutchinson 1929a, 59–61, 66, plan 3; Barnett 1976, 25, n. 3. The "Persian Gulf" reliefs showed "sea surrounded by flat land covered with date palms" (L. W. King, quoted in Barnett 1976, 25). Concerning their fate, Thompson wrote, "I cannot trust my memory about it, but my recollection is that it was damaged, and, as far as I can remember, it was reburied and not moved, and in any case it could not be in England, as it was Turkish property" (Weidner and Furlani 1939, 37). A relief fragment showing "a dead buffalo in a stream" (BM 135751), illustrated by G. Smith, may be from this facade, as he reported it was found "in the western part of the palace, near the edge of the mound" (G. Smith 1875, 148).

27. Thompson and Hutchinson 1929a, 66, 69, caption to plan 4.

28. R. C. Thompson and M. E. L. Mallowan, "The British Museum Excavations at Nineveh, 1931–32," *Liverpool Annals of Archaeology and Anthropology* 20 (1933): 72–74, pl. CVI right.

29. el-Wailly 1965, 6; el-Wailly 1966, c; Madhloom 1967, 78f.; Madhloom 1968, 50; Salman 1970, c-d. The scale indicators in Madhloom's plan (1967, pl. IX) are inaccurate—the true scale is neither that of the scale bar (1:600), nor the printed figure (1:200), but rather roughly 1:311. The plan also omits Slabs 1–4 in Room I, though these were found *in situ* (el-Wailly 1966, Arabic section, fig. 5, following p. 1); omits

the "buttresses and recesses" reported in Room I (Salman 1970, d); and gives an arrangement of slabs in Room III that does not correspond with Layard's plans and observations (Layard 1849a, vol. 2, 136).

30. Layard 1849a, vol. 2, 137f.; Layard 1851, 75:C; Layard 1853a, 138; Turner 1970, 178–80; Reade 1979b, 92. In Layard's second plan of H some slab numbers were used twice: narrative Slabs 1–7 at the north, from the first campaign; and throne-room facade Slabs 1–12 at the south, from the second.

31. For the two casts of Elamite horsemen Reade (1967, 44, n. 10) assigned to Court H (Paterson 1915, pl. 98, nos. 31, 32), see Layard 1849a, vol. 1, appendix III, nos. 84, 85. The subject of these casts closely matches Layard's description of Slabs 4–7 from Court H and does not accord with what is known of any other reliefs excavated during his first campaign at Nineveh. The originals may have been two slabs showing horsemen that were badly damaged by workmen after Layard's departure (Ross 1902, 56).

32. Layard 1853a, 135f.; Madhloom 1968, 50.

33. Layard 1849a, vol. 2, 137.

34. Ibid., 125–30; Turner 1970, 189; Madhloom 1967, pl. IX.

35. Layard 1849a, vol. 2, 125. Sargon's Room VII—Loud, Frankfort, and Jacobsen 1936, fig. 71; Assurbanipal's Room M—Barnett 1976, fig. 7, text-plate 6. Despite Layard's assertion to the contrary, 1.75 m of the south wall of Room I was in fact preserved. Madhloom exposed the bases of three wall slabs overlooked by Layard that form the southeast corner of the room (personal observation).

36. Madhloom 1967, pl. IX; Turner 1970, 186.

37. Layard 1849a, vol. 2, 126f.; Turner, 1970, 185f.; Reade 1979a, 34.

38. Layard 1849a, vol. 2, 136; Madhloom 1967, pl. IX.

39. Turner 1970, 189f., pl. XXXVIII.

40. Layard 1849a, vol. 2, 124f.; Madhloom 1967, pl. IX; el-Wailly 1966, c; Turner 1970, 192. A better-preserved image of two eunuchs operating a balance is on Slab 3 from Room 13 in Sargon's palace at Khorsabad (Botta and Flandin 1849, vol. 2, 140).

41. Layard 1849a, vol. 2, 124.

42. Ibid., 130–34. Madhloom 1967, pl. XII:A (west and south walls); Madhloom 1969, Arabic section, pl. 20:B before p. 1 (east and north walls).

43. Turner 1970, 188; Loud and Altman 1938, pls. 75–76; Layard 1849a, vol. 2, 133.

44. Layard 1849a, vol. 2, 134f.; Layard 1853a, 69–71, 102–17; Gadd 1936, 226.

45. The numbers of the slabs here called 60 and 58 are not entirely certain (see figs. 57, 58). Layard (1853b, 2) says figure 57 was "found detached from the rest, but was probably No. 61." The right edge of figure 57, however, does not align well with the left edge of Slab 62 (see fig. 56), and the transition from mountainous to marshy terrain is missing. Figure 57 must therefore be Slab 60. Figure 58 would then be Slab 58, with the intervening (lost) Slab 59 showing a sledge. This identification of Slabs 58 and 60 was apparently first proposed by Reade (1978, 55).

46. Reade 1979b, 87; Layard 1849a, vol. 2, 132; Madhloom 1967, pl. IX.

47. Layard 1853a, 229.

48. Ibid., 229f.

49. Turner 1970, 194–96, pl. XL:f.

50. Layard 1853a, 228.

51. Ibid., 228f.

52. Turner 1970, 196, 202, pl. XL:d.

53. Layard 1853a, 73f.

54. Ibid., 72f.

55. Ibid., 73. Uncarved or roughly carved slabs near doorways were also found in Assurbanipal's North Palace, Room M, Slab 22, and Room R, Slabs 1–2 (Barnett 1976, pls. 36, 41).

56. Layard 1849a, vol. 2, 135.

57. Ibid., 136; Turner, 1970, 194f., 208.

58. Layard 1849a, vol. 2, 135; Gadd 1936, 163f.; Reade 1967, 44f., pl. 12.

59. Layard 1853a, 230, 438–41.

60. Ibid., 230–33.

61. Ibid., 230f.; Reade 1979b, 110. Chiseling off existing relief: Layard 1853a, 104, 138, 342. Assurbanipal in the Southwest Palace: see chapter 6.

62. Layard 1853a, 442.

63. Ibid., 442; Turner 1970, 200–202, pl. 45.

64. Layard 1853a, 442–44.

65. Ibid., 445f. This stone, NA$_4$.^{d}ŠE.TIR, is discussed in chapter 5.

66. Layard 1853a, 462.

67. Ibid., 446–60.

68. Ibid., 445.

69. Ibid., 445.

70. Ibid., 149. The numbering of the slabs is problematic—Layard's "Slabs 5–13" actually include twelve slabs, and the slab divisions in his drawings, which seem to have been based primarily on compositional breaks, often do not correspond with those of the originals.

71. Layard 1853a, 148–53. Behind the king is an archaic type of chariot, identical to examples shown in ninth-century reliefs, which M. Wolff suggested was ceremonial (*Archiv für Orientforschung* 11 [1936–37]: 231–34).

72. Turner 1970, 200–202, pl. XLV:b.

73. Layard 1853a, 445.

74. Ibid., 342.

75. Ibid., 347.

76. Ibid., 344, opp. 345.

77. Ibid., 344–47; G. Smith 1875, 144f. Barnett (1976, 6, note 2) incorrectly asserted that these tablets were found in Rooms LX and LXI. Layard's unpublished jour-

nal, however, fully corroborates his published claim that they were from XL and XLI (quoted in Barnett 1976, 6, note 3).

78. Layard 1853a, 342; Reade 1967, 44.

79. Layard 1853a, 582–84. The caption to Layard 1853b (p. 33) states that the reliefs illustrated there were from Room LXIII, but this is a misprint. Their original locations—given correctly in Layard 1853a (pp. 582–84) and in the unpublished original drawings (British Museum, WAA, Or. Dr., vol. 1, 65–66, and vol. 4, 54)—were Room XLIII, Slabs 2 and 4 (Layard 1853b, 33c and b) and Room XLVI, Slabs 9–11 and 13–14 (Layard 1853b, 33a and d).

80. Layard 1853a, 583.

81. Layard 1849a, vol. 2, 135f. These deities, on Slab 5 (Layard 1849b, 75), were oddly posed—they neither sat nor stood, but straddled the poles on which they were carried in a pose appropriate only for riding.

82. Layard 1853a, 583f.; see note 79.

83. Layard 1853a, 584; Turner 1970, 194–99, 207–9.

84. Layard 1853a, 103, 119. On Slab 11 was a tree, in which "were birds and two nests containing their young. The sculptor probably introduced these accessories to denote the season of the year" (Layard 1853a, 119; Layard 1853b, 40). This is unique in Sennacherib's published reliefs.

85. Layard 1853a, 103. The idealized nature of Layard's plans is stressed by Geoffrey Turner in his manuscript, which he kindly shared with me, on the Southwest Palace plan, to be included in Bleibtreu, Barnett, and Turner (forthcoming).

86. Layard 1853a, 104f., 118.

87. Ibid., 104f., 338.

88. Ibid., 338–40.

89. Quote: ibid., 67f. Cf. Layard 1849a, vol. 2, 139f.; Ross 1902, 144–52.

90. Layard 1849a, vol. 2, 140; Ross 1902, 149, 151.

91. Albenda 1986, pls. 24, 27–33, 68, figs. 29, 45, 48.

92. Layard 1853a, 68f.

93. Turner 1970, 196, n. 99. Sennacherib states that he set up statues of couchant animal figures in the doors of the shrines (Luckenbill 1924, 106:30–107:36, 119:24–120:27). In his forthcoming study of the palace plan, Turner suggests that these may have been the "small crouching lions" Layard reported in Door *b* of LI(s) (Layard 1853a, 68f.; Turner, as in note 85).

94. Paterson 1915, 12.

95. Layard 1853a, 460.

96. Ibid., 153–59, 460–62; K. A. Kitchen, *The Third Intermediate Period in Egypt* (Warminster, 1973), 378–80.

97. Layard 1853a, 584–86.

98. Ibid., 586.

99. Ibid., 586.

100. Ibid., 586.
101. Ibid., 588.
102. Ibid., 586–88.
103. Ibid., 586.
104. Ibid., 645.
105. Ibid., 589.
106. Ibid., 338.

Chapter 4

1. Layard 1853a, 589.

2. Neither text carries a date. For the date of the earlier text, see chapter 7, note 2. The later text was apparently composed in late 694 or in 693, as the latest events it mentions occurred in the first part of the sixth campaign (Levine 1982, 46).

3. 703/702, 702, 694, 694/693 texts: Luckenbill 1924, 96:76–78, 100:50–54, 106:6–12, 119:18–20 (variant "F1" = IIIR, 13:iv:1). 700 text: B. Evetts, "On Five Unpublished Cylinders of Sennacherib," *Zeitschrift für Assyriologie* 3 (1888): 316:77 to 317:82. 697 text: G. Smith 1878, 14, 151, "Cylinder C."

4. Luckenbill 1924, 111:64; Reade 1970, 65. Independent support of this was provided by F. M. Fales, who derived a value of 27.5–28cm for a half-cubit on the basis of Assyrian records giving the heights of children of various ages (*Censimenti e catasti di epoca neo-assiria* [Rome, 1973], 121).

5. In 1989 I checked Layard's figure for the east-west dimension of the palace with a 50-meter tape. Two tries by two different people, measuring from the throne-room facade to the west edge of the mound, gave figures of 197 and 199m, showing that this aspect of Layard's plan is very accurate. I could not check the north-south dimension as there are no exposed features to measure from.

6. Layard 1849a, vol. 2, 137f.; Layard 1853a, 135–38.

7. See chapter 3, note 16.

8. Thompson and Hutchinson 1929a, 65f.; Thompson and Hutchinson 1929b, 135, no. 122, M, N. Thompson's hand copy of the text clearly reads É *nak-kap-ti* (1929b, pl. LII, no. 122:N:2). According to CAD 1980, vol. N/1 184f., *nakkaptu* designates the temple (on the sides of the head). A type of stone called *nakkaptu* (NA₄.SAG.KI) is attested only in lexical lists. A full account of the 1989 excavations will be included in the Nineveh preliminary report. For the problem of the date of the fifth campaign, see chapter 7, note 24.

9. Direct distance of 293.5 m measured while surveying during 1989 season at Nineveh. On the plan of Thompson and King (my figure 45), this distance is approximately 308 m.

10. The elevation of the *bīt nakkapti* threshold is nearly the same as that of the base of the throne-room bull (1.09 m difference).

11. Using a 50-meter tape, two tries by two different people gave distances of 334 and 338 m.

12. Reade 1970, 90.

13. Reade 1970, 74; Reade 1978, 54, fig. 4.

14. Luckenbill 1924, 105:v:91-vi:5, 118:16 to 119:17. Translation: Luckenbill 1927, §§ 386, 409.

15. There is considerable variation in the length that different copies of the building account give for the "west" (i.e., north) inner front, behind the Ishtar Temple ziggurat. The smallest value is 383 cubits, on copies dating to 700 B.C. (Luckenbill 1924, 102:78, "Rassam Cylinder"; G. Smith 1878, 150:78, "Cylinder B"). Two other versions, the dates of which are lost, give figures of 386 cubits (not 393 as erroneously stated in Luckenbill 1924, 102, n. 2) and 400 cubits (Schroeder 1922, no. 120:78). The largest value, 443 cubits, is on a cylinder dating to 697 B.C. (G. Smith 1878, 151, "Cylinder C"). With a single exception (162 instead of 176 cubits for the "north" front in G. Smith 1878, 150:77, "Cylinder B"), the remaining measurements are constant in all these versions. Evidently only the "west" portion of the palace platform continued to expand between 700 and 697 B.C. Perhaps the suite of rooms that extends to the west of Court LXIV, including LXIX to LXXI, was built during this period.

16. Such irregular plans are much more common in the actual excavated remains of late Assyrian buildings than they are in the regularized groundplans published by their nineteenth-century excavators. For examples, see Khorsabad, Nabu temple ("H") and Residences L and M (Loud and Altman 1938, pl. 70); and Nineveh, Nabu temple (my fig. 45).

17. Sargon II: Lie 1929, 76:13 to 79:7; Luckenbill 1927, § 73. Sennacherib: Luckenbill 1924, 96:79 to 97:86; Luckenbill 1927, §§ 366–67. Sculptures of "mountain sheep" are not mentioned in later Sennacherib texts (Lie 1929, 78:3; Luckenbill 1924, 97:85). The GAR (or NINDA, = 12 cubits; CAD 1964, vol. A/1 245) is used by Sargon (Weissbach 1918, 182:38–40), but only rarely hereafter by Sennacherib (Luckenbill 1924, 95:73, 113:viii:8). Even the name "Palace without Rival" is taken from Sargon (Lie 1929, 76:14; Luckenbill 1924, 96:79).

18. Sargon II: Lie 1929, 78:4–5. Sennacherib: Luckenbill 1924, 97:86. This passage presents some difficulties. About these wall slabs Sargon says, "*ṣi-ru-uš-šin ab-šim*" (upon them I depicted (captive peoples)). The equivalent passage in Sennacherib's text substitutes "*qé-reb-ši-in is-si-ha,*" (on them they carved?). Forms similar to *is-si-ha* are attested for the verbs *sehû*, "to become rebellious," and *esēhu*, "to assign" (CAD 1984, vol. S, 208a; von Soden 1965, 248a), but neither of these makes sense here. Von Soden (1965, 249a) suggested the verb form in question be emended to *e!-si-iq!?* (*esēqu*: "to incise a relief"), but Erle Leichty's collation of the text at my request shows that *is-si-ha* is correct. It seems likely, nonetheless, that *esēqu*, which is sometimes written *esēku*, is the verb intended by the scribe. Perhaps the signs in question here are intended to be read *es-si-ku₆*. More likely, the scribe may here be confusing *esēqu* with

the more common and phonetically similar *esēhu* (CAD 1958, vol. E, 329, s.v. *"esēku"*). The earliest clearly attested appearance of *esēqu* with the meaning "to incise a relief" is in texts of Esarhaddon (CAD 1958, vol. E, 331f.). In Sennacherib's period, the distinction between *esēhu* and *esēqu* in this context might not yet have been clear to the scribe.

19. Luckenbill 1924, 109:56. The Sargon II parallel is Lie 1929, 76:13–14.

20. Reade (as in chapter 3, note 24), 33f.

21. Borger 1979, vol. 1, 64f. It would be impossible to estimate how many individual cylinders are represented by Borger's list of duplicates without first examining all of the fragments.

22. Eponym Canon C[b]7: [. . .] É.GAL MÚR URU [*ša ni-na-a* . . .] (Ungnad 1938, 435). See also Luckenbill (1924, 117:7) and J. N. Postgate, "URU.ŠE = *kapru*," *Archiv für Orientforschung* 24 (1973): 77.

23. Five campaigns, smaller dimensions: Room I, Door *d* (Layard 1851, 59–62; Russell 1985, 20–22, 499–504); inscribed cylinders (Luckenbill 1924, "E1," 103–16; Heidel 1953). Six campaigns, larger dimensions: Room I, Door *a* (Luckenbill 1924, "F1," 21, 66–76, 117–25).

24. Inscription: Appendix 1, Room XXXIII, Door *p* (Layard 1853a, 445). Though copies of several different editions of the annals and building accounts written between 700 and 694 B.C. survive, none of these have yet been adequately published (see Reade 1975, 191f.; Borger 1979, vol. 1, 65). If G. Smith's (1878, 15, 151) publication of "Cylinder C," dated 697 B.C., is to be trusted, then the palace building account did not take its final form until after 697.

25. Jerusalem Prism: Ling-Israel, P., "The Sennacherib Prism in the Israel Museum—Jerusalem," in *Bar-Ilan Studies in Assyriology Dedicated to Pinhas Artzi*, edited by J. Klein and A. Skaist (Ramat Gan, Israel, 1990), 213–48. Taylor Prism: Luckenbill 1924, 128:36–38, variant "H1"; Borger 1979, 86:vi:[25]–[26]. The Taylor Prism is dated 20 Addaru (twelfth month, usually February–March; Borger 1979, 87). A prism excavated by Thompson in the "House of Sennacherib's Son" (R. C. Thompson, "A Selection from the Cuneiform Historical Texts from Nineveh," *Iraq* 7 [1940]: 89–93) and dated by Reade to 691–689 B.C. (1975, 193) may briefly mention the Southwest Palace before turning to a description of the waterworks and city wall. As with the Nebi Yunus cylinders, this is presumably a statement that the palace was finished.

26. That greatest of Assyrian treasure hunters, Hormuzd Rassam, tells us that upon discovering an Assurbanipal prism in a wall of the North Palace, he proceeded "to break down every wall that seemed likely to contain relics of the past" in both the North and Southwest palaces (Rassam 1897, 222).

Chapter 5

1. The colossus in figure 48 is not inscribed, but it is the best-preserved Sennacherib example and shows what the less fortunate examples in the palace originally looked like.

2. Clarke and Engelbach 1930; R. Naumann, *Architektur Kleinasiens,* 2d ed. (Tübingen, 1971), 33–43.

3. Halule: Luckenbill 1924, 82:34. Aqueduct: W. A. Wigram, *The Cradle of Mankind* (London, 1914), 122; W. Bachmann, *Felsreliefs in Assyrien (Wissentschaftliche Veröffentlichungen der deutschen Orient-Gesellschaft,* LII), Leipzig, 1927, 4 (my translation) and Taf. 2; Jacobsen and Lloyd 1935, 13, 44–46.

4. Layard 1853a, 116, 133, 206; Place and Thomas 1867, vol. 1, 230, 232 (my translation). The chemical composition and characteristics of the Assyrian limestone and alabaster are discussed by R. M. Boehmer, "Gipsstein," *Reallexikon der Assyriologie,* vol. 3 (Berlin, 1968), 379f.

5. Luckenbill 1924, 104:65, 118:9; Heidel 1953, 154:3. For stone identification, see Thompson 1936, 158f.

6. Layard 1853a, 110; Luckenbill 1924, 104:65 to 105:78. Luckenbill's footnote on p. 104, which identifies the "they" of 104:65–66 as the captives who transport the stone, is misleading; "they" are surely the "predecessors" of 104:61 (see translations in Heidel 1953, 182, n. 2; and CAD 1964, vol. A/1, 286b, s.v. *"aladlammû"*). Note that the Tastiate reference occurs in the middle of the description of the old palace: 104:56 to 105:84. Heidel (1953, 182) likened this passage to a description of bronze casting where Sennacherib compared the outmoded technique of his predecessors to his own superior procedure (Luckenbill 1924, 108:80 to 109:88).

7. Layard 1849a, vol. 2, 102–4.

8. For an account of the force and unpredictability of the Tigris flood, see Layard (1853a, 204). A letter to Sargon II reports the sinking of a colossus that was too heavy for the boats that carried it (S. Parpola, *The Correspondence of Sargon II, Part I: Letters from Assyria and the West* [*State Archives of Assyria,* I], Helsinki, 1987, no. 119).

9. Several letters that appear to date from the reign of Sargon II refer to the transport of colossi from Tastiate and also mention the city of Adia, which seems to be another stone source (Waterman 1930, vol. 2, no. 1362; Parpola [as in note 8], nos. 120, 150). One of the letters referring to Adia is from the crown prince, Sennacherib, which suggests that he was involved in colossus procurement for his father's palace (ibid., no. 32).

10. Mentions of Balaṭai in Sennacherib texts: Luckenbill 1924, 108:62f., 108:78 (and duplicates 121:50, 122:13; Heidel 1953, 160:79, 162:5), 126a:3, 126c:2, 129:63, 132:74; Thompson and Hutchinson 1929b, 135, no. 122N:10; Schroeder 1922, no. 121:9. Location of Balaṭai: Forrer 1919, 106; E. Unger, "Balâṭâ," *Reallexikon der Assyriologie,* vol. 1 (Berlin, 1932), 394. For medieval Balad, see J. M. Fiey, "Balad et le Béth 'Arabayé Irakien," *Orient Syrien* 9 (1964): 189–232.

11. Epigraphs labeling Balaṭai: Appendix 1, Court VI, Slabs 60, 66, and 68. Bibliography of the Court VI reliefs: the fullest studies are Reade (1978, 55–60), who examined them for evidence for the location of the Balaṭai quarry; and Russell 1987. Naumann (as in note 2), 37f., figs. 15–17; and Clarke and Engelbach (1930, 90) refer

to the series briefly in their discussions of stone transport in Asia Minor and Egypt. For additional bibiography, see note 20 below.

12. *Correspondence Etc. on Excavations in Nineveh and Babylon* (a collection of unpublished letters kept by the Department of Western Asiatic Antiquities, British Museum), 331. I am grateful to Julian Reade for bringing this passage to my attention. For Jikan, see Place and Thomas 1867, vol. 2, 150f.; R. Killick and M. Roaf, "Excavations in Iraq, 1981–82," *Iraq* 45 (1983): 213 and map 3; and H. Fujii and H. B. al-Aswad, separate articles in *Researchs on the Antiquities of Saddam Dam Basin Salvage and Other Researches,* Mosul, ca. 1987, 62–67 and Arabic section, 71–78. None of these brief reports mentions Rawlinson's quarries, which must now be inundated by the Saddam Dam reservoir.

13. Reade 1978, 60. Pamela Gerardi of The University Museum, Philadelphia, informs me that while "in the district of Balaṭai" is the usual translation of the passage *ina erṣet Balaṭai* (CAD 1958, vol. E, 311f.), the literal meaning of *erṣetu* is "earth." "In the earth of Balaṭai" may therefore be preferable, especially since this is a quarry dug into the ground.

14. Luckenbill 1924, 63–66, 127d:6.

15. Luckenbill 1924, 127d, 132:73; CAD 1968, vol. A/2, 451, s.v. *"ašnan"*; Reade 1978, 60.

16. Reade 1978, 60; Galter, Levine, and Reade 1986, 31, no. 20; Layard 1853a, 446, 459; Rawlinson 1861, vol. 1, 7:E; Luckenbill 1924, 127d.

17. This confirms the definition of *apsasītu* suggested in CAD 1968, vol. A/2, 194a: "perhaps the sphinx." Actual examples from the time of Esarhaddon were found by Layard in the Southwest Palace at Nimrud (Barnett and Falkner 1962, pls. CVIII–CXI). Rooms XXIX and XXX: Layard 1853a, 445f.

18. Luckenbill 1924, 108:59, 121:48; Heidel 1953, 160:77; Thompson and Hutchinson 1929b, 135, no. 122N:4; also see J. N. Postgate, "URU.ŠE = *kapru,*" *Archiv für Orientforschung* 24 (1973): 77. Luckenbill's (1924, 108:72–73) translation of this passage—"Great slabs of breccia I fashioned and cut free on both sides, in their mountain"—is incorrect. CAD 1971, vol. K, 354, translates: "I cut out both stones in their quarry," and a variant text confirms this reading (Russell 1985, 506:24). For identification of stone, see Reade 1970, 94; Layard 1853a, 68f.; Thompson 1936, 193.

19. Luckenbill 1924, 107:55–56, 108:65–71, 121:43; Heidel 1953, 160:74; Thompson and Hutchinson 1929b, 135, no. 122M:1. Identification of stone: Thompson 1936, 146–48; CAD 1956, vol. G, 104–6; von Soden 1966, 293a. Location of Mt. Ammanana: M. Cogan, ". . . From the peak of Amanah," *Israel Exploration Journal* 34 (1984): 255–59.

20. Layard (1853a, 110) misinterpreted this scene as the raising of the palace foundation platform, but the representation and caption clearly show that the subject is a quarry. Layard's error was perpetuated by Paterson (1915, 6), Gadd (1936, 171), and B. Hrouda, "Der assyrische Palastbau nach zeitgenössischen Darstellungen," *Bonner Jahrbücher* 164 (1964): 15–26. The true subject was recognized by V. Scheil, "Bas-

relief avec inscription de Sennachérib," *Recueil de Travaux* 15 (1893): 148f., and E. Strommenger, "Zu den sogenannten Palastbaureliefs des Sanherib," *Berliner Jahrbuch für Vor- und Frühgeschichte* 6 (1966): 111–14.

21. Appendix 1, Court VI, Slabs 66 and 68. This image confirms the translation "bull colossus with human head," given in CAD 1964, vol. A/1, 286.

22. Clarke and Engelbach 1930, 13–19; K. Bittel and R. Naumann, *Boğazköy-Hattuša*, I (*Wissenschaftliche Veröffentlichungen der deutschen Orient-Gesellschaft*, LXIII), Stuttgart, 1952, Taf. 54b.

23. Nimrud: Layard 1853a, 195; Khorsabad: see note 26.

24. CAD 1982, vol. Q, 299–300, translates *qulmû* as "(an ax)." This is clearly correct in some contexts, as where it is used to designate a tool for cutting trees, but in other contexts it is used as a digging implement and for cutting stone. This tool could hardly have had the same form for all these uses; evidently *qulmû* refers to a class of edged and/or pointed tools. *Akkullu* is translated in CAD 1964, vol. A/1, 276–77, as "(a hammer-like tool)." This word also occurs in a variety of contexts, but in each case it seems to refer to a pick or mattock.

25. Place and Thomas 1867, vol. 1, 86–88; Place is incorrect in identifying the location of the hoard as Room 84 (see Loud and Altman 1938, 55). "Mason's pick": Place and Thomas 1867, vol. 3, pl. 71:5–7; Loud and Altman 1938, 99:213–17, pl. 62. It is not clear from metallographic analysis whether these crude objects are tools, or merely iron ingots (R. Pleiner, "The Technology of Three Assyrian Iron Artifacts from Khorsabad," *Journal of Near Eastern Studies* 38 (1979): 89f.; and J. E. Curtis et al., "Neo-Assyrian Ironworking Technology," *Proceedings of the American Philosophical Society* 123 (1979): 376f., 389f.). For the weight of these "picks," see R. Pleiner and J. Bjorkman, "The Assyrian Iron Age," *Proceedings of the American Philosophical Society* 118 (1974): 295, n. 17. For a description of the use of the quarryman's pick in modern Egypt, see Clarke and Engelbach (1930, 17). "Mattock": Place and Thomas 1867, vol. 3, pl. 71:4; see Layard (1853a, 194) for a similar example from Nimrud.

26. Place and Thomas 1867, vol. 1, 84, 86; vol. 3, pls. 70:7–9, 71:8.

27. Layard 1853a, 195; D. Oates, "The Excavations at Nimrud (Kalhu), 1961," *Iraq* 24 (1962): 17. For Assyrian iron tools that could have been used for stoneworking—including picks, saws, hoes, axes, adzes, sledges, wedges, chisels, and chains—see J. E. Curtis, "An Examination of Late Assyrian Metalwork with Special Reference to Material from Nimrud," Ph.D. diss., University of London, Institute of Archaeology, 1979, 131–35, 139–41, 146f., 251; and Pleiner and Bjorkman (as in note 25), 283–313. Metallographic analyses of several excavated iron tools are in Pleiner (as in note 25), 83–91; and Curtis et al. (as in note 25), 369–90.

28. Layard 1853a, 203. I had previously thought of levers only as lifting devices. A bit of experimentation showed, however, that as a lever pivots on its fulcrum it exerts thrust both forward and upward. This simultaneous raising and pushing at the rear, combined with the pull of the teams in front, appears to have been necessary to overcome the initial friction of a forty- to fifty-ton stone block at rest. Once underway, the

pull of the teams in front was probably sufficient to keep it moving, at least over hard level terrain.

29. Laessøe, who believed that this bull had been brought by raft from the quarry at Tastiate, argued that these devices were part of a drydock system used to facilitate the unloading of the colossi (J. Laessøe, "Reflexions on Modern and Ancient Oriental Water Works," *Journal of Cuneiform Studies* 7 (1953): 19–21). This seems inconsistent with the location of this scene at the beginning of the transport sequence, however, and the inscription labels this image as the quarry at Balaṭai, from which colossi were evidently brought only by land. Reade noted these objections and suggested instead that they were being used in conjunction with a dam to divert water temporarily from a small stream so that the sledge could cross (Reade 1978, 57–59). This may be, but a crude bridge would seem to be a less complex solution to such a problem.

30. For sledges, rollers, tracks, and sleepers, see Clarke and Engelbach (1930, 89–91).

31. Loud, Frankfort, and Jacobsen 1936, fig. 58.

32. Luckenbill 1924, 122:26 to 123:30.

33. Layard 1853a, 107.

34. Luckenbill 1924, 121:49–123:31.

35. It is ironic that the sole surviving Assyrian account of the circumstances of Sennacherib's murder implicates his colossi. The precise reading of this unfortunately laconic passage is uncertain, but it appears that he was either stabbed to death between a pair of them or perhaps crushed to death beneath one (Streck 1916, vol. 2, 38:70–71; S. Parpola, "The Murderer of Sennacherib," in *Death in Mesopotamia* (*Mesopotamia*, VIII), edited by B. Alster [Copenhagen, 1980], 175).

Chapter 6

1. Layard 1853a, 589.

2. Room XXXIII: Gerardi 1988. Assurbanipal: Falkner 1952–1953b, 247–49; Hrouda 1965, 115–17; Reade 1979b, 110. Reade (1972, 90; 1979b, 109f.) feels that some of the uninscribed reliefs in the Southwest Palace are sufficiently unlike both Sennacherib and Assurbanipal to warrant an atribution to one of Assurbanipal's successors, Sinsharishkun (?–612 B.C.). This latter category is here grouped with Assurbanipal, to which it is much more closely related than to Sennacherib.

3. B. Berenson, *The Italian Painters of the Renaissance* (London, 1952), 199.

4. Assurbanipal's name is not included in the Room I epigraph, but the subject (Ituni) is certainly his and the text is duplicated on an Assurbanipal epigraph collection tablet (Gerardi 1988, 22f.). Similarly, the broken epigrah on Room V¹/T¹, Slab F does not include Assurbanipal's name, but its beginning (*a-na-[ku . . .*]) only occurs in his reign (ibid., 5, 7, 28).

5. Falkner 1952–1953b, 247–49; Hrouda 1965, 115–17; Nagel 1967, 31–39.

6. Hrouda 1965, 95 and Taf. 26–27; Madhloom 1970, 14, 18, and plates 1–7. Note that this observation applies only to Assyrian chariots; enemy chariots in the ninth century may have eight or more spokes (Madhloom 1970, 14).

7. Falkner 1952–1953a, 30. Sennacherib: SWP:I, V, X, XXXVI, LXX. Assurbanipal: NP:M, V^1/T^1; SWP:XXXIII.

8. Ibid.; Hrouda 1965, 116. Sennacherib: SWP:I, V, XXXVI. Assurbanipal: NP:M; SWP:XXXIII.

9. Falkner 1952–1953b, 249. Sennacherib: SWP:I, V, VI, XXXVI. Assurbanipal: NP:M, V^1/T^1; SWP:XXXIII.

10. Hrouda 1965, 116. Sennacherib: SWP:I, V, VI, XXXVI. Assurbanipal: NP:M, V^1/T^1.

11. Falkner 1952–1953b, 249. Sennacherib: SWP:V, XXXVI. Assurbanipal: NP:M, V^1/T^1; SWP:XXXIII.

12. Hrouda 1965, 116. Sennacherib: SWP:V, XXXVI. Assurbanipal: NP:M, V^1/T^1.

13. Reade 1972, 100f., 108. Sennacherib: SWP:VI, XXXVI, LXX. Assurbanipal: NP:M; V^1/T^1.

14. Falkner 1952–1953b, 248. Assurbanipal: NP:I, M, V^1/T^1; SWP:XXXIII.

15. Falkner 1952–1953b, 249. Assurbanipal: NP:I, M, V^1/T^1; SWP:XXXIII.

16. M. Shapiro, "Style," in *Anthropology Today,* edited by A. L. Kroeber (Chicago, 1953), 289.

17. Falkner 1952–1953b, 247. Sennacherib: SWP:LXX. Assurbanipal: NP:I, M, S^1, SWP:XXXIII.

18. Falkner 1952–1953a, 34. Sennacherib: SWP:I, V, VI, X, XXXVI. Assurbanipal: NP:I, M, S^1; SWP: XXXIII.

19. Ibid., 30; Nagel 1967, 25. Sennacherib: SWP:V, VI, XXXVI, LXX. Assurbanipal: NP:M, S^1; SWP:XXXIII.

20. Nagel 1967, 25f. Sennacherib: SWP:I, V, VI, XXXVI. Assurbanipal: NP:M, V^1/T^1; SWP:XXXIII.

21. Nagel 1967, 18–22. Sennacherib: SWP:I, V, VI, XXXVI, LXX. Assurbanipal: NP:M, S^1, V^1/T^1; SWP:XXXIII.

22. Sennacherib: SWP:I, V, VI, XXXVI. Assurbanipal: NP:I, M.

23. Nagel 1967, 22f. Sennacherib: SWP:V, X, XXXVI. Assurbanipal: NP:V^1/T^1.

24. Nagel 1967, 24. The example illustrated here is from Room F, where Assurbanipal's name was not recorded, but it is identical to less well-preserved examples in NP:I and M.

25. Nagel 1967, 24. Assurbanipal: NP:M, V^1/T^1.

26. Falkner 1952–1953b, 247. Sennacherib: SWP:LXX. Assurbanipal: NP:M, S^1.

27. Nagel 1967, 27–30; Reade 1979b, 97f.

28. Streck 1916, vol. 2, 84:51–56; Luckenbill 1927, § 835.

29. North Palace: K:1–2, S:1, T:2. Southwest Palace: VI:Door *a*; XXXI: Door *o*; and XLIX: detached.

30. Reade 1967, 43, n. 7; Nagel 1967, 38; Barnett 1976, 55f.

31. Reade 1967, 44.

32. Nagel 1967, 24.

33. See note 30.

34. Layard 1853a, 444.

35. Reade (see note 2) has observed that in the reliefs from Court XIX and Room XXVIII the king is shown participating in the campaign and his attendants are wearing armor, unlike in similar scenes from the North Palace. Because of these differences, Reade assigned these sculptures to Sinsharishkun, who also campaigned in Babylonia and who may have repaired the Southwest Palace. This attribution must remain speculative, however, since no authenticated relief of Sinsharishkun exists with which the Court XIX and Room XXVIII examples might be compared. The slight differences that distinguish these reliefs from those of the North Palace may be attributable to a change in fashion, different artists, or the passage of time within the reign of Assurbanipal, rather than to the accession of a new monarch.

Chapter 7

1. Wäfler 1975; Reade 1979b, 91–93.

2. Text in S. Smith 1921. Transliteration and translation in Luckenbill 1924, 48–55, 94–98. Translation only in Luckenbill 1927, §§256–67, 363–71. For dates, see Levine 1982, 29–37, and J. A. Brinkman, *Prelude to Empire* (Philadelphia, 1984), 57–59.

3. Luckenbill 1924, 52:38. Appendix 1, Room LXX.

4. Appendix 1, Room III. The earliest account of the first campaign lists by name eighty-eight "strong, walled cities of Chaldea" captured by Sennacherib at that time. Among these were thirty-three from Bīt-Dakkuri, a large Chaldean district extending down the Euphrates just south of Borsippa (Luckenbill 1924, 52:36–39, 54:50). This area should have included Dilbat, on the Euphrates some ten kilometers south of Borsippa. It is puzzling, however, that Dilbat, which Tiglath-pileser III calls *māhāzu la šanān* ("unrivaled cult city"; Rost 1893, vol. 1, 56:11), was not mentioned in this list by name. It may be that despite its resistance, Dilbat, an important and time-honored urban center, was omitted from this list because Sennacherib did not consider it a Chaldean tribal city (for the dynamics of urban Babylonian and tribal Chaldean populations in southern Mesopotamia, see Brinkman, as in note 2, 9–15).

5. Reade, 1979b, 91f.; Levine 1982, 40f. See Appendix 2 for full references for the decoration in each room.

6. Text in Layard 1851, pls. 63–64. Transliteration and translation in Luckenbill 1924, 55–60, 99–101. Translation only in Luckenbill 1927, §§ 269–82, 372–78. For duplicates, see Borger 1979, vol. 1, 64.

7. Luckenbill 1924, 68:16; Levine 1973–74, 100f., 104–6, 116f.; J. E. Reade, "Kassites and Assyrians in Iran," *Iran* 16 (1978): 140f.

8. Levine 1982, 37–39; Luckenbill 1924, 55:60.

9. Luckenbill 1924, 58:25, 67:10. Appendix 1, Room LX. For the location of Bīt-Kubatti, see Levine 1973, 313–15.

10. Appendix 1, Room XIV. Waterman 1930, vol. 2, no. 891:5. Though this epigraph is broken, comparison with the Room III, Slab 8 epigraph shows that only a single sign, the city determinative URU, is missing in front of the city name (Wäfler 1975, vol. 1, 281f.). For Urzana, who was defeated during Sargon II's eighth campaign, see Lie (1929, 26:149–54) and Luckenbill (1927, §§ 22, 169–75). Though Alamu must be within fleeing distance of Muṣaṣir, which is northeast of Assyria, its precise location is unknown.

11. Appendix 1, Room V. Lie 1929, 16:98. For other occurrences of the name, see Parpola (1970, 23, 126). It may be the same as Elenzaš (ibid., 123).

12. This epigraph was misattributed by Layard as "No. 2, Chamber G," i.e., Room III (1851, 75:E), but it is plainly visible today on Slab 11 of Room V (formerly designated "C"). Evidently Layard or his publisher here mistook his notation "C, 11" for "G, II."

13. Layard 1853a, 460.

14. Wäfler 1975, vol. 1, 266–82. Wäfler (p. 267) observed that the convention of distinguishing easterners by skin cloaks occurred already in the Akkadian period in the well-known stele of Naram-Sin, where they are worn by defeated easterners, the Lullubi. In Sargon's Room 2, skin cloaks were worn by the inhabitants of the labeled cities of Harhar, Tikrakka, Bīt-Bagaia, Kišesim, and Ganguhtu; in Room 13, Muṣaṣir; and in Room 14, Pazaši (for references, see chapter 2, note 26). So consistent was the use of this convention, that skin cloaks were considered sufficient identification for the unlabeled easterners in the tribute processions from Room 10 (Botta and Flandin 1849, vol. 2, pls. 122–136).

15. Reade 1979b, 92f.

16. Layard (1853a, 71) felt the landscape represents Armenia, Media, or Kurdistan, which would be consistent with the second campaign.

17. Unless the archers at Lachish were conscripts from the time of Sargon II as suggested, but then rejected, by J. E. Reade, in "Elam and Elamites in Assyrian Sculpture," *Archäologische Mitteilungen aus Iran*, n.s. 9 (1976): 99.

18. Appendix 2, Rooms XLIII, XLVI, XLVII. Layard 1853a, 584; Reade 1979b, 92.

19. Na'aman 1979, 64–70. For the rather complicated state of publication of this cylinder and its duplicates, see Borger (1979, vol. 1, 64f.) and for an edition of the text, ibid., 68–77. Translation: Luckenbill 1927, §§ 239–240. Concerning his apparent lack of success in Judah, one could argue that Sennacherib was not really interested in capturing Jerusalem itself, but rather used this campaign to reduce Judah's border forts and to bring the area into the Assyrian sphere of influence as a buffer state between Assyria and Egypt, as he apparently also made Ellipi a buffer against Elam in the second campaign. On the third campaign and Egypt, see F. Yurco, "Sennacherib's Third Campaign and the Coregency of Shabaka and Shebitku," *Serapis* 6 (1980): 221–40 (reference courtesy of William J. Murnane).

20. II Kings 18:13–14, 17; Isaiah 36: 1–2, 37:8. Luckenbill 1924, 32:19. The excavated remains of Tell ed-Duweir, ancient Lachish, also confirm that Sennacherib's seige was a success (Ussishkin 1982).

21. Appendix 1, Room I, Slabs 1 and 4a; el-Wailly 1965, 6.

22. Layard 1853a, 445; Wäfler 1975, vol. 1, 56f. At Khorsabad, turbans seem to be one type of standard headgear for westerners, as in Room 5, Slabs 10–11 (with epigraph identifying Ekron; Botta and Flandin 1849, vol. 2, pl. 93) and Room 10 (ibid., pls. 122–29, upper register).

23. Galleys: Reade 1979b, 92. Woman's headdress: Wäfler 1975, vol. 1, 112f. Reversed Phrygian bonnet: Layard 1853a, 582 (the captive cited is on Room I, Slab 13); Wäfler 1975, vol. 1, 180, 185; Reade 1979b, 93.

24. The date of the fifth campaign is sometimes given incorrectly as 699 B.C (Liverani 1981, 236, notes 15–16; Levine 1982, 53), repeating an error of King (1909, 11f.) and Luckenbill (1924, 61), who misdated to 698 the eponymous campaign against Cilicia that followed Sennacherib's fifth royal campaign (corrected in Luckenbill 1927, § 285). The true date of the Cilician campaign is the eponymy of Šulum-bēl, 696 B.C. (Ungnad 1938, 456). Furthermore, a foundation prism in the British Museum (K 1674), dated 697, includes the fourth campaign but not the fifth, which must therefore have taken place that year (L. W. King, *Catalogue of the Cuneiform Tablets in the Kouyunjik Collection, Supplement* [London, 1914], 223; collated by me).

25. In the Central Palace of Tiglath-pileser III, one wall relief series has a blank text register, presumably because the king died before the inscription was added to the already finished reliefs (Reade 1979b, 72–75).

26. Appendix 1, Court VI.

27. Wäfler 1975, vol. 1, 57–59, 179f.

28. Ibid., vol. 1, 58f.

29. R. D. Barnett, "The Siege of Lachish," *Israel Exploration Journal* 8 (1958): 164.

30. Reade 1979b, 91. Layard (1853a, 651) observed "Each room appears to have been dedicated to some particular event."

31. Luckenbill 1924, 66:3 (my translation). A similar opposition may have occurred already in the throne room (B) of Assurnasirpal II where western campaigns are shown on the south wall and eastern campaigns (possibly) on the north wall (Winter 1981, 15, 19). Sennacherib here maintains this principle of opposition, but transfers it from the throne room to the larger, and perhaps more public, spaces of the courtyards.

32. Reade 1979b, 93. Reade suggests that deportation was also the subject of the reliefs in Room XLVI, and perhaps XLIV and XLVII, but Layard's drawings and descriptions leave considerable doubt in these cases (Appendix 2, Rooms XLIV, XLVI, XLVII). The mixture of easterners and westerners in Room XLIII recalls Room 10 in Sargon's palace, a corridor lined with reliefs showing processions of eastern and western tributaries (see notes 14 and 22 above).

33. Reade 1967, 43–45; Read 1979b, 92. J. A. Brinkman reminds me that at the time the palace was apparently being completed (693–691 B.C.), Babylonia had rebelled from Assyria and was successfully resisting recapture. Babylonia might therefore have been an inappropriate subject for any rooms being decorated during this final phase of construction (private communication, letter of 14 February 1989).

34. And later, the throne room (M) of Assurbanipal's North Palace. The programmatic implications of showing a mixture of campaigns in the throne room are discussed by Winter (see note 31 above).

Chapter 8

1. The components of the audience for Sennacherib's palace reliefs, and their possible degree of familiarity with earlier decorative conventions, will be investigated in chapters 9 and 10.

2. For an analysis of the debts that Assurnasirpal II's palace decoration owed to earlier Near Eastern visual conventions, see Winter (1981, 6–15). The question of whether Fort Shalmaneser should be termed a "palace" is considered in chapter 2, note 10.

3. Turner 1970, 181–94, pl. XXXVIII. "Fort Shalmaneser": Mallowan 1966, vol. 3, pl. VIII (also Pritchard 1969, no. 881).

4. The original layout of Tiglath-pileser III's palace decoration cannot be determined, as the palace plan has not been recovered.

5. Meuszyński 1979.

6. Exceptions are the genies of Room I in Assurnasirpal's Northwest Palace at Nimrud (see fig. 14; Layard 1849a, vol. 1, 387; Reade 1965, 133), and the processions of Room 10 in Sargon's palace at Khorsabad (see fig. 123), both of which are in two registers. On Slabs 13 and 23, located opposite the main door and behind the throne base in Assurnasirpal's throne room (B), the height of the figures is only two-thirds of the height of the slab (Budge 1914, pl. 11).

7. The single exception to the rule of narrative composition in two registers is the timber transport scene from the northeast end of Facade "n" in Sargon's palace at Khorsabad, which is composed in a single register (see fig. 107). This image is discussed in detail later.

8. This is the subject of chapter 9.

9. For illustrations, see note 36 below.

10. According to his building account, Tiglath-pileser III's palace was decorated with bull and lion colossi and with apotropaic wall reliefs (Luckenbill 1926, § 804; Rost 1893, vol. 1, 76:29–31). Reliefs showing winged genies were reported, but no drawings were made and only one fragment survives (Layard 1851, captions to pls. 29, 65, 71–72a; Barnett and Falkner 1962, 33, pl. CIV). Winged human-headed bulls carved in low relief were also found (Barnett and Falkner 1962, xiv, 18, 25f., pl. CVII).

11. *Oxford English Dictionary,* compact edition, 1971, Oxford, s.v. "tradition," sense 5.

12. See chapter 2, note 10.

13. Though it is clear from the surviving remains that Tiglath-pileser III's relief decoration was modeled on Assurnasirpal II's, it can only be postulated that the same might hold true for the plan of Tiglath-pileser's palace, which is unknown.

14. The precise date of the foundation of the capital at Kalhu is uncertain, but the approximate date may be deduced from Assurnasirpal II's annals. The royal campaign of the king's fourth year originated from Nineveh, while that of the sixth year started from Kalhu (the point of origin of the fifth-year campaign is not recorded; Grayson 1976, §§ 560, 577). The earliest edition of the annals from Nimrud, on the "Nimrud Monolith," records the first five campaigns, followed by the account of the founding of the capital at Kalhu (ibid., §§ 617–19), and the later Ninurta Temple annals also include the building at Kalhu immediately following the account of the fifth year (ibid., § 576). For the foundation date of Dur Sharrukin, see Tadmor (1958, 85, 94).

15. *Oxford English Dictionary* (as in note 11), s.v. "inovation," sense 1.

16. For many years the only synthetic studies of Mesopotamian apotropaic figures and associated texts were Woolley (1926), van Buren (1931), and Gurney (1935). This situation has changed dramatically in recent years with the appearance of important new works by Rittig (1977), Reade (1979a), Kolbe (1981), Green (1983, 1986), and Wiggerman (1983, 1986); and these are to be joined by R. S. Ellis, *Domestic Spirits: Apotropaic Figurines in Mesopotamian Buildings (Occasional Publications of the Babylonian Fund,* 3), Philadelphia. In the discussion that follows, the prevailing opinions concerning each of these apotropaic types is briefly summarized with full references to the relevant sources. I have not, however, attempted to discuss fully the issues raised by each type, nor to reconcile opposing views, as this would require a lengthy digression and is, in any case, largely beyond my philological capabilities.

17. For full references, see Appendix 2:

Human-headed winged genie: Court H, Door *a;* Court VI, Doors *a, c, d, e, g, k;* Court XIX, Door *h;* Room LXX, Door *a* (Reade 1979a, 35f.; Kolbe 1981, 14–30, "Variant A"; Wiggerman 1986, 129–50).

Bull colossi: Court H, Doors *a, c;* Room I, Doors *d, e;* Court VI, Doors *a, d, g, k;* Court XIX, Doors *h, l;* Room XXXIV, Doors *b, l;* Room LX, Door *a;* West Facade (this type of figure is called *aladlammû*—Appendix 1, Court VI, Slabs 60, 66; Reade 1979a, 41; Kolbe 1981, 1–14).

Fish-cloaked genie: Room XXIV, Door *d;* Room XXXVIII, Doors *g, i;* Room LX, Door *b;* Court LXIV, Doors *b, h* (this is one type of *apkallu*—Gurney 1935, 53:44, 67:15–20; Rittig 1977, 80–93; Reade 1979a, 38f.; Kolbe 1981, 14–30, "Variant C"; Green 1983, 89f.; *idem,* "The Chronology and Identity of the Fish-cloaked Human Figure in Mesopotamian Art," XXXIIe Rencontre Assyriologique Internationale, Münster, 8–12th July, 1985, *compte rendu,* in press; Wiggerman 1986, 152–55).

Hero strangling lion: Court H, Door *a;* West Facade (Reade 1979a, 38; Kolbe 1981, 89–96; Wiggerman 1983, 100, 102).

Eagle-headed genie: Court VI, Door *i;* Room XIV, Door *a* (this is another type of *apkallu* = "sage"—Gurney 1935, 51:36, 65:12; Rittig 1977, 70–77; Reade 1979a, 39; Kolbe 1981, 14–30, "Variant B"; Green 1983, 88f.; Wiggerman 1986, 151f.). It is not clear how Layard distinguished this last type from the human-headed ones, as in both cases he reported that only the lower portions remained. Presumably (one hopes) he found fragments of the heads.

18. For full references, see Appendix 2:

Horned-crowned long-haired figure: Room I, Door *f;* Room XXXI, Doors *n,o* (van Buren 1931, 51; Rittig 1977, 44–48; Reade 1979a, 36; Kolbe 1981, 116–21; Green 1983, 92; Wiggerman 1986, 125–27).

Lion-headed eagle-footed figure: Room I, Door *f;* Court VI, Doors *a, i;* Room XXXI, Doors *n, o;* Hall XLIX, Comments; Room LX, Door *b;* Room LXX, Door *b* (van Buren 1931, 51f.; Rittig 1977, 103–10; Reade 1979a, 39f.; Kolbe 1981, 108–15, 222f.; Green 1983, 90f; *idem,* 1986, Wiggerman 1986, 294–98 and *passim*).

Six-curled figure: Court H, Door *a;* Court VI, Doors *a, d, g, k* (van Buren 1931, 43f., 52; Rittig 1977, 51–58; Reade 1979a, 38; Kolbe 1981, 96–108; Green 1983, 91f.; Wiggerman 1983; *idem,* 1986, 286–88). A similar six-curled hero was found at the citadel gate at Khorsabad, but his attributes were the lion and curved stick (*gamlu?*), rather than a standard (Botta and Flandin 1849, vol. 1, pls. 4, 46–47). For the *gamlu,* a tool used by exorcists, see Wiggerman (1986, 121f.).

Human-headed lion-footed figure: Room XIV, Door *a* (Rittig 1977, 78f.—incorrectly identified as scorpion-man; Reade 1979a, 40—incorrectly identified as *urmah-lilu;* Kolbe 1981, 132–36; A. Green 1985, 76f.; Wiggerman 1986, 101–3, 299–302; Barnett 1976, pls XXVI, LIV).

It is, of course, possible that some of these "new" types had already appeared in destroyed portions of Sargon's palace reliefs, but there seems to be no evidence for this.

19. "Sacred trees" in Sargon's palace: Botta and Flandin 1849, vol. 1, pl. 80; vol.2, pls. 116, 119, 139, 144.

20. For full references, see Appendix 2:

Human-headed or winged lions: Room XIX, Door *a;* Room XXIV, Door *c;* Room LXIV, Door *a.*

Sphinxes: Court H, Door ? (not on Layard's plans).

Winged sphinxes/lions: Room XXXIII, Door *p.* For the inscription, see Appendix 1, Room XXXIII, Door *p.* Reade (1972, 111) identified its original location.

21. CAD 1968, vol. A/2, 193. Layard's (1853a, 230) statement that the "lower part" of the human-headed lions in Court XIX, Door *a,* was inscribed suggests that these were standing figures, with the inscription in its usual space between the legs. Reade's (1979a, 42, n. 164) suggestion that Layard reserved the term "sphinx" for crouching figures seems questionable in view of the latter's description of the Room XXXIII co-

lossi both as "sphinxes" and "lions." In Door *a* of Esarhaddon's Southwest Palace at Nimrud, the doorjamb lions were standing, while those located in the doorway, apparently as column bases, were recumbent (Barnett and Falkner 1962, pls. CVIII, CIX).

22. Reade 1979a, 42; Winter 1982, 367f.; Pritchard 1969, fig. 648; W. Orthmann, *Untersuchungen zur späthethitischen Kunst,* Bonn, 1971, pls. 50b, 63e, 64d.

23. Rost 1893, vol. 1, 72:rev.:18; Lyon 1883, 44:68; Luckenbill 1924, 97:82; Streck 1916, 88:102; Luckenbill 1926, § 804, and 1927, §§ 73, 366, 837. On the *bīt-hilāni,* see Winter 1982, 357–64; and J. Börker-Klähn, "Der *bīt-hilāni* im *bīt šahūri* des Assur-Tempels," *Zeitschrift für Assyriologie* 70 (1980): 258–73.

24. G. Smith 1875, 78; Mallowan 1966, vol. 1, 226f., figs. 188–92; Botta and Flandin 1849, vol. 2, pls. 152–54, and vol. 5, 168f. Examples from houses in Assur may also predate Sennacherib, but this is uncertain (C. Preusser, *Die Wohnhäuser in Assur* [*Wissenschaftliche Veröffentlichung der Deutschen Orient-Gesellschaft,* LXIV], Berlin, 1954, 33, 58, Taf. 15, 28, 29). These figurines are collected and analyzed in van Buren (1931), Rittig (1977), Wiggerman (1986), Green (1983, 1985, 1986), and in Green's "A Note on the Assyrian 'Goat-fish', 'Fish-man' and 'Fish-woman'," *Iraq* 48 (1986): 25–30.

25. A number of these texts are presented by S. Smith, in Woolley (1926, 695–713), by Gurney (1935), by Rittig (1977, 151–83); by P. Hibbert, in Kolbe (1981, 193–209); and by Wiggerman (1986). The fullest description of the figurines is in an undated text from Assur, published by Ebeling (1920, no. 298), which is translated by Smith, in Woolley (pp. 695–701), Gurney (pp. 64–75), and Rittig (pp. 151–70); by Hibbert, in Kolbe (pp. 193–207); and collated by Wiggerman (pp. 87–93). The dated texts are Gurney's Text III (discussed by Wiggerman, pp. 220–222) and Text I (also edited by Wiggerman, pp. 18–44).

26. Botta and Flandin 1849, vol. 1, pls. 24, 29.

27. Sargon II: Botta and Flandin 1849, vol. 2, pl. 154. For a bibliography of this type, see note 18. E. Ebeling ("Talim," *Archiv für Orientforschung* 5 [1928–1929]: 218f.) identified these figurines with some described in the texts, but misread their name as *ta-lim,* "younger brother" (Ebeling 1920, no. 298:obv.:43), an error perpetuated by Gurney (1935, 52 n. 4, 68:43), Rittig (1977, 156:43), Reade (1979a, 38 n. 133), and Kolbe (1981, 96–108). The reading NUN!.ME! (= *apkallu*) was proposed by B. Landsberger in *Sam'al* (Ankara, 1948, 95 n. 227), and the dictionaries agree. On the basis of collation of Ebeling's text and comparison with two better-preserved duplicates, Wiggerman (1983, 91; 1986, 346:43) read *làh-me,* but admitted that in another duplicate (K7823, iii. 49) the signs look like NUN.ME. Edith Porada suggests that the *lahmu* may be a type of *apkallu* and that the two terms may be used interchangeably (personal conversation). This would resolve the epigraphic difficulties and requires further investigation. Wiggerman translates *lahmu* (in CAD "(a monster)") as "hairy one" on the basis of its similarity to the adjective *lahmu* ("hairy, shaggy"; CAD 1973, vol. L, 41).

28. Akkadian examples: H. Frankfort, *Cylinder Seals* (London, 1939), 60, 86f., pls. XVIII:k, XXI:c; Pritchard 1969, fig. 693; and note the similar figures on a Middle As-

syrian altar of Tukulti-Ninurta I from Assur (ibid., fig. 577). Spade: C. B. F. Walker, in Reade 1979a, 38, n. 133; Hibbert, in Kolbe 1981, 195:43; Wiggerman 1983, 92; *idem*, 1986, 88:43, 172, 346:43.

29. Sargon II example: Botta and Flandin 1849, vol. 2, pls. 152, 152bis. For a bibliography of this type, see note 18. Woolley 1926, 695:no. 7, 698:41; Green 1983, 91; *idem*, 1986, 153f.

30. Khorsabad example: Botta and Flandin 1849, vol. 2, pl. 153:b. For a bibliography of this type, see note 18. Earlier examples of hairstyle: Frankfort (as in note 28), pls. XX:d, XXI:c, XXV:c. Reade comments on the antiquity of this hairstyle, though without citing specific examples (1979a, 36). Lulal: Wiggerman 1986, 125–27.

31. Wiggerman 1986, 102f.; Gurney 1935, 52:51. For a bibliography on this type, see note 18. The figurine in figure 101 was found in Phase E of the Burnt Palace in a box by the east jamb of the door connecting the main court (18) and throne room (8) (D. Oates and J. Reid, "The Burnt Palace and the Nabu Temple; Nimrud, 1955," *Iraq* 18 [1956]: 27, fig. 2). In the same box was a *lahmu* figurine. A similar pair was in the box by the west jamb (details kindly provided by Anthony Green).

32. The fourth Sargon figurine type is a bull man, which Wiggerman identifies as the *kusarikku* ("bull/bison man") of the figurine texts (Botta and Flandin 1849, vol. 2, pls 153:a and c; Rittig 1977, 98–103; Reade 1979a, 40; Wiggerman 1986, 103f., 303–14). While this type has not been reported on Sennacherib's palace reliefs, it may yet turn up—Rassam says it occurred together with a fish-cloaked *apkallu* on reliefs from Room I, Door *b*, in Assurbanipal's North Palace at Nineveh, and the same group recurs on a door jamb of Palace S at Pasargadae (H. Rassam, in Barnett 1976, 42; Green 1983, 92).

33. It should be noted, however, that some of the ritual texts prescribe that certain apotropaic figures are to be "drawn in the gates," suggesting that the carving of figures in these locations may be but a durable variation of a common practice (Wiggerman 1986, 72f., 78:1, 194, 229–31).

34. It continued in use as a garment decoration, as evidenced by the embroidered tunic of Assurbanipal in the lion hunt reliefs from the North Palace (R. D. Barnett and A. Lorenzini, *Assyrian Sculpture in the British Museum* [Toronto 1975], pls. 105, 116, 127).

35. Assurnasirpal II: Court D/E (Meuszyński 1981, 31–34, pls. 5–6); Sargon II: court facades L, N, n, m, Rooms 9, 10, 12 (Botta and Flandin 1849, vol. 1, pls. 10–11, 24–25, 29–30, 42; vol. 2, pls. 121, 122, 138).

36. Assurnasirpal II: Budge 1914, pls. 12, 19, 42; Barnett and Falkner 1962, pl. CXV. Sargon II: Botta and Flandin 1849, vol. 2, pls. 107–14; Albenda 1986, figs. 76–78. Assurbanipal: Barnett 1976, pls. A, E. Because of similarities to passage A/R in Assurbanipal's North Palace, Reade suggested that the reliefs of Sennacherib's Room LI(n) show processions "to and from the hunt" (Barnett 1976, text-plate 8, pls. 2, 39; Reade 1972, 100f.). The evidence is incomplete, however: there are records of only the lower end of A/R and only the upper end of LI(n), and while the subjects of the

surviving A/R reliefs clearly belong to the hunt, this connection in Room LI(n) is much less clear.

37. Assurnasirpal's Room G: Meuszyński 1971. Brandes (1970) argues that the Room G subject is ceremonial lustration. Sargon's Rooms 2 and 7: Botta and Flandin 1849, vol. 1, pl. 52; vol. 2, pl. 107. Assurbanipal: Barnett 1976, pl. LXIV.

38. Barnett and Falkner 1962, pl. CXIV. Assurnasirpal describes the cutting of trees on Mt. Amanus for transport to Nineveh (Grayson 1976, § 586). It is also possible, however, that these trees are being cut down as part of the destruction of an enemy city (ibid., § 587).

39. Reade 1979a, 30.

40. Assurnasirpal II: Grayson 1976, §§ 581, 600, 681. Assurbanipal: Luckenbill 1927, §§ 896, 935, 986. It must be noted that Sargon II's surviving texts do not mention hunts, but the hunts in his Room 7 are neither dangerous, numerous, nor prominently displayed, as were the hunts of Assurnasirpal II and Assurbanipal. For Sargon, the hunt may have had only recreational value and not played an important role in his royal self-image.

41. In addition to stressing the importance of his new quarry at Balaṭai, discussed in chapter 5, Sennacherib claimed to have invented a new means of casting bronze figures and a new type of structure for a well (Luckenbill 1924, 108:vi:80–109:vii:19, 110:45–49; Luckenbill 1927, §§ 411–13).

Chapter 9

1. For a discussion of the differences between Renaissance perspective *construction* and ancient perspective *representation*, see E. Panofsky, *Early Netherlandish Painting* (Cambridge, Mass., 1953), vol. 1, 3–12. For studies of Assyrian spatial conventions, see Groenewegen-Frankfort (1951, 170–81), Reade (1980a), and Russell (1987, 523–28).

2. The spacing of the eyes in bifocal vision results in two slightly different views of nearby objects; in the case of distant objects this effect is unnoticeable. The result is that near objects appear more three-dimensional than far ones. Head movement causes near objects to appear to remain stationary while far ones seem to move along: the greater the distance, the greater the apparent movement.

3. G. Boccaccio, *The Decameron*, translated by R. Aldington (New York, 1930), 6th day, 5th tale.

4. C. de Brosses, *Lettres familières écrites d'Italie*, 1739–40, as quoted in E. Baccheschi, *The Complete Paintings of Giotto* (New York, 1966), 10.

5. The height of a standing figure in a relief is, of course, relative and can be varied to meet the requirements at hand. I believe, however, that in the reliefs of Assurnasirpal II, Tiglath-pileser III, and Sargon II, the scale of the principal figure, the king, could not have been much reduced without making him too small to recognize easily. In other words, I suggest that the maximum height of the register was essentially also the

minimum height that would permit the ready recognition of the figure of the king from anywhere in the throne room. The exception is the timber transport scene from Court VIII of Sargon II's palace at Khorsabad.

6. One could argue here that the audience would instinctively read these images conceptually, ranking the figures hierarchically according to their size, and therefore would not be disturbed by the mixture of figures of different scales (Schapiro 1969, 235–37). The resulting "hierarchy," however, would itself be confusing, since figures of the same rank (i.e., Assyrian infantrymen) are regularly shown in widely differing scales in a single composition. The factor governing size here is clearly their place in the composition, rather than their place in a social or military hierarchy.

7. Notice Budge (1914, pls. 20a, 23b), where the king is larger than his attendants, who are larger than other soldiers, who are larger than captives. The same sort of ranking may be observed, more subtly, for Tiglath-pileser III (Barnett and Falkner 1962, pls. LXXXII-LXXXV) and in the captive punishment scenes of Sargon II (Botta and Flandin 1849, vol. 2, pls. 83, 116). This form of ranking is discussed by H. Schäfer (*Principles of Egyptian Art,* 4th ed., translated by J. Baines [Oxford, 1974; 1st ed., 1919], 231–34) and by Schapiro (1969, 236f.).

8. Panofsky (as in note 1), 223, 305, n. 2.

9. The term "viewpoint" is somewhat inaccurate here, since the mural format obliges the viewer continually to shift position in order to comprehend the composition and precludes a single viewpoint. Instead, we should think in terms of multiple viewpoints that run horizontally across the composition, paralleling the movement of the viewer (Groenewegen-Frankfort 1951, 4, 176f.). Despite this limitation, the term "viewpoint" has been retained in the discussion that follows, primarily because the use of alternative terminology—for example, "viewing level" or "viewing angle"—might have proven cumbersome and obscure.

10. Groenewegen-Frankfort 1951, 173f.

11. In this context, Groenewegen-Frankfort noted that, spatially, Assurnasirpal's most successful composition shows the Assyrian army marching in front of a city wall (Room B, Slab 8: Budge 1914, pl. 22b; Groenewegen-Frankfort 1951, 174). Here the city wall serves as a curtain that simultaneously creates a shallow foreground stage space and eliminates any need for background space.

12. Budge 1914, pls. 13b, 21, 22a.

13. Barnett and Falkner 1962, pls. VI, VII, XXVII, XXX, XXXIV, LXX. Groenewegen-Frankfort 1951, 175, pl. LXX:B.

14. Barnett and Falkner 1962, pls. XXVI, XLI, LXVII. Not all of these reliefs display a consistent viewpoint, however; there is a "hovering" dead person in pl. XVII.

15. Ibid., pls. X, XL, XCI.

16. Climbing mound face: Botta and Flandin 1849, vol. 1, pl. 70; vol. 2, pls. 145, 147. Hovering dead: ibid., vol. 1, pls. 58–60.

17. Albenda (1983) has reconstructed and analyzed this relief series. Several points of her interpretation are reexamined by E. Linder ("The Khorsabad Wall Relief: A

Mediterranean Seascape or River Transport of Timbers?" *Journal of the American Oriental Society* 106 [1986]: 273–81).

18. The relatively unimportant role of diminution in a composition with a high, distant viewpoint may perhaps best be appreciated by referring to more modern, "correct," perspective images with similar viewpoints, such as Albrecht Altdorfer's *Battle of Issus* (1529) and Camille Pissarro's *Place du Théâtre Français* (1895), both of which are illustrated in H. Gardner, *Art through the Ages*, 8th ed. (New York, 1986), figs. 18–32, 21–56.

19. See chapter 5, note 9.

20. See modern reconstruction in Ussishkin 1982, fig. 9.

21. Ibid., 119–26.

22. Barnett, as in chapter 7, note 29. I owe the second observation to Professor Nadav Na'aman.

23. This is not, strictly speaking, an innovation, as the idea of specificity in narrative reliefs is a well-established neo-Assyrian tradition, beginning with the reliefs of Assurnasirpal II (Winter 1981, 14f.; J. E. Reade, "Texts and Sculptures from the North-West Palace, Nimrud," *Iraq* 47 [1985]: 212f.). What is different here is the much greater *degree* of specificity, which should have made the subjects of Sennacherib's reliefs more readily recognizable than those of his predecessors.

24. The same sort of perspective was apparently found in Room LX (Layard 1853a, 460), and a few inverted trees are found in Room XLVIII (Layard 1853b, pl. 40), though these may be intended as trees cut by the Assyrian plunderers. A similar perspective sometimes occurs in Egyptian painting, especially when a pool of water is depicted (cf. the tomb of Rekhmire, illustrated in Pritchard 1969, no. 115), but I am not aware of other examples in Mesopotamia.

25. Levine 1973–1974, 3f., 100.

26. Possible inverted mountains: Layard 1853a, 460. Upright mountains: Rooms V, VI, XIV, XXXII, XLV.

27. Transliteration in Luckenbill 1924, 67:10; my translation. Viewers familiar with the old convention shown in figure 117 would, of course, automatically read these bumps as "mountains" and would therefore have no difficulty following the narrative. For this audience, Sennacherib's new convention is no more successful than the old in conveying the nominal idea of "mountains." Sennacherib's convention *is* superior, I believe, in its use of relative scale to express the text's adjectival nuances ("difficult, extremely rough").

28. Reade 1980a, 73.

29. Slabs 63–64. Groenewegen-Frankfort 1951, 177, pl. LXXIII. One of the Tiglath-pileser III reliefs cited above is an earlier, somewhat tentative, example of the use of figures (sheep) to define space, while later examples are to be found in some hunting reliefs of Assurbanipal (ibid., pls. LXX:B, LXXIX:A). The Sennacherib relief would seem to be somewhat more daring than either of these other examples in its use of human figures, rather than just animals, as spatial indicators.

30. Luckenbill 1924, 120–24. See also the claims made in the *bīt akīti* titulary, discussed in chapter 11.

31. These two texts are discussed in chapter 4, note 18. In a somewhat similar passage, Esarhaddon states that in the Nineveh *ekal māšarti* (arsenal), victories against hostile regions were commemorated in sculpture, but the text does not specify that this sculpture was on wall slabs, that is, *askuppāti* (Borger 1956, 62, A:VI:28–29).

32. E. H. Gombrich cites examples of the difficulties experienced by "primitives" in interpreting post-Renaissance perspective (*Art and Illusion*, 3d ed. [Princeton, 1969], 267–69). Such difficulties may not, however, have applied for Sennacherib's less sophisticated perspective, which does not employ such potentially confusing conventions as converging orthogonals, foreshortening, and diminution between figures in foreground and background.

Winter (1981, 29f.) observes that historical narrative reliefs become compositionally more complex over the period from Assurnasirpal II to Sennacherib. She also notes the increasingly diverse audience garnered by the expansion of the empire, but does not consider the implications of this complexity for that audience. I would argue that the end result of this greater compositional "complexity" in narrative reliefs is an image that may have been more readily perceptible to the untrained eye of someone outside the palace circle than were earlier examples, thereby rendering the message intelligible to a wider range of receivers.

33. Ulai River battle: Reade 1979b, Taf. 17–18; H. Frankfort, *The Art and Architecture of the Ancient Orient*, 1st paperback ed. (Harmondsworth, 1970), fig. 208. North Palace reliefs: ibid., fig. 204; Barnett 1976, *passim*.

34. The issue of sequence in Assyrian art was first raised by Groenewegen-Frankfort (1951, 6, 174), and further pursued by H. G. Güterbock ("Narration in Antolian, Syrian, and Assyrian Art," *American Journal of Archaeology* 61 [1957]: 62–71) and Reade (1979b).

35. Budge 1914, pls. 23, 24a, 18b. The lower part of Slab 6 is completely preserved only in Layard's drawing, published by Weidner and Furlani (1939, fig. 58).

36. Band II: King 1915, pls. VII-XII. Other examples: Bands I, III, IV, and VIII (King 1915). The various types of sequences in Shalmaneser's gate reliefs are discussed fully by Reade (1979b, 65–69).

37. Barnett and Faulkner 1962, pls. XXXII, XXXIV, IV, VI, VII, VIII; Reade 1968, 70f. For an excellent analysis of this relief series, see E. Auerbach, "Emphasis and Eloquence in the Reliefs of Tiglath-pileser III," *Iraq* 51 (1989): 79–84.

38. Room 2, Slabs 2–12: Botta and Flandin 1849, vol. 1, pls. 52–59bis. Other similar sequences: Room 2, Slabs 25–29, upper register (ibid., vol. 1, pl. 52); Room 5, Slabs 5–13, lower register (ibid., vol. 2, pl. 85); Room 13, Slabs 1–7, lower register (ibid., vol. 2, pl. 139); Room 14, Slabs 10–12, lower register (ibid., vol. 2, pl. 144). Room 7: ibid., vol. 2, pls. 107–14; Reade 1979b, 83; E. Guralnik, "Composition of Some Narrative Reliefs from Khorsabad," *Assur* 1, no. 5 (1976):57–79.

39. Room XIV, Alammu: S. Smith 1938, pl. LVI. Other examples are in Rooms III,

XVII, XXXI, XXXII, XXXIX, XLV, XLVIII, LXIX, and LXX (see Appendix 2 for references).

40. Botta and Flandin 1849, vol. 1, pl. 52 (Room 2); vol. 2, pl. 85 (Room 5).

41. Notably in Rooms I, V, XXIV, XXXVIII, LI(s), and LXV (see Appendix 2).

42. Layard 1849a, vol. 2, 130–34.

43. This same technique of varying landscape detail to indicate passage through space was used earlier in Band X of Shalmaneser III's Balawat gates. The lower register of this band shows the expedition to the source of the Tigris that commences in flat land, continues beside a river, and concludes in the mountains (King 1915, pls. LV-LX).

44. Luckenbill 1924, 121:49–50.

45. Ulai River battle: see note 33. Lion hunts: Barnett 1976, pls. XLVI-LIII, LVI-LIX.

Chapter 10

1. Reade (1979c, 335–39) and Winter (1981, 22, 29–31, and 1983, 27) raised questions about the nature of the audience for neo-Assyrian palace decoration, but neither attempted a comprehensive investigation of the components of that audience. The textual evidence in this chapter is presented in the best available translation; when no adequate translation was available, I translated it myself. References to transliterations of the best-preserved exemplars are given in the notes.

2. D. J. Wiseman, "A New Stela of Aššur-naṣir-pal II," *Iraq* 14 (1952):24–44, pls. 2–11. Translation in Grayson 1976, § 676–82.

3. "men and women from all districts of my land": ERÍN.MEŠ MÍ.MEŠ *qa-ri-ú-te šá pi-rík* KUR-*ia gab-bi-šá*; "Foreign dignitaries, envoys": LÚ.MAH.MEŠ LÚ *šap-ra-a-te*; "people of the city Kalhu": ZI.MEŠ *šá* URU *kal-hi*; "functionaries from all my palaces": LÚ *za-ri-qi*-MEŠ *šá* É.GAL.MEŠ-*a kàl-li-ši-na* (Wiseman, as in note 2, pl. 11:141–48; Grayson 1976, § 682).

4. Sargon II and Esarhaddon describe similar ceremonies at the dedication of their new palaces. These are discussed below.

5. Grayson 1976, § 682.

6. Ibid., §§ 620–23.

7. Ibid., § 705.

8. Weissbach 1918, 184:82–84; Luckenbill 1927, §§ 51, 90. The same request is contained on two foundation tablets of precious materials (ibid., §§ 111, 115).

9. Weissbach 1918, 184:54–56; Luckenbill 1927, § 87. Somewhat shorter forms of this passage are in ibid., §§ 74, 94, 98, and 101. For the equivalent passage in the palace annals, see Lie 1929, 79:7. Sargon also invited the gods into the Northwest Palace at Nimrud after he restored it (Winckler 1889, vol. 1, 172:19; Luckenbill 1927, § 138).

10. Text in Winckler 1889, vol. 2, pl. 36:177–79; transliteration and translation in CAD 1964, vol. A/1, 278b, and Lie 1929, 81:14–15; translation also in Luckenbill 1927, § 74.

"kings from (foreign) lands": *mal-ki ma-ti-tan*;

"governors of my land": LÚ.EN *pa-ha-ti* KUR-*ia* (the "EN" sign is absent from Winckler's edition, pl. 36:178, but present in the other versions);

"overseers": LÚ *ak-li*;

"commanders": LÚ *šá-pi-ri*;

"nobles": LÚ.NUN.MEŠ;

"high officials": LÚ *šu-ut* SAG.MEŠ;

"elders of Assyria": LÚ.AB.BA.MEŠ KUR *aš + šur*-KI

11. Winckler 1889, vol. 1, 144:37–38; Luckenbill 1927, § 98 (shorter version from Room 14 in ibid., § 87). Sargon II also held a festival for "the people of Assyria" after restoring Assurnasirpal's palace (ibid., § 138; Winckler 1889, vol. 1, 172:20).

12. Weissbach 1918, 180:27–28; Luckenbill 1927, §§ 48, 72, 83, 98, 99, 102.

13. Reade (1979c, 332–34) distinguished four categories of foreigners represented on the reliefs: independent equals, independent inferiors, uncivilized tribes, and tributaries. He observed that whenever an enemy or tributary state became an Assyrian province, it ceased to be represented in the reliefs.

14. Gods: Luckenbill 1924, 98:92, 116:65–68, 125:49–50; future kings: ibid., 98:93, 116:77–85; "the people of my land": *ba-hu-la-te* KUR-*ia* (ibid., 116:74–76, 125:51).

15. Ibid., 95:71.

16. Chaldeans and Arameans: ibid., 51:24. Hilakku and Que: ibid., 61:61–62:85. Mannea: according to Parpola (1970, 236f.) this is the only mention of Mannea in any Sennacherib text.

17. Sargon II in Mannea (3rd, 6th, 7th, and 8th campaigns): Luckenbill 1927, §§ 6, 10, 12, 19, 56; Que (7th and 13/14th campaigns): ibid., §§ 16, 18, 42; Hilakku (9th campaign): ibid., §§ 25, 55, 80.

18. Luckenbill 1924, 95:72.

19. Dur Sharrukin dates: Tadmor 1958, 94, 97.

20. Luckenbill 1924, 95, n. 14. The same list appears in the building account that accompanies the annals of the first five campaigns (ibid., 104:52–53).

21. Luckenbill 1924, 117:6.

22. Levine 1973, 312–17.

23. Luckenbill 1924, 94:67.

24. Ibid., 60:56–58. A later inscription records similar unsolicited donations after the destruction of Babylon from the kings of Dilmun (Bahrain) and Sab'a, sent to Assur for the construction of the "Temple of the New Year's Festival" (ibid., 137:39–41, 138:48–50).

25. In a passage that foreshadows this one, Sargon II records that the kings of Dil-

mun and Iatnana (Cyprus) sent voluntary tribute to Sargon at Babylon in the course of his thirteenth campaign, to the south, but in each case the presence of elements of the Assyrian army in the vicinity seems to have been the stimulus (Luckenbill 1927, §§ 41, 44, 70; Winckler 1889, 126:144–149).

26. Future kings, gods: Luckenbill 1927, §§ 694, 699; Borger 1956, 63, A:VI:44–45, and 65, A:VI:65–74; "all of the magnates and people of my land": LÚ.GAL.MEŠ *ù* UN.MEŠ KUR-*ia ka-li-šú-nu*—Borger 1956, 63, A:VI:49. I cannot agree with Kinnier Wilson (1972, 43, 90–92) that *nišē māti-ia* here refers to foreign workers; the phrase clearly denotes the people of Assyria ("my land").

27. Arsenal: Luckenbill 1927, §§ 690, 697–98; Borger 1956, 59, A:V:47–49. "Letter to Assur": Luckenbill 1927, § 606; Borger 1956, 106:21.

28. L. = Luckenbill 1927; B. = Borger 1956. Na'id-Marduk: L., § 510; B., 47, B:II:32–39. Hazael and Laialê: L., §§ 518a, 536, 538; B., 53, A:IV:6–18, and 57, B:III:41–56. Elamite and Guti princes: L., § 524; B., 58–59, A:V:26–33. Medians: L., § 540; B., 54–55, A:IV:32–45.

29. Luckenbill 1927, §§ 836, 838; Streck 1916, vol. 2, 88:89–95, 90:108–15. The *bīt redûti* is almost certainly to be identified with Assurbanipal's North Palace at Nineveh, since its building account was on a cylinder from the foundations of that palace (Barnett 1976, 5f.).

30. L. = Luckenbill 1927; S. = Streck 1916, vol. 2. Egypt: L., §§ 774, 905; S., 14:8–9. Arvad: L., §§ 780, 848, 912; S., 18:63–67. Tabalu: L., §§ 781, 848, 911; S., 18:68–74. Hilakku: L., § 782; S., 18:75–80. Lydia: L., §§ 784, 909–10; S., 20:95–110. Mannea: L., § 786; S., 24:11–26:26. Babylonia: L., § 789; S., 28:82–30:95. Nabatea: L., §§ 822, 870, 880; S., 134:45–136:57.

31. Kinnier Wilson, 1972, was not well-received by reviewers. Its worst flaws—its incomplete publication of the texts and lack of indexes—were rectified by Dalley and Postgate, 1984. See the reviews by A. K. Grayson, *Journal of Cuneiform Studies* 26 (1974):130–32; W. von Soden, *Zeitschrift für Assyriologie* 66 (1974): 129f.; P. Garelli, "Remarques sur l'Administration de l'Empire Assyrien," *Revue d'Assyrioloqie et d'Archéologie orientale* 68 (1974): 129–40; Parpola 1976; R. A. Henshaw, "Late Neo-Assyrian Officialdom," *Journal of the American Oriental Society* 100 (1980): 283–305; and G. van Driel, "Wine Lists and Beyond?" *Bibliotheca Orientalis* 38 (1981): 259–72.

32. The tablets were found in a wine magazine (SW 6) and in rooms NE 48–49. The earlier group corresponds to Parpola's (1976, 170) Groups II and III, while the later is his Group I, which was redated by Dalley and Postgate (1984, 22f.).

33. Kinnier Wilson 1972, #3:i10; Dalley and Postgate 1984, #141:r.12, both dating about 784 B.C.

34. "Magnates" (GAL.MEŠ): Kinnier Wilson 1972, 32–43; von Soden 1972, 934f., "*rabiānum.*" Parpola (1976, 171f.) rightly objected to Kinnier Wilson's translation of this word as "emirs." K.8669: K. F. Müller, "Das assyrische Ritual," *Mitteilungen der Vorderasiatisch-Ägyptischen Gesellschaft* 41, no. 3 (1937): 59–89, pl. I-III. The section listing the officials is Müller, 61:1–20.

35. Kinnier Wilson 1972, 43.

36. Botta and Flandin 1849, vol. 1, pls. 52, 57–66.

37. Reade 1980b, 85f. For Room G, see Meuszyński 1971, 32–50. Brandes (1970, 153f.), on the contrary, argues that the subject of Room G is ceremonial lustration. No such ambiguity attends the Room 2 banquet reliefs in Sargon's palace.

38. Kinnier Wilson 1972, 45, 89, 100–105; #1:ii15; #21:r.14; #22:5. Henshaw (as in note 31, 301), however, observed that a number of people in this "guest list" seem to be of lower ranks.

39. Kinnier Wilson 1972, 6, 44, 46, #3:i10; #4:17; #8:r.4; #18:r.19.

40. Kinnier Wilson 1972, 46, #4:r.8', #23:3, #18:r.14. This title, *ša* UGU É-*a/an-ni*, does not occur in the later group, but appears in a tablet of ca. 615 B.C. (Dalley and Postgate 1984, #40:9).

41. These people are listed in both groups of wine lists. "Eunuchs": Kinnier Wilson 1972, 46f.; Dalley and Postgate 1984, 284 (GAL.SAG), 286 (SAG.MEŠ). "Bodyguard": Kinnier Wilson 1972, 48f.; Dalley and Postgate 1984, 31–33, 39, 286 (*qurbūtu* and *ša* GÌR^(II)).

42. Chief scribe (LÚ.A.BA.É.GAL): Kinnier Wilson 1972, 62, #12:3', #19:21; the title reappears in tablets dating ca. 639 and 626 (Dalley and Postgate 1984, #55:10', #59:13, #73:3). Foreign scribes: Kinnier Wilson 1972, 62f., #9:r.18–20; #10:r.7; #13:12'; 21:r.8'; Dalley and Postgate 1984, #134:14'.

43. Mallowan 1966, vol. 1, 172; vol. 3, plan VIII.

44. Kinnier Wilson 1972, 78–87. "Palace servants" (LÚ.ÌR.É.GAL): ibid., #1:iii:8–10. "Cook" (LÚ.MU): ibid., #1:iii:11. "Bread bakers": Dalley and Postgate 1984, 285 (NINDA). These workers are designated by the signs LÚ.GAR, usually transcribed LÚ.NINDA. The Akkadian equivalent is unknown; CAD 1964, vol. A/1, 296, suggested *alahhinu*, while J. N. Postgate ("The Place of the *Šaknu* in Assyrian Government," *Anatolian Studies* 30, [1980]: 68) preferred *muraqqi'u*. Kinnier Wilson's (1972, 45) identification of these people as "governors" (LÚ.GAR can also be read *šaknu*) is made unlikely by their context (among the kitchen staff) and by the absence of the expected phonetic complement.

45. Diviners (LÚ.HAL.MEŠ): Kinnier Wilson 1972, 74f.,; Assyrian: #6:22, #8:28b, #13:r.8', #15:12, #16:32, #20:10'; Kassite: #12:4'; #20:11'; Dalley and Postgate 1984, #120:obv. 16'. In the only possible occurrence of Kassite diviners on a later group list, the name of the profession is completely lost (Kinnier Wilson 1972, #13:20'). Bird augurs (LÚ *da-gíl* MUŠEN.MEŠ); Kinnier Wilson 1972, #3:i4–5; Dalley and Postgate 1984, #145(=NWL #3):iv:5.

46. Kinnier Wilson 1972, 76–78; Dalley and Postgate 1984, 285 (LÚ/MÍ.NAR.MEŠ). For Kummuh, add Kinnier Wilson 1972, #1:iii:7.

47. "Wine steward": Dalley and Postgate 1984, 284 (LÚ.GAL.GEŠTIN); Kinnier Wilson 1972, 71. "Deputy" (*šanû*): ibid., 71, #8:11, #21:10a'.

48. Original texts in Kinnier Wilson (1972) and Dalley and Postgate (1984). Several names were restored by Parpola (1976, 167f.): #4—Muṣaṣir (*not* Egypt), Šupria;

#11—Tabalu; #13—Sangibutu (*not* Singir); #14—Manisa; #23—Šupria (*not* Suhu), Tabalu, Malatya.

49. Dalley and Postgate 1984, 24, #143:ii:9'-12', #145:iv:26.

50. *targumannu:* Kinnier Wilson 1972, 94, #18:r.8. Reade (1979c, 336) suggested the possibility of guided tours of the palace, and Paley (1983, 53) implied the same.

51. Postgate 1974, 119f. Occurrences of *madattu* in the annals have been collected by N. B. Janowska, "Some Problems of the Economy of the Assyrian Empire," in *Ancient Mesopotamia,* ed. I. M. Diakonoff (Moscow, 1969), 253–76 (translated from *Vestnik Drevnej Istorii,* no. 1, 1956, 28–46).

52. Postgate 1974, xx, 121.

53. ABL 252; trans. Postgate 1974, 271:4–5, 273:37.

54. ND 2777; trans. *Iraq* 21 (1959): 174:5–7; cited in Postgate 1974, xx.

55. ABL 241, 242; trans. Postgate 1974, 267:6'-7', 268:8–12.

56. LÚ.MAH.MEŠ. Postgate 1974, 123–25. See also CAD 1962, vol. Ṣ, 213, s. v. "*ṣīru* A."

57. They are: Anqarruna (Ekron), Arabia, Bīt-Ammān, Egypt, Elam, Gaza, Judah, Kummuh, Mannea, Marqasi, Moab, Nabatea, Que, Sam'al, Šupria, Tabalu, Edom, Zikirtu. References from Postgate (1974, 124). In addition, there is also mention of horses from Malatya, perhaps as tribute (ibid., 17f.).

58. Ibid., 125f., with examples. Note also Waterman 1930, vol. 1, 221:10, 411:rev.:5. This seems to have been the usual term for royal audience for any purpose, not confined only to tribute delivery.

59. ABL 948:rev.:5–10; trans. Postgate 1974, 126.

60. *Door d:* Slabs D–3 to D–6, and D–8, published in Meuszyński 1979, 5–13, figs. 1–5; Slab D–7 illustrated in Budge 1914, pl. XXVIII. *Door c:* Slabs E–1 to E–4, in Meuszyński 1981, 32, Taf. 6.

61. *Throne-room outer court:* Botta and Flandin 1849, vol. 1, pls. 29, 36–39. *Corridor 10:* ibid., vol. 2, pls. 122–36.

62. Postgate 1974, 126f. Postgate here observes that the same subject recurs in the reliefs of the "audience hall" at Persepolis.

63. In procession reliefs from a number of the Assyrian palaces, the king is shown attended by a variety of officials and servants who would have formed one part of the audience for the reliefs when the king was in residence at the palace. It is beyond the scope of this study to attempt to identify these individuals, many of whom must, however, also have figured in the Nimrud wine lists. For some preliminary remarks concerning these individuals, see Reade (1972). These officials have also been studied by Michelle Marcus, "A Study of Types of Officials in Neo-Assyrian Reliefs: Their Identifying Attributes and Their Possible Relationship to a Bureaucratic Hierarchy," M.A. thesis, Columbia University, 1981.

64. Assurnasirpal's Ninurta and Ishtar temples (Mallowan 1966, vol. 1, 84–92), Sargon's Rooms 161–98, and Sennacherib's Rooms LI(s)–LIX (see chapter 3, note 93).

65. Kinnier Wilson 1972, #1:iii:2, #18:25.

66. For the question of the *visual* literacy of various components of the audience, see chapter 9, note 32.

67. Paley, who first noted this function of epigraphs, likened them to captions that refresh the memory of docents in churches and museums (Paley 1983, 53).

Chapter 11

1. A shorter version of a portion of this chapter appeared in Russell 1987, 530–37. For a summary of the various editions of Sennacherib's texts, see Borger 1979, vol. 1, 64–68; augmented in part by Reade 1975, 189–96.

2. Liverani 1981, 234–36. The actual situation is not quite as straightforward as Liverani indicates. The title "king of the four quarters" first occurs in an edition omitted by Liverani that records only the first four campaigns and therefore omits the campaign to the north (British Museum, WAA, K 1674; published in C. Bezold, *Keilinschriftliche Bibliothek,* Berlin, 1890, II, 80, no. A2). The date of this text, however, is 697 B.C. (month not preserved), meaning that it was probably inscribed during or immediately after the fifth campaign, which took place in 697 (see chapter 7, note 24). Thus the "four quarters" title is already justified, even though the body of the text fails to support the claim.

3. Liverani 1981, 240f. This title also first appears in a text written at the time the campaign in question was in progress, and which therefore does not record the campaign itself (ibid., 241, n. 20).

4. Ibid., 244f.

5. Luckenbill 1924, 21, 66–76, 117–25. Luckenbill designated the Door *a* text "F1," and the Door *c* text "I1." Translation only in Luckenbill 1927, §§ 300–22 (F1), 407–16 (I1). For further information on these bulls, see Galter, Levine, and Reade 1986; and Russell, forthcoming. For an analysis of the significance of the palace dimensions in these texts, see chapter 4.

6. The date of the *composition* of these texts is less certain. Levine (1973, 312–17) has demonstrated that the account of the second campaign in the Door *a* text must have been composed before 700 B.C. The titulary too contains some elements that suggest it is a transitional formulation, originally composed before 697 B.C. (Liverani 1981, 240f., 244). The titulary of Door *c* is generally reckoned to be of rather late date (Liverani 1981, 240, 247; Luckenbill 1924, 117, n. 1), partly on the basis of similarities with the titulary of an inscription from Nebi Yunus (Luckenbill's "H4") composed between 691 (battle of Halule) and 689 B.C. (destruction of Babylon).

7. Sennacherib's published foundation texts never start with the word "palace," even if they were intended for burial in the palace foundations (see Bezold, as in note 2, 80, n. 2).

8. Tadmor 1981, 25f.

9. Just such a genealogy occurs in a derogatory passage of a Babylonian "declara-

tion of war": "Sennacherib, son of Sargon, offspring of a house slave" (P. Gerardi, "Declaring War in Mesopotamia," *Archiv für Orientforschung* 33 [1986]: 36:7).

10. Luckenbill 1924, 66:1, 117:1.

11. Liverani 1981, 235.

12. Transliteration in Luckenbill 1924, 66:1–3; my translation. Liverani 1981, 236, 240.

13. Transliteration in Luckenbill 1924, 117:1–6; my translation. Liverani 1981, 240–43.

14. Tadmor 1981, 25f. Tadmor observes that, with only three exceptions (Tiglath-pileser III, Sargon II, Sennacherib), every Assyrian king's texts present *both* a genealogy and a claim of divine election. This dual affirmation of legitimacy is a very old Mesopotamian tradition, dating back at least to the Early Dynastic period. See, for example, the inscription on the "Stela of the Vultures" of Eannatum of Lagash; translated in J. Cooper, *Reconstructing History from Ancient Inscriptions: the Lagash-Umma Border Conflict (Sources from the Ancient Near East, II, No. 1)*, Malibu, 1983, 45:i–v.

15. Transliteration in Luckenbill 1924, 76:1–6; my translation.

16. Transliteration in Luckenbill 1924, 24:16–19; translation in Liverani 1981, 2f.

17. Liverani 1981, 242, n. 21. See also Liverani 1979, 311. Appendix 1, Room I, Slab 1. Barnett 1956, 91.

18. Transliteration in Luckenbill 1924, 135:9 to 136:19; my translation. The inscription refers to the destruction of Babylon and consequently must date after 689 B.C.

19. As with the dual affirmation of legitimacy in the royal titulary (see note 14), this combination of references to new buildings and irrigation works likewise has a long history in Mesopotamian royal inscriptions, occurring already in the Early Dynastic period in an inscription of Urnanshe of Lagash (translated in Cooper, as in note 14, 44:i–vi). Laura O'Rourke, a senior at Barnard College, reminds me that this same short text also recounts the king's military conquests. According to Redman, "these activities may be symbolic of the two realms of authority that concerned early kings and that brought them to power: war and water" (C. Redman, *The Rise of Civilization*, San Francisco, 1978, 306). Sennacherib's titularies demonstrate his interest in affirming his authority in these traditional realms.

20. Luckenbill 1927, § 54.

21. Liverani 1979, 308f.

22. Full accounts of Sennacherib's deeds are in the texts the titularies of which are discussed here. Though as "historical" accounts they lend themselves to a variety of often widely divergent interpretations, they do seem to confirm in a general way the self-portrait presented in the titularies. Sennacherib's annals (Luckenbill 1924, 23–93) depict the king's reign as a remarkably peaceful and stable period for the Assyrian empire. The majority of the Assyrian empire was apparently at peace for most of Sennacherib's reign; with the exception of Babylonia, he never campaigned twice in the same region. Sennacherib devoted a considerable part of his energy and resources to

erecting civic works. At Nineveh he built the Southwest Palace, the largest known Assyrian palace; the *bīt kutalli*, or armory; a great city wall some twelve kilometers in curcuit with eighteen gates; and roads, bridges, canals, and orchards. At Assur he rebuilt several important temples and added the *bīt akīti*, the "Temple of the New Year's Festival" (ibid., 94–155). Among Sennacherib's most remarkable accomplishments were the great irrigation projects for Nineveh, the courses for which are still marked by royal stelae—as at Bavian, Maltai, and Faida—and by spectacular feats of engineering such as the aqueduct at Jerwan (Reade 1978; Jacobsen and Lloyd, 1935).

23. II Kings 20:12–13; trans. *New English Bible,* New York, 1971. Cited in Paley 1983, 53.

24. Luckenbill 1924, 128:38.

25. Appendix 2, Court XIX, Door *h;* and Room XXXIV, Doors *b* and *1.* Reconstruction in Ussishkin 1982, fig. 60. It is difficult to judge how clear the Lachish siege would have appeared to a viewer standing in Door *h* of Court XIX. According to Layard's plan, the distance from Door *h* to the Lachish siege slab in Room XXXVI was some 130 feet, and the perception difficulties imposed by distance would have been compounded by the differential in lighting between the bright sunlight of Court XIX and the presumably dim interior of Room XXXVI, deep in the palace. Thus, the colossi serve simultaneously to attract the viewer's attention to a scene that may have been nearly invisible from the outside and to mark the path to a clearer view of it.

26. Both the Assyrian (Luckenbill 1924, 70:28–32) and biblical (II Kings 19:35–36; II Chronicles 32:21) accounts agree that Jerusalem did not fall.

27. These observations do not apply in the same degree to epigraphs, which are sufficiently short and simple to be readily interpreted for visitors by whoever is serving as their tour guide.

28. Reade 1979c, 339.

29. P. Garelli, "La Propagande Royale Assyrienne," *Akkadica* 27 (1982): 26. Parpola (as in chapter 5, note 35), 171–82.

30. It is possible, however, that for at least some suites of rooms the sequence of passage through space would have been governed by a particular ceremonial function, now unknown, which that suite served.

31. II Kings 18:13, 17; 19:8.

32. Ussishkin 1982, 50–54.

33. John Barth, "Life-Story," in *Lost in the Funhouse,* paperback ed. (New York, 1969), 118.

34. Liverani 1981, 234f.

35. Reade 1979c, 339.

36. Liverani 1979, 302.

37. Transliteration in Luckenbill 1924, 124:43 to 125:47; my translation. For identification of the swamp, see Jacobsen and Lloyd 1935, 35, n. 20.

38. Transliterations in Luckenbill 1924, 97:88, 115:43–45; my translations.

39. Appendix 1, Court VI, Slab 66. Some of the captives are identifiable on the basis of costume as westerners (Wäfler 1975, vol. 1, 57–59, 179f.), but the remainder display no identifying characteristics and could be from anywhere.

40. For the idea of the capital as the center of the realm, see Liverani 1979, 306–9; Liverani 1981, 235; Winter 1981, 19f. On the dynamics of deporting populations for use as labor in royal building projects, see B. Oded, *Mass Deportations and Deportees in the Neo-Assyrian Empire* (Wiesbaden, 1979), 54–59, 89–91, 110f.

41. This door, designated *a* in Layard's plan, is to be distinguished from throne-room Door *a*, whose titulary was discussed above.

42. To military conquest and tribute, the ideal order exemplified by Assurnasirpal II's palace reliefs adds a third component: service to the gods (Winter 1981, 20f.).

BIBLIOGRAPHY

ALBENDA, P.

1976–77   "Landscape Bas-Reliefs in the *Bīt-Ḫilāni* of Ashurbanipal." *Bulletin of the American Schools of Oriental Research* 204:49–72; and 205:29–48.

1978   "Assyrian Carpets in Stone." *Journal of the Ancient Near Eastern Society* 10:1–34.

1983   "A Mediterranean Seascape from Khorsabad." *Assur* 3, no. 3, 103–36.

1986   *The Palace of Sargon, King of Assyria (Éditions Recherche sur les Civilizations. Synthèse,* XXII). Paris.

BARNETT, R. D.

1956   "Phoenicia and the Ivory Trade." *Archaeology* 9:87–97.

1958   "The Siege of Lachish." *Israel Exploration Journal* 8:161–64.

1963   "Altorientalische Altertümer in London." *Archiv für Orientforschung* 20:197–200.

1969   "Ezekiel and Tyre." *Eretz-Israel* 9:6–13.

1976   *Sculptures from the North Palace of Ashurbanipal at Nineveh.* London.

BARNETT, R. D., AND M. FALKNER

1962   *The Sculptures of Aššur-naṣir-apli II (883–859 B.C.), Tiglath-pileser III (745–727 B.C.), Esarhaddon (681–669 B.C.) from the Central and South-west Palaces at Nimrud.* London.

BLEIBTREU, E., R. D. BARNETT, AND G. TURNER.

forthcoming   "The Southwest Palace of Sennacherib at Nineveh" (complete publication of British Museum sculptures and drawings relating to Sennacherib's palace).

BORGER, R.

1956   *Die Inschriften Asarhaddons, Königs von Assyrien (Archiv für Orientforschung Beiheft,* IX). Graz.

1979   *Babylonisch-Assyrische Lesestücke (Analecta Orientalia,* LIV). 2d ed. 2 vols. Rome (1st ed.: Rome, 1963).

BOTTA, P. E., AND E. FLANDIN.
1849–50   *Monument de Ninive.* 5 vols. Paris.

BRANDES, M. A.
1970   "La salle dite 'G' du palais d'Assurnasirpal II à Kalakh, lieu de
                 cérémonie rituelle." In *Actes de la XVIIe Recontre Assyriologique
                 Internationale*, 147–54. Gembloux.

BUDGE, E. A. W.
1914   *Assyrian Sculptures in the British Museum: Reign of Ashur-nasir-pal,
                 885–860 B.C.* London.

BUREN, E. D. VAN
1931   *Foundation Figurines and Offerings.* Berlin.

CAD
1956–84   *The Assyrian Dictionary of the Oriental Institute of the University of
                 Chicago.* Chicago.

CLARKE, S., AND R. ENGELBACH
1930   *Ancient Egyptian Masonry.* London.

DALLEY, S., AND J. N. POSTGATE
1984   *The Tablets from Fort Shalmaneser (Cuneiform Texts From Nimrud,
                 III).* London.

EBELING, E.
1920   *Keilschrifttexte aus Assur, Religiösen Inhalts*, II (*Wissenschaftliche
                 Veröffentlichung der Deutschen Orient-Gesellschaft*, XXXIV). Leip-
                 zig.

FALKNER, M.
1952–53a   "Die Reliefs der assyrischen Könige. Zweite Reihe: 1. Zehn as-
                 syrische Reliefs in Venedig." *Archiv für Orientforschung* 16:25–34.
1952–53b   "Die Reliefs der assyrischen Könige. Zweite Reihe: 4. Zwei as-
                 syrische Reliefs in Durham." *Archiv für Orientforschung* 16:246–
                 51.

FILIPPI, W. DE
1977   "The Royal Inscriptions of Aššur-Nāṣir-Apli II (883–859 B.C.): A
                 Study of the Chronology of the Calah Inscriptions Together with
                 an Edition of Two of These Texts." *Assur* 1 (no. 7):123–69.

FORRER, E.
1919   *Provinzeinteilung des assyrisches Reiches.* Berlin.

GADD, C. J.
1936   *The Stones of Assyria.* London.
1938   "A Visiting Artist at Nineveh in 1850." *Iraq* 5:118–22.

GALTER, H. D., L. D. LEVINE, AND J. E. READE
1986   "The Colossi of Sennacherib's Palace and Their Inscriptions."
                 Annual Review of the Royal Inscriptions of Mesopotamia Project
                 4:27–32.

GERARDI, P.

1988   "Epigraphs and Assyrian Palace Reliefs: The Development of the
        Epigraphic Text." *Journal of Cuneiform Studies* 40:1–35.

GOOSSENS, G.

1949   "Fragment de Relief de Sennachérib." *Bulletin des Musées Royaux
        d'Art et d'Histoire,* series 4, 21:60–64.

1950   "Relief de Sennachérib." *Bulletin des Musées Royaux d'Art et
        d'Histoire,* series 4, 22:86–88.

GRAYSON, A. K.

1976   *Assyrian Royal Inscriptions. Part 2: From Tiglath-pileser I to
        Ashur-nasir-apli II (Records of the Ancient Near East,* II). Wies-
        baden.

GREEN, A.

1983   "Neo-Assyrian Apotropaic Figures." *Iraq* 45:87–96.

1985   "A Note on the 'Scorpion-man' and Pazuzu." *Iraq* 47:75–82.

1986   "The Lion-Demon in the Art of Mesopotamia and Neighbouring
        Regions." *Baghdader Mitteilungen* 17:141–254.

GROENEWEGEN-FRANKFORT, H. A.

1951   *Arrest and Movement: An Essay on Space and Time in the Represen-
        tational Art of the Ancient Near East.* London.

GURNEY, O. R.

1935   "Babylonian Prophylactic Figures and Their Rituals." *Annals of
        Archaeology and Anthropology* 22:31–96.

HALL, H. R.

1928   *Babylonian and Assyrian Sculpture in the British Museum.* Paris.

HEIDEL, A.

1953   "The Octagonal Sennacherib Prism in the Iraq Museum." *Sumer*
        9:117–88.

HROUDA, B.

1965   *Die Kulturgeschichte des assyrischen Flachbildes (Saarbrücker Bei-
        träge zur Altertumskunde,* II). Bonn.

HULIN, P.

1963   "The Inscriptions on the Carved Throne-Base of Shalmaneser
        III." *Iraq* 25:48–69.

JACOBSEN, T., AND S. LLOYD

1935   *Sennacherib's Aqueduct at Jerwan (Oriental Institute Publications,*
        XXIV). Chicago.

KING, L. W.

1909   *Cuneiform Texts from Babylonian Tablets in the British Museum,*
        XXVI. London.

1915   *The Bronze Reliefs from the Gates of Shalmaneser, King of Assyria,
        B.C. 860–825.* London.

KING, L. W., AND E. A. W. BUDGE
1902   *Annals of the Kings of Assyria*, I. London.

KINNIER WILSON, J. V.
1972   *The Nimrud Wine Lists: A Study of Men and Administration at the Assyrian Capital in the Eighth Century, B.C. (Cuneiform Texts from Nimrud,* I). London.

KOLBE, D.
1981   *Die Reliefprogramme religiös-mythologischen Charakters in neuassyrischen Palästen (Europäische Hochschulschriften,* XXXVIII/3). Frankfurt am Main.

LAESSØE, J.
1959   "Building Inscriptions from Fort Shalmaneser, Nimrud." *Iraq* 21:38–41.

LAYARD, A. H.
1849a   *Nineveh and Its Remains.* 2 vols. London.
1849b   *Monuments of Nineveh from Drawings Made on the Spot.* London.
1851   *Inscriptions in the Cuneiform Character from Assyrian Monuments.* London.
1853a   *Discoveries in the Ruins of Nineveh and Babylon.* London.
1853b   *A Second Series of the Monuments of Nineveh.* London.

LEGAC, Y.
1907   *Les Inscriptions d'Aššur-naṣir-aplu III.* Paris.

LEVINE, L. D.
1973   "The Second Campaign of Sennacherib." *Journal of Near Eastern Studies* 32:312–17.
1973–74   "Geographical Studies in the Neo-Assyrian Zagros." *Iran* 11:1–27; and 12:99–124.
1982   "Sennacherib's Southern Front: 704–689 B.C." *Journal of Cuneiform Studies* 34:28–58.

LIE, A. G.
1929   *The Inscriptions of Sargon II, King of Assyria. Part I: The Annals.* Paris.

LIVERANI, M.
1979   "The Ideology of the Assyrian Empire." In *Power and Propaganda (Mesopotamia,* VII), ed. M. T. Larsen, 297–317. Copenhagen.
1981   "Critique of Variants and the Titulary of Sennacherib." In *Assyrian Royal Inscriptions: New Horizons in Literary, Ideological, and Historical Analysis,* ed. F. M. Fales, 225–57. Rome.

LOUD, G., AND C. B. ALTMAN
1938   *Khorsabad, Part II: The Citadel and the Town (Oriental Institute Publications,* XL). Chicago.

LOUD, G., H. FRANKFORT, AND T. JACOBSEN

1936   *Khorsabad, Part I: Excavations in the Palace and at a City Gate* (*Oriental Institute Publications,* XXXVIII). Chicago.

LUCKENBILL, D. D.

1924   *The Annals of Sennacherib* (*Oriental Institute Publications,* II). Chicago.

1926   *Ancient Records of Assyria and Babylonia,* I. Chicago.

1927   *Ancient Records of Assyria and Babylonia,* II. Chicago.

LYON, D. G.

1883   *Keilschrifttexte Sargon's.* Leipzig.

MADHLOOM, T.

1967   "Excavations at Nineveh, 1965–67." *Sumer* 23:76–79.

1968   "Nineveh, 1967–68 Campaign." *Sumer* 24:45–51.

1969   "Nineveh, 1968–69 Campaign." *Sumer* 25:44–49.

1970   *The Chronology of Neo-Assyrian Art.* London.

1972   *Naynawa* (*Historical Monuments in Iraq,* I. In Arabic). Baghdad.

MALLOWAN, M. E. L.

1966   *Nimrud and Its Remains.* 3 vols. London.

MEISSNER, B., AND P. ROST

1893   *Die Bauinschriften Sanheribs.* Leipzig.

MEUSZYŃSKI, J.

1971   "Contribution to the Reconstruction of the Northwest Palace in Kalḫu." *Études et Travaux* 5:32–51.

1979   "La façade de la salle du trône au Palais Nord-Ouest à Nimrud." *Études et Travaux* 11:5–13.

1981   *Die Rekonstruktion der Reliefdarstellungen und ihrer Anordnung im Nordwestpalast von Kalḫu (Nimrud),* (*Baghdader Forschungen,* II). Mainz am Rhein.

NA'AMAN, N.

1979   "Sennacherib's Campaign to Judah and the Date of the *LMLK* Stamps." *Vetus Testamentum* 29:61–86.

NAGEL, W.

1967   *Die neuassyrischen Reliefstile unter Sanherib und Assurbanaplu* (*Berliner Beiträge zur Vor- und Frühgeschichte,* XI). Berlin.

PALEY, S. M.

1976   *King of the World: Ashur-nasir-pal II of Assyria, 883–859 B.C.* Brooklyn.

1983   "Assyrian Palace Reliefs: Finished and Unfinished Business." In *Essays on Near Eastern Art and Archaeology in Honor of Charles Kyrle Wilkinson,* ed. P. Harper and H. Pittman, 48–58. New York.

PARPOLA, S.

1970   *Neo-Assyrian Toponyms (Alter Orient und Altes Testament,* VI). Neukirchen-Vluyn.

1976   Book review: "J. V. Kinnier Wilson, *The Nimrud Wine Lists.*" *Journal of Semitic Studies* 21:165–74.

PATERSON, A.

1915   *Assyrian Sculptures: Palace of Sinacherib.* The Hague.

PLACE, V., AND F. THOMAS

1867–70   *Ninive et l'Assyrie.* 3 vols. Paris.

PORADA, E.

1945   "Reliefs from the Palace of Sennacherib." *Bulletin of the Metropolitan Museum of Art,* n.s., 3:152–60.

POSTGATE, J. N.

1974   *Taxation and Conscription in the Assyrian Empire,* (*Studia Pohl, series maior,* III). Rome.

PRITCHARD, J. B.

1969   *The Ancient Near East in Pictures Relating to the Old Testament.* 2d ed. Princeton (1st ed.: Princeton, 1954).

RASSAM, H.

1897   *Asshur and the Land of Nimrod.* New York.

RAWLINSON, H. C.

1861   *Cuneiform Inscriptions of Western Asia,* I. London.

1870   *Cuneiform Inscriptions of Western Asia,* III. London.

READE, J. E.

1965   "Twelve Ashurnasirpal Reliefs." *Iraq* 27:119–34.

1967   "Two Slabs from Sennacherib's Palace." *Iraq* 29:42–48.

1968   "The Palace of Tiglath-pileser III." *Iraq* 30:69–73.

1970   "The Design and Decoration of Neo-Assyrian Public Buildings." Ph.D. diss. Cambridge, King's College.

1972   "The Neo-Assyrian Court and Army: Evidence from the Sculptures." *Iraq* 34:87–112.

1975   "Sources for Sennacherib: The Prisms." *Journal of Cuneiform Studies* 27:189–96.

1976   "Sargon's Campaigns of 720, 716, and 715 B.C.: Evidence from the Sculptures." *Journal of Near Eastern Studies* 35:95–104.

1978   "Studies in Assyrian Geography. Part 1: Sennacherib and the Waters of Nineveh." *Revue d'Assyriologie et d'Archéologie orientale* 72:47–72, 157–75.

1979a   "Assyrian Architectural Decoration: Techniques and Subject-Matter." *Baghdader Mitteilungen* 10:17–49.

1979b   "Narrative Composition in Assyrian Sculpture." *Baghdader Mitteilungen* 10:52–110.

1979c	"Ideology and Propaganda in Assyrian Art." In *Power and Propaganda* (*Mesopotamia*, VII), ed. M. T. Larsen, 329–43. Copenhagen.
1980a	"Space, Scale, and Significance in Assyrian Art." *Baghdader Mitteilungen* 11:71–74.
1980b	"The Architectural Context of Assyrian Sculpture." *Baghdader Mitteilungen* 11:75–87.
1983	*Assyrian Sculpture.* Cambridge, Mass.

RITTIG, D.

1977	*Assyrisch-babylonische Kleinplastik magischer Bedeutung vom 13.-6. Jh. v. Chr.* (*Münchener Universitäts-Schriften Phil. Fachbereich,* 12. *Münchener Vorderasiatische Studien,* 1). Munich.

ROSS, H. J.

1902	*Letters from the East, 1837–1857.* London.

ROST, P.

1893	*Die Keilschrifttexte Tiglat-Pilesers III.* 2 vols. Leipzig.

RUSSELL, J. M.

1985	"Sennacherib's 'Palace without Rival': A Programmatic Study of Texts and Images in a Late Assyrian Palace." Ph.D. diss. University of Pennsylvania, Philadelphia.
1987	"Bulls for the Palace and Order in the Empire: The Sculptural Program of Sennacherib's Court VI at Nineveh." *Art Bulletin* 69:520–39.
1989	"Review of Pauline Albenda, *Palace of Sargon.*" *Bulletin of the American Schools of Oriental Research* 276:88–92.
forthcoming	"Neo-Assyrian Palace Inscriptions: Their Content and Architectural Context" (working title of book-length manuscript).

SALMAN, I.

1970	"Foreward: Nineveh." *Sumer* 26:c–d.

SCHAPIRO, M.

1969	"On Some Problems in the Semiotics of Visual Art: Field and Vehicle in Image-Signs." *Semiotica* 1:223–42.

SCHRAMM, W.

1973	*Einleitung in die assyrischen Königsinschriften,* II. Leiden.

SCHROEDER, O.

1922	*Keilschrifttexte aus Assur, historischen Inhalts,* II (*Wissenschaftliche Veröffentlichung der Deutschen Orient-Gesellschaft,* XXXVII). Leipzig.

SHUKRI, A.

1956	"Conservation and Restoration of Assyrian Sculpture at Nimrud." *Sumer* 12: Arabic section, 133–34.

SMITH, G.

1871   *History of Assurbanipal, Translated from the Cuneiform Inscriptions.*
            London.

1875   *Assyrian Discoveries.* London.

1878   *History of Sennacherib.* London.

SMITH, S.

1921   *The First Campaign of Sennacherib.* London.

1938   *Assyrian Sculptures in the British Museum from Shalmaneser III to
            Sennacherib.* London.

SMITH, W. S.

1960   "Two Assyrian Reliefs from Canford Manor." *Bulletin of the Mu-
            seum of Fine Arts* 58:44–57.

SODEN, W. VON

1965–81   *Akkadisches Handwörterbuch.* 3 vols. Wiesbaden.

STRECK, M.

1916   *Assurbanipal und die letzten assyrischen Könige bis zum Untergang
            Niniveh's.* 3 vols. Leipzig.

TADMOR, H.

1958   "The Campaigns of Sargon II of Assur: A Chronological-
            Historical Study." *Journal of Cuneiform Studies* 12:22–40, 77–
            100.

1981   "History and Ideology in the Assyrian Royal Inscriptions." In
            *Assyrian Royal Inscriptions: New Horizons in Literary, Ideological,
            and Historical Analysis,* ed. F. M. Fales, 13–33. Rome.

THOMPSON, R. C.

1936   *A Dictionary of Assyrian Chemistry and Geology.* Oxford.

THOMPSON, R. C., AND R. W. HUTCHINSON

1929a   *A Century of Exploration at Nineveh.* London.

1929b   "Excavations on the Temple of Nabu at Nineveh." *Archaeologia*
            79:103–48.

TURNER, G.

1970   "The State Apartments of Late Assyrian Palaces." *Iraq* 32:177–
            213.

UNGNAD, A.

1938   "Eponymen." *Reallexikon der Assyriologie* 2:412–57. Berlin.

USSISHKIN, D.

1982   *The Conquest of Lachish by Sennacherib.* Tel Aviv.

WÄFLER, M.

1975   *Nicht-Assyrer neuassyrischer Darstellungen (Alter Orient und Altes
            Testament, XXVI).* 2 vols. Neukirchen-Vluyn.

el-WAILLY, F.

1965   "Foreward: Nineveh." *Sumer* 21:4–6.

1966   "Foreward: Nineveh." *Sumer* 22:b–c.

WATERMAN, L.

1930–36   *Royal Correspondence of the Assyrian Empire.* 4 vols. Ann Arbor.

WEIDNER, E. F.

1932–33   "Assyrische Beschreibungen der Kriegs-Reliefs Assurbanaplis." *Archiv für Orientforschung* 8:175–203.

WEIDNER, E. F., AND G. FURLANI

1939   *Die Reliefs der assyrischen Könige* (*Archiv für Orientforschung Beiheft,* IV). Berlin.

WEISSBACH, F. H.

1918   "Zu den Inschriften der Säle im Palaste Sargon's II. von Assyrien." *Zeitschrift der Deutschen Morgenländischen Gesellschaft* 72:176–85.

WIGGERMANN, F. A. M.

1983   "Exit *Talim!* Studies in Babylonian Demonology, I." *Jaarbericht Ex Oriente Lux* 27 (1981–1982):90–105.

1986   *Babylonian Phrophylactic Figures: The Ritual Texts.* Amsterdam.

WINCKLER, H.

1889   *Die Keilschrifttexte Sargon's.* 2 vols. Leipzig.

WINTER, I. J.

1981   "Royal Rhetoric and the Development of Historical Narrative in Neo-Assyrian Reliefs." *Studies in Visual Communication* 7 (no. 2):2–38.

1982   "Art as Evidence for Interaction: Relations between the Assyrian Empire and North Syria." In *Mesopotamien und seine Nachbarn,* ed. H. J. Nissen and J. Renger, 355–82. Berlin.

1983   "The Program of the Throneroom of Assurnasirpal II." In *Essays on Near Eastern Art and Archaeology in Honor of Charles Kyrle Wilkinson,* ed. P. O. Harper and H. Pittman, 15–31. New York.

WOOLLEY, C. L.

1926   "Babylonian Prophylactic Figures." *Journal of the Royal Asiatic Society,* 689–713.

INDEX

Page numbers of illustrations are in **boldface** type.

337

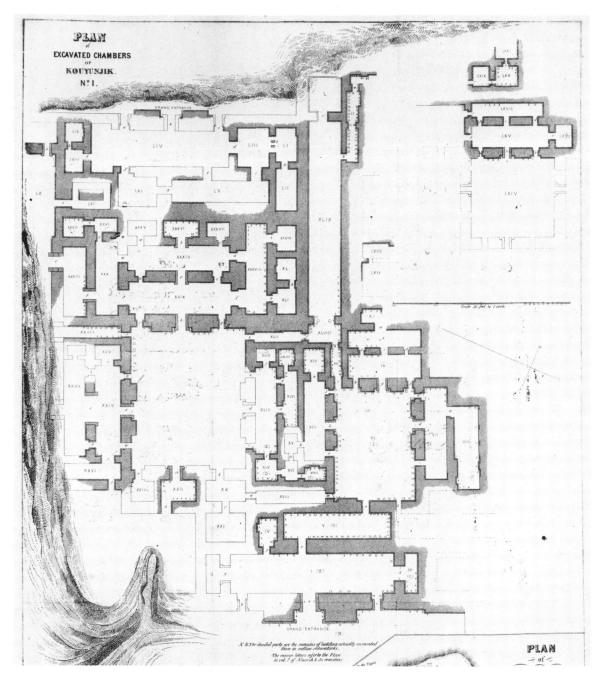

Layard's second plan of the Southwest Palace, Nineveh (from Layard 1853a, opp. 67).

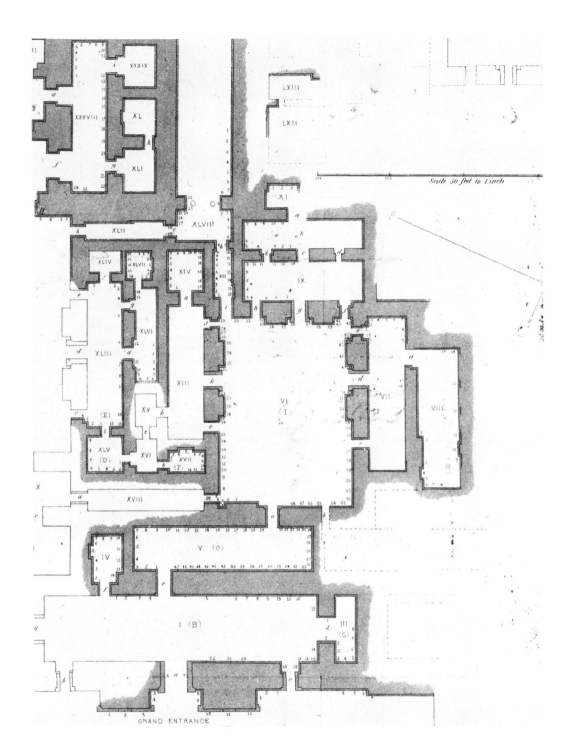

Scale 50 feet to 1 inch

GRAND ENTRANCE

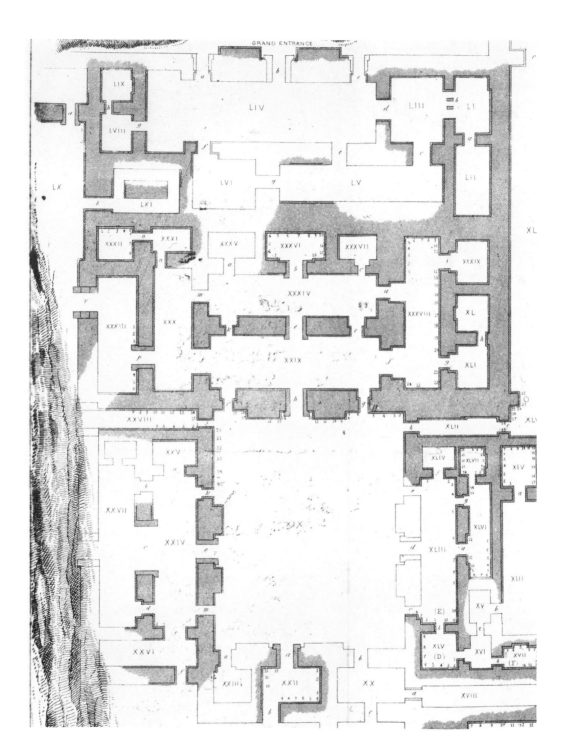

GRAND ENTRANCE

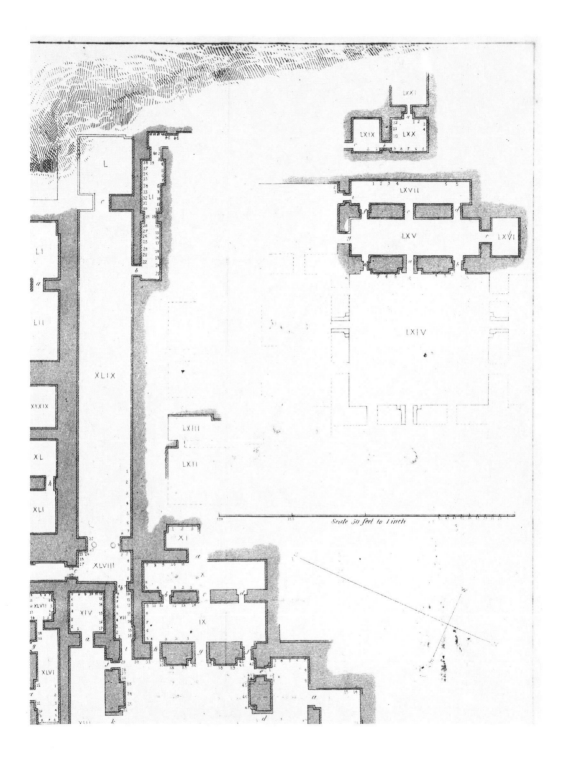

Scale 50 feet to 1 inch

Map of the ancient Near East at the time of Sennacherib (drawn by Denise Hoffman).

Mountains   ■ Canal   ▲ Rock carving